# The Face of Jesus, the Martyr and the Reciprocity of Abiding Love

*Anthropological Considerations in Spiritual Theology Based Upon the Pontifical Writings of Pope Saint John Paul the Great*

J. Marianne Siegmund

En Route Books and Media, LLC
Saint Louis, MO

ENROUTE
Make the time

En Route Books and Media, LLC
5705 Rhodes Avenue
St. Louis, MO 63109

Contact us at
contactus@enroutebooksandmedia.com

Cover photo by Gregorini Demetrio, CC BY-SA 3.0,
https://commons.wikimedia.org/w/index.php?curid=128271762

Copyright 2024 J. Marianne Siegmund

ISBN-13: 979-8-88870-274-1 and 979-8-88870-275-8
Library of Congress Control Number: 2024951115

All rights reserved. No part of this book may be reproduced, stored in a retrieval system, or transmitted in any form, or by any means, electronic, mechanical, photocopying, or otherwise, without the prior written permission of the author.

To all the martyrs of Holy Mother Church,
past, present and to come,
especially to the martyrs of the Colosseum, the Circus Maximus
and the First Martyrs of Rome
in honor of Jesus Christ King of Martyrs for whom they shed their
blood in union with Mary, the Queen of Martyrs, her
Most Chaste Spouse, Saint Joseph,
and their faithful servant of the servants of Christ,
Pope Saint John Paul the Great


In profound gratitude to my parents, without whom this work
would not have been possible

*"Misericordias Domini in aeternum cantabo."*
Psalm 88:2

# Table of Contents

Preface ............................................................................................. vii
    Why Martyrdom? ..................................................................... viii
    What This Book Is Not .............................................................. ix
    What This Book Is .................................................................... xii

Introduction ..................................................................................... 1

Chapter One: A Sketch of John Paul's Concept of the Human Person ...... 5
    The Significance of *Gaudium et Spes* ........................................ 6
    Anthropological Considerations ................................................ 10
    John Paul's Interpretation of *Gaudium et Spes* 22 ..................... 12

Chapter Two: *Gaudium et Spes* and the "Mystery of Man" ................ 17
    John Paul's Interpretation of the "Mystery of Man" .................. 20
    The Fundamental Goodness of the Human Person ..................... 22
    "The Mystery of the Father and His Love" ................................ 26
    The Passion of Christ Reveals the Father's Love ....................... 32

Chapter Three: John Paul's Opening Address at Puebla .................... 41
    Two Objections to Citing the *Opening Address* at Puebla ......... 45
    The Person's Ontological Dependence Upon His Creator .......... 48
    The Futility of the Human Person's Existence When Fragmented from God ............................................................................... 56
    The Church Safeguards the Truth of the Human Person ............ 60

Chapter Four: *Fides et Ratio* and the Human Person ....................... 65
    The Person's Rational Nature Distinguishes Him from the Rest of Visible Creation ..................................................................... 68

The "Transcendent Capacity of Human Reason" .................................. 74

Chapter Five: One "Finds Oneself" Through Self-Gift .................... 81
    John Paul's Notion of the Human Person as Self-Gift ...................... 89
    The Gift-Character of the Human Person ............................................ 93
    The Holy Spirit Enables the Person to Make a "Sincere Gift" of Himself ................................................................................................ 98
    The Opening of One's "I" to Another Who is Suffering ................. 102
    Concluding Remarks ........................................................................... 105

Chapter Six: The Theme of Martyrdom in the Pontificate of John Paul II:
    Setting the Theological Context for a Discussion of Martyrdom ... 109
    Martyrdom in the Pontifical Writings of Pope Saint John Paul II. 114
    *Veritatis Splendor*: John Paul's Primary Teaching on Martyrdom. 120

Chapter Seven: *Veritatis Splendor* and the Sacrifice of the Martyrs ....... 123
    The Martyr's Relation to the Catholic Church ................................ 125
    "By the Sacrifice of His Life" .............................................................. 128
    Death Rather Than "An Act Contrary to Faith or Virtue" .............. 131
    "Obey God Rather Than Men" .......................................................... 134
    *Veritatis Splendor* and Safeguarding the Good of the Human Person ........................................................................................................... 135
    The Sacrifice of the Martyr is a Gift of Self to Holy Mother Church ........................................................................................................... 137

Chapter Eight: The Morality of Human Acts and the Existence of Intrinsically Evil Acts ......................................................................... 141
    "The Object of the Human Act" and the Existence of Intrinsically Evil Acts ................................................................................................. 142
    Truth's Splendor: Jesus Christ ............................................................ 145

# Table of Contents

The "Essential Bond Between Truth, the Good and Freedom" ....... 147

**Chapter Nine: John Paul's Description of Human Freedom: Christ Crucified "Reveals the Authentic Meaning of Freedom"** ............... 153
Human Freedom and the Integrity of the Person ......................... 158
A Development of One's "Primordial Vocation" ........................... 164

**Chapter Ten: From Human Freedom to Human Dignity** ....................... 169
A Definition of Human Dignity ...................................................... 170
The Interplay Between Freedom and Dignity in Regard to the Martyr ............................................................................................. 173
The Concept of Witness ................................................................ 178
The Martyr's Attitude Toward Human Dignity ........................... 182
Human Dignity and Conscience ................................................... 189
The "Acceptance of Truth is the Condition for Authentic Freedom" ....................................................................................... 192
Final Prelude to John Paul's Central Passages on Martyrdom ....... 201

**Chapter Eleven: Descriptions of the Term *Martyr*** ............................... 209
Martyrdom is "the exaltation of the inviolable holiness of God's law" ................................................................................................. 214
Martyrdom and "fidelity to God's holy law" ................................ 217
The Literal or Metaphorical Use of "Martyr" ............................... 224
Is Susanna a Confessor of God's Holy Law? ................................ 225
Saint John the Baptist and the Compelling Impetus of Truth ........ 229
The Martyr Accepts Death to "Profess…Faith and…Love for Christ" ............................................................................................. 231

**Chapter Twelve: Martyrdom Affirms the "Inviolability of the Moral Order"** ................................................................................................. 237

Martyrdom is "the Exaltation of a Person's Perfect 'Humanity' and of True 'Life'" ................................................................. 239
The "Inviolability of the Moral Order" .............................................. 250
"Out of Love of Physical Life," Do Not "Lose the Very Reason for Living" ........................................................................................ 258
The Catholic Church Interprets and Safeguards Moral Norms ..... 266
"Maintaining a Harmony Between Freedom and Truth" ............... 269
Conclusions to John Paul's Thought in *Veritatis Splendor* ............ 270
Veritatis Splendor and Martyrdom ..................................................... 276

Chapter Thirteen: Additional Encyclicals on Martyrdom ..................... 283
*Redemptoris Missio*: Bearing "Witness to One's Faith in Jesus Christ" ............................................................................................................ 283
"Ut Unum Sint" and the "Supreme Demand of Faith" ................... 287
"Fides et Ratio:" The Martyrs "Declare What we Would Like to Have the Strength to Express" ................................................................. 292

Chapter Fourteen: Additional Texts on Martyrdom: Martyrdom as an "Extraordinary Fruitfulness for the Building Up of the Church" ... 299
A "Sign of That Greater Love Which Sums Up All Other Values" 302
Martyrdom "Reveals to the World the Very Essence of the Christian Message" ........................................................................................... 307
The Martyr's Resplendent Character ................................................. 309

Chapter Fifteen: Contemplating Christ's Face and the Death of the Martyr ............................................................................................... 313
John Paul's Explanation of the Term *Contemplating the Face of Christ* ................................................................................................. 314
The Self-Emptying of Jesus Christ ...................................................... 319

The "Treasure" and "Joy" of Holy Mother Church: Contemplating Christ's Face ................................................................. 327
The Contemplation of Christ's Face is a Reciprocity of Abiding Love ............................................................................. 331
Trinitarian Implications of Contemplating the Face of Christ ....... 337

Chapter Sixteen: Contemplating the Face of Christ with Mary ............. 343
Contemplating the Face of Christ Opens One to "The Mystery of Trinitarian Life" ................................................................. 347
*Rosarium Virginis Mariae* and "The Truth About Man" ............... 350
Contemplating Christ with Mary "in the Living Sacrament of His Body and His Blood" .......................................................... 353

Chapter Seventeen: The Martyr's Death is a Contemplation of the Face of Christ ............................................................................ 359
An Objective Articulation of the Martyr's Death ........................... 366
An Objective Articulation of Contemplating Christ's Face ............ 368
The Martyr's Death is a Contemplation of Christ's Face ............... 371
The Martyr's Death is a Visible Proclamation of Christ's Face ...... 373
The Martyr's Death Expresses a Life "Distinguished…in the Art of Prayer" ............................................................................... 376

Chapter Eighteen: Summarizing the Project ...................................... 381
Correlating Martyrdom and Contemplation of Christ's Face with *Gaudium et Spes* 22 .......................................................... 381
Correlating Martyrdom and Contemplation of Christ's Face with *Gaudium et Spes* 24 .......................................................... 388
Martyrdom and Contemplating the Face of Jesus Christ ............... 393
The Difference Between the Martyr and the Saintly Non-Martyr . 400

Chapter Nineteen: Concluding Remarks............................................................405
  Implications of the Martyr's Death as a Contemplation of the Face of Christ ................................................................................................................. 405
  The Martyr's Death Expresses a Contemplative Element in Proclamation ..................................................................................................... 405
  Martyrdom and Prayer.................................................................................... 409
  The Martyr's Contribution Toward the Transformation of the World................................................................................................................. 415
  The Transforming Impetus of Love ............................................................. 415
  Martyrdom Makes t/Truth "Visible" to the World ...................................... 419
  Sacrificing One's Corporeal Life Points Toward the Primacy of the Spiritual Life..................................................................................................... 421
  The Martyr's Death Expresses Human Relationships in a New Light ................................................................................................................. 422

Chapter Twenty: A Final Exhortation from John Paul II......................... 425

Bibliography ............................................................................................................. 427

# Preface

When I began doctoral studies at the Pontifical University of Saint Thomas Aquinas in Urbe (Angelicum) in Rome in the fall of 2005, Pope John Paul II had passed away about six months earlier. Postcards of John Paul II waving "goodbye" and Pope Benedict XVI waving "hello" lined the giftshops for tourists to easily access.[1] Pilgrims and tourists alike purchased memorabilia and visited the late Pontiff's tomb in Saint Peter's Basilica, located in the crypt at that time. The presence of the great John Paul seemed to permeate the city by his absence.

Having lived much of my life under the Pontificate of John Paul, I have long studied his thought. On two separate occasions, 1991 and 2005-2009, I lived near the Colosseum, so close, as a matter of fact, that I could see it from my window on one of them (1991). Almost every day, I would walk past the Colosseum, where countless men and women gave their lives in witness to Jesus

---

[1] Throughout this work, "John Paul" refers to Saint John Paul II. The title, "the Great," has been attached to very few pontiffs in the history of the Church. Since it is bestowed by popular acclaim and not by a formal declaration of Holy Mother Church, my title serves as a small contribution for the title, "the Great," to be applied to St. John Paul II. The pontiffs who have been declared "the Great" in the history of the Church are Pope Saint Leo the Great, who reigned from 440-461, Pope Saint Gregory the Great, who reigned from 590 to 604, and Pope Saint Nicholas the Great, who reigned from 858-867. Note, as well, that with every instance of the word, *Church*, in this work, I mean the one, holy, Catholic and Apostolic Church founded by Jesus Christ, which subsists in the Catholic Church.

Christ, many centuries ago. Consequently, I easily connected the thought of Pope Saint John Paul II and martyrdom, thus making it the subject of my doctoral dissertation.

This work is a revised, updated version of my doctoral dissertation, earned at the Angelicum in 2009. My original title was *Contemplating the Face of Christ: A Spiritual Reading of Martyrdom in the Pontifical Writings of Pope John Paul II*. I successfully defended the work at 5:00 PM on June 11, which was the Solemnity of the Body and Blood of our Lord Jesus Christ that year. Had I not been defending my dissertation, I would have been participating in the annual Pontifical Eucharistic Procession from Saint John Lateran to Saint Mary Major. In addition, the classroom at the Angelicum where I defended my work was the same room used by the Holy Father, then Karol Wojtyła, when he defended his own dissertation, *Doctrina de Fide Apud S. Joannem a Cruce* (*Faith According to Saint John of the Cross*), in 1948.

Because I have updated the text, I subtracted the standard dissertation coversheet, removed the Imprimatur, and deleted the director's name (Fr. Luke Buckles, O.P.), and the Reader's name (Fr. Paul Murray, O.P.).

**Why Martyrdom?**

The topic of martyrdom has drawn the attention of numerous twentieth century writers, perhaps because of the sheer number of martyrs in the last two centuries. In this work, however, I do not focus upon one particular martyr or a select group of martyrs, either past or present. Instead, I highlight the fact that martyrdom

Preface

itself is "a sign of that greater love, which sums up all other values."[2] It expresses a gift of self that is contemplative in nature and love is at the very heart of that act.

This work focuses upon a spiritual reading of martyrdom in the pontifical writings of Pope Saint John Paul II, which features its contemplative and anthropological dimensions. Since "our witness…would be hopelessly inadequate if we ourselves had not first contemplated His face," my articulation of the martyr's death as a contemplation of the face of Christ and of the person as a contemplator of His holy face, is of prime concern to all.[3] At the conclusion of this work, it is my hope that the reader will see how truly the martyrs proclaim the words of Saint Paul. "For God, who commanded the light to shine out of darkness, hath shined in our hearts, to give the light of the knowledge of the glory of God, in the face of Christ Jesus" (2 Corinthians 4:6).[4]

**What This Book Is Not**

The term *martyrdom* expresses numerous realities among those who use the word. The Holy Father implies that a martyr is not

---

[2] John Paul II, *Incarnationis Mysterium* 13.
[3] John Paul II, *Novo Millennio Ineunte* 16.
[4] Unless otherwise noted, Biblical citations are from the following version. *The Holy Bible* Douay Rheims Version, Revised by Bishop Richard Challoner in 1749-1752 (Rockford, IL: Tan Books and Publishers, Inc., 1989).

necessarily a full member of the Catholic Church.[5] Thus, one would presume that the death of the non-Catholic martyr is also a contemplation of Christ's face. Because the martyr dies to uphold objective truth, and thus, the objective moral law, he may or may not be a full member of the Catholic Church. Nonetheless, the Church founded by Jesus Christ "subsists in the Catholic Church" and He entrusted His teachings to the Church for safekeeping.[6]

Whether the martyr believes in the fullness of the Church's teachings, he witnesses to the objective moral law, which the Catholic Church safeguards. Since the moral law is objective—it is true for all people of all time—each person, regardless of religious denomination, must be willing to die to defend it.

In *Veritatis Splendor*, John Paul implies that the martyrs of which he speaks are those the Catholic Church acknowledges. For example, in paragraph 27, he claims that the Church puts into practice the "precepts and love" of Christ "in the sacrifice of her martyrs." Elsewhere, John Paul teaches that the "Bishop of Rome is the Bishop of the Church which preserves the mark of the martyrdom of Peter and of Paul."[7] Further, in *Christifideles Laici* 39, the Pontiff indicates that the martyr's death "constitutes a source of extraordinary fruitfulness for the building up of the Church."

---

[5] The Conciliar document, *Lumen Gentium*, defines full, visible membership in the Church in paragraph 14, with additional specifications in paragraphs 8 and 15.

[6] Second Vatican Council, *Lumen Gentium* 8. See also Pope Paul VI, *Mysterium Ecclesiae* 6-7.

[7] John Paul II, *Ut Unum Sint* 90.

These passages and other similar texts offer additional justification for my focus upon the martyr from a Catholic perspective.

One might raise the following objection. In *Veritatis Splendor* 76, John Paul states that the martyrs are those "holy men and women of the Old and New Testaments, who are considered such because they gave their lives rather than perform this or that particular act contrary to faith or virtue." One might argue that the Old Testament martyrs are *not* Catholic, since, although the Church is prefigured in the Old Testament, these people lived before the Catholic Church came into full existence. Thus, one might contend that my reason for focusing upon the martyr as a full member of the Catholic Church is unfounded.

To the above objection, I respond as follows. Given that the Old Testament concerns people living before the time of Christ, I reaffirm my commitment to speak primarily of the martyr who is Catholic, maintaining that John Paul does so himself, although he is necessarily concerned with the ecumenical dimension of martyrdom as Sovereign Pontiff. In addition, the "holy men and women of the Old and New Testaments, who are considered such" *are* "considered [as] such" precisely *because* the Catholic Church holds them to be so, whether formally, through canonization, or informally, such as parents naming their children after holy people from the Old or New Testaments.

In my discussion of how John Paul regards martyrdom, then, I note the fact that, because the martyr dies to uphold objective truth, and thus, the objective moral law, a martyr need not be a full member of the Catholic Church.⁸ Even still, my explication of the martyr understood from the Roman Catholic perspective, from John Paul, himself, highlights a spiritual dimension of martyrdom, which describes its contemplative aspect. The area of ecumenism and martyrdom, with the profusion of distinctions it would require, is a worthy task for a future study.⁹

**What This Book Is**

The human person's redemption is "accomplished in the death and Resurrection of Jesus," which is anchored in the Incarnation of the Son of God, the Second Person of the Blessed Trinity Made Flesh.¹⁰ Consequently, from the beginning of his pontificate, John Paul ponders the Year of Great Jubilee and he wants to celebrate it

---

⁸ John Paul's encyclical, *Veritatis Splendor*, especially paragraph 82, illuminates the fact that not all martyrs have full membership in the Catholic Church. Thus, they are regarded as witnesses to the Faith.

⁹ For more on the ecumenical dimension of martyrdom, see John Paul II, *Ut Unum Sint* 1, 84 and John Paul II, *Tertio Millennio Adveniente* 37. See also John Paul II, *Regina Coeli* (7 May 2000) and John Paul II, Homily "Ecumenical Commemoration of the Witnesses to the Faith in the Twentieth Century" (7 May 2000). Note the fact that the May 7 Commemoration was an ecumenical Liturgy of the Word. Pope Saint John Paul II gathered in the Roman Colosseum with the Greek Orthodox Metropolitan Gennadios and the Rev. Dr. Ishmael Noko of the Lutheran World Federation to honor 12,692 confessors and martyrs [George Weigel, *The End and the Beginning Pope John Paul II – The Victory of Freedom, the Last Years, the Legacy* (New York, NY: Doubleday, 2010), 232-233].

¹⁰ John Paul II, *Incarnationis Mysterium* 6.

on a grand scale.¹¹ In fact, the Jubilee Year is a "hermeneutical key" for understanding his papacy.¹² Even more, contemplating the face of Christ is the "core" of the Jubilee's "legacy" and John Paul highlights the martyr as a witness to Christ.¹³ In this work, my claim that the martyr's death reveals the face of Christ to others *must*, then, play a specific role in the legacy of the Year of Great Jubilee.

In his *Bull of Indiction* announcing the Year of Great Jubilee, the Holy Father enumerates "signs, which attest to the faith and foster the devotion of the Christian people" such as the pilgrimage, the holy door, the indulgence and reconciliation with God.¹⁴ The last one he lists is the martyr who is "a sign of that greater love which sums up all other values."¹⁵ Not only does John Paul see martyrdom as the "supreme glorification of human dignity," but also, he highlights martyrdom as a significant factor for the Christian as he enters the third millennium.¹⁶

Although perhaps forgotten by the passing of years, an extraordinary Pope has implemented an explicit plan for the 2000th anniversary of Christ's birth, the Year of Great Jubilee. That plan includes the Pontiff's desire that the Church remains "anchored in the testimony of the martyrs and jealously guard their memory."¹⁷

---

¹¹ See, for example, John Paul II, *Redemptor Hominis* 1. See also John Paul II, *Dominum et Vivificantem* 2, 9-54, 56, 60.

¹² John Paul II, *Tertio Millennio Adveniente* 23.

¹³ John Paul II, *Novo Millennio Ineunte* 15.

¹⁴ John Paul II, *Incarnationis Mysterium* 7.

¹⁵ John Paul II, *Incarnationis Mysterium* 13.

¹⁶ John Paul II, *Dominum et Vivificantem* 60; John Paul II, *Incarnationis Mysterium* 13.

¹⁷ John Paul II, *Incarnationis Mysterium* 13.

An examination of martyrdom within his pontifical writings not only sheds new light on his highly significant pontificate, but it also unfolds a spiritual treasure for the people of God.

In my study, I elucidate the concept of martyrdom according to John Paul, who indicates that the martyr is a witness to Christ's teachings.[18] Martyrdom depicted as such offers a clarity that allows the reader to grasp the martyr's way of living in the fullness of truth for which he dies. Such a death offers a fresh way to think about proclamation, prayer, and the human person by showing how John Paul understands two seemingly unrelated topics: *martyrdom* and the *contemplation of the face of Christ*.

Focusing upon the death of the martyr highlights John Paul's concept of the human person. Specifically, he uses the Conciliar term, the *mystery of man*.[19] Suggesting that the death of the martyr is a contemplation of the face of Christ offers a novel understanding of martyrdom, which highlights truth and engages John Paul's original term, *contemplating the face of Christ*.

Through a study of the Holy Father's texts, one can draw numerous insights on the contemplative dimension of the human

---

[18] *Redemptoris Missio* 45 offers an excellent example of the Pope's description of the martyr as a witness. "The supreme test is the giving of one's life, to the point of accepting death in order to bear witness to one's faith in Jesus Christ. Throughout Christian history, martyrs, that is, 'witnesses,' have always been numerous and indispensable to the spread of the Gospel. In our own age, there are many: bishops, priests, men and women religious, lay people--often unknown heroes who give their lives to bear witness to the faith. They are *par excellence* the heralds and witnesses of the faith" [John Paul II, *Redemptoris Missio* 45].

[19] Second Vatican Council, *Gaudium et Spes* 22.

person. Some of the principle contributions regard the listening dimension of proclamation and prayer as a revelation of the truth of the human person. Further, I note that martyrdom, itself, is prayer. Several reasons that support this idea hinge upon the fact that the martyr's death implies that his whole being is directed toward God. The martyr's death, which shows his complete immersion in t/Truth, corresponds to the truth of the human person that my reading of the Pope's anthropology highlights.

# Introduction

At the dawn of the new millennium, Pope John Paul II reflects that the people of today, "perhaps unconsciously, ask believers not only to 'speak' of Christ, but in a certain sense to 'show' Him to them."[1] For John Paul, the believer shows the face of Christ to others only after he has first contemplated it himself.[2]

How does this showing of Christ take place? If the believer shows Christ to others by contemplating, or by radiating graces received after contemplation, or by both, then showing Christ to others is letting Christ show Himself through one's cooperation with divine grace. What, then, does it mean to contemplate Christ's face?

According to John Paul, the *"contemplation of the face of Christ* [is] Christ considered in His historical features and in His mystery, Christ known through His manifold presence in the Church and in the world and confessed as the meaning of history and the light of life's journey."[3] One might ask, then, whether contemplating Christ's face transforms the believer, somehow enabling him to radiate Christ. Even still, is it possible to perceive the effects of one's contemplation of Christ's face? If so, what are those effects? If radiating Christ is a consequence of having contemplated His face, then how is that radiance manifested?

---

[1] John Paul II, *Novo Millennio Ineunte* 16.
[2] John Paul II, *Novo Millennio Ineunte* 16.
[3] John Paul II, *Novo Millennio Ineunte* 15.

## 2    *The Face of Jesus, the Martyr and the Reciprocity of Abiding Love*

To ponder the showing of Christ's face to others, I focus upon the martyr, whom one might highlight as an example of such contemplation. The leading example of contemplating the face of Christ, is Mary, our Blessed Mother and the Queen of Martyrs. As John Paul explains, "the contemplation of Christ has an incomparable model in Mary. ... No one has ever devoted himself to the contemplation of the face of Christ as faithfully as Mary."[4] Although I focus upon the martyr, Mary is assuredly the preeminent contemplator of the face of her Divine Son. Of course, everything good and beautiful that I highlight concerning the martyr is also true of the Perpetual Virgin of Nazareth, the holy Mother of God, Mary, who is the Immaculate Conception.

A key task in my work is to illustrate that the death of the martyr signifies an attitude toward human dignity that refuses to betray the truth of the human person. In one of the most relevant texts, the Holy Father claims that martyrdom is "fidelity to God's holy law, witnessed to by death."[5] This death affirms "the inviolability of the moral order [and it] bears splendid witness"[6] to the "holiness of the Church,"[7] to "the holiness of God's law and to the

---

[4] John Paul II, *Rosarium Virginis Mariae* 10.

[5] John Paul II, *Veritatis Splendor* 93. Throughout the present work, I refer to "God's law" or to "the teachings of Christ." In the Old Testament context, "God's law" refers to the Decalogue. By "God's law" or "Christ's teachings" in a New Testament context, I mean "the Commandments of God and the charity of Christ," which recalls the Beatitudes, as well as the precepts of the Church [John Paul II, *Veritatis Splendor* 110].

[6] John Paul II, *Veritatis Splendor* 92.

[7] John Paul II, *Veritatis Splendor* 93.

inviolability of the personal dignity of man."[8] Martyrdom "is also the exaltation of a person's perfect 'humanity' and of true 'life,'"[9] and it "represents the high point of the witness to moral truth."[10]

By highlighting the fact that martyrdom is an affirmation of "the inviolability of the moral order" and "the high point of the witness to moral truth," one might surmise that truth plays a crucial role in the Holy Father's notion of martyrdom.[11] It is precisely that concept of martyrdom, witnessing to moral truth by death, which describes the martyr as a prime example of one who lives in the truth.[12] On account of the martyr's "eloquent and attractive example of a life completely transfigured by the splendor of moral truth," I suggest that his death, which makes known the holiness of his Church, reveals the face of Christ.[13]

Based upon John Paul's understanding of *martyrdom*, the *martyr*, and *contemplating Christ's face*, I argue that the martyr's death is a contemplation of Christ's face and this contemplation shows Christ to others. Although John Paul does not connect the martyr's death with the contemplation of Christ's face or even suggest that the two concepts are related, I perceive a correlation between the two that offers a new understanding of both *martyrdom* and *contemplating Christ's face*. To support my interpretation of the Pontiff's thought entails, among other considerations, a conscientious

---

[8] John Paul II, *Veritatis Splendor* 92.
[9] John Paul II, *Veritatis Splendor* 92.
[10] John Paul II, *Veritatis Splendor* 93.
[11] John Paul II, *Veritatis Splendor* 92, 93.
[12] John Paul II, *Fides et Ratio* 5; John Paul II, *Veritatis Splendor* 88, 93.
[13] John Paul II, *Veritatis Splendor* 93.

analysis of his understanding not only of *martyrdom* and *contemplating the face of Christ*, but also, of the human person. By examining the Pope's texts on both martyrdom and contemplation of the face of Christ, then, I bring out the relation between the two concepts, which is the thesis I defend: the martyr's death is a contemplation of Christ's face.

My project highlights an objective dimension of martyrdom, which remains true whether, at the actual moment of death, the martyr is actively and consciously contemplating the face of Christ. By discussing the objective dimension of the martyr's death, I do not mean to suggest that the martyr is solely defined as a contemplator of Christ's face, nor do I argue that martyrdom is the *only* way, or even the *best* way, in which one might radiate the contemplation of Christ's face. I do not claim that the martyr is somehow a *better* contemplator than a saint who is not a martyr, since every believer is to contemplate the face of Christ.

The objective description of martyrdom as a contemplation of Christ's face means that the martyr's death shows Christ to others. According to John Paul's texts, which describe the two concepts independently from each other, I claim that the martyr's death is an example of what it means to contemplate the face of Christ. The martyr's death is a contemplation of Christ's face and that death shows Him to others.

# Chapter One

## A Sketch of John Paul's Concept of the Human Person

In his Jubilee Bull, *Incarnationis Mysterium*, John Paul directs the Church to meditate upon martyrdom. Further, in *Novo Millennio Ineunte*, the Pope speaks of the contemplation of Christ's face as the "core" of the Jubilee's legacy, and he reflects upon this "legacy" at greater length in chapter four of this Apostolic Letter. In addition, *Novo Millennio Ineunte* also contains references to the theme of martyrdom.

In addition to both *Incarnationis Mysterium* and *Novo Millennio Ineunte*, texts connected to the Jubilee, such as *Tertio Millennio Adveniente* and *Rosarium Virginis Mariae*, provide additional evidence that both martyrdom and contemplating Christ's face play a key role in John Paul's thought on the Year of Great Jubilee. For example, *Tertio Millennio Adveniente* 37 speaks of martyrdom, while *Rosarium Virginis Mariae*, which is to be read "in continuity with" *Novo Millennio Ineunte*, cites the contemplation of Christ's face in numerous paragraphs.[1]

John Paul's *Homily* of 6 January 2001 and "To the Youth of the World on the Occasion of the XIX World Youth Day" are other examples that indicate the centrality of contemplating Christ's face and martyrdom, in connection with the Year of Great Jubilee, as a

---

[1] John Paul II, *Rosarium Virginis Mariae* 3. Examples of contemplating Christ's face in *Rosarium Virginis Mariae* include the following: 1, 3, 9, and 10.

focus for the Church. Even still, to leap to the conclusion that martyrdom is an expression of contemplating Christ's face merely by linking certain Jubilee passages, cannot be done. It needs further justification.

The Jubilee itself, with its very reason of existence being the event of the Incarnation, celebrates the human person, as well, for the "whole of human history… stands in reference to [Christ]."[2] Rather than presenting a comprehensive study of John Paul's notion of the person, however, I offer a concise depiction of it that serves as a foundation upon which to build my interpretation of martyrdom and contemplating Christ's face. Focusing upon the human person underlies the first part of my project, then, and it sets the stage for my ensuing argument, in which I begin to justify my claim that the martyr's death is a unique instance of contemplating Christ's face.

## The Significance of *Gaudium et Spes*

Developing John Paul's anthropology begins with the suggestion that its grounding lies in Jesus Christ, who "fully reveals man

---

[2] John Paul II, *Incarnationis Mysterium* 1. Convincing evidence shows that the Year of Great Jubilee not only celebrates the human person, but also that it intrinsically engages John Paul's thought on the person, as well. The question is this. If the Jubilee exists to both commemorate and contemplate the mystery of the Incarnation, as John Paul affirms in *Incarnationis Mysterium* 1, how does his notion of the human person involve Jesus Christ? As I show in the present section, the Pope's anthropology is rooted in Jesus Christ, who "fully reveals man to man himself" [Second Vatican Council, *Gaudium et Spes* 22].

# Chapter One: A Sketch of John Paul's Concept of the Human Person

to man himself." It is precisely because Jesus is true God and true Man that He makes known the mystery of the human person *to* the person, himself. John Paul incorporates this teaching from *Gaudium et Spes* 22 into his pontificate because "having an exact concept of God" leads to "the true concept of man."[3]

The Pontiff explains, "In Jesus Christ the history of salvation finds its culmination and ultimate meaning."[4] Because Christ is "of one being with the Father," He is "the one who reveals God's plan for all creation and for man in particular."[5] Further, by His Incarnation and salvific death, Christ reveals "the mystery of the Father and His love" to each person.[6] The Christological emphasis in John Paul's anthropology, then, is a fundamental element to which I shall return.

If one has a faulty understanding of the Creator, then one misunderstands the human person, as well.[7] With the Christological foundation of John Paul's anthropology, concretized in his fre-

---

[3] John Paul II, *Augustinum Hipponesem* Chapter II 2.
[4] John Paul II, *Incarnationis Mysterium* 1.
[5] John Paul II, *Tertio Millennio Adveniente* 4.
[6] John Paul II, *Tertio Millennio Adveniente* 4. As I show in a subsequent section, God's love is intimately connected with the concept of the martyr's death radiating the face of Jesus Christ.
[7] This comment refers to *Gaudium et Spes* 36: "Creatura enim sine Creatore evanescit [Without the Creator, the creature vanishes]." Note the force of the word, *evanesco*: "vanish, fade out, become vapid or dissipated, die." If knowledge of the Creator is faulty or incomplete, one likewise misunderstands the human person, who stands at the pinnacle of God's *visible* creation. The invisible Angels are of a higher order than the human person. Nevertheless, a proper understanding of the person becomes *dissipated* or even *dies*, if one has a wrong notion of God.

quent mention of *Gaudium et Spes* 22 and 24, one finds a plethora of teaching concerning the notion of the human person, his dignity and freedom, his redemption by Jesus Christ and his unique calling to be a child of the Father. My aim is to make use of certain indispensable facets of the Pope's anthropological thought that show how martyrdom and how contemplating Christ's face describe a contemplative dimension of the human person.

A central foundation of John Paul's solicitude for the human person is *Gaudium et Spes* 22: "only in the mystery of the Incarnate Word does the mystery of man take on light." A second fundamental text, paragraph 24 of the same document, indicates that, because the human person is the "only creature on earth which God willed for itself, [he] cannot fully find himself except through a sincere gift of himself." Using several passages that convey the Holy Father's interpretation of *Gaudium et Spes* 22 and 24, then, provide the specific elements of his thought that develop a concise explanation of his teaching concerning the human person, which brings his contemplative dimension to the fore.

Positing that John Paul's central, anthropological claims stem from *Gaudium et Spes* 22 and 24, however, requires clear evidence. Another initial challenge is defending the legitimate objection that, since the Conciliar texts do not comprise his own pontifical writing, they cannot serve as the basis of his anthropological claims.

At first glance, arguing that the Conciliar texts should not serve as a foundation for developing John Paul's anthropology may seem valid. In the specific work that follows, however, *Gaudium et Spes* 22 and 24 clearly do form a pivotal theme in his Christological no-

Chapter One: A Sketch of John Paul's Concept of the Human Person    9

tion of the human person.⁸ Further, the Pontiff highlights the first chapter of *Gaudium et Spes*, quotes paragraph 22, and claims that "the climactic section" of this first chapter, paragraph 22, is "one of the constant reference-points" of his teaching.⁹ He also refers to *Gaudium et Spes* 24 in several noteworthy passages.

Because John Paul often refers to these Conciliar texts when speaking about the human person, I argue that they do, in fact, reveal a vital concept in his thought: Christ "fully reveals man to himself" as a person who finds himself when he makes "a sincere gift of himself." Upon conclusion of the present chapter, then, my groundwork is prepared for the ensuing argument, in which I begin to justify my claim that the martyr's death is a contemplation of Christ's face.

---

⁸ John Paul often refers to *Gaudium et Spes* 22 and 24. For examples of his references to *Gaudium et Spes* 22, see the following documents by Pope Saint John Paul II. *Christifideles Laici* 36; *Dominum et Vivificantem* 53; *Dives in Misericordia* 1; *Evangelium Vitae* 2, 104; *Fides et Ratio* 13; *Incarnationis Mysterium* 1; *Gratissimam Sane* 2 (three times), 13, 19; *Mane Nobiscum Domine* 6; *Novo Millennio Ineunte* 23, 49; *Pastores Dabo Vobis* 72; *Redemptor Hominis* 8-10, 13, 18; *Redemptoris Mater* 4 (twice), 46; *Redemptoris Missio* 10, 18, 28 (twice); *Rosarium Virginis Mariae* 25; *Salvifici Doloris* 31; *Sollicitudo Rei Socialis* 47; *Tertio Millennio Adveniente* 4, 52; *Veritatis Splendor* 2, 28, 73. For references to *Gaudium et Spes* 24 in John Paul's thought, see the following. *Christifideles Laici* 40; *Dominum et Vivificantem* 59 (twice), 62; *Evangelium Vitae* 96; *Familiaris Consortio* 22; *Gratissimam Sane* 8, 9 (three times), 11, 12, 19; *Mulieris Dignitatem* 7, 18, 20, 30; *Pastores Dabo Vobis* 44; *Redemptor Hominis* 13; *Salvifici Doloris* 28; *Ut Unum Sint* 26, 28; *Veritatis Splendor* 13, 86.

⁹ John Paul II, *Fides et Ratio* 60.

## Anthropological Considerations

Christian anthropology hinges upon the fact that the person is created in the image of God.[10] In order to elucidate this claim, I select points from John Paul's interpretation of *Gaudium et Spes* 22 and 24, which are particularly apropos to my reading of his thought on martyrdom. In my analysis of the Pope's reflection on *Gaudium et Spes* 22, I first discuss his construal of the *mystery of man* in *Redemptor Hominis* 8-10 by noting that the person is created in the image and likeness of God, that he is newly created in Christ through His redemptive death, and that God loves the human person He creates.

My second illustration of John Paul's reading of *Gaudium et Spes* 22 describes the person's dependence upon God for his existence *as* a human being, and it stresses his unique dignity among the rest of creation. I primarily rely upon the Pope's *Opening Address* at the Puebla Conference, although I also refer to *Dominum et Vivificantem* 36.

My third portrayal of John Paul's interpretation of *Gaudium et Spes* 22, further expounds upon the person's creation in the image of God by showing that his way of being a human person differentiates him from among the rest of creation and it dictates his

---

[10] John Paul II, *Mulieris Dignitatem* 6; John Paul II, *Opening Address* at the Puebla Conference, 28 January 1979 (9). The term "image and likeness" refers to Genesis 1:26-27. Due to my frequent mention of this text, and, because repeated citations of an often-quoted text makes reading cumbersome, I do not give the Biblical reference unless it is part of a whole sentence, which I am quoting.

capacity to transcend the world in which he lives. Using *Fides et Ratio* 60 and *Augustinum Hipponesem* to expound upon this point, I suggest that the human person is open to the transcendent because he is rational. The person's openness to the transcendent, to God Himself, is crucial in order to grasp his contemplative nature. If, as John Paul maintains, the person is created in God's image and likeness on account of his immense love, and, if the person is thus essentially open to the transcendent by his very nature, then his thirst for God is innate. Subsequently, I explain that thirst, sometimes described as contemplative, in essence, is present in the death in the martyr.

The second part of my analysis on the human person illustrates John Paul's interpretation of *Gaudium et Spes* 24. Created by God's love, the person is also created for love. One finds himself by giving himself to another. For John Paul, one's concrete encounter with the love of God in Jesus Christ is imperative. In my study, I maintain that John Paul's reflection on *Gaudium et Spes* 24 is a way of bringing to the fore the human person's capacity of giving himself to another human person.

At the conclusion of this chapter, a preliminary thought, still to be argued, is to surmise that the martyr (martyrdom) and contemplating Christ's face connect because they (presumably, but still to be proved) illuminate papal teaching on the human person. Further, John Paul's interpretation of *Gaudium et Spes* 22 and 24 indicates that his anthropology is Christocentric; it is firmly rooted in

Jesus Christ who, "by His Incarnation," unites Himself with each human person.[11]

## John Paul's Interpretation of *Gaudium et Spes* 22

John Paul's frequent reference to *Gaudium et Spes* 22 seems to suggest that it is a fundamental key to his understanding of the human person. Because he quotes the inception of this paragraph and calls it "one of the constant reference points" of his teaching, I aim to show that it forms the crux of his thought on the person from three different dimensions.[12]

Paragraphs 8-10 of John Paul's first encyclical, *Redemptor Hominis*, explain the first dimension of the human person, which is based upon his interpretation of *Gaudium et Spes* 22. Since the Conciliar document indicates, "Christ fully reveals man to himself," I discuss this "revelation" according to the Pope's reading of the *mystery of man* in *Redemptor Hominis* 8-10. This *mystery* maintains that the person, created in the image and likeness of God, is newly created in Christ because of the Father's love for him. It is precisely *because* the human person is created in the image and likeness of God and *because* he is newly created by Jesus Christ in the first place, that his life is meaningless without reference to God. The emptiness of one's life when separated from his Creator leads to my second remark on John Paul's interpretation of *Gaudium et Spes* 22.

---

[11] Second Vatican Council, *Gaudium et Spes* 22 quoted in John Paul II, *Redemptor Hominis* 13.

[12] John Paul II, *Fides et Ratio* 60.

In the *Opening Address* at the Puebla Conference, the Holy Father emphasizes the futility of one's life when severed from God. Here, he brings to the fore the person's openness to the Transcendent—to God—specifically on account of his creation by God. The person's openness to the Absolute, who is God Himself, is a truth that flows from his creation because, as the Pope maintains, one cannot find authentic happiness without reference to God, who is his Creator. The central concern from *Gaudium et Spes* 22 that John Paul highlights at the Puebla Conference, then, is the human person's fundamental openness to God, who creates him.

The *mystery of man* specifies that he is created in God's image and likeness and he is newly created in Christ. At the same time, this *mystery* also indicates that one's life is futile when severed from God. These two dimensions of the *mystery of man* bring to the fore his uniqueness among other living creatures and they locate the inexhaustible mystery of the human person in the fact that he is created in God's image and likeness. As a creature, then, the person is essentially open to God. The fundamental openness of the human person to God testifies to his ability to transcend the material world in which he lives.

The notion of human transcendence offers a third interpretation of *Gaudium et Spes* 22 because it shows that one's capacity to transcend the world is ultimately rooted in one's creation in God's image. John Paul offers an example of this teaching in *Fides et Ratio* 60, where he explains that the "transcendent capacity of human reason" is due to the fact that the person is created in the image of God; his way of being a human person is to exist as a rational being. Further, human rationality indicates the person's innate dignity and freedom. Moreover, John Paul's continual reiteration of the person's distinction from the rest of visible creation, on account of his rational nature, suggests the immensity and grandeur of God's love for him that is also manifested in the Passion and death of Jesus.

Investigating John Paul's analysis of *Gaudium et Spes* 22 in three instances, *Redemptor Hominis* 8-10, the *Opening Address* at the Puebla Conference, and *Fides et Ratio* 60, provides a succinct and partial synopsis, to be completed with *Gaudium et Spes* 24, of my abridgment concerning his thought on the human person. The Pope's interpretation of *Gaudium et Spes* 22 shows that it is not only a constant point of reference for him, but also, and, more importantly, it indicates *how* Christ reveals the human person to himself. In other words, the nature of the person—the very mystery of his being—is illuminated by Jesus Christ because Christ makes the love that God the Father has for the person tangible by His Passion and death.

My extrapolation of the Pope's interpretation of *Gaudium et Spes* 22 contributes to his notion of martyrdom for several reasons. First, the Holy Father's concept of the person as a creature in the image of God highlights human rationality. In turn, human rationality brings out the contemplative dimension of the person: because one is rational, one can transcend the visible, everyday world in which one lives. Thus, one can reflect upon questions such as who he is, where he is going, and what life and suffering really mean. One's ability to transcend the visible world also indicates that the person can think of God, and one can pray.

## Chapter One: A Sketch of John Paul's Concept of the Human Person

If the human person is created in the image of God, then dependence upon God is inscribed in his very being. This idea helps to show that the martyr's death reveals much more than the sublime dignity of the human person. In fact, the death of the martyr reveals, as I argue below, that authentic humanism bears witness to the truth of the human person, created and redeemed by God, and called to share in His divine life.

# Chapter Two

## *Gaudium et Spes* and the "Mystery of Man"

*Gaudium et Spes* 22 is an exceptionally rich Conciliar passage. Although lengthy, I offer the entire citation. My analysis of John Paul's interpretation of *Gaudium et Spes* 22 focuses upon one of its key phrases: the *mystery of man*.

> The truth is that only in the mystery of the Incarnate Word does the mystery of man take on light. For Adam, the first man, was a figure of Him who was to come, namely Christ the Lord. Christ, the final Adam, by the revelation of the mystery of the Father and His love, fully reveals man to man himself and makes his supreme calling clear. It is not surprising, then, that in Him all the aforementioned truths find their root and attain their crown.
>
> He who is 'the image of the invisible God' (Colossians 1:15), is Himself the perfect man. To the sons of Adam, He restores the divine likeness which had been disfigured from the first sin onward. Since human nature as He assumed it was not annulled, by that very fact it has been raised up to a divine dignity in our respect too. For by His Incarnation the Son of God has united Himself in some fashion with every man. He worked with human hands, He thought with a human mind, acted by human choice and loved with a human heart. Born of the Virgin Mary, He has truly been

made one of us, like us in all things except sin (Hebrews 4:15).

As an innocent lamb He merited life for us by the free shedding of His own Blood. In Him God [the Father] reconciled us to Himself and among ourselves; from bondage to the devil and sin He delivered us, so that each one of us can say with the Apostle: The Son of God 'loved me and gave Himself up for me' (Galatians 2:20). By suffering for us He not only provided us with an example for our imitation, He blazed a trail, and if we follow it, life and death are made holy and take on a new meaning.

The Christian man, conformed to the likeness of that Son who is the firstborn of many brothers, received 'the first-fruits of the Spirit' (Romans 8:23) by which He becomes capable of discharging the new law of love. Through this Spirit, who is 'the pledge of our inheritance' (Ephesians 1:14), the whole man is renewed from within, even to the achievement of 'the redemption of the body' (Romans 8:23): 'If the Spirit of Him who raised Jesus from the death dwells in you, then He who raised Jesus Christ from the dead will also bring to life your mortal bodies because of His Spirit who dwells in you' (Romans 8:11). Pressing upon the Christian to be sure, are the need and the duty to battle against evil through manifold tribulations and even to suffer death. But, linked with the paschal mystery and patterned on the dying Christ, he will hasten forward to resurrection in the strength which comes from hope.

## Chapter Two: *Gaudium et Spes* and the "Mystery of Man"

> All this holds true not only for Christians, but for all men of good will in whose hearts grace works in an unseen way. For, since Christ died for all men, and since the ultimate vocation of man is, in fact, one and divine, we ought to believe that the Holy Spirit in a manner known only to God offers to every man the possibility of being associated with this Paschal Mystery.
>
> Such is the mystery of man, and it is a great one, as seen by believers in the light of Christian revelation. Through Christ and in Christ, the riddles of sorrow and death grow meaningful. Apart from His Gospel, they overwhelm us. Christ has risen, destroying death by His death; He has lavished life upon us so that, as sons in the Son, we can cry out in the Spirit: Abba, Father.[1]

From beginning to end, *Gaudium et Spes* 22 speaks of the *mystery of man* made clear "in the mystery of the Incarnate Word" and by "believers in the light of Christian revelation." Elucidating the term, *mystery of man*, serves as the lens through which I reflect upon John Paul's interpretation of *Gaudium et Spes* 22: because the human person is created out of the love of God, and love is made visible in the Incarnate Word, he is newly created in Christ. Any attempt to understand the person apart from this Love, who is God, is not possible.[2]

---

[1] Second Vatican Council, *Gaudium et Spes* 22.

[2] By capitalizing *Love*, I emphasize the Johannine teaching of God as Love [1 John 4:8, 16].

To say that the *mystery of man* takes on light by the Incarnation is to suggest that the human person, who *is* the mystery, cannot be understood except through Jesus Christ. Created out of the love of God, one's life is meaningless without reference to His divine, creative love. My first elucidation of John Paul's notion of the human person, then, reflects upon the *mystery of man* in the Pope's first encyclical, to which I now turn.

## John Paul's Interpretation of the "Mystery of Man"

In *Redemptor Hominis* 8-10, I see three intimately connected truths, rooted in Sacred Scripture, upon which the Pope relies. These Scripture-based truths explain John Paul's reading of *Gaudium et Spes* 22's term, the *mystery of man*. The first truth is that the person is created by God in His image and likeness. Since John Paul stresses the fact that the human person's creation in God's image forms the "immutable basis of all Christian anthropology," this first Scripture-based truth is a theme to which I refer throughout this work.[3]

Second, the human person, redeemed by Christ's Precious Blood, is created anew in Jesus Christ (cf. Colossians 1:13-17, 21-22).[4] At certain moments, the Pontiff's elucidation of the human

---

[3] John Paul II, *Mulieris Dignitatem* 6. The Pontiff sees Christian anthropology as "the Christian truth about man" [John Paul II, *Homily*: 19 October 1982 (3)].

[4] John Paul II, *Redemptor Hominis* 8.

# Chapter Two: *Gaudium et Spes* and the "Mystery of Man"

person as a creature focuses upon image and likeness.[5] At other times, he stresses a different aspect of God's creation of the human person, such as his fundamental goodness.[6] Regardless of the specific dimension of the person's creation by God, which John Paul accentuates at any given moment, the crucial point for him is the fact that God creates the human person in His image, out of nothing.

In *Redemptor Hominis* 8-10, I draw attention to a third Scripture-based truth, which elucidates the *mystery of man*. This truth highlights the human person as a being who is loved by God: "God shows His love for us in that while we were yet sinners, Christ died for us" (Romans 5:8 RSVCE).[7] Another passage also underscores the human person as a creature who is loved by God: "For God so loved the world, as to give His only begotten Son; that whosoever believeth in Him, may not perish but may have life everlasting" (John 3:16.).[8] While these passages indicate Christ's redemptive

---

[5] In the passage I am considering, John Paul focuses upon the human person, created in God's image and likeness, in *Redemptor Hominis* 8 and 9.

[6] The Holy Father emphasizes the fundamental goodness of the human person throughout *Redemptor Hominis* 8-10.

[7] In *Redemptor Hominis* 8-10, John Paul does not cite Romans 5:8. Instead, in *Redemptor Hominis* 8 he refers to Romans 5:12-21 and in paragraph 9 he cites Romans 5:11. I offer Romans 5:8 above because both of the texts, to which the Pontiff refers, expound upon Romans 5:8. Again, the point is that by His death, Christ reconciles the human person to God. "For if while we were enemies we were reconciled to God by the death of His Son, much more, now that we are reconciled, will we be saved by His life" [Romans 5:10 RSVCE].

[8] John Paul quotes John 3:16 in *Redemptor Hominis* 8 and 10.

love for the person, particularly revealed in the Passion and death of Jesus, I distinguish it from one's re-creation in Christ in order to highlight the immense love of God for His human creature. Although that love logically dictates that the person become a new creation in Christ, I separate these truths in order to expound upon them and to more closely unite them in the end.

In my reading of *Redemptor Hominis* 8-10, then, I show that John Paul's interpretation of the Conciliar term, *mystery of man*, relies upon these three Scripture-based truths. Being created by God in His image and being created anew in Jesus Christ manifest, according to John Paul, God's love for the human person. God's love is particularly evident in the Passion and death of Jesus. Therefore, because the Pope interweaves these three truths, I do as well. While speaking of them necessarily involves distinguishing these concepts, my analysis of *Redemptor Hominis* 8-10 shows that they also comprise an intimately related whole in the Pontiff's thought.

## The Fundamental Goodness of the Human Person

In the first chapter of Genesis, one reads of the person's creation by God: "Let us make man to our image and likeness" (Genesis 1:26). Instead of opening *Redemptor Hominis* 8 by citing this well-known Scripture passage, however, John Paul immediately directs one's attention to God's affirmation of the goodness of His creation: having created "all the things that He had made," God saw that "they were very good" (Genesis 1:31).

## Chapter Two: *Gaudium et Spes* and the "Mystery of Man"

Elaborating upon the goodness of God's creation, the Pontiff observes that the "good has its source in wisdom and love."[9] Thus, when sin enters the world and creation becomes "subjected to futility" (Romans 8:20), Jesus Christ reconciles the human person to God the Father by drawing him back to the "divine Source of wisdom and love," from whom he is created.[10] The Pontiff highlights the fact that in Jesus, the person finds his "original link with the divine Source of wisdom and love" after sin enters the world with the fall of Adam.[11] As if commenting directly on *Gaudium et Spes* 22, John Paul speaks of Christ, the new Adam, who restores the person to God's friendship: "As this link was broken in the man Adam, so in the man, Christ, it was reforged."[12] Thus, the human person is not only created in God's image and likeness, but also, he is newly created in Christ, the new Adam, by His redemptive act (cf. Romans 5:14).[13]

After a brief reflection on how the world of today is "subjected to futility," the Pope focuses upon the pinnacle of visible creation, which is the human person.[14] Referring to the Second Vatican Ecumenical Council—and here, his remarks precede his citation of

---

[9] John Paul II, *Redemptor Hominis* 8.

[10] John Paul II, *Redemptor Hominis* 8.

[11] John Paul II, *Redemptor Hominis* 8. In this section of *Redemptor Hominis* 8, John Paul quotes Genesis 1:26-30 and Romans 8:20 (cf. 8:19-22).

[12] John Paul II, *Redemptor Hominis* 8. Here, John Paul cites Romans 5:12-21.

[13] John Paul II, *Redemptor Hominis* 8.

[14] John Paul II, *Redemptor Hominis* 8.

*Gaudium et Spes* 22—John Paul comments upon the *mystery of man*, which the Council brings to light.

According to the Pontiff, the Council analyzed the human person in two ways: first, "by penetrating like Christ the depth of human consciousness and [second,] by making contact with the inward mystery of man," expressed by "the word *heart*."[15] John Paul connects both Conciliar reflections on the human person by specifying the link between Christ and the human person: "Christ, the Redeemer of the world, is the One who penetrated in a unique, unrepeatable way into the mystery of man and entered his *heart*, thus uniting Himself "in a certain way…with each man."[16] By restoring to the person "that likeness to God which had been disfigured ever since the first sin," Christ, "the perfect man," raises human nature to "a dignity beyond compare."[17] The fact that the remainder of *Redemptor Hominis* 8 references *Gaudium et Spes* 22 further implies that the paragraph is a commentary upon it.

In *Redemptor Hominis* 8, the Pope speaks of the creation of the human person not in terms of image and likeness, but rather, as an affirmation of the goodness of God's creation. The Pope holds together these two truths: that God created the person in His image and likeness, and that the human person, whom God creates, is good. Affirming the goodness of the human person's existence is crucial to John Paul's thought precisely because the person, togeth-

---

[15] John Paul II, *Redemptor Hominis* 8.
[16] John Paul II, *Redemptor Hominis* 8.
[17] John Paul II, *Redemptor Hominis* 8.

## Chapter Two: *Gaudium et Spes* and the "Mystery of Man"

er with the rest of creation, has been "subjected to futility" on account of the fall.[18]

One might describe the "futility," which the human person experiences because of sin, as the meaninglessness of human life when it is severed from God, who is the source of life. After explicating John Paul's interpretation of *Gaudium et Spes* 22 in *Redemptor Hominis* 8-10, I return to this sense of "futility," the emptiness of human life when cut off from God, with my remarks on John Paul's *Opening Address* at the Puebla Conference.

The three Scripture-based truths I draw from *Redemptor Hominis* 8 are not only present, but they also specify the following truths concerning John Paul's notion of the human person. First, God's creation of the person indicates that his very existence is good, in and of itself. The great good of human life underscores the command that one is not to take innocent human life. Second, with his explicit mention of *Gaudium et Spes* 22, John Paul alludes to the person's being created anew in Jesus Christ. Although he develops this point in greater depth with *Redemptor Hominis* 9-10, his remark about Christ penetrating one's heart is telling: not only does Jesus Christ penetrate the *mystery of man* because "all things were made through Him" (John 1:3), but also, He pervades that mystery by the fact that He became Incarnate.[19]

A final remark about *Redemptor Hominis* 8 concerns John Paul's reflection upon the *mystery of man* by noting what I have identified as the third Scripture-based truth: God manifests His

---

[18] John Paul II, *Redemptor Hominis* 8.
[19] John Paul II, *Redemptor Hominis* 8.

love for the human person in the redemptive love of Jesus Christ. The Holy Father shows Christ's redemptive love for the human person in *Redemptor Hominis* 8 by first noting the goodness of His creation, which finds "its source in wisdom and love."[20] The human person, then, is created out of the immense love of God from the very beginning.

John Paul builds upon the foundation of God's love for the person by explaining that Christ, his Redeemer, visibly manifests that love by restoring him to the Father's friendship after sin enters the world. The *mystery of man* is noteworthy, then, because it signifies the dignity one has as a being who is created good by God, and who is restored to the source of that goodness, the "wisdom and love" of God, after sin pierces human history. The fundamental goodness of the human person and the drama of sin in human life point to Jesus, who redeems him. The redemption of Jesus reveals the Father's love.

## "The Mystery of the Father and His Love"

John Paul opens *Redemptor Hominis* 9 by noting that he is continuing his commentary upon the Conciliar teaching just rendered in the preceding paragraph. In fact, the specific point of *Gaudium et Spes* 22 that I see the Pope elucidating in *Redemptor Hominis* 9 is "the revelation of the mystery of the Father and His love" for the human person. Exactly how the Pope describes the Father and His love for the person becomes clear with the subsequent analysis.

---

[20] John Paul II, *Redemptor Hominis* 8.

## Chapter Two: *Gaudium et Spes* and the "Mystery of Man"

In *Redemptor Hominis* 9, the Holy Father's interpretation of *Gaudium et Spes* 22 returns to the creation of the human person. This time, he cites the Genesis text regarding one's creation in the image and likeness of God; he does so, however, only through explicit mention of Jesus Christ, who "became our reconciliation with the Father" (Romans 5:11; Colossians 1:20).[21]

In a masterful blend of the three Scripture-based truths that I am claiming substantiate the Pope's interpretation of the Conciliar term, *mystery of man,* John Paul expresses the human person's creation and being created anew by Jesus, through the love of the Father made visible in Christ's redemptive death on the Cross. Here, the Pope expresses the *mystery of man,* which term encapsulates the three Scriptural truths of one's creation and being created anew in Jesus out of the Father's love.

> As we reflect again on this stupendous text from the Council's teaching, we do not forget even for a moment that Jesus Christ, the Son of the living God, became our reconciliation with the Father (Romans 5:11, Colossians 1:20). He it was, and He alone, who satisfied the Father's eternal love, that Fatherhood that from the beginning found expression in creating the world, giving man all the riches of creation, and making him 'little less than God' (Psalms 8:6), in that he was created 'in the image and after the likeness of God' (Genesis 1:26). ...The redemption of the world—this tremendous mystery of love in which creation is renewed—is,

---

[21] John Paul II, *Redemptor Hominis* 9.

at its deepest root, the fullness of justice in a human heart—the heart of the first-born Son—in order that it may become justice in the hearts of many human beings, predestined from eternity in the first-born Son to be children of God (Romans 8:29-30; Ephesians 1:8) and called to grace, called to love.

In this passage, John Paul highlights God's creation of the person by focusing upon his re-creation through Jesus Christ, who reveals the Father's love. By calling attention to the fact that Jesus "became our reconciliation with the Father," the Pope emphasizes His redemptive act in terms of love: Jesus satisfies "the Father's eternal love."[22] Thus, John Paul links Christ's death with the Father and His love by seeing His love, poured out on the Cross, as "a fresh manifestation of the eternal fatherhood of God" and of His love for the person.[23] In Jesus, the Father draws near to each human being; the Son restores the person to the Father's friendship and makes of him a new creation as a child of God.

John Paul continues to interweave the three Scripture-based truths I have identified as his interpretation of the *Gaudium et Spes* 22 term, the *mystery of man*, in this encyclical text: the human person, created by God in His image and likeness and created anew in Jesus Christ, is revealed as a being known and loved by the Father. In the rest of *Redemptor Hominis* 9, the Pope elucidates this love, which "does not draw back before anything that justice requires in

---

[22] John Paul II, *Redemptor Hominis* 9.
[23] John Paul II, *Redemptor Hominis* 9.

## Chapter Two: *Gaudium et Spes* and the "Mystery of Man"

Him." The most explicit, visible expression of the Father's love for the human person is the fact that He sent "His only begotten Son" (John 3:16) to restore each person to the Father's friendship (cf. 1 Timothy 2:5-6).

Depicting the abyss of the Father's love for the human person, then, John Paul reiterates its sublimity before returning to the subject of one's re-creation in Christ, on account of His salvific love. John Paul explains the depth of God's love for the human person.

> Above all, love is greater than sin, than weakness, than the 'futility of creation' (Romans 8:20); it is stronger than death; it is a love always ready to forgive, always ready to go to meet the prodigal son (Luke 15:11-32), always looking for 'the revealing of the sons of God' (Romans 8:19), who are called 'to the glory that is to be revealed' (Romans 8:18).[24]

Here, John Paul holds two truths together: first, the infinite love of God for the human person, and second, the concrete perception of His eternal love made visible in Jesus Christ. The Passion and death of Jesus on the Cross manifests the love of God the Father, and, through His Son's Cross, John Paul emphasizes that the Father draws near to each human person. The Pope explains the Father's "drawing near" to the person, through the Cross of Jesus, as the "revelation of the Father."[25]

---

[24] John Paul II, *Redemptor Hominis* 9.
[25] John Paul II, *Redemptor Hominis* 9.

This revelation of the Father and outpouring of the Holy Spirit [that the Cross reveals], which stamp an indelible seal on the mystery of the Redemption, explain the meaning of the Cross and death of Christ. The God of creation is revealed as the God of redemption, as the God who is 'faithful to Himself' (1 Thessalonians 5:24), and faithful to His love for man and the world, which He revealed on the day of creation.[26]

In *Redemptor Hominis* 9, then, I see a continuation of John Paul's explication of the Conciliar expression, the *mystery of man*, in his focus on Jesus, who "satisfied the Father's eternal love." Quoting Saint Paul's Second Letter to the Corinthians, the Holy Father teaches, "For our sake God [the Father] made Him [the Son] to be sin who knew no sin" (2 Corinthians 5:21)."[27] By restoring the human person to Himself through Jesus Christ, the Father reveals both the depth of His love for the human person and the magnitude of one's calling to live in God's friendship. The Pope explains, God "made" Christ, the innocent Lamb, "to be sin (2 Corinthians 5:21)" in order "to reveal the love that is always greater than the whole of creation, the Love that is … [God] Himself, since "God is Love" (1 John 4:8, 16)."[28] His Christological intent is telling because the Cross, through which the Son redeems the human person, becomes a visible expression of the love of the eternal Father. The Pontiff elucidates this point in the following manner.

---

[26] John Paul II, *Redemptor Hominis* 9.
[27] John Paul II, *Redemptor Hominis* 9.
[28] John Paul II, *Redemptor Hominis* 9.

## Chapter Two: *Gaudium et Spes* and the "Mystery of Man"

The redemption of the world—this tremendous mystery of love in which creation is renewed—is, at its deepest root, the fullness of justice in a human heart—the heart of the first-born Son—in order that it may become justice in the hearts of many human beings, predestined from eternity in the first-born Son to be children of God and called to grace, called to love.[29]

John Paul continues his commentary on the Conciliar text in *Redemptor Hominis* 9. Since *Redemptor Hominis* 9 unites both God the Father's creation and Christ's re-creation of the human person by His redemptive death, which reveals the Father's love, one might also affirm that it elucidates *Gaudium et Spes* 22.[30] The specific point that John Paul reflects upon is that the Son reveals the Father's love: "Christ, the final Adam, by the revelation of the mystery of the Father and His love, fully reveals man to man himself and makes his supreme calling clear."[31]

The human person's "supreme calling" is to be a child of the Heavenly Father precisely because he has been restored to His friendship by the redemptive work of Jesus. The Holy Father concludes *Redemptor Hominis* 9 by putting a name to the "revelation

---

[29] John Paul II, *Redemptor Hominis* 9.

[30] The Pontiff's words in this paragraph indicate his intent to speak of *Gaudium et Spes* 22. "As we reflect again on this stupendous text from the Council's teaching, we do not forget even for a moment that Jesus Christ, the Son of the living God, became our reconciliation with the Father (Romans 5:11, Colossians 1:20)" [John Paul II, *Redemptor Hominis* 9].

[31] Second Vatican Council, *Gaudium et Spes* 22.

of love [which] is also described as mercy:" Jesus Christ is the "form and name" of the Father's revelation of love and mercy.

## The Passion of Christ Reveals the Father's Love

In *Redemptor Hominis* 10, the Pontiff reaches the heart of the expression, *mystery of man,* by developing the concept of the Father's love for the human person. In fact, *Redemptor Hominis* 10 draws together the three Scripture-based truths that illuminate John Paul's reading of the *Gaudium et Spes* 22 term, *mystery of man*. These three truths, the person's creation by God and his being created anew in Jesus Christ, and third, God's love for the person, are united in one pivotal thought: the Father reveals His love for the human person in the Passion and death of Christ.

One might argue that the love of God sums up these three truths, rooted in Sacred Scripture, in the first place. This is a valid objection. God's love for the human person is unquestionably evident in His creation of him: "For if man exists, it is because God has created him though love, and through love continues to hold him in existence."[32] In a similar way, creating the person anew in Jesus Christ also manifests God's love. "In the creation of the world and of man, God gave the first and universal witness to His almighty love and His wisdom, the first proclamation of the 'plan of His loving goodness,' which finds its goal in the new creation in Christ."[33]

---

[32] *Catechism of the Catholic Church* 27.
[33] *Catechism of the Catholic Church* 315.

## Chapter Two: *Gaudium et Spes* and the "Mystery of Man"

Although it is emphatically true that the concept of God's love is able to recapitulate any number of theological ideas, John Paul's remarks in *Redemptor Hominis* 10 suggest that he sees the love of the Father, which Jesus Christ manifests, as the culmination of the *mystery of man*. The human person is vivified and given new life, as the text explains, in the mystery of the Father's love that one encounters in Jesus Christ.

The person, according to John Paul's elucidation in *Redemptor Hominis* 8-9, is created in the Love who is God, Himself.[34] Having seen in *Redemptor Hominis* 9 that Jesus reveals "the mystery of the Father and His love" by His redemptive death, one might consider *Redemptor Hominis* 10 as an interpretation of *how* the "mystery of man take[s] on light" in the "mystery of the Incarnate Word."

The specific point that initiates John Paul's teaching on the *mystery of man* is the human person's essential need for love. In *Redemptor Hominis* 10, the Holy Father holds together both the person's need for love and the meaninglessness of his life when he regards himself as severed from the love of God. John Paul begins with love, perhaps initially understood as human love, and then he immediately draws that love upward to the divine: the human person is created anew in Christ's love. The Pope expresses these thoughts as follows.

---

[34] John Paul quotes 1 John 4:8, 16 in *Redemptor Hominis* 9, but he also explicates the love of God for the human person in His creative act of making him and restoring him to His friendship, as I have shown above with *Redemptor Hominis* 8.

Man cannot live without love. He remains a being that is incomprehensible for himself, his life is senseless, if love is not revealed to him, if he does not encounter love, if he does not experience it and make it his own, if he does not participate intimately in it. This…is why Christ the Redeemer 'fully reveals man to himself.'[35]

John Paul explains one's encounter with the love of God Incarnate in Jesus Christ as "the human dimension of the mystery of the redemption."[36] Seen in the light of Jesus, it is in "this dimension man finds again the greatness, dignity and value that belong to his humanity."[37] What John Paul highlights in *Redemptor Hominis* 10 is that the love of Christ, made visible by His death, confirms the magnitude of His love. The love that Christ reveals also indicates the dignity and worth of the human person. Elsewhere, the Pope notes that the Incarnation is the "most radical and elevating affirmation of the value of every human being," since, by His Incarnation, Christ unites Himself with each human person.[38]

*Redemptor Hominis* 10 suggests that the Pope's intention is to offer an analysis of *Gaudium et Spes* 22. Christ "reveals man to himself" because He shows him his own worth as a human person. He makes known the *mystery of man* by revealing to him that he is to become a child of God the Father. Further, Christ makes known

---

[35] John Paul II, *Redemptor Hominis* 10.
[36] John Paul II, *Redemptor Hominis* 10.
[37] John Paul II, *Redemptor Hominis* 10.
[38] John Paul II, *Christifideles Laici* 37; Second Vatican Council, *Gaudium et Spes* 22 quoted in John Paul II, *Redemptor Hominis* 13.

## Chapter Two: *Gaudium et Spes* and the "Mystery of Man"

one's adoptive sonship in His own Flesh by restoring him to the Father's friendship through His death on the Cross (cf. Romans 8:14-25; Galatians 4:5-7).

The Pope emphasizes the human person's re-creation in Christ, "in the mystery of the redemption," when he says, "man becomes newly 'expressed' and, in a way, is newly created."[39] That "new expression" of the human person takes place through his contact with Jesus. John Paul implies that the person's "new expression" becomes stifled by "immediate, partial, often superficial, and even illusory standards and measures of his being" that do not lead to an authentic understanding of oneself.[40] Instead, the Pontiff accentuates, together with the Conciliar document, the indispensability of Jesus Christ, who is the one to reveal the human person to himself. One must encounter Christ in order to understand both himself and the mystery of who he is as a human person.

John Paul explains the totality of approach with which one must seek Christ in order to understand oneself. Relentlessly, the person must "with his unrest, uncertainty and even his weakness and sinfulness, with his life and death, draw near to Christ."[41] The Pope stresses the fact that, for the human person to "find" himself, to let Christ reveal him to himself, the person must "enter into Him with all his own self [and], he must 'appropriate' and assimilate the whole of the reality of the Incarnation and Redemption."[42]

---

[39] John Paul II, *Redemptor Hominis* 10.
[40] John Paul II, *Redemptor Hominis* 10.
[41] John Paul II, *Redemptor Hominis* 10.
[42] John Paul II, *Redemptor Hominis* 10.

The Pontiff's key assertion, regarding the person's entrance into Christ's Incarnation and Redemption, highlights the intimate love Christ has for each human person and the need for him to "encounter…experience…[and to] participate" in the love that Jesus reveals to him. Exactly *how* the human person encounters Christ governs the rest of *Redemptor Hominis* 10, and, broadly speaking, the entirety of my project, as well. The place to begin one's reflection concerning the person's "entrance into Christ," then, is to continue my careful analysis of this paragraph.

John Paul indicates what happens when a person enters into Christ "with all his own self."[43] Such a person "bears fruit not only of adoration of God but also of deep wonder at himself."[44] Marveling at Christ's love not only evokes the person's adoration and gratitude to God for "so great a Redeemer," but it also illuminates one's own dignity and stature by showing the Father's regard for the human person by sending His Son in the first place.[45] According to John Paul, the "name for that deep amazement at man's worth and dignity" is the "Gospel…the Good News…[and] Christianity."[46]

John Paul notes that the Gospel, or the "amazement at man's worth and dignity," specifies the Church's solicitude of the person. Further, he explains that the "amazement at man's worth and dignity," which one might call the Gospel-amazement of the person,

---

[43] John Paul II, *Redemptor Hominis* 10.

[44] John Paul II, *Redemptor Hominis* 10.

[45] *Exsultet* at the Easter Vigil quoted in John Paul II, *Redemptor Hominis* 10.

[46] John Paul II, *Redemptor Hominis* 10.

## Chapter Two: *Gaudium et Spes* and the "Mystery of Man"

determines the mission of the Church in the world. Because Christianity understands the Father's high regard for human life, not only as Creator, but also by sending the Son as Redeemer, the Church never ceases to promote the welfare of the human person. The Pope depicts the connection between the Gospel-amazement of the human person and Jesus Christ in the following manner.

> This amazement, which is also a conviction and a certitude—at its deepest root it is the certainty of faith, but in a hidden and mysterious way it vivifies every aspect of authentic humanism—is closely connected with Christ. It also fixes Christ's place—so to speak, His particular right of citizenship—in the history of man and mankind.[47]

Gospel-amazement of the human person is "a conviction and a certitude" of Christ's abiding presence in the world because it testifies to the presence of Jesus on earth in human history, beginning with the Incarnation. The person continues to be loved by God [the Father] as human history unfolds throughout time. Further, "amazement at man's worth and dignity," which is the love that the Father has for His creature, is essential for the Pope's anthropology because, for him, it "vivifies every aspect of authentic humanism."[48]

With the Pontiff's mention of "amazement at man's worth and dignity" and Christ's presence "in the history of man," one hears an echo of the Conciliar document. Continuing his commen-

---

[47] John Paul II, *Redemptor Hominis* 10.
[48] John Paul II, *Redemptor Hominis* 10.

tary on *Gaudium et Spes* 22, John Paul seems to be speaking of the following passage, which reminds the reader of Christ's physical, tangible, earthly presence among people in human history. The section of *Gaudium et Spes* 22 below highlights the totality of Christ becoming human "like us in all things except sin" (Hebrews 4:15).

> Since human nature as He assumed it was not annulled, by that very fact it has been raised up to a divine dignity in our respect too. For by His Incarnation the Son of God has united Himself in some fashion with every man. He worked with human hands, He thought with a human mind, acted by human choice and loved with a human heart. Born of the Virgin Mary, He has truly been made one of us, like us "in all things except sin" (Hebrews 4:15).[49]

John Paul concludes *Redemptor Hominis* 10 with words expressing his pastoral affection for the human race. He explains that the Church, "unceasingly contemplating the whole of Christ's mystery," is fully convinced that the "Redemption that took place through the Cross has definitively restored his dignity to man and given back meaning to his life in the world."[50] Although the meaning of the person's life on earth "was lost to a considerable extent

---

[49] Second Vatican Council, *Gaudium et Spes* 22.
[50] John Paul II, *Redemptor Hominis* 10.

## Chapter Two: *Gaudium et Spes* and the "Mystery of Man"

because of sin," in Christ, he is "definitively restored to his dignity."[51]

John Paul specifically notes that the Church's task is to direct the human person to God, through Jesus Christ. The Pontiff explains the Church's essential duty throughout human history is "to direct man's gaze, to point the awareness and experience of the whole of humanity towards the mystery of God, to help all men to be familiar with the profundity of the Redemption taking place in Christ Jesus."[52] When the human person is directed to the Father through Jesus, it affects the very core of his being: "man's deepest sphere is involved—we mean the sphere of human hearts, consciences and events."[53]

My elucidation of *Redemptor Hominis* 8-10, then, suggests that it is one of John Paul's interpretations of the Conciliar expression, *mystery of man*. The Holy Father's depiction of the *mystery of man* in *Redemptor Hominis* 8-10 might be construed as rooted in three Scripture-based truths: that the human person is created by God, he is created anew in Jesus Christ, and he is a being who is deeply loved by God. The love of God—and John Paul emphasizes the Father's love—is visible in Christ's redemptive death on the Cross. Since the person's creation and re-creation, indeed, his very existence, depends upon the love of God the Father manifest in Jesus Christ, when the person is severed from the Father by his own doing, his very existence loses its essential meaning.

---

[51] John Paul II, *Redemptor Hominis* 10.
[52] John Paul II, *Redemptor Hominis* 10.
[53] John Paul II, *Redemptor Hominis* 10.

# Chapter Three

## John Paul's Opening Address at Puebla

At the beginning of my section on John Paul's notion of the human person, I state that his frequent mention of *Gaudium et Spes* 22 suggests it plays a vital role in his thought. Further, I indicate that the Conciliar text forms the core of his teaching on the person from three perspectives. The first standpoint, rooted in *Redemptor Hominis* 8-10, expounds upon Christ revealing the person to himself as one who is created by God, recreated in Jesus Christ, and loved by the Heavenly Father. As I describe above, Jesus makes the love of the Father visible by His Passion and death. A second perspective, which highlights *Gaudium et Spes* 22 in John Paul's thought on the human person, follows directly from the first. To extrapolate this second dimension, I primarily rely upon John Paul's *Opening Address* at the Puebla Conference, although I also cite *Dominum et Vivificantem* 36.

The second perspective on *Gaudium et Spes* 22 concerns, for John Paul, what he regards as the basis of Christian anthropology. The Holy Father first notes that the "Church possesses the truth about the human being" on account of the Gospel.[1] For John Paul, the *truth of the human person* is located in an anthropology, the "primordial assertion" of which is that he is "the image of God and cannot be reduced to a mere fragment of nature or to an anony-

---

[1] John Paul II, *Opening Address* at Puebla, 28 January 1979 (I.9).

mous element in the human city."² A consistent thinker, he elsewhere refers to the human person's creation by God, in His image and likeness, as the "immutable basis of all Christian anthropology."³

John Paul construes this "irreplaceable foundation" of Christian anthropology in language that personalizes and makes interiorly palatable one's creation in the image of God.⁴ Assimilating the human person's creation in terminology that expresses the intimate, personal reality of the human being, he describes each one as a "single, unique, and unrepeatable, someone thought of and chosen from eternity, someone called and identified by name."⁵ The singularity of the human person expressed by John Paul at Puebla, then, shows that Jesus reveals the individual to himself as a personal being of incomparable pre-eminence. This unrivaled, personal excellence of the human being encompasses two additional facets, and the Puebla *Address* sheds light on both of them.

The first facet of John Paul's Christian anthropology, which highlights the singular standing of every human being, builds upon his insistence in *Redemptor Hominis* 8-10 that God loves the person He creates. In my reading of the Puebla *Address*, the Holy Father claims that it is precisely because of God's personal, creative

---

² John Paul II, *Opening Address* at Puebla, 28 January 1979 (I.9).

³ John Paul II, *Mulieris Dignitatem* 6. For John Paul, Christian anthropology is "the Christian truth about man" [John Paul II, *Homily* 19 October 1982 (3)].

⁴ John Paul II, *Opening Address* at Puebla, 28 January 1979 (I.9).

⁵ John Paul II, *Opening Address* at Puebla, 28 January 1979 (I.9).

and redemptive love for the human being that elicits the futility of human existence if he lives without reference to God.

The emptiness of the human person's life, when undertaken apart from the One who created him, contributes to a second interpretation by the Pope of the Conciliar text. John Paul's insight specifies that Christ's revelation of the person to himself includes an explicit intimacy of being "thought of...chosen...called and identified by name" by his Creator.⁶ Elsewhere, the Holy Father explains a similar point: because the person is a creature, he is constituted "in a unique, exclusive and unrepeatable relationship with God Himself."⁷

On account of this profoundly intimate and personal Creator, the human person can only be fulfilled, at his deepest, interior level, by God. John Paul brings out the futility of human life when severed from God—and, consequentially, the person's innate uniqueness among the rest of creation—in his *Opening Address* at Puebla, which fittingly serves as my text for evaluating this claim.

The futility of human life when envisaged apart from God, however, is only one of the two facets that depict one's personal uniqueness. The second dimension that sheds light on the singular standing of the person is God becoming Man: by His Incarnation,

---

⁶ John Paul II, *Opening Address* at Puebla, 28 January 1979 (I.9).

⁷ John Paul expresses this thought in his Wednesday Catechesis, *Man An Woman He Created Them: A Theology of the Body*, with his discussion of man's original solitude. "Man is 'alone:' that means that he, through his own humanity, through what he is, is constituted at the same time in a unique, exclusive and unrepeatable relationship with God Himself" [John Paul II, General Audience 24 October 1979 (2)].

Jesus manifests the truth of the human being and the Catholic Church safeguards that truth. As John Paul often stresses, by taking on Flesh, "the Son of God, in a certain way united Himself with each man."[8]

Guarding the truth of the person, the Church brings out the unique marvel of each human being by continually accentuating human "worth and dignity" in contemporary society.[9] Rather than highlighting Church teaching on issues such as social justice or the defense of innocent human life, however, I specifically draw attention to her defense of human "worth and dignity" from its Christological source: the mystery of the Incarnate Word, who illuminates the mystery of the person and secures one's inestimable significance by taking on Flesh.[10]

Explaining John Paul's interpretation of *Gaudium et Spes* 22 with these two perspectives—the person's creation by God in *Redemptor Hominis* 8-10 and his incomparable, personal distinction in the Puebla *Address*—is crucial for developing his thought on the martyr and contemplating Christ's face because both aspects suggest the unrivaled existence of the human person among the rest of creation.[11] The love of God, manifest in each person's creation and

---

[8] Second Vatican Council, *Gaudium et Spes* 22 quoted in John Paul II, *Redemptor Hominis* 13.

[9] John Paul II, *Redemptor Hominis* 10.

[10] John Paul II, *Redemptor Hominis* 10; Second Vatican Council, *Gaudium et Spes* 22. As the Pontiff makes clear in *Redemptor Hominis* 10, "amazement at man's worth and dignity," which I describe above, is a vital aspect of his anthropology.

[11] *Fides et Ratio* 60 encapsulates a third interpretation of *Gaudium et Spes* 22.

# Chapter Three: John Paul's Opening Address at Puebla

re-creation, then, indicates both his unparalleled, personal existence and his ultimate fulfillment in God.

The person's creation by God as a "single, unique, and unrepeatable someone" confirms his inherent dignity, freedom, and calling to be a child of God. In fact, "based on the uniqueness and irrepeatability" of each human person, his dignity is his "indestructible property."[12] Human dignity and human freedom play a key role in the Pope's understanding of martyrdom, as I explain below.

## Two Objections to Citing the *Opening Address* at Puebla

At Puebla, John Paul claims that the Church safeguards Christ's teaching on the intimate union between the human person and Christ. Before expounding upon this claim, however, one might raise two objections. First, because the Puebla *Address* is delivered in a pastoral context, since the Pope speaks "as a brother to his very beloved brothers," who are bishops, why am I focusing upon it?[13] Second, why is it appropriate to use the Puebla text, which is less weighty than encyclicals and other papal documents, in my present work?

Responding first to the objection concerning the pastoral context of the Puebla *Address*, I answer in the following manner. Concisely put, to qualify a document as primarily *pastoral* rather than

---

[12] John Paul II, *Christifideles Laici* 37.

[13] John Paul II, *Opening Address* at Puebla, 28 January 1979 (I.9). By *pastoral*, I mean implementing truths of the Faith with daily living.

*theological*, specifies an inherent relevance of the text to one's life.[14] It conveys the truth it signifies so that one may directly apply it to various situations in life. Thus, to identify a document as *pastoral* does not indicate that a text or context is devoid of Church teaching and other theological truths. In fact, the Pope comments upon the reality that truth "offers a solid basis" so that it may have its proper, practical application in daily life.[15] The following section from the Puebla *Address*, then, reveals both its pastoral setting and it upholds the relevance of truth to daily life.

> It is a great consolation for the universal Pastor to see that you come together here, not as a symposium of experts or a parliament of politicians or a congress of scientists or technologists (however important such meetings may be), but rather as a fraternal gathering of Church pastors. As pastors, you keenly realize that your chief duty is to be teachers of the truth: not of a human, rational truth but of the truth that comes from God. That truth includes the principle of authentic human liberation: 'You will know the truth, and

---

[14] My point is not to declare which, of the various texts I cite, are *pastoral* or *theological*, as if the two could be opposed to each other in the first place; they cannot. Instead, given the role that the Puebla *Address* plays in my work, I note the fact that truth *is* pastoral. In other words, living the truth, which the Catholic Faith professes, is both a pastoral and a moral living of the theological truths taught by the Church. As I describe below, the martyr's death is a vibrant living of the truth of the Faith.

[15] John Paul II, *Opening Address* at Puebla, 28 January 1979 *Introduction*.

### Chapter Three: John Paul's Opening Address at Puebla

the truth will set you free' (John 8:32). It is the one and only truth that offers a solid basis for an adequate "praxis."[16]

I note the pastoral dimension of the *Opening Address* at Puebla then, because it directly concerns a point I raise in this section: that the Church safeguards the *mystery of man* on account of Christ's Incarnation. To affirm that the Church protects the truth of the human person through Christ's Incarnation both raises and answers objections regarding pastoral context because she applies the truth she received from Christ directly to the human person. In other words, the Catholic Church ensures the "radical and elevating affirmation" of each person since, "by His Incarnation," Christ unites Himself with each human person.[17] I mention the pastoral context of the Puebla *Address*, then, because John Paul speaks to the ecclesial safekeeping of the truth of the human person, which, in fact, secures the unfolding of an authentic Christian humanism.

Granted the validity of focusing upon this *Address*, which is both pastoral and theological, the second objection remains. Why is the Puebla *Address*, which is minor among other papal documents, a significant reference? The *Opening Address* at Puebla does not contain the level of importance that an encyclical carries.

To the above question, I answer as follows. The various truths upon which John Paul expounds in the *Opening Address* dictates its inclusion in my project. Its central themes concern the Church's

---

[16] John Paul II, *Opening Address at Puebla*, 28 January 1979 *Introduction*.

[17] John Paul II, *Christifideles Laici*, 37; Second Vatican Council, *Gaudium et Spes* 22.

task of safeguarding the human person, in all his inherent uniqueness, as the being created in God's image. Further, the *Address* brings out the person's matchless, personal distinction on account of his creation in the image of God. Although a seemingly minor text, the *Address* is a notable instance of John Paul's interpretation of the *mystery of man* in the Conciliar document, which specifies: "Only in the mystery of the Incarnate Word does the mystery of man take on light."[18] Thus, it aptly serves my intended goal.

## The Person's Ontological Dependence Upon His Creator

John Paul regards the human person's dependence upon his Creator as a central theme of Christian anthropology. At Puebla, the Pope makes it clear that the foundation of one's dependence is rooted in the Genesis text: "God created man in His own image, in the image of God He created him; male and female He created them" (Genesis 1:27).[19] My work with the Puebla *Address*, then,

---

[18] Second Vatican Council, *Gaudium et Spes* 22.

[19] John Paul II, *Opening Address* at Puebla, 28 January 1979 (I.9). At times, the Pope explains that being created in the "image and likeness of the personal God" means that the human person is "a rational being (*animal rationale*)" [John Paul II, *Mulieris Dignitatem* 6]. See also the following documents of John Paul II: *Mulieris Dignitatem* 7; *Fides et Ratio* 88; *Veritatis Splendor* 38, 43, 73. In other places, John Paul elucidates the person's creation in terms of his inability to "attain fulfillment apart from this image and likeness" [John Paul II, *Mulieris Dignitatem* 5]. See also two other works of his: *Mulieris Dignitatem* 11 and *Homily* 15 August 1991 (4-6)]. In still another place, the Pope reflects that the person is in the image and likeness of God because he is "a rational and free creature capable of knowing God and loving Him" [John Paul II, *Mulieris Digni-*

## Chapter Three: John Paul's Opening Address at Puebla

naturally returns to the fundamental notion of one's creation in the image of God, which is the first point I highlight with *Redemptor Hominis* 8-10. The human person's creation in God's image (*imago Dei*) forms, for John Paul, the crux of one's existence as a human being. In other words, because the person is a creature, he depends upon his Creator.

I see the Puebla *Address* as a second expression of John Paul's thought regarding *Gaudium et Spes* 22, because it describes this crucial factor in Christian anthropology: the human person's creation in the image of God. The Holy Father elaborates upon one's dependence on God, because of his creation in His image, with *Dominum et Vivificantem*. In my reading of this encyclical, I believe John Paul builds upon the person's dependence upon his Creator, to which the Puebla *Address* speaks, on account of one's creation in the image of God. The Pope explains this thought in the following passage.

> Having been called into existence, the human being—man and woman—is a creature. The 'image of God,' consisting of rationality and freedom, expresses the greatness and dignity of the human subject, who is a person. But this person-

tatem 7]. John Paul also elucidates "image and likeness" in terms of existing in relation to another. He explains this point as follows: "Being a person in the image and likeness of God thus also involves existing in a relationship, in relation to the other 'I.' This is a prelude to the definitive self-revelation of the Triune God: a living unity in the communion of the Father, Son and Holy Spirit. ... Only in this way can we understand the truth that God in Himself is Love (cf. 1 John 4:16)" [John Paul II, *Mulieris Dignitatem* 7].

al subject is also always a creature: in his existence and essence he depends on the Creator.[20]

From the above quotation, then, one might surmise that being created in the image of God not only means that the person is rational and free, but also, it specifies that he depends upon the Creator for his very life and existence in the world as a human person.[21] One's dependence upon his Creator is, therefore, an ontological reality. In other words, the person's dependence upon God is due to the fact that he exists *as* a human person.[22] Because the human person exists *as a creature*, he is ontologically dependent upon his Creator for both his existence and his essence. In short, the person depends upon God *that* he is (existence) *as* he is (essence).

Rooted in the mystery of the Incarnation, the Pope locates the foundation of Christian anthropology—his ontological dependence upon the Creator—in the visible moment of the Incarnation, at Christ's birth.[23] The Incarnation specifies the person's ontological dependence upon his Creator because all are created through Him (John 1:3), out of His great love, and because, "with each one Christ has united Himself for ever through this mystery [of Re-

---

[20] John Paul II, *Dominum et Vivificantem* 36.

[21] John Paul II, *Dominum et Vivificantem* 36.

[22] One's existence as a human person who is created in the image of God, and thus, ontologically dependent upon Him, makes an objective statement about the nature of his existence. The ontological claim concerning the person's dependence upon the Creator does not speak to the subjective manner in which the person feels about his existence in the image and likeness of God.

[23] John Paul II, *Opening Address* at Puebla, 28 January 1979 (I.9).

demption]," which the Incarnation makes possible.²⁴ Further, since he is created in the image and likeness of God, the Incarnation shows that the person's dependence upon the Creator makes each human a unique, unrepeatable being who is loved by God. He explains as follows.

> I made especially pointed reference to this irreplaceable foundation of the Christian conception of the human being in my *Christmas Message*: 'Christmas is the feast of the human being. …Viewed in quantitative terms, the human being is an object of calculation. …But at the same time the human being is single, unique, and unrepeatable, someone thought of and chosen from eternity, someone called and identified by name.'²⁵

According to the Pope's analysis, the Christian understanding of the human being draws upon his remarkable difference from the rest of creation. If each person is "single, unique, and unrepeatable," then he is unique among all human beings.²⁶ Rather than supposing the person to be a random creation or an unknown entity, he is a rational being, deliberately created, chosen, and identified by his Creator as a being who is distinctively loved by God in an "unrepeatable" way. The Pontiff explains that the person, "in his unique unrepeatable human reality…keeps intact the image and

---

²⁴ John Paul II, *Redemptor Hominis* 13.
²⁵ John Paul II, *Opening Address* at Puebla, 28 January 1979 (I.9).
²⁶ John Paul II, *Opening Address* at Puebla, 28 January 1979 (I.9).

likeness of God Himself."²⁷ Not only is each person created in God's image and likeness, then, as if that were some intangible, vague reality, but also the Holy Father emphasizes that each human being, personally created by God, is known and loved by God.

To specify the manner of human existence in extraordinarily intimate terms indicates how highly God looks upon each human person as His own. As John Paul explains, being loved by God is not only fundamental to human existence as a creature in the image of God, but also, it specifies his "capacity of having a personal relationship with God," which the Puebla *Address* highlights.²⁸ John Paul describes the cherished relationship that God desires to have with the person as that which follows upon his existence as a creature in God's image. The Pope describes elsewhere that the "constitutive properties of human nature" are properties that flow from the very gift of being created in the image and likeness of God.²⁹ The capacity of having a relationship with God, then, flows from one's being—from the very way in which God creates him to be.

> [I]n his own humanity [man] receives as a gift a special 'image and likeness' to God. This means not only rationality and freedom as constitutive properties of human nature, but also, from the very beginning, the capacity of having a personal relationship with God, as 'I' and 'you,' and there-

---

²⁷ John Paul II, *Redemptor Hominis* 13.
²⁸ John Paul II, *Dominum et Vivificantem* 34.
²⁹ John Paul II, *Dominum et Vivificantem* 34.

fore the capacity of having a covenant, which will take place in God's salvific communication with man."[30]

At Puebla, then, the Pontiff reiterates that each human being is a "single, unique, and unrepeatable, someone thought of and chosen from eternity, someone called and identified by name."[31] Because "by His Incarnation, the Son of God has united Himself in some fashion with every man," the person, created in God's image, is not only a "single, unique, and unrepeatable" person, but he also has an incomparable dignity.[32]

Noting that the person is "the high point of the whole order of creation in the visible world," the Conciliar teaching especially brings to light his unrivaled dignity.[33] Since "human nature as [Christ] assumed it was not annulled, by that very fact it has been raised up to a divine dignity."[34] This insightful description of the human person emphasizes both human distinction and divine love.[35]

As I explain above, the Pope sees one's creation by God in His image and likeness as the "immutable basis of all Christian anthropology," and as the "irreplaceable foundation" of the Christian

---

[30] John Paul II, *Dominum et Vivificantem* 34.

[31] John Paul II, *Opening Address* at Puebla, 28 January 1979 (I.9).

[32] Second Vatican Council, *Gaudium et Spes* 22; John Paul II, *Redemptor Hominis* 13; John Paul II, *Opening Address* at Puebla, 28 January 1979 (I.9).

[33] John Paul II, *Mulieris Dignitatem* 6.

[34] Second Vatican Council, *Gaudium et Spes* 22.

[35] By "human distinction," I mean that which differentiates the person from other creatures.

concept of the person.[36] Thus, one might deduce that John Paul's notion of Christian anthropology particularly stresses the intimate union between Creator and creature: not only is the person created in God's image and likeness, but also each individual person is a singular expression of divine love. Moreover, according to the Pontiff's Puebla *Address*, Christ reveals the human person to himself as someone intimately known and uniquely loved by God. Calling each by name, God personally knows and loves everyone (cf. Isaiah 49:1). This unparalleled, personal distinction of the human being ensures his identity as a creature who, because he is made in the image and likeness of God, is also personally known and loved by God.

The foundation of Christian anthropology, then, which the Pope brings out at Puebla, is that the person's creation in the image of God specifies his ontological dependence upon his Creator. The person cannot be other than he is.

In sum, the intimate language with which John Paul expresses the basis of Christian anthropology suggests several key factors. First, it indicates the person's exceptional reality among the rest of visible creation. Created in the image of God, the person ontologically depends upon Him for his existence *as* a human person.

Second, it underlines the esteem and affection that God has for the person, with whom He desires to have an intimate relationship. Again, the basis for that relationship is one's creation in the image of God. Further, the central factor of Christian anthropology sug-

---

[36] John Paul II, *Mulieris Dignitatem* 6; John Paul II, *Opening Address at Puebla*, 28 January 1979 (I.9).

gests that God anticipates a response from the person. That response, which entails a manner of living that encapsulates his entire being, brings to the fore the person's free will to embrace his dependence upon God.[37]

Finally, because the person depends upon God for his existence as a human being, Christian anthropology dictates the irreducibility of the person to anonymity. In my next section, I emphasize the fact that the human person cannot be separated from the source of his creation, who is God.

According to John Paul, then, the basis of Christian anthropology first concerns the human person's unique mode of existence, created in the image of God, and second, it involves his explicit manner of existence as a rational being who is unique and unrepeatable. Although one might wonder whether I am stipulating a dual foundation of Christian anthropology, these two facets—the person's creation in God's image and his rational, unrepeatable uniqueness—are two ways of expressing a single reality. In other words, *because* the person is created in the image of God, each is a rational, singular, and irreplaceable human person. The person's unique singularity is a truth of the human person that follows upon his creation in God's image and likeness.

---

[37] By faith, the person responds to God who reveals Himself. He is to do so with his entire being. "You shall love the Lord your God with all your heart, and with all your soul, and with all your mind" (Matthew 22:37 RSVCE). I discuss the subject of faith with *Veritatis Splendor* below.

## The Futility of the Human Person's Existence When Fragmented from God

Among various texts that support his claim, that one's life is meaningless when severed from God, John Paul's *Opening Address* at the Puebla Conference continues to be an excellent source for further reflection. The *Address* to the Third General Assembly of CELAM in Puebla de los Angeles is significant to my argument because it hinges upon the truth that, since the human person is created in God's image, he cannot be understood apart from God.[38]

In his first apostolic journey abroad, John Paul opens his discussion on the unique, personal distinction of the human person by explaining that the "truth we owe to human beings is first and foremost a truth about themselves."[39] The Pope justifies this statement by noting that, in today's world, with its "inadequate view of the human being," the truth about the human person is obscure.[40] While so much has been written about the human person, para-

---

[38] John Paul II, *Opening Address* at Puebla, 28 January 1979 (I.9).

[39] In John Paul's first apostolic journey abroad, he visited the Dominican Republic, Mexico and the Bahamas. For a complete listing of his addresses during his visit (25 January through 1 February 1979), see the official website of the Holy See [www.vatican.va].

[40] At the time of his *Opening Address*, liberation theology was a point of contention among the participants. Regarding the Pope's speech, contemporary North American author, George Weigel, writes that John Paul had the opportunity to influence what "post-Vatican II Catholicism would be in Latin America—a question now focused through the intense debate over 'liberation theology'" [Weigel, *Witness to Hope*, 282].

doxically, he is more confused than ever about the meaning of his existence and the final end of human life.

The Pontiff explains contemporary confusion about the truth of the human person: this is the "age of people's deepest anxieties about their identity and destiny; it is the age when human beings have been debased to previously unsuspected levels, when human values have been trodden underfoot as never before."[41] What explains the present denigration of the human person to such an appalling degree?

John Paul suggests that the concept of the person's futility lies in the "paradox" of atheistic humanism: when the human person is "severed from an essential dimension of [his] being—the Absolute [God]—[he is] thus confronted with the worst possible diminution of [his] being."[42] To explicate this reduction of the human person, the Holy Father not only underscores one's ontological dependence upon God, but he also emphasizes the necessity of looking to Christ in order to understand the human person.

John Paul focuses upon Christ Jesus by arguing that *Gaudium et Spes* 22 "goes to the heart of the problem" when it teaches, "Only in the mystery of the Incarnate Word does the mystery of man take on light."[43] Because He unites Himself with every person "by His Incarnation," Christ reveals the person's unique status.[44]

The Holy Father's intimate portrayal of God's creative act, in vibrant terms of a "single, unique, and unrepeatable, someone,"

---

[41] John Paul II, *Opening Address* at Puebla, 28 January 1979 (I.9).
[42] John Paul II, *Opening Address* at Puebla, 28 January 1979 (I.9).
[43] John Paul II, *Opening Address* at Puebla, 28 January 1979 (I.9).
[44] Second Vatican Council, *Gaudium et Spes* 22.

directly counteracts the anonymity of the human person, who is often reduced "to a mere fragment of nature."[45] As the Pope highlights at Puebla, the essential core of Christian anthropology stipulates that, on account of his creation in God's image, the person "cannot be reduced to a mere fragment of nature or to an anonymous element in the human city."[46] His reason for asserting this futility lies in the fact that, since God created the person in His image and likeness, his life only takes on meaning when it is directed toward God.[47]

Since the human person is created in the image of God, he depends upon his Creator for his existence as a human person. Any

---

[45] John Paul II, *Opening Address* at Puebla, 28 January 1979 (I.9).

[46] John Paul II, *Opening Address* at Puebla, 28 January 1979 (I.9). With this remark, John Paul refers to *Gaudium et Spes* 12 and 14.

[47] John Paul II, *Opening Address* at Puebla, 28 January 1979 (I.9). Several other examples from John Paul II include: *Mulieris Dignitatem* 5; *Novo Millennio Ineunte* 54; *Sollicitudo Rei Socialis* 30; *Tertio Millennio Adveniente* 7; *Veritatis Splendor* 73, 84. Further, when citing *Gaudium et Spes* 22, John Paul often explains that the mystery of the human person, illumined by the Incarnation, cannot be understood without reference to God. I am not suggesting, however, that the comprehensive whole of the Pontiff's claims, which involve the futility of one's existence when severed from God, are necessarily contained in his references to *Gaudium et Spes* 22. Rather, in several instances, the Pope mentions the meaninglessness of one's existence when severed from God in conjunction with *Gaudium et Spes*, such as the following, in addition to his *Opening Address* at Puebla: *Dominum et Vivificantem* 29; *Dives in Misericordia* 1; *Fides et Ratio* 12, 60. The Holy Father's occasional allusion to the futility of one's life when severed from God, spoken in conjunction with several references to *Gaudium et Spes* 22, ordains its inclusion in my presentation of his anthropology.

attempt to reduce the person to a lesser entity is akin to tearing him out of his own personhood. Diminishing the human person to a "mere fragment of nature" so confuses his existence that it detaches him from his identity so much so that he sees no difference between himself and the rest of creation.[48] This profound reduction of the human person divides him from his mode of existence as a rational being and so thoroughly separates him from who he is, that he comes to regard himself, albeit, perhaps unconsciously, as an unknown, unidentified, anonymity in the world.[49]

If one's concept of the person fails to take into account his relation to God, then his own understanding of himself necessarily falls short. Because he has been fragmented from the fundamental cause of his being, one's understanding of his essential nature becomes confused and meaningless. In the Puebla *Address*, the Holy Father points to the section of *Gaudium et Spes* 22 that calls attention to the *mystery of man* in light of Jesus Christ. In fact, John Paul's interpretation of the Conciliar document at Puebla explains further Christ's illumination of the human person.

---

[48] John Paul II, *Opening Address* at Puebla, 28 January 1979 (I.9).

[49] See, for example, the following documents of Saint John Paul II: *Christifideles Laici* 6; *Laborem Exercens* 7; *Tertio Millennio Adveniente* 36; *Evangelium Vitae* 22; *Ecclesia in Europa* 9, 44. Further, in both *Evangelium Vitae* 24 and *Veritatis Splendor* 93, the Pope indicates that the confusion between good and evil is "an extremely serious and mortal danger" [John Paul II, *Evangelium Vitae* 24] and "the most dangerous crisis which can afflict man" [John Paul II, *Veritatis Splendor* 93].

## The Church Safeguards the Truth of the Human Person

At Puebla, the Holy Father clearly emphasizes the role of the Church in proclaiming the truth of the human person. Noting its pastoral dimension, John Paul stipulates that revealing the truth of the person offers "the best service to human beings."[50] He explains, however, that the Church not only has "the right and the duty to proclaim the truth about the human being," but she also receives this truth from the Incarnate Word, "who knew 'what was in man's heart' (John 2:25)."[51] Elsewhere, John Paul explains that speaking about Jesus, who reveals to the human person who he is, expresses "the chief way for the Church" because Jesus is "our way 'to the Father's house' (John 14:1) and...the way to each [person]."[52]

John Paul further portrays the intimate relationship between Christ, the Church, and the human person. Far from being an ambiguous, distant structure, the Church is, in fact, a vibrant, living reality that passionately loves her Founder, Jesus, and earnestly seeks to defend the truth He has entrusted to her.

> On this way leading from Christ to man, on this way on which Christ unites Himself with each man, nobody can halt the Church. This is an exigency of man's temporal welfare and of his eternal welfare. Out of regard for Christ and in view of the mystery that constitutes the Church's own life, the Church cannot remain insensible to whatever

---

[50] John Paul II, *Opening Address* at Puebla, 28 January 1979 (I.9).
[51] John Paul II, *Opening Address* at Puebla, 28 January 1979 (I.9).
[52] John Paul II, *Redemptor Hominis* 13.

serves man's true welfare, any more than she can remain indifferent to what threatens it. ...She is at once a sign and a safeguard of the transcendence of the human person.[53]

The Church, as John Paul explains, is fundamentally involved in safeguarding the truth regarding the human person. Because the person is created for God, the Church's task is to protect the person's pathway to the Father through Christ. While the context of the Puebla speech necessarily calls for the pastoral voice of the Church, the Pope clearly specifies a central truth regarding his concept of the human person. This vital truth is that, because the person is created in God's image, considering him apart from the manner in which he is created deprives him of the dignity he possesses. As guardian and protector of the Sacred Deposit of the Faith, the Church both ensures and proclaims the truth of the human person, which Christ makes known to her.[54]

Implying that Christ manifests the truth of the person through the Church He founded focuses upon John Paul's reference to the Gospel. As I comment above with *Redemptor Hominis* 8-10, the Holy Father describes the term, *Gospel*, as the name for the "amazement at man's worth and dignity."[55] In his Puebla *Address*, the Pope explains that, on account of the Gospel—and, I might add, because of this "amazement at man's worth and dignity"[56]— the Church "possesses the truth about the human being." Combin-

---

[53] John Paul II, *Redemptor Hominis* 13.
[54] Second Vatican Council, *Dei Verbum* 10.
[55] John Paul II, *Redemptor Hominis* 10.
[56] John Paul II, *Redemptor Hominis* 10.

ing these two dictums of the Pope, one might specify that the truth about the human person commands nothing less than astonishment—sheer wonder—at the mystery of who he is. Jesus illuminates the truth of the human person through the Church He founded and continues to guide through the Holy Spirit. The Pope explains these thoughts as follows.

> Thanks to the Gospel, the Church possesses the truth about the human being. It is found in an anthropology that the Church never ceases to explore more deeply and to share. The primordial assertion of this anthropology is that the human being is the image of God and cannot be reduced to a mere fragment of nature or to an anonymous element in the human city.[57]

At Puebla, John Paul's interpretation of *Gaudium et Spes* 22 focuses upon fact that, because the person is created in "the image of God," regarding him as anything less divides him from the dignity he possesses. Further, being created in the image and likeness of God implies that human life takes on meaning *in* God because the person is created *for* God, who is Love, and who is the person's beginning and final end (cf. 1 John 4:8, 16; Revelation 21:6).

John Paul's Puebla remarks hinge upon the person's creation in God's image, which he highlights when he discusses both the person's futility apart from God and the Church's task of safeguarding the truth of the human person. The Pope's solicitous care for the

---

[57] John Paul II, *Opening Address* at Puebla, 28 January 1979 (I.9).

# Chapter Three: John Paul's Opening Address at Puebla

human person underscores both his "unique, and unrepeatable" existence and God's preferential love for him as "someone thought of and chosen from eternity."[58] The *Opening Address* at Puebla shows, in unambiguous language, that the object of the Church's care is the human person in his "unique unrepeatable human reality, which keeps intact the image and likeness of God Himself."[59]

As I will point out in a moment, the Church's solicitude for the human person leads to *Gaudium et Spes* 24, which is the second text that comprises a central core of the Pope's anthropology. Before turning to this notable analysis, however, a final dimension of John Paul's interpretation of *Gaudium et Spes* 22 remains for discussion.

My last point concerns the importance John Paul heeds to human transcendence. *Fides et Ratio* 60 offers a significant contribution to my sketch of the Pope's anthropology because it concisely expresses the person's distinction from the rest of creation on account of his rationality, which provides him with the capacity to transcend the visible, material world in which he lives.

---

[58] John Paul II, *Opening Address* at Puebla, 28 January 1979 (I.9).
[59] John Paul II, *Redemptor Hominis* 13.

# Chapter Four

## *Fides et Ratio* and the Human Person

As the core of John Paul's anthropology stipulates, the person's creation in the image of God (*imago Dei*) specifies his ontological dependence upon Him. *Fides et Ratio* 60 brings out this truth, which the Puebla *Address* emphasizes, but with a complementary difference: the human person's creation in the image of God is the bedrock upon which human transcendence lies. My central concern in this chapter is to show that human transcendence, rooted in one's rational nature, is due to his creation in the image of God.

Among the many texts that highlight the person's transcendent nature, *Fides et Ratio* 60 contains fundamental elements for explicating John Paul's thought on the person because it indicates that the foundation of human transcendence lies in his creation in the image of God. Together with the Puebla *Address*, then, one learns that being created in the image of God not only specifies human dependence upon Him for his existence *as* a person, but it also expresses that dependence based upon his rationality: the person has the capacity to transcend the world in which he lives. *Fides et Ratio* 60 plays a significant role in my work because it marks human transcendence as the distinguishing characteristic between the person and the rest of visible creation.

In *Fides et Ratio* 60, John Paul draws upon the Second Vatican Ecumenical Council in order to apply it to his present study on the relationship between faith and reason. He opens paragraph 60 by referring to chapter one of the first part of *Gaudium et Spes* (12-22), which is entitled, "The dignity of the human person."[1] In the Pope's opinion, this first chapter of *Gaudium et Spes* "amounts to a virtual compendium of...biblical anthropology."[2]

My extrapolation of *Fides et Ratio* 60 links the following extract from *Gaudium et Spes* 22 with a further remark on the human person: he is differentiated from visible creation on account of his transcendent nature. John Paul's special mention of *Gaudium et Spes* suggests that the following extract occupies a privileged position in his ensuing thought.

> The truth is that only in the mystery of the Incarnate Word does the mystery of man take on light. For Adam, the first man, was a figure of Him who was to come, namely Christ the Lord. Christ, the final Adam, by the revelation of the mystery of the Father and His love, fully reveals man to man himself and makes his supreme calling clear.[3]

---

[1] Since paragraph 22 of *Gaudium et Spes* concludes the opening chapter, one might presume it contains the culmination of preceding Conciliar thought on the human person. It is not surprising that the Pontiff begins *Fides et Ratio* 60 by stating the prime significance of this Conciliar document, which seems to exemplify his own thought on the person. In this paragraph, he specifically refers to *Gaudium et Spes* 22 as "one of the constant reference points" of his teaching, as I mention above [John Paul II, *Fides et Ratio* 60].

[2] John Paul II, *Fides et Ratio* 60.

[3] Second Vatican Council, *Gaudium et Spes* 22 quoted in John Paul II, *Fides et Ratio* 60.

# Chapter Four: *Fides et Ratio* and the Human Person

In the Pontiff's analysis of *Fides et Ratio* 60, the first chapter of *Gaudium et Spes* concerns three points. First, it reiterates the inestimable worth of the human person, who is created in the image of God. Second, the Conciliar document "explains the dignity and superiority of the human being over the rest of creation, and [third, it] declares the transcendent capacity of human reason."[4] The Pope also mentions atheism, and the document identifies the "flaws of its philosophical vision…especially in relation to the dignity and freedom of the human person."[5] Although *Fides et Ratio* 60 draws upon each one of these areas, I focus upon what I see as the crucial addition for examining John Paul's teaching on the person: the supremacy of "the human being over the rest of creation," on account of the "transcendent capacity of human reason."[6]

My specific task, then, is to show that *Fides et Ratio* 60 comments upon the *mystery of man* and Christ's revelation of the human person to himself by offering a key principle that illustrates John Paul's interpretation of *Gaudium et Spes* 22. That principle, which contributes toward my sketch of his anthropology, is human distinction from the rest of visible creation based upon his transcendent nature.

The person's singularity among visible creation is a truth that follows upon his creation in the image of God.[7] Human transcend-

---

[4] John Paul II, *Fides et Ratio* 60.
[5] John Paul II, *Fides et Ratio* 60.
[6] John Paul II, *Fides et Ratio* 60.
[7] In this part of *Fides et Ratio* 60, the Pope cites *Gaudium et Spes* 14-15 in relation to transcendence. Shortly thereafter, he points to the "cli-

ence flows from the heart of the Pope's anthropology, which is the person's creation in the image of God. For the sake of clarity, I first discuss the person's preeminence among creation. Second, I consider the fact that rationality enables him to transcend the world in which he lives.

## The Person's Rational Nature Distinguishes Him from the Rest of Visible Creation

John Paul teaches that the person's creation in the "image and likeness of the personal God" means that he is ontologically dependent upon his Creator for his existence as a human person.[8] An additional factor, which I touch upon in the Puebla account, is the person's unique irrepeatability that testifies to the profundity of God's creative love for him.

The Pontiff's insistence upon the human person's "dignity and superiority...over the rest of creation" in *Fides et Ratio* 60 further refines his concept of human distinction, on account of his creation in the image of God, by emphasizing his rationality as the basis for human transcendence. Continuing my reflection upon John Paul's interpretation of *Gaudium et Spes* 22, then, being created in the image of God means the human person is unique among visible creation because he is the sole entity whom God chose to create in

---

matic section of the chapter," extracting the lines from paragraph 22, to which I refer above.

[8] John Paul II, *Mulieris Dignitatem* 6; John Paul II, *Opening Address at Puebla*, 28 January 1979 (I.9); John Paul II, *Dominum et Vivificantem* 36.

# Chapter Four: *Fides et Ratio* and the Human Person

this (rational) manner. Thus, the person's "supreme calling" is likewise distinct from the rest of creation.⁹

In *Fides et Ratio* 60, the crucial factor that the Pope highlights is that, because the person is created in the image of God, he has a rational nature; his variance from the rest of visible creation is evident in his rationality.¹⁰ Although *Fides et Ratio* 60 offers this principle, another text, *Augustinum Hipponesem*, expounds upon its meaning. Admittedly, John Paul highlights themes from the works of Saint Augustine in this document. Nevertheless, the Pope acknowledges Augustine's influence, and he encourages study of the "thought of an incomparable man whose children and disciples we all are in a certain fashion, both in the Church and in the western world itself."¹¹

---

⁹ John Paul II, *Fides et Ratio* 60.

¹⁰ One might find it interesting to note that John Paul indirectly supports the point that the person's rationality differentiates him from the rest of creation in his exhortation to study philosophy. In particular, the Pope speaks of the prime importance of philosophical formation, not only for seminarians, but also for the whole of Christian education [John Paul II, *Fides et Ratio* 60].

¹¹ John Paul II, *Augustinum Hipponesem* Chapter IV. John Paul provides further evidence of his own esteem for Augustine and concord with his thought when he affirms that "the exact and heartfelt knowledge of his life awakens the thirst for God, the attraction of Christ, the love for wisdom and truth, the need for grace, prayer, virtue, fraternal charity, and the yearning for eternal happiness" [John Paul II, *Augustinum Hipponesem Introduction*]. Moreover, he reiterates his concurrence with previous Pontiffs when he reaffirms his own desire that the works of the saint be studied: "I too have added my voice to those of my predecessors, when I expressed my strong desire 'that his philosophical, theological and spiritual doctrine be studied and spread, so that he may continue . . . his

In his Apostolic Letter, *Augustinum Hipponesem*, John Paul clarifies how the person's rational nature distinguishes him from the rest of visible creation, and he states why it makes such a difference. Referring to the Conciliar term that I am discussing, *the mystery of man*,[12] John Paul defends, with Augustine, the fact that the human person's greatness lies in his ability to enjoy God.[13] The person is in the "image of the One whom he is capable of enjoying, and whose partner he can become."[14] Since the person is created in the image of God, his capacity to enjoy God "'is in the soul of man,

---

teaching in the Church, a humble but at the same time enlightened teaching which speaks above all of Christ and love'" [John Paul II, *Augustinum Hipponesem* Introduction].

[12] John Paul II, *Augustinum Hipponesem* Chapter II 2 Chapter IV.

[13] John Paul II, *Augustinum Hipponesem* Chapter II 2. In *Gaudium et Spes* 12, one reads that, among all of visible creation, only the human person "has the capacity of knowing and loving his Creator," because he is created in the image of God. "Sacrae enim Litterae docent hominem 'ad imaginem Dei' creatum esse, capacem suum Creatorem cognoscendi et amandi, ab eo tamquam dominum super omnes creaturas terrenas constitutum, ut eas regeret, eisque uteretur, glorificans Deum" [Second Vatican Council, *Gaudium et Spes* 12]. In addition, the ability to enjoy God also results in joy for the creature. The Doctor of the Church, Saint Therese of the Child Jesus and of the Holy Face, elucidates joy as follows: "joy isn't found in the material objects surrounding us but in the inner recesses of the soul. One can possess joy in a prison cell as well as in a palace. The proof is this: I am happier in Carmel even in the midst of interior and exterior trials than in the world surrounded by the comforts of life, and even the sweetness of the paternal hearth" [Saint Therese of Lisieux, *Story of a Soul* translated by John Clarke, OCD (Washington, D.C.: Institute of Carmelity Studies Publications, 1976), 137].

[14] John Paul II, *Augustinum Hipponesem* Chapter II 2.

## Chapter Four: *Fides et Ratio* and the Human Person

which is rational or intellectual...immortally located in his immortality,' and therefore, the sign of his greatness: 'he is a great nature, because he is capable of enjoying the highest nature and of becoming its partner.'"[15] Hinging upon the truth of one's creation in the image of God, then, his rationality differentiates him from visible creation because it enables him to enjoy his Creator.[16]

In *Augustinum Hipponesem*, John Paul brings out the idea that rationality makes the person unique among the rest of visible creation because he is capable of seeking for the truth and hoping to find it.[17] The Pontiff further elaborates upon this insight by explaining that seeking the truth helps one to transcend the visible world, and—what is central for the Pope—it helps the person to

---

[15] John Paul II, *Augustinum Hipponesem* Chapter II 2.

[16] John Paul II, *Augustinum Hipponesem* Chapter II 2. Indeed, the human person is "the only creature on earth which God willed for itself" [Second Vatican Council, *Gaudium et Spes* 24]. The English translation of *itself*, however, is often confusing. In the Latin, *seipsam*, is translated as *itself*, which is feminine because it refers to *creature* [*creatura*]. Since one cannot say *man* is willed by God for *herself*—the feminine gender of *creatura* being lost in the English—it is translated in the neuter, as *itself*. A more comprehensible translation of the text is as follows. "This likeness reveals that the person, who is the only creature on earth whom God wills [voluerit] for [propter] himself, is not able to find himself except through a sincere gift of himself. [Haec similitudo manifestat hominem, qui in terris sola creatura est quam Deus propter seipsam voluerit, plene seipsum invenire non posse nisi per sincerum sui ipsius donum"].

[17] John Paul II, *Augustinum Hipponesem* Chapter IV.

grasp the *mystery of man*.¹⁸ John Paul recounts the thought of Augustine on this point.

> He [Augustine] teaches therefore that one must seek the truth 'with piety, chastity and diligence,' in order to overcome doubts about the possibility of returning into oneself, to the interior realm where truth dwells; and likewise to overcome the materialism which prevents the mind from grasping its indissoluble union with the realities that are understood by the intelligence, and the rationalism that refuses to collaborate with faith and prevents the mind from understanding the 'mystery' of the human person.¹⁹

What *Augustinum Hipponesem* brings to light, then, is how the human person's creation in the image of God makes him unique among visible creation. The person's rational nature distinguishes him because he is able to enjoy his Creator.²⁰ In addition, *Augustinum Hipponesem* accentuates the point that one's rationality specifies that the person is able to seek and to find the truth.²¹ The person can hope. He can hope to find the truth and he can hope for what he desires.

One might ask the reason for the Pontiff's emphasis upon the human person's differentiation from the rest of visible creation. Of

---

[18] John Paul II, *Augustinum Hipponesem* Chapter IV; Second Vatican Council, *Gaudium et Spes* 22.
[19] John Paul II, *Augustinum Hipponesem* Chapter IV.
[20] John Paul II, *Augustinum Hipponesem* Chapter II 2.
[21] John Paul II, *Augustinum Hipponesem* Chapter IV.

# Chapter Four: *Fides et Ratio* and the Human Person

what importance is human uniqueness? The person's distinction is significant because rationality is a facet of being human that "makes possible" God becoming man.[22] John Paul sees Jesus Christ as central to authentic Christian anthropology because such an anthropology is "founded on the person of Christ, which will bring the dynamism of the creation and redemption to bear on reality and on the correct solution to the problems of life."[23]

The human person's creation in the image of God indicates that rationality specifies his way of being human. His rational nature dictates his capacity to receive truth. Thus, the person's creation in God's image not only stipulates his differentiation from the visible world, but it also expresses a dimension of being human that "allows" the Son to become man.

Because the person's distinctiveness among creation is often confused or negated in contemporary society, calling particular attention to one's "dignity and superiority . . . over the rest of creation," in a manner that stresses his rational nature, is a substantial contribution toward the Christian concept of the person. Reflecting upon John Paul's interpretation of *the mystery of man* highlights rationality as a significant factor of his creation in the image of God, and thus, of his exclusivity among visible creation.

---

[22] I put quotation marks around "makes possible" since God can do anything, except that which contradicts His nature. Since "human nature was assumed, not absorbed," by the Incarnation, the Son could not assume the nature of an irrational creature because it would contradict His nature. See Vatican Council I, *Dei Filius* 4 (Denzinger 3017).

[23] John Paul II, *Ex Corde Ecclesiae* 33.

In agreement with the Pontiff's analysis of Augustine, I maintain that rationality is the basis of one's ability to enjoy God.[24] Rationality includes, of course, the ability to pray. The human person can raise his mind and heart to the Father in love. What lies at the heart of his enjoyment of God, then, is love.

The person's delight in God which, in addition to rationality, indicates the capacity for contemplation, is key to understanding the martyr's death as a contemplation of Christ's face. I discuss the nature of contemplation, according to John Paul's understanding of the term, *contemplating the face of Christ*, below. For the moment, however, having reflected upon the superiority of the human person "over the rest of creation," I next consider the "transcendent capacity of human reason."[25]

## The "Transcendent Capacity of Human Reason"

As I suggest, the person's creation in the image of God specifies his "dignity and superiority…over the rest of creation" and, based upon human rationality, it indicates his capacity for transcendence.[26] In other words, the human person's reason enables him to transcend the visible, material world in which he lives. The fact that the person is open to the transcendent is vital to John Paul's teaching because it implies his spiritual capacity. Elsewhere, John

---

[24] John Paul II, *Augustinum Hipponesem* Chapter II 2.
[25] John Paul II, *Fides et Ratio* 60.
[26] John Paul II, *Fides et Ratio* 60.

## Chapter Four: *Fides et Ratio* and the Human Person

Paul describes human transcendence in terms of Augustine's restless thirst for God.[27]

John Paul insists upon the fact that human knowledge is not "limited strictly to the world of sense experience."[28] He defines human transcendence as the ability of the mind to reach beyond the visible, material world.[29] Because the person can think beyond (transcend) the material world, he is also able to desire what lies beyond the present world.[30] Conversely, because the person desires the infinite, his thinking transcends the world in which he lives.

One of John Paul's particularly enlightening explanations of *transcendence* is in his encyclical, *Centesimus Annus*. He explains human transcendence when commenting upon the fact that truth is objective. Indeed, he maintains that the desire for truth "is part

---

[27] John Paul II, *Pastores Dabo Vobis* 45.

[28] John Paul II, *Fides et Ratio* 83.

[29] John Paul II, *Fides et Ratio* 83. Elsewhere, the Pope acknowledges that the Fathers of the Church "fully welcomed reason which was open to the absolute [John Paul II, *Fides et Ratio* 41]. Further, the Pope uses the word *transcend* in the sense of *reaching beyond* when he writes concerning the Incarnation, "to enter into 'the fullness of time' means to reach the end of time and to transcend its limits, in order to find time's fulfillment in the eternity of God" [John Paul II, *Tertio Millennio Adveniente* 9].

[30] John Paul alludes to the idea that a person is able to think beyond, or transcend, the world in which he lives when he discusses human suffering. In *Salvifici Doloris*, the Pope writes that when a person "discovers the salvific meaning of suffering," he becomes a "completely new person" and that new understanding of oneself confirms "the spiritual greatness which in man surpasses the body in a way that is completely beyond compare" [John Paul II, *Salvifici Doloris* 26].

of human nature itself."[31] Because truth is exterior to the mind, the human person is able to reach "his full identity" when he adheres to the truth by the way he lives.[32] The Pope describes the transcendent nature of truth as follows.

> Totalitarianism arises out of a denial of truth in the objective sense. If there is no transcendent truth, in obedience to which man achieves his full identity, then there is no sure principle for guaranteeing just relations between people. ... If one does not acknowledge transcendent truth, then the force of power takes over, and each person tends to make full use of the means at his disposal in order to impose his own interests or his own opinion, with no regard for the rights of others. ... Thus, the root of modern totalitarianism is to be found in the denial of the transcendent dignity of the human person who, as the visible image of the invisible God, is therefore by his very nature the subject of rights which no one may violate—no individual, group, class, nation or State.[33]

Since John Paul maintains that human transcendence involves what lies beyond the tangible world, then one might suggest that he implies Christ reveals the human person to himself as a being who

---

[31] John Paul II, *Fides et Ratio* 3.

[32] John Paul II, *Centesimus Annus* 44. See also John Paul II, *Veritatis Splendor* 84-89. The Pope comments upon the same quotation in *Veritatis Splendor* 99.

[33] John Paul II, *Centesimus Annus* 44.

## Chapter Four: *Fides et Ratio* and the Human Person

desires fulfillment beyond what is immediately and tangibly present. Again, to say that Christ reveals the person to himself is to specify that He makes known who the person is and what concerns his ultimate fulfillment. To be sure, Christ reveals one's destiny and one's "supreme calling" to each person.[34]

John Paul affirms that human transcendence is "the basis of the essentially religious dimension of the human person," and this dimension "can be grasped and recognized by reason itself."[35] The person's religious dimension specifies that he is essentially open to God: "The human individual is open to transcendence, to the Absolute; he has a heart which is restless until it rests in the Lord."[36] The crux of his argument is that the truth of the human person, who is created and redeemed in Christ, dictates his openness not only to visible reality, but also to that which lies beyond his immediate grasp.[37] Concisely put, the human person's creation in God's image means he is able to transcend the world in which he lives and thus, he is essentially open to God. Creation in the image of God also signifies that the human person can only be fulfilled by God.

John Paul understands the truth of the human person as his creation in God's image and his redemption by Christ. Further, the

---

[34] Second Vatican Council, *Gaudium et Spes* 22 quoted in John Paul II, *Fides et Ratio* 60.

[35] John Paul II, *Pastores Dabo Vobis* 45.

[36] John Paul II, *Pastores Dabo Vobis* 45.

[37] John Paul II, *Pastores Dabo Vobis* 45. The text reads as follows: "Every human being, as God's creature who has been redeemed by Christ's Blood, is called to be reborn 'of water and the Spirit' (John 3:5) and to become a 'son in the Son'" [John Paul II, *Pastores Dabo Vobis* 45].

*mystery of man* dictates his fundamental openness to God, regardless of whether the person knows it. In other words, human transcendence confirms one's ontological dependence upon God: because he is created by God, he can only be fulfilled by God.

Earlier in the same document, the Pope teaches that the "truth of Christian Revelation, found in Jesus of Nazareth, enables all men and women to embrace the 'mystery' of their own life."[38] This statement refers to *Gaudium et Spes* 22, where one learns that Christ's Incarnation brings the *mystery of man* to light. The dimension of the human person that *Fides et Ratio* 15 illuminates is his ability to be challenged by the absolute truth of Christian revelation. Absolute truth triggers human transcendence by inciting the person to reach beyond himself.

The person is not only open to the transcendent because of his creation by God, but also the truth beckons one to go beyond oneself, to reality that lies beyond one's immediate, tangible grasp. The provocation that the absolute truth evokes, then, reveals that it not only incites one's openness to the transcendent, but also, it respects human autonomy and human freedom. The significant factor is that absolute truth has the power to summon the person beyond himself. The person has the capacity to see beyond the visible, material world in which he lives.

Since the person's transcendent capacity is rooted in the fact that he is created in the image of God, human transcendence also testifies to God's own transcendent nature. Elsewhere, John Paul

---

[38] John Paul II, *Fides et Ratio* 15. The ideas in this paragraph and the following paragraph extrapolate upon *Fides et Ratio* 15.

explains God's transcendence as a gift, in conjunction with his teaching on the Holy Spirit: "The Triune God, who 'exists' in Himself as a transcendent reality of interpersonal gift, giving Himself in the Holy Spirit as gift to the human person, transforms the human world from within, from inside hearts and minds."[39] Thus, the person's transcendent capacity is a reality that flows from his creation by God, in His image, for God is "a transcendent reality of interpersonal ."[40]

---

[39] John Paul II, *Dominum et Vivificantem* 59.
[40] John Paul II, *Dominum et Vivificantem* 59.

# Chapter Five

## One "Finds Oneself" Through Self-Gift

Three vital documents concerning John Paul's notion the human person, *Redemptor Hominis* 8-10, the *Opening Address* at Puebla, and *Fides et Ratio* 60, serve to illuminate his interpretation of *Gaudium et Spes* 22, which I claim focuses on the *mystery of man*. These texts emphasize the person's creation in the image of God and what it signifies. Again, the "immutable basis of all Christian anthropology," as John Paul sees it, lies in the fact that the person is created in the image of God.[1] One may reasonably maintain, therefore, that *Gaudium et Spes* 22 forms the nucleus of the Pontiff's insight regarding the human person.

In *Redemptor Hominis* 8-10, I extrapolate the Pope's interpretation of the *mystery of man* using three truths rooted in Sacred Scripture: first, the person is created in the image and likeness of God; second, he is newly created in Christ through His redemptive death; and third, God loves the human person He creates. Given the fact that one's creation in the image of God is imperative to Christian anthropology, it is fitting to examine this foundation in the first point of my first text and it is a vital factor to which I continually refer.

Since the "primordial assertion" of Christian anthropology maintains that the person is created in the image of God, man is

---

[1] John Paul II, *Mulieris Dignitatem* 6.

ontologically dependent upon his Creator.² My second illustration of John Paul's analysis of *Gaudium et Spes* 22 describes human dependence upon God for one's existence *as* a person. To underscore this truth, I rely upon John Paul's *Opening Address* at the Puebla Conference, which highlights the person's incomparable dignity and God's desire for intimacy with Him. The Holy Father brings out the Church's task of proclaiming the truth about the person, and this truth compels sheer astonishment at the mystery of who he is. As I show above, the *Address* calls attention to the impossibility of reducing the person to "a mere fragment of nature" and it explains the futility of his life when it is severed from God.

The third point I make, which illustrates John Paul's interpretation of *Gaudium et Spes* 22, shows that both human distinction from the rest of creation and the foundation of human transcendence lie in the fact that the person is created in the image of God.³ Using *Fides et Ratio* 60 together with *Augustinum Hipponesem*, I expound upon the notion that human transcendence confirms one's ontological dependence upon God: having been created by God, one can likewise only be fulfilled by Him. Further, I show that the human person is not only capable of enjoying God, but also, that his rationality means he is able to search for the truth and he can hope to find it.⁴

The person is open to the transcendent, then, because he is rational; having been created in the image of God, absolute truth im-

---

² John Paul II, *Opening Address* at Puebla, 28 January 1979 (I.9); John Paul II, *Dominum et Vivificantem* 36.

³ John Paul II, *Fides et Ratio* 60.

⁴ John Paul II, *Augustinum Hipponesem* Chapter II 2; Chapter IV.

pels human transcendence to reach beyond oneself.[5] Analyzing certain texts leads to the conclusion that one's creation in the image of God specifies both his ontological dependence upon Him and, based upon human rationality, it denotes the person's capacity for transcendence.

Again, the truth of the human person is based in a Christian anthropology that affirms the person's creation in the image of God. The three points I summarize above, extrapolated from John Paul's insight on *Gaudium et Spes* 22, support and expound upon this fundamental component of Christian anthropology. Now, an additional factor deserves consideration.

The Holy Father holds that the "essential truth concerning man," and "one of the key points of all Christian anthropology," is that the person finds himself "through a sincere gift of himself."[6] This truth places *Gaudium et Spes* 24 next to paragraph 22 as a vital component to Christian anthropology because it shows that the person discovers who he is when he gives himself to another. According to the Pope, this Biblically based anthropology provides that "man discovers himself as belonging to Christ and discovers that in Christ he is raised to the status of a child of God" the Father.[7] Thus, he more easily comprehends "his own dignity as man, precisely because he is the subject of God's approach and presence, the subject of the divine condescension, which contains the pro-

---

[5] John Paul II, *Fides et Ratio* 15.
[6] *To the Youth of the World* 14; John Paul II, *Salvifici Doloris* 28; Second Vatican Council, *Gaudium et Spes* 24.
[7] John Paul II, *Dominum et Vivificantem* 59.

spect and the very root of definitive glorification."[8] In other words, because the Father gives Himself to the human person, his response to God means he receives even more from Him: divine adoption.

My next task, then, examines John Paul's interpretation of *Gaudium et Spes* 24. The Pope highly regards *Gaudium et Spes* 24 since he asserts that it summarizes "the whole of Christian anthropology" and that it is "the structural basis of biblical and Christian anthropology."[9] Several instances of John Paul's interpretation of *Gaudium et Spes* 24, in conjunction with my work on *Gaudium et Spes* 22, suggest that both paragraphs form a bedrock of his thought on the person.

My following analysis of John Paul's interpretation of *Gaudium et Spes* 24 serves to extrapolate his thought on the person from three perspectives. These points stress the giving of oneself to God and to others. Further, they complement my work on *Gaudium et Spes* 22 and they advance that work in the following ways.

First, with *Redemptor Hominis* 8-10, I show above that John Paul regards the person's creation in the image of God as an essential point—the foundational basis—of Christian anthropology.[10]

---

[8] John Paul II, *Dominum et Vivificantem* 59. Earlier in this encyclical, John Paul explains that, through grace, the human person "is called and made 'capable' of sharing in the inscrutable life of God" [John Paul II, *Dominum et Vivificantem* 9].

[9] John Paul II, *Dominum et Vivificantem* 59; John Paul II, *Mulieris Dignitatem* 7.

[10] John Paul II, *Redemptor Hominis* 8-10. The Pope specifies that one's creation in the image of God is central to his concept of Christian

## Chapter Five: One "Finds Oneself" Through Self-Gift

Now I add the fact that being created in the image of God is a *gift* that the human person receives from his Creator.[11] And, because the *imago Dei* is a gift each person receives from God, it indicates that being a gift for another is intrinsic to the nature of the human person as such.[12]

Underlying the fact that the person's creation in God's image is a gift, that gift requires a response from the person: one is to "seek the truth and to adhere to it once it is known."[13] Indeed, living in the truth compels one to *be* who he *is*. Texts that particularly enable me to stress God's gift of creation in the *imago Dei* are *Mulieris Dignitatem* 7 and *Dominum et Vivificantem* 34.

Second, with John Paul's *Opening Address* at Puebla, I explain above that being created in the image of God means that the human person is ontologically dependent upon his Creator for his existence *as* a human being. Because the person is created by God, any attempt to separate the person from God results in his sense of emptiness and futility. With John Paul's interpretation of *Gaudium et Spes* 24, I now explain the person's ontological dependence upon God as an intimate relationship between God and the human person using *Dominum et Vivificantem* 59.

---

anthropology in *Mulieris Dignitatem* 6 and in his *Opening Address* at Puebla, 28 January 1979 (I.9).

[11] John Paul II, *Dominum et Vivificantem* 34.

[12] From a subjective perspective, accepting one's ontological dependence upon God facilitates the person's awareness of his own exalted status, namely, his dignity as a child of the Heavenly Father. Acknowledging one's creation in God's image as a gift also stipulates how the human person is to love others: by making a gift of himself to God and to others.

[13] John Paul II, *Veritatis Splendor* 34.

Third, with the *Fides et Ratio* text and other supporting documents, I describe the person's rational nature as the basis of his distinction from among the rest of visible creation. Moreover, his rationality enables him to transcend the visible, material world in which he lives.[14] With *Gaudium et Spes* 24, I demonstrate that rationality is coupled with the person's ability and desire for communion with another, and that communion opens the person to the other as a gift. *Salvifici Doloris* 28 is particularly helpful in explicating the person's fundamental openness to another person, which suggests that giving oneself to another entails willingness to suffer for and with another human person.

To adequately comment upon the Pontiff's interpretation of *Gaudium et Spes* 24, I offer the complete passage below.

> God, who has fatherly concern for everyone, has willed that all men should constitute one family and treat one another in a spirit of brotherhood. For having been created in the image of God, who "from one man has created the whole human race and made them live all over the face of the earth" (Acts 17:26), all men are called to one and the same goal, namely God Himself.
>
> For this reason, love for God and neighbor is the first and greatest Commandment. Sacred Scripture, however, teaches us that the love of God cannot be separated from love of neighbor: 'If there is any other Commandment, it is summed up in this saying: Thou shalt love thy neighbor as

---

[14] John Paul II, *Augustinum Hipponesem* Chapter IV.

# Chapter Five: One "Finds Oneself" Through Self-Gift

thyself. ... Love therefore is the fulfillment of the Law' (Romans 13:9-10; cf. 1 John 4:20). To men growing daily more dependent on one another, and to a world becoming more unified every day, this truth proves to be of paramount importance.

Indeed, the Lord Jesus, when He prayed to the Father, 'that all may be one . . . as We are one' (John 17:21-22) opened up vistas closed to human reason, for He implied a certain likeness between the union of the divine Persons, and the unity of God's sons in truth and charity. This likeness reveals that man, who is the only creature on earth which God willed for itself, cannot fully find himself except through a sincere gift of himself (cf. Luke 17:33).[15]

---

[15] Second Vatican Council, *Gaudium et Spes* 24. "Deus, qui paternam curam omnium habet, voluit ut cuncti homines unam efficerent familiam fraternoque animo se invicem tractarent. Omnes enim creati ad imaginem Dei, qui fecit 'ex uno omne genus hominum inhabitare super universam faciem terrae' (Acts 17:26), ad unum eumdemque finem, id est ad Deum ipsum, vocantur. Quapropter dilectio Dei et proximi primum et maximum mandatum est. A Sacra autem Scriptura docemur Dei amorem a proximi amore seiungi non posse: '... si quod est aliud mandatum, in hoc verbo instauratur: Diliges proximum tuum sicut teipsum... Plenitudo ergo legis est dilectio' (Romans 13:9-10; cf. 1 John 4:20). Quod vero hominibus magis in dies ab invicem dependentibus atque mundo magis in dies unificato maximi comprobatur esse momenti. Immo Dominus Iesus, quando Patrem orat ut 'omnes unum sint..., sicut et nos unum sumus' (John 17:21-22), prospectus praebens humanae rationi impervios, aliquam similitudinem innuit inter unionem personarum divinarum et unionem filiorum Dei in veritate et caritate. Haec similitudo manifestat hominem, qui in terris sola creatura est quam Deus propter seipsam voluerit, plene seipsum invenīre non posse nisi per

The following points offer John Paul's interpretation of *Gaudium et Spes* 24. First, being created in the image of God is a gift; second, one's ontological dependence upon God describes a profound relationship of intimacy between God and the person; third, the person's capacity for communion with another opens him to suffer for another. The Pontiff's interpretation of *Gaudium et Spes* 24,

---

sincerum sui ipsius donum" (Luke 17:33). As I explain above, the translation of *seipsam* as *itself* is confusing, since the person is either male or female. "Haec similitudo manifestat hominem, qui in terris sola creatura est quam Deus propter seipsam voluerit, plene seipsum invenire non posse nisi per sincerum sui ipsius donum." Again, the precise and logical translation of the passage is as follows. "This likeness reveals that the person, who is the only creature on earth whom God wills [voluerit] for [propter] *himself*, is not able to find [invenire] himself except through a sincere gift of himself." The notion of "finding oneself," might seem vague or ambiguous to the contemporary reader. The word *invenire* perhaps best translates as *find*; however, it can also mean *come upon, find out*, or *discover*. Thus, one might explain the Conciliar insight as follows. A person discovers who he is as a human being precisely through giving himself to another. The connotation is that one comes to see who he is when he gives himself to another. One might ask what it means to give oneself to another, whether that *other* be God, or another human person. In Sacred Scripture, a similar idea concerns losing oneself, or losing one's life to preserve it. *Gaudium et Spes* 24 cites Luke 17:33 after expressing the idea of self-gift. The following passages carry the same meaning: Matthew 16:25; Mark 8:35; Luke 9:24. Coupled with the Conciliar text, then, one might answer that giving oneself to another, in freedom and in love, protects and preserves one's own identity as a human person. Elsewhere, John Paul identifies finding oneself, which is the Council's notion of "self-discovery," as "self-realization" [John Paul II, *Mulieris Dignitatem* 7].

Chapter Five: One "Finds Oneself" Through Self-Gift          89

then, fittingly serves as the second indispensable basis for analyzing his thought on the human person.

**John Paul's Notion of the Human Person as Self-Gift**

In his pontifical writings that comment upon *Gaudium et Spes* 24, John Paul focuses upon the human person as a gift.[16] The Pon-

---

[16] In his article on John Paul's use of *Gaudium et Spes* 24, Pascal Ide reflects upon the centrality of giving in his thought: "Le don est un concept central de la pensée de Jean-Paul II" [Pascal Ide, *Une Théologie du Don: Les occurrences de Gaudium et Spes, n. 24, §3 chez Jean-Paul II (premiére partie)* in Anthropotes 17/1 (2001) 149-178, p. 149]. Henceforth, this first part of Ide's article will be referred to as *Une Théologie du Don (premiére partie)*. Ide also remarks that John Paul offers his "first complete citation of the passage [Second Vatican Council, *Gaudium et Spes* 24], on February 2, 1979," with his homily on the Feast of the Presentation [Ide, *Une Théologie du Don (premiére partie)*, 150]. The Pope's reference to the Conciliar paragraph at the inception of his pontificate suggests that it plays an important role in his thought. Although the theology of giving is a domain in itself, my work on the martyr's self-gift contributes to the notion of giving, which includes laying down his life for those who put him to death. I develop this thought with *Salvifici Doloris* 28. For more information on notion of giving in theology, see Jean-Luc Marion, *Étant Donné: Essai d'une Phénoménologie* (Paris: Presses Universitaires de France, 1997); Rev. William D. Virtue, Doctoral Dissertation, Pontificia Università S. Tommaso d'Aquino, Teologia: *Mother and Infant: The Moral Theology of Embodied Self-giving in Motherhood in Light of the Exemplar Couplet Mary and Jesus Christ* (Romae: Pontificia Studiorum Universitas, 1995). For interesting studies on the concept of gift in theology and other fields, see *Le don*: Colloque interdisciplinaire: Lyon, 24-25 Novembre 2001, Sous la présidence de Jean-Luc

tiff grounds his thought on the gift-character of the human person in the Conciliar dictum, that he is the only creature on earth that God desires for his own sake; he finds himself through self-giving. His thought on self-giving is, in turn, rooted in "the truth about the image and likeness of God," which has its grounding in paragraph 22 of the Conciliar document.[17] The Holy Father's interpretation of *Gaudium et Spes* 24 helps show that the person is both intrinsically constituted as a gift (the objective notion of the person as gift, having been given himself by God), and the person is one who finds himself by giving himself (the subjective dimension of the person as gift).

In the Conciliar teaching that the human person finds himself by making a sincere gift of himself, Pascal Ide, of the Congregation for Catholic Education, offers a careful analysis of *sincere* in his article, *Une Théologie du Don*. He focuses upon the word's etymology, which specifies, "*sincerum* comes from *sine cira*, [meaning] without wax." He elaborates as follows.

> Originally, *sincerity* referred to the quality of honey which had not been made more profitable by the addition of wax. Transferred from the realm of objects to the human [personnes] world, this term has come to mean the pure (unmixed) nature of an attitude, a word, etc. 'Sincerity means purity, explains Father Cottier; sincerity is transparency to

---

Marion avec la participation de Jean-Noël Dumont, et al. (Lyon: Éditions de l'Emmanuel, Le Collège Supérieur, 2001).

[17] John Paul II, *Mulieris Dignitatem* 7.

truth.' Consequently, a sincere gift will be a gift devoid of any expectation of personal benefit.[18]

The notion of sincerity as a pure attitude, which specifies the human person's transparency to truth, suggests that one who lives in truth possesses a clarity, or inner radiance that allows the truth to be visible in him. In other words, the person who lives in the truth has a luminosity that, of its very nature, communicates its radiance to others regardless of whether one speaks. The sincere gift of oneself, then, suggests that the person's inner transparency involves standing in the truth of oneself before God.

With *Gaudium et Spes* 22 above, one learns that Christ reveals the human person to himself. The brief analysis of *sincere* from paragraph 24 of the same document suggests that the person not only stands in the truth of who he is before God, but also that his transparency to the truth is evident to others. To make the notion of *transparency* more concrete, one might posit that it specifies the person's openness to another human being.

---

[18] Ide, *Une Théologie du Don (premiére partie)*, 152. Since I refer to the concept of sincerity as "transparency to truth" in my subsequent work, I offer the original language for the passage quoted above. "A l'origine, la sincérité désigne la qualité d'un miel qui n'est pas mélangé à de la cire en vue de bénéfices illicites. Transféré du monde des choses au monde des personnes, ce terme signifie le caractère non mélangé d'une attitude, d'une parole, etc. 'sincérité signifie pureté, explique le Père Cottier; la sincérité est la transparence à la vérité.' Un don sincère sera par conséquent un don pur de toute recherche de soi" [Ide, *Une Théologie du Don (premiére partie)*, 152].

In my reading of the Pope's analysis, I bring out the fact that God wants the human person to *be* who he *is*.[19] The person's transparency, or openness to another, helps explicate the Pope's thought because *being* the person one *is* means standing in truth before God and before another. As I show with *Gaudium et Spes* 22, the person is a rational being, created in the image of God and redeemed by Jesus Christ. John Paul's reflection upon *Gaudium et Spes* 24 shows that, because the person is created in the image of God, he is a gift from God. Thus, for a person to *be* who he *is* from a subjective aspect, one gives oneself to another (to God or to another person) as a gift.

In Ide's insightful article, *Une Théologie du Don*, he identifies in John Paul the notion of the Trinity as the "supreme model of the gift" for the human person, made in His image, because "life in the Trinity, communion between the divine Persons [is] where giving and receiving are total, without introducing any inequality."[20] John Paul expresses the same idea of the Trinity as a model for human giving, in the quotation I offer below, from *Mulieris Dignitatem*. The point is this. Because the person is created in God's image and likeness, he receives his existence *as a human being* from God.[21]

---

[19] The key texts I examine above, which particularly articulate this point, are John Paul II, *Redemptor Hominis* 8-10, John Paul II, *Opening Address* at Puebla, 28 January 1979, John Paul II, *Fides et Ratio* 60 and 15, as well as John Paul II, *Augustinum Hipponesem*, Chapters II, IV.

[20] Ide, *Une Théologie du Don (premiére partie)*, 171.

[21] As I note above, the Pope explains that "Having been called into existence, the human being—man and woman—is a creature. ... [The person] in his existence and essence...depends on the Creator" [John Paul II, *Dominum et Vivificantem* 36].

# Chapter Five: One "Finds Oneself" Through Self-Gift

To reiterate a text already given, John Paul specifically teaches that each person, "in his own humanity receives as a gift a special 'image and likeness' to God."[22] The person's creation, his very existence *as* a person, is a *gift* from God. His way of being human is living as a gift *from* God *to* others. Because the person is himself a gift created by God in the objective sense, he can only find himself—he can only *become* who he really *is* from a subjective dimension—through making a gift of himself to another person.[23] As Ide notes, John Paul clearly states that, while the human person is created to give, self-giving transcends one's own capabilities; it requires grace.[24]

**The Gift-Character of the Human Person**

---

[22] John Paul II, *Dominum et Vivificantem* 34. I discuss this notion with John Paul's interpretation of *Gaudium et Spes* 22, using the *Opening Address* at Puebla, 28 January 1979.

[23] While I highlight the distinction between the objective and subjective notion of self-gift, Ide stresses the difference between the realization that one finds himself by making himself a gift and the possibility of being a gift for another person. He identifies the problem as follows: "Of course one can argue that man can only find himself by giving himself, but if he finds himself in the act of giving it means that as long as he hasn't given, he has not found himself. In technical terms, realization [réalisation] is one thing, possibility [possibilité] another" [Ide, *Une Théologie du Don, (premiére partie)*, 153].

[24] Ide, *Une Théologie du Don, Les occurrences de Gaudium et Spes, n. 24, §3 chez Jean-Paul II (seconde partie)* in *Anthropotes* 17/2 (2001) 313-344, p. 328. Henceforth, the second part of Ide's article will be cited as *Une Théologie du Don (seconde partie)*.

In *Mulieris Dignitatem* 7, John Paul brings out the objective reality of the gift-character of the person, in addition to the subjective aspect of one finding oneself through self-giving. In addition, he emphasizes the human person's manner of existing in relation to another person, which further qualifies his notion of self-gift.[25] The Holy Father elucidates these thoughts by noting that being a "person in the image and likeness of God…involves existing in a relationship, in relation to the other 'I.'"[26] Again, the model of relationship finds its grounding in the Trinitarian God, who is "a living unity in the communion of the Father, Son, and Holy Spirit."[27]

When speaking of the "unity of the Trinity: unity in communion," John Paul clearly refers to the "unity of the two" in marriage, but he also employs this concept to describe the person's existence in the image and likeness of God.[28] Since I explicated the notion of image and likeness with *Gaudium et Spes* 22, I simply mention it here to draw out the person's intrinsic relation to another person, which relation signifies his innate gift-character.

In God, the "unity of the divinity," the Three Persons exist in divine relationship. In the human person, created male and female, the "unity of the two" is not only a sign of "interpersonal communion," but it also shows a "likeness to the divine communion." John

---

[25] Although I often specify the person's relation to another human person, I also—and so does the Pope—mean to affirm one's relation to God, as well.

[26] John Paul II, *Mulieris Dignitatem* 7.

[27] John Paul II, *Mulieris Dignitatem* 7.

[28] John Paul II, *Mulieris Dignitatem* 7.

## Chapter Five: One "Finds Oneself" Through Self-Gift

Paul explains, "To be human means to be called to interpersonal communion."[29]

The fundamental dimension of one's call to interpersonal communion is marriage, for the "whole of human history unfolds within the context of this call."[30] John Paul explains this idea in the following passage.

> In this [human] history, on the basis of the principle of mutually being 'for' the other, in interpersonal 'communion,' there develops in humanity itself, in accordance with God's will, the integration of what is 'masculine' and what is 'feminine.'[31]

John Paul connects the notion of being "for" another person not only in human history, but also, he specifically highlights salvation history. At this point, the Holy Father has prepared the setting for a discussion on the Conciliar teaching of self-giving. Again, the point I emphasize concerns the notion of the person as a gift for another person, on account of one's creation by God.

Following the Council's text, the Pope focuses upon the Scripture passage from Christ's prayer "that all may be one...as we are one (John 17:21-22)" in order to show the grounding of his teach-

---

[29] Quotations in this paragraph refer to John Paul II, *Mulieris Dignitatem* 7.
[30] John Paul II, *Mulieris Dignitatem* 7.
[31] John Paul II, *Mulieris Dignitatem* 7.

ing.³² John Paul highlights the passage in *Gaudium et Spes* 24 that speaks of "a certain likeness between the union of the divine Persons and the union of God's children in truth and charity." He brings out the notion of *gift* by explaining that this "likeness reveals that man, who is the only creature on earth which God willed for its [his] own sake, cannot fully find himself except through a sincere gift of self."

Continuing his reflection upon *Gaudium et Spes* 24, the Pontiff elaborates upon the fact that being willed "for one's own sake" means being a human person. He describes the person as one who comes to know who he is—his own self-realization—when he makes a gift of himself. The following text brings the heart of his position to the fore.

> With these words, the Council text [*Gaudium et Spes* 24] presents a summary of the whole truth about man and woman—a truth which is already outlined in the first chapters of the Book of Genesis, and which is the structural basis of biblical and Christian anthropology. Man—whether man or woman—is the only being among the creatures of the visible world that God the Creator 'has willed for [his] own sake;' that creature is thus a person. Being a person means striving towards self-realization (the Council text speaks of self-discovery), which can only be achieved 'through a sin-

---

³² Second Vatican Council, *Gaudium et Spes* 24 quoted in John Paul II, *Mulieris Dignitatem* 7. The quotations in this paragraph and the next are John Paul's references to *Gaudium et Spes* 24 in *Mulieris Dignitatem* 7.

cere gift of self.' The model for this interpretation of the person is God Himself as Trinity, as a communion of Persons. To say that man is created in the image and likeness of God means that man is called to exist 'for' others, to become a gift.[33]

Being created in the image of the Trinitarian God, then, signifies both the person's innate gift-character (objective dimension) *and* the person's call to self-giving (the subjective aspect). By concentrating upon the human person's discovery of self through "the sincere gift" of himself, John Paul stresses one's intrinsic openness to God.

The human person's innate openness to God, on account of his creation in God's image and likeness, indicates God's gift of Himself to each human person. His self-gift to the person—one's creation in God's image—specifies the importance of the human person's own self-giving. The foundation of one's gift of self, then, as *Mulieris Dignitatem* 7 helps explain, is rooted in one's creation (*imago Dei*). The innate gift-character of the person flows from God, in whose image one is created.

John Paul's interpretation of *Gaudium et Spes* 24, which specifies that the person's creation in the image of God is a gift given to him by God, deserves additional explanation. *Dominum et Vivificantem* 59 and *Salvifici Doloris* 28 offer further comment upon the Pope's interpretation of *Gaudium et Spes* 24 and the gift-character of the human person.

---

[33] John Paul II, *Mulieris Dignitatem* 7.

## The Holy Spirit Enables the Person to Make a "Sincere Gift" of Himself

In *Dominum et Vivificantem* 59, John Paul offers a second interpretation of *Gaudium et Spes* 24. He begins by noting that the Holy Spirit enables one to understand his own humanity, which he specifies as a full realization of his creation in the image and likeness of God. He explains that the "intimate truth of the human being has to be continually rediscovered in the light of Christ who is the prototype of the relationship with God."[34]

The Holy Father stresses the Spirit's activity in helping the person to know this "truth of his being," namely, that God creates the person for his own sake and that his full self-discovery occurs through his sincere gift of self to another.[35] By the power of the Holy Spirit, one comes to the "effective knowledge and full implementation" of the truth of one's being: each person is to rediscover "in Christ the reason for 'full self-discovery through a sincere gift of himself' to others."[36]

In addition to the Spirit helping one to know and understand—in the light of Christ—what it means to be created in the image and likeness of God, John Paul brings out a second aspect that leads toward self-discovery, which is the concept of self-gift. He explains as follows.

---

[34] John Paul II, *Dominum et Vivificantem* 59.
[35] John Paul II, *Dominum et Vivificantem* 59.
[36] John Paul II, *Dominum et Vivificantem* 59.

## Chapter Five: One "Finds Oneself" Through Self-Gift

There also has to be rediscovered in Christ the reason for 'full self-discovery through a sincere gift of himself' to others, as the Second Vatican Council writes: precisely by reason of this divine likeness which 'shows that on earth man…is the only creature that God wishes for himself' in his dignity as a person, but as one open to integration and social communion.[37]

In the next section of *Dominum et Vivificantem* 59, John Paul defines the "truth about man." Here, he returns to the fact that the person's sincere gift of himself is rooted in the Trinity, "who 'exists' in Himself as a transcendent reality of interpersonal gift."[38] Citing *Gaudium et Spes* 24, the Pontiff mentions the "certain likeness between the union of the divine Persons and the union of the children of God in truth and charity," to which I refer above.[39] In a moment, I show how the "truth about man," as John Paul understands it, and as this passage infers, concerns the dignity to which the human person is summoned, namely, his calling to be a child of God the Father. Reiterating a point from his first encyclical, *Redemptor Hominis*, the Pope teaches that, since "man is the way of

---

[37] John Paul II, *Dominum et Vivificantem* 59.
[38] John Paul II, *Dominum et Vivificantem* 59.
[39] Second Vatican Council, *Gaudium et Spes* 24 quoted in John Paul II, *Dominum et Vivificantem* 59. I offer a definition of the Pontiff's understanding of "truth of man" below, which is in *Dominum et Vivificantem* 59. I also offer additional clarification of this term, appropriate to the present study.

the Church, this way passes through the whole mystery of Christ, as man's divine model."[40]

At this point, John Paul integrates *Gaudium et Spes* 24 more deeply into his thought, particularly regarding the gift of self. One's self-gift enables the person to better understand his own dignity, due to his status as a child of the Heavenly Father. The person who "discovers himself as belonging to Christ" learns that "in Christ he is raised to the status of a child of God" the Father.[41] The Pope emphatically states that Christian anthropology might be summarized by the gift of self because, on account of that gift, one learns of his "definitive glorification."[42]

Christian anthropology is summed up in the person finding "himself through a sincere gift of self," then, for two reasons. First, based on the Gospel, the person learns he belongs to Christ. Second, he "discovers that, in Christ, he is raised to the status of a child of God."[43] He realizes his own dignity as a child of the Father because the Father comes to him and the Father glorifies him by making him His adopted child. Indeed, the person is "the subject of the divine condescension."[44] John Paul explains as follows.

---

[40] John Paul II, *Dominum et Vivificantem* 59. As I mention with the Pope's interpretation of *Gaudium et Spes* 22, John Paul speaks of Christ uniting Himself with each person, on account of His Incarnation. Recall, as well, that the Pope also speaks of Jesus as the way for the Church and the way for each person, in *Redemptor Hominis* 13, to which I refer in the present sentence.

[41] John Paul II, *Dominum et Vivificantem* 59.

[42] John Paul II, *Dominum et Vivificantem* 59.

[43] John Paul II, *Dominum et Vivificantem* 59.

[44] John Paul II, *Dominum et Vivificantem* 59.

Along this way the Holy Spirit, strengthening in each of us 'the inner man,' enables man ever more 'fully to find himself through a sincere gift of self.' These words of the Pastoral Constitution of the Council can be said to sum up the whole of Christian anthropology: that theory and practice, based on the Gospel, in which man discovers himself as belonging to Christ and discovers that in Christ he is raised to the status of a child of God, and so understands better his own dignity as man, precisely because he is the subject of God's approach and presence, the subject of the divine condescension, which contains the prospect and the very root of definitive glorification.[45]

Combining the above quotation with the Pontiff's description of the "truth about man," one learns the following. John Paul indicates that the "truth about man" points to "a certain likeness between the union of the divine Persons and the union of the children of God in truth and charity."[46] In other words, the "truth about man" specifies that, in Jesus Christ, the human person "is raised to the status of a child of God" the Father.[47]

---

[45] John Paul II, *Dominum et Vivificantem* 59.

[46] Second Vatican Council, *Gaudium et Spes* 24 quoted in John Paul II, *Dominum et Vivificantem* 59.

[47] John Paul II, *Dominum et Vivificantem* 59. Elsewhere, John Paul describes the "truth about man" by claiming that the "Church receives 'the meaning of man' from Divine Revelation" [John Paul II, *Centesimus Annus* 55]. One might also understand the "meaning of man" as the "truth of man," or rather, the "truth of the human person." In *Centesimus Annus*, John Paul refers to his teaching on the person in his first encycli-

Living in accord with the truth of the human person dictates his obedience to that truth. He lives as a child of the Father faithful to the Commandments, because the law of God speaks to the good of the human person. As the Pontiff explains, "man, living a divine life, is the glory of God, and the Holy Spirit is the hidden dispenser of this life and this glory."[48]

## The Opening of One's "I" to Another Who is Suffering

In *Gaudium et Spes* 24, the Council Fathers teach that the person "cannot fully find himself except through a sincere gift of himself." With *Dominum et Vivificantem* 59, John Paul clearly enunciates that the sincere gift of self summarizes "the whole of Christian anthropology" on account of the Father raising the person to the status of an adopted child through Jesus Christ.

In *Salvifici Doloris* 28, the Pope employs the Parable of the Good Samaritan to show the gift of self as an opening one's "I" to another person who suffers.[49] Here, as well, the Holy Father affirms

---

cal. In *Redemptor Hominis* 13, John Paul expresses his hope "that each person may be able to find Christ, in order that Christ may walk with each person the path of life, with the power of the truth about man and the world that is contained in the mystery of the Incarnation and the Redemption and with the power of the love that is radiated by that truth" [John Paul II, *Redemptor Hominis* 13]. The "truth about man" is that one "learn(s) to know other human beings, in order to become more fully human through [one's] capacity for 'self-giving'" [John Paul II, *To the Youth of the World* 14].

[48] John Paul II, *Dominum et Vivificantem* 59.
[49] John Paul II, *Salvifici Doloris* 28.

## Chapter Five: One "Finds Oneself" Through Self-Gift

that the gift of self is "one of the key points of all Christian anthropology." With *Salvifici Doloris* 28, then, one comes to see a crucial perspective of John Paul's interpretation of self-gift.

Commenting on the Parable of the Good Samaritan, John Paul reflects upon the concept of being a neighbor to another person. The parable shows that a neighbor is "the person who carried out the Commandment of love of neighbor." The Good Samaritan has compassion on the suffering of another human person. Thus, being a Samaritan is being a neighbor to another person. It characterizes the relationship one must possess toward another who suffers. Each person must "stop" beside the other suffering person. John Paul explains this "stopping" beside another human person as an "availability" and an "interior disposition of the heart" with the following passage.

> This stopping does not mean curiosity but availability. It is like the opening of a certain interior disposition of the heart, which also has an emotional expression of its own. The name 'Good Samaritan' fits every individual who is sensitive to the sufferings of others, who 'is moved' by the misfortune of another.[50]

The Pope speaks of one's "availability" toward the other as a stopping "beside the suffering of another person," sensitive to his affliction and moved by it. "If Christ, who knows the interior of man, emphasizes this compassion, this means that it is important

---

[50] John Paul II, *Salvifici Doloris* 28.

for our whole attitude to others' suffering."[51] Cultivating this "sensitivity of heart...bears witness to compassion towards a suffering person."[52] Further, the Pope explains that, at times, one's compassion toward another who suffers "remains the only or principal expression of our love for and solidarity with the sufferer."[53]

While compassion is essential, it is to become "an incentive to actions aimed at bringing help" for the suffering person.[54] Thus, John Paul defines the Good Samaritan as "one who brings help in suffering, whatever its nature may be."[55] The Holy Father further clarifies this "help" as being "effective." The following passage, which expresses these thoughts and concludes the paragraph, is vital to my account of martyrdom that follows.

> He puts his whole heart into it, nor does he spare material means. We can say that he gives himself, his very 'I,' opening this 'I' to the other person. Here we touch upon one of the key points of all Christian anthropology. Man cannot 'fully find himself except through a sincere gift of himself.' A Good Samaritan is the person capable of exactly such a gift of self.[56]

---

[51] John Paul II, *Salvifici Doloris* 28.
[52] John Paul II, *Salvifici Doloris* 28.
[53] John Paul II, *Salvifici Doloris* 28.
[54] John Paul II, *Salvifici Doloris* 28. That "incentive to actions" might be interpreted as the martyr's willingness to die.
[55] John Paul II, *Salvifici Doloris* 28.
[56] John Paul II, *Salvifici Doloris* 28.

Through the opening of his 'I' to the other person, John Paul not only explicitly mentions *Gaudium et Spes* 24, but he also brings to the fore "one of the key points of all Christian anthropology."[57] The person's "opening of a certain interior disposition of the heart," in imitation of Christ whose Flesh was opened on Calvary (John 19:34), is implied by the martyr's death, which encompasses another person who is suffering even more than himself: the perpetrators of his martyrdom.

**Concluding Remarks**

In these first five chapters, my depiction of John Paul's concept of the human person yields several conclusions. First, because of the Pontiff's concern for the person, he interprets *Gaudium et Spes* 22 and 24 in a manner that highlights one's creation by God, in His image, as a being imbued with human reason. Second, not only is the human person created in the image of God, but also, he is loved by Him. Further, the person has the God-given gift of human reason, with its transcendent capacity to know God and to know oneself. These conclusions about the human person suggest that John Paul's reading of *Gaudium et Spes* 22 and 24 highlights an anthropology that is grounded decisively in the Incarnation.

Expounding upon how John Paul interprets *Gaudium et Spes* 22 and 24 reveals that his anthropology is solidly established upon the Incarnation for the following reasons. The Pope defines an an-

---

[57] In my ensuing discussion on martyrdom, I return to John Paul's interpretation of *Gaudium et Spes* 24 as the opening of one's "I" to another person who is suffering.

thropology based upon Incarnation as one which, "reaching beyond its own limitations and contradictions, moves toward God Himself, indeed toward the goal of 'divinization.'"[58] Indeed, to imply that the person's "divinization" is rooted in the Incarnation is to specify *how* Christ "fully reveals man to man himself and makes his supreme calling clear."[59] In other words, the person's highest calling is to be "divinized."

John Paul explicates "divinization" in the following manner: "This [divinization] occurs through the grafting of the redeemed onto Christ and their admission into the intimacy of the Trinitarian life. ... [I]t is only because the Son of God truly became man that man, in Him and through Him, can truly become a child of God."[60] A succinct way of defining "divinization," then, is to say that the human person becomes a child of God the Father. Saint Paul explains the person's call to become a child of the Father in the context of the Incarnation, which is the only way to understand this mystery, insofar as it is possible to do so.

---

[58] John Paul II, *Novo Millennio Ineunte* 23.

[59] Second Vatican Council, *Gaudium et Spes* 22.

[60] John Paul II, *Novo Millennio Ineunte* 23. In *Christian Faith and Human Understanding*, contemporary philosopher Msgr. Sokolowski comments upon John Paul's themes of truth and faith, particularly in *Veritatis Splendor* and *Fides et Ratio*. He shows that living as "adopted sons of the Father is based on truth, not on blind obedience, and hence it elevates our rational personhood, our agency in truth" [Msgr. Robert Sokolowski, *Christian Faith and Human Understanding* (Washington, D.C.: Catholic University Press, 2006), 210].

## Chapter Five: One "Finds Oneself" Through Self-Gift

> But when the time had fully come, God sent forth His Son, born of woman, born under the law, to redeem those who were under the law, so that we might receive adoption as sons. And because you are sons, God has sent the Spirit of His Son into our hearts, crying, 'Abba! Father!' So, through God you are no longer a slave but a son, and if a son then an heir (Galatians 4:4-7).

John Paul unites his reflections on the human person's divinization in Jesus, "the new man" and *Gaudium et Spes* 22: "God and man that He is, He reveals to us also the true face of man, 'fully revealing man to man himself.'"[61] An anthropology based upon the Incarnation, then, encapsulates Christ's revelation to the human person as one who is called to be a child of the eternal Father.

Given the fact that John Paul's anthropology is grounded in the Incarnation, which his emphasis on the Conciliar texts seems to indicate, yields another result, as well. His anthropology, because it is Christocentric, is itself centered upon the very reason for the Jubilee's existence. Since the Holy Father's concept of the person flows from Jesus becoming man, it is plausible to suggest that it informs his underlying theme of the Jubilee year.

---

[61] John Paul II, *Novo Millennio Ineunte* 23. In this paragraph, the Pope offers two Scriptural citations that refer to Jesus, "who is 'the new Man' (cf. Ephesians 4:24; Colossians 3:10)." Note, as well, that the words in *Gaudium et Spes* 22 are sometimes translated as "Christ, the new Adam" (*Christus, novissimus Adam*), which is, in fact, a literal translation [Second Vatican Council, *Gaudium et Spes* 22].

The Holy Father's remarks upon the goodness of the human person, which describe one of his interpretations of *Gaudium et Spes* 22, help to show in the next part of my work that the martyr's acceptance of death affirms "the inviolability of the personal dignity of man."[62] In addition, the Holy Father's emphasis on the gift-character of the person that *Gaudium et Spes* 24 underscores, plays a key role to understanding martyrdom as "the exaltation of a person's perfect 'humanity' and of true 'life'" because one finds himself by making "a sincere gift of himself."[63]

---

[62] John Paul II, *Veritatis Splendor* 92.
[63] John Paul II, *Veritatis Splendor* 92; Second Vatican Council, *Gaudium et Spes* 24.

# Chapter Six

## The Theme of Martyrdom in the Pontificate of John Paul II: Setting the Theological Context for a Discussion of Martyrdom

Having presented a description of John Paul's anthropology in the first part of this book, I now offer a specific theological context with which to discuss his concept of martyrdom. A person who is a martyr is typically regarded not only as a prime example of a believer, but also as an exemplary imitator of Christ.[1] As a "witness to

---

[1] The Greek word for martyr, μάρτυς, in ancient texts, means *witness*, or a *victim of religious persecution*. An example of the martyr being a firm believer and an imitator of Christ include the following. Pope Saint Leo the Great teaches, "Yet the martyrs also have done great service to all men, in that the Lord who gave them boldness, has used it to show that the penalty of death and the pain of the cross need not be terrible to any of His followers, but might be imitated by many of them" [Pope Saint Leo the Great: *Sermons*: Sermon LXXXV: On the feast of Saint Lawrence the martyr (3), (August 10)]. While the purpose of this treatise is not to trace the history of how the word has evolved, Rino Fisichella explains that the term *martyrdom* "begins to be stabilized" with the *Martyrium Polycarpi* around 155 [René Latourelle, Rino Fisichella, eds., *Dictionary of Fundamental Theology*, 621]. In *Martyrium Polycarpi*, Polycarp's death is described as martyrdom precisely because "it was in accord with the Gospel of Christ" [19.1, quoted in René Latourelle, Rino Fisichella, eds., *Dictionary of Fundamental Theology*, 621]. From 155 onward, claims Fisichella, "being a martyr…is identified with giving one's life for the truth of the Gospel" [René Latourelle, Rino Fisichella, eds., *Dictionary of*

the truth of the faith and of Christian doctrine," he "endures death through an act of fortitude."[2] Further, the Catholic Church teaches that martyrdom is "the supreme witness given to the truth of the faith: it means bearing witness even unto death [*ūsque ad mortem*]."[3]

---

*Fundamental Theology*, 621]. Furthermore, he notes a theological development in the *Martyrium Polycarpi*: The term *martyr* is applied to Christ and thus, the martyr is one who, "by following Christ's example…witnesses to perfect charity" [René Latourelle, Rino Fisichella, eds., *Dictionary of Fundamental Theology*, 623]. Perhaps the most intriguing statement in this entry, worthy of development in a future study, is that the Church herself is "by nature a martyr" [René Latourelle, Rino Fisichella, eds., *Dictionary of Fundamental Theology*, p. 620].

[2] *Catechism of the Catholic Church* 2473. Prior to engaging the thought of the Pontiff on martyrdom, I offer an authoritative and concise statement regarding the Church's concept of martyrdom. Because the *Catechism of the Catholic Church* offers a brief and lucid definition of martyrdom, I employ these texts before delving into Papal thought.

[3] "*Martyrium* testimonium est supremum veritati fidei perhibitum; ipsum denotat testimonium quod ūsque ad mortem procedit" [*Catechism of the Catholic Church* 2473]. In English, the words "even unto death" seem to indicate that, while martyrdom *can* include death, it does not necessarily *require* it. The Latin, however, with the preposition *ad*, connotes a real movement toward death (*ad mortem*), which results completely (*ūsque*) in the cessation of life. The Latin, then, brings out the fact that it is precisely the witness of martyrdom, itself, which advances entirely (*ūsque*) *toward* death, and results *in* death. In other words, what comprises martyrdom is its full and complete movement toward its "physical" object, which is death. The spiritual object, is, of course, fidelity to God in His teaching through the Church, and in His "word," by keeping His Commandments (cf. John 8:31-32; 14:15; 15:12).

If martyrdom entails witnessing to "the truth of the faith and of Christian doctrine," how does contemplating the face of Christ enter it?[4] By forfeiting his life, the martyr, having perhaps first contemplated the face of Christ, might show Christ to others by choosing to die rather than to act against "the truth of the faith and of Christian doctrine."[5]

Does *martyrdom itself* somehow reveal the face of Christ? On one hand, since a person cannot *make* himself a martyr, how can martyrdom be his consciously willed act? On the other hand, if being martyred is *not* one's deliberately willed act, how can one freely accept death for the sake of the Gospel? In other words, if there is not a specific act of the martyr's will in accepting martyrdom, how is he an ideal believer and not a victim of circumstance?

In order to answer these questions, I need to show that martyrdom comprises more than its obvious dimension of passively undergoing death. To be sure, the martyr is not a victim of circumstance, who, finding no means of escape, has no other option but death. Consequently, this section of my work brings out the notion that *being* martyred contains within it one's willing acceptance of death. The person's voluntary consent to die, rather than to act against "the truth of the faith and of Christian doctrine," is an act of the martyr's will.[6]

With his opening remark in *Fides et Ratio*, the Holy Father speaks of the centrality of faith and reason to the human contemplation of truth. The Pope's claim serves as a springboard to my

---

[4] *Catechism of the Catholic Church* 2473.
[5] *Catechism of the Catholic Church* 2473.
[6] *Catechism of the Catholic Church* 2473.

description of martyrdom in his thought because, in my reading of John Paul, martyrdom expresses both faith and reason. Martyrdom concerns the intellect since it expresses the faith of the martyr and the teachings of the holy Catholic Faith. In addition, martyrdom engages one's reason, for the martyr's action, a choice of the will, is in accord with truth.

My present chapter unfolds how John Paul's initial statement in *Fides et Ratio* sheds light on his portrayal of martyrdom, which I subsequently explain as a contemplation of Christ's face. Although the Holy Father does not specifically express the martyr's death as a contemplation of Christ's face, the task of the present moment indicates his understanding of martyrdom. Thus, it sets the ground for a correlation of his thought on the two concepts of martyrdom and the contemplation of the face of Jesus. The exact words of *Fides et Ratio* provide the context.

> Faith and reason are like two wings on which the human spirit rises to the contemplation of truth; and God has placed in the human heart a desire to know the truth—in a word, to know Himself—so that, by knowing and loving God, men and women may also come to the fullness of truth about themselves.[7]

---

[7] John Paul II, *Fides et Ratio* Prior to the *Introduction*. With the text above, John Paul offers the following Scripture citations: cf. Exodus 33:18; Psalms 27:8-9; 63:2-3; John 14:8; 1 John 3:2. In this quotation, John Paul speaks of the "truth about themselves," meaning, the *truth about the human person*. In fact, he often mentions, as my work shows, the term, *truth about man*. The human person comes to know who he is by know-

As I mention above, martyrdom traditionally means that the person witnesses "to the truth of the faith and of Christian doctrine" and that he "endures death through an act of fortitude."[8] With the *Catechism's* definition of martyrdom, then, one presupposes the martyr's own faith, and one regards his actions to be in accord with human reason since it is contrary to reason to deny what one knows to be true.

John Paul explains that the martyr's death "represents the high point of the witness to moral truth."[9] His witness to moral truth not only presupposes his faith and the teachings of the Catholic Church, but it also verifies that his death is in accord with human reason.[10] Thus, while the martyr might subjectively contemplate

---

ing and loving God, as the Pope teaches in the quotation above. The more one learns who he is the closer is his union with God. John Paul expresses this union elsewhere, by citing *Gaudium et Spes* 24. He explains that the prayer of Jesus, "that all may be one...as we are one (John 17:21-22)" implies a "certain likeness between the union of the Divine Persons, and the union of God's children in truth and charity" [Second Vatican Council, *Gaudium et Spes* 24 quoted in John Paul II, *Ut Unum Sint* 26 and *Dominum et Vivificantem* 59]. John Paul identifies this close union between God and the person as "the truth about man" in *Dominum et Vivificantem* 59, explaining that this truth "passes through the whole mystery of Christ, as man's divine model" [John Paul II, *Dominum et Vivificantem* 59]. Elsewhere, the Pope defines the term as follows: "the *truth of the person* [is] what the person is and what the person reveals from deep within" (John Paul II, *Fides et Ratio* 3). I discuss the term, *truth of the human person*, at greater length above.

[8] *Catechism of the Catholic Church* 2473.

[9] John Paul II, *Veritatis Splendor* 93.

[10] By claiming that the martyr's death is in accord with human reason, I presuppose that the martyr is not an insane person who is acting

the face of Christ, his death must suggest something beyond the subjective domain and in the objective realm.

As I make clear, martyrdom brings to the fore the contemplative dimension of the human person. I claim that the human desire to know and to live the truth shines forth in the martyr's acceptance of death to uphold the very objectivity of truth, and thus, of the moral law, as well. But, if the martyr's death radiates truth, one might ask if—or how—the non-martyr embodies the same contemplation.

To push the point further, how is the martyr's death, as a radiation of truth, different from the non-martyr's death? Does the death of a saintly non-martyr also show the Truth, who is Jesus, to others? To suggest that the non-martyr does not radiate truth *as much* or *as well* as does the martyr, is to miss the depth of the argument I intend to develop. If my claim concerns an objective reality—and it does—then showing Christ's face must also describe a dimension of every human person and not just the martyr. My work in the present section probes these questions in some detail.

## Martyrdom in the Pontifical Writings of Pope Saint John Paul II

At the beginning of this work, I indicate my intent of describing the martyr's death as a contemplation of Christ's face according to John Paul's definition of *martyr (martyrdom)* and *contemplating the face of Christ*. Further, I explain that the first stage of my work

---

outside of human reason. In the present work, I explain that the martyr's death is in accord with human reason because it is consonant with the *truth of the human person.*

## Chapter Six: The Theme of Martyrdom in the Pontificate of JP II

comprises an analysis of the human person, which I address by examining John Paul's interpretation of *Gaudium et Spes* 22 and 24. Having elucidated several vital elements of the Pope's notion of the person, I now focus upon his explanation of martyrdom using the most significant texts.

The pontifical writings of John Paul contain more references to martyrdom than one might presume at first glance. For example, the Holy Father focuses upon martyrdom in the Jubilee Year by exhorting the faithful to "remain anchored in the testimony of the martyrs and jealously guard their memory."[11] To this end, the Pope requested an updated *Roman Martyrology*, which was published in 2004. A second example concerns the Holy Father's pontificate, itself, during which he canonized 482 saints and beatified some 1,300 people, many of whom were martyrs. A final example, the Pontiff's lengthy reference to martyrdom in *Veritatis Splendor*, serves as the starting point for my discussion of his significant texts on the subject.

The next stage of my project, then, entails a careful presentation of passages that depict John Paul's understanding of martyrdom. After citing a text, I offer my own interpretation, and I connect it with previous ideas presented.

Note that *Veritatis Splendor*, the Pope's most extensive explication on martyrdom, is an encyclical. Thus, it contains his most authoritative teaching on the subject. At the same time, I consider other relevant documents, which develop my elucidation of *Veritatis Splendor*. Following a careful and extensive reflection on this

---

[11] John Paul II, *Incarnationis Mysterium* 13.

encyclical, I discuss other significant passages where John Paul speaks of martyrdom. These texts include *Redemptoris Missio, Ut Unum Sint, Fides et Ratio,* and *Christifideles Laici,* among others.

A final point concerns the Aristotelian distinction between the *literal* and *metaphorical* use of a word. Applying this distinction to the terms *martyr* and *martyrdom* highlights the fact that they signify a variety of meanings. In the present section, I define and explain *martyrdom* in its literal sense, thus distinguishing it from a metaphorical employment of the term.

In the *Topics*, Aristotle offers a definition for the literal meaning of a word in his analysis of *sameness*.[12] By distinguishing various ways in which the person can speak of *sameness*, Aristotle alludes to the literal meaning of a word. The "most literal" use of a word is its most "primary use."[13] Characterizing the literal function of a word as its most "primary use" means that the literal sense is the first, or the strictest sense, in which the word is understood.

In my present work, I speak of *martyr* and *martyrdom* in the literal sense of these words. To be clear, the most "primary," or literal meaning of the word *martyr* specifies "fidelity to God's holy law, witnessed to by death."[14] The most "primary" aspect of *mar-*

---

[12] Aristotle, *Topics* Book I 103a6-103a38. Aristotle speaks of the *literal* meaning in which a word can be used far less than he mentions the *metaphor*.

[13] Aristotle, *Topics* Book I 103a6-103a38.

[14] John Paul II, *Veritatis Splendor* 93. As I indicate in my *Introduction* in chapter one, I explain that Christians are united in a common martyrology, and that implying the martyr is a Catholic offers an unhindered clarity to my discussion. Speaking within this context, then, I note that the literal meaning of the term *martyr* implies Church recognition of the

*tyrdom* in the literal sense, then, necessarily comprises the physical death of a human person who gives his life in order to remain faithful to God's law "rather than perform this or that particular act contrary to faith or virtue."[15] In other words, death is endured out of reverence for what the Church teaches concerning what one is to believe (faith) or how one is to act (Commandments).

Aristotle describes how a word can be used either as a metaphor or metaphorically, in the *Poetics*,[16] *Rhetoric*,[17] and *Topics*.[18]

---

person's death as a statement of "fidelity to God's holy law" [John Paul II, *Veritatis Splendor* 93]. As my unfolding of John Paul's understanding of martyrdom continues, I add further qualifications to the definition of martyrdom offered in the present sentence above.

[15] John Paul II, *Veritatis Splendor* 76, 93. In my subsequent elucidation of martyrdom, John Paul brings out the fact that one's "voluntary acceptance of death" is sufficient to qualify one as a martyr [John Paul II, *Veritatis Splendor* 91]. I explain this qualification when discussing *Veritatis Splendor* 91.

[16] Aristotle, *Poetics* 1457b1-1458a8; *Poetics* 1458a18-1459a8.

[17] Aristotle, *Rhetoric* Book III, 1405a4-1405a33; Book III, 1410b6-1410b36; Book III, 1412a10-1412a17; and Book. III, 1412a18-1412b32.

[18] Aristotle, *Topics* Book VI, 139b32-140a2; Book VI, 140a6-140a17 and Book VII, 154a12-154a23. With the conclusion of this sentence, I acknowledge that there is a difference between a word that is a metaphor and using a word metaphorically. In my study of Aristotle's appropriate texts on this subject, I find that his weightier passages speak of *metaphor* rather than a *metaphorical* use of a word. These texts are enumerated in footnotes below. Given the fact that *metaphor* is a noun and that *metaphorical* is an adjective, by describing Aristotle's definition of *metaphor*—by application—one understands the sense in which he uses *metaphorical*. Further, the following paragraphs adequately enlighten the reader concerning the distinction I offer between a *literal* and a *metaphorical* use of the words *martyr* and *martyrdom*.

Setting aside the nuances and intricate details, I find that his remarks about the metaphor and the metaphorical use of a word can be summarized in two points. First, a word used as a metaphor indicates both a similarity and a dissimilarity to its subject. The second point brings out the fact that a metaphor adds a depth of perspective that the literal meaning of a word cannot convey. Below, I highlight Aristotle's texts, which describe these two points.

The crux of Aristotle's definition specifies that a metaphor "must be drawn…from things that are related to the original thing, and yet not obviously so related."[19] In other words, there is a similarity and a dissimilarity to the subject indicated. Aristotle notes this distinction as follows.

On one hand, a metaphor makes "what it signifies to some extent familiar because of the likeness involved."[20] Elsewhere, he stresses a parallel thought by affirming that metaphors "must be fitting, which means that they must fairly correspond to the thing signified."[21]

On the other hand, Aristotle accentuates the fact that a metaphor uses a word in a way "as though it were something different" than it actually is.[22] Although he makes several differentiations

---

[19] Aristotle, *Rhetoric* Book III, 1412a10-1412a17.

[20] Aristotle, *Topics* Book VI, 140a6-140a17.

[21] Aristotle, *Rhetoric* Book III, 1405a4-1405b33. In the same passage, Aristotle further emphasizes the importance of *similitude* by indicating that, if one uses a metaphor, he "must draw them not from remote but from kindred and similar things, so that the kinship is clearly perceived as soon as the words are said" [Aristotle, *Rhetoric* Book III, 1405a4-1405b33].

[22] Aristotle, *Topics* Book VII, 154a12-154a23.

about a metaphor in the *Poetics*, the vital notion that Aristotle reiterates is that "a good metaphor implies an intuitive perception of the similarity in dissimilars."²³ Again, the significant factor that Aristotle highlights is that a metaphor expresses similitude and dissimilitude with the subject to which it refers.

Aristotle's second point concerning a *metaphor* is quite perceptive. In the *Rhetoric*, he explains that, while "ordinary words convey only what we know already, it is from metaphor that we can best get hold of something fresh."²⁴ His insight on how a metaphor expresses a new idea is apropos to various connotations of *martyr* and *martyrdom*. Using the word *martyrdom* in a metaphorical sense, to explain the deprivation of private property, for example, offers the listener the possibility of grasping a new idea. In this instance, one comes to a deeper understanding of the hardship inflicted upon a person and upon a family, due to the deprivation of private property, by considering it a suffering akin to martyrdom.

In a metaphorical sense of acquiring a "fresh" idea, one might apply the term *martyrdom* to various sufferings endured under persecution, such as the inability to hold public office, the denial of purchasing land, or the inability of obtaining sufficient resources for sustaining life.²⁵ Speaking metaphorically, one might refer to

---

²³ Aristotle, *Poetics* 1458a18-1459a8.

²⁴ Aristotle, *Rhetoric*, Book III, 1410b6-1410b36. See also Aristotle, *Rhetoric* Book III, 1412a18-1412b32.

²⁵ In a particularly telling passage in Sacred Scripture, Jesus speaks to His disciples of the reward they will receive for their fidelity to Christ and to the Gospel. In promising His followers a "hundred times" as many "houses and brethren and sisters, and mothers, and children, and lands,"

these sufferings as a martyrdom, which brings to the fore a vivid sense of the injustice inflicted. Another example might include calling a *martyr* one who endures various human sufferings, such as severe illness. Using the words *martyr* or *martyrdom* to signify something other than "fidelity to God's holy law, witnessed to by death," then, is a valid, but a metaphorical, application of the terms.[26] In the present context, I note and explain any apparent discrepancy of my claim that John Paul speaks of *martyrdom* in a literal sense of the term.

## *Veritatis Splendor*: John Paul's Primary Teaching on Martyrdom

In *Veritatis Splendor*, John Paul teaches that living the truth radiates a brilliance, or a "splendor" that "shines forth … in man, created in the image and likeness of God (cf. Genesis 1:26)."[27] This central theme of the document, in my opinion, is unmistakably depicted in the person who is a martyr. I begin to substantiate my claim that the martyr radiates truth in the present section, and I

---

He nonetheless assures them that they will receive persecution, as well, "and in the world to come life everlasting" [Mark 10:30]. See also Matthew 5:10-12, 10:22-24; Luke 21:12; 1 Peter 4:13-16.

[26] John Paul II, *Veritatis Splendor* 93. For a metaphorical use of the term, *martyrdom*, see the Irish teaching on three forms of martyrdom in Stokes and Strachan, "Old Irish Homily" in *Thesaurus Paelaeohibernicus: A Collection of Old-Irish Glosses, Scholia, Prose and Verse* 8 Vols. (Cambridge: 1903), II, 246-47. See also: Sulpitius Severus, *Letters of Undoubted Authenticity* Letter II: To the Deacon Aurelius and Saint John Chrysostom, *Homily VIII: Colossians iii*, 5-7.

[27] John Paul II, *Veritatis Splendor* Prior to the *Introduction*.

## Chapter Six: The Theme of Martyrdom in the Pontificate of JP II

further explicate the unique dimensions of this radiance in the following section.

In *Veritatis Splendor*, John Paul portrays martyrdom as the pinnacle of the human person's moral life, and the "supreme witness" to which one might be called.[28] Further, he maintains that martyrdom concerns the chief expression of human dignity and human freedom.[29] At the conclusion of my work on *Veritatis Splendor*, I offer an initial explication of why I maintain that the martyr's death describes this central theme of truth shining forth in the human person.

A crucial factor in upholding my position highlights the fact that the martyr's death is a gift offered in "fidelity to God's holy law" and an "eloquent and attractive example of a life completely transfigured by the splendor of moral truth."[30] These concepts illuminate not only my proximate concern of showing that the martyr's death radiates truth, but also, they contribute to the ultimate point I wish to make: the martyr's death is a contemplation of Christ's face.

In order to put forth the Holy Father's understanding of martyrdom in *Veritatis Splendor*, I document and expound upon each instance of the term *martyr* or *martyrdom* by following the paragraph order of the encyclical. Further, because *Veritatis Splendor* is an expansive work, not all elements specifically address my concern. Thus, I summarize important concepts, such as conscience,

---

[28] John Paul II, *Veritatis Splendor* 89.

[29] The Holy Father speaks of martyrdom as an expression of dignity and freedom in *Veritatis Splendor* 90-94, as I describe below.

[30] John Paul II, *Veritatis Splendor* 93.

the object of a moral act, intrinsically evil acts, the human good, human dignity, human freedom, and faith as they apply to my subject. After the detailed work of each reference to *martyrdom* in *Veritatis Splendor* is complete, I offer an initial explanation of why I maintain that the martyr is the person who, by the very way that he gives his life, unmistakably radiates the splendor of truth.

The notions of human dignity and human freedom, which I expound upon as they arise in the present chapter, lay the foundation for claiming that the martyr radiates the Truth who is Christ to others on account of the action of the Holy Spirit. The human person's resistance to untrue propositions and his testimony to truth becomes clear in one's acceptance of death.

One's willingness to suffer death is a key to distinguishing the martyr's death as a contemplation of Christ's face from the pious non-martyr's death. Because the martyr is willing to die, his voluntary acceptance of death reveals his interior docility to the Holy Spirit, which one might only presume in the death of the saintly non-martyr. Thus, my presentation of *Veritatis Splendor* includes apropos remarks from *Dominum et Vivificantem*, in addition to other pontifical writings, since these texts help to distinguish the martyr from the non-martyr. Further, these passages stress the dignity and freedom of the person that assist in my presentation of *Veritatis Splendor*.

# Chapter Seven

## *Veritatis Splendor* and the Sacrifice of the Martyrs

In *Veritatis Splendor* 27, John Paul speaks of the Church's responsibility of "promoting and preserving the faith and the moral life."[1] He expounds upon the Conciliar teaching that affirms the Magisterium as the authentic interpreter of Sacred Scripture by explaining this responsibility as a revelation of the "Church, in her life and teaching, [as]…'the pillar and bulwark of the truth' (1 Timothy 3:15), including the truth regarding moral action."[2]

The Church directs "man's gaze to…the mystery of God," and the Pontiff's assertion in *Veritatis Splendor* 27 is written with the same intent to serve the human person.[3] In the encyclical, John Paul affirms that the Magisterium is obligated, "in fidelity to Jesus Christ and in continuity with the Church's tradition," to "help man in his journey towards truth and freedom."[4] In fact, the Holy Father wrote *Veritatis Splendor* in order to guard the human person against the prevalent errors of the day, which seek to threaten him.[5]

---

[1] John Paul II, *Veritatis Splendor* 27.

[2] John Paul II, *Veritatis Splendor* 27.

[3] John Paul II, *Redemptor Hominis* 10. In *Veritatis Splendor*, John Paul particularly emphasizes the Church's responsibility of defending the integrity of the human person. See, for example, John Paul II, *Veritatis Splendor* 13, 72, 73, 79, 101, 116.

[4] John Paul II, *Veritatis Splendor* 27.

[5] In my presentation of *Redemptor Hominis*, I mention the Church's responsibility of safeguarding the truth of the human person [John Paul

In light of the Church's task of defending the integrity of the person, a task entrusted to the Church by Christ himself, the Pope speaks of martyrs.

> In the Holy Spirit, the Church receives and hands down the Scripture as the witness to the 'great things' which God has done in history (cf. Luke 1:49); she professes by the lips of her Fathers and Doctors the truth of the Word made Flesh, puts His precepts and love into practice in the lives of her saints and in the sacrifice of her martyrs, and celebrates her hope in Him in the Liturgy. By this same Tradition Christians receive 'the living voice of the Gospel,' as the faithful expression of God's wisdom and will.[6]

---

II, *Redemptor Hominis* 10]. Here again, with *Veritatis Splendor*, the Pope speaks out in defense of human freedom. To be more specific, John Paul's stated purpose for writing this encyclical is "to set forth, with regard to the problems being discussed, the principles of a moral teaching based upon Sacred Scripture and the living Apostolic Tradition, and at the same time to shed light on the presuppositions and consequences of the dissent which that teaching has met" [John Paul II, *Veritatis Splendor* 5]. At the conclusion of his work, the Pontiff reiterates the importance of *Veritatis Splendor* by stating his intent, which is the "reaffirmation of the universality and immutability of the moral Commandments, particularly those which prohibit always and without exception intrinsically evil acts" [John Paul II, *Veritatis Splendor* 115].

[6] John Paul II, *Veritatis Splendor* 27.

## Chapter Seven: *Veritatis Splendor* and the Sacrifice of the Martyrs

**The Martyr's Relation to the Catholic Church**

*Veritatis Splendor* 27 contains several implications for martyrdom. In particular, I note the fact that the martyr is a member, at least broadly understood, of the Catholic Church, which was founded by Jesus Christ. Second, I show that the Church's task of "promoting and preserving the faith and the moral life" of the human person implies the fact that obedience to Church teaching is one of the means by which one is not only "promoted and preserved," but also made holy.[7] The person's sanctification, then, results in part from his obedience to Church teaching.

My extrapolation of *Veritatis Splendor* 27 concerns the implication that the martyr is a member of the Catholic Church. My reason for stating this inference consists in the following. The Holy Father mentions the martyrs together with the Fathers, Doctors, and saints of the Church, who "receive 'the living voice of the Gospel,' as the faithful expression of God's wisdom and will."[8] Thus, one might understand that the Fathers and Doctors of the Church, as well as the saints and the martyrs, are a "faithful expression of God's wisdom and will."[9] They hand on the unchangeable truth of God's love for the human person and the truth of the Gospel message itself.

---

[7] John Paul II, *Veritatis Splendor* 27. In addition to the sanctification that results in the human person from his obedience to Church teaching, other ways in which he is made holy include prayer and the worthy reception of the sacraments.

[8] John Paul II, *Veritatis Splendor* 27.

[9] John Paul II, *Veritatis Splendor* 27.

Another aspect of the martyr in *Veritatis Splendor* 27, which likewise indicates that he is at least an implicit member of the Church broadly understood, involves the following. To say that the martyr puts the "precepts and love [of Christ] into practice" by the "sacrifice" of his life is to imply the guiding hand of the Magisterium.[10]

Another factor in *Veritatis Splendor* 27 is that John Paul speaks of the Church's solicitous care of her members, and, as I have just explained, the martyrs possess at least a broad membership. Along with all members of the Church, the martyr is guided by the authority and responsibility of the Magisterium, which "promotes and preserves the faith and the moral life" of the human person.[11] Consider the verbs that John Paul uses in order to put forth various actions of the Church. In the one sentence containing the word *martyrs*, he indicates that the Church *receives* and *hands down*, she *professes* and *celebrates*, and she *puts into practice* the precepts and the love of Christ.[12] The Church's task of "promoting and preserving the faith and the moral life" of the human person corresponds to a similar passage from *Redemptor Hominis*.[13]

From *Redemptor Hominis* 10, one recalls that the "Church's fundamental function in every age…is to direct man's gaze, to point the awareness and experience of the whole of humanity towards the mystery of God, to help all men to be familiar with the

---

[10] John Paul II, *Veritatis Splendor* 27.
[11] John Paul II, *Veritatis Splendor* 27.
[12] John Paul II, *Veritatis Splendor* 27.
[13] John Paul II, *Veritatis Splendor* 27; John Paul II, *Redemptor Hominis* 10.

# Chapter Seven: *Veritatis Splendor* and the Sacrifice of the Martyrs

profundity of the Redemption taking place in Christ Jesus."[14] With this passage, I now bring out the Holy Father's thought that, directing the person toward God the Father through Jesus is the Church's task. Indeed, it is the Church's honor. The responsibility of the Church in leading the human person to the Heavenly Father through Jesus also affects one's "deepest sphere," including his heart and his conscience.[15] The teaching of the Church is one of the means by which she leads the human person to the Father through Jesus.

Another factor that *Redemptor Hominis* 10 teaches is that the central focus of the Church is the care of the human person. As *Veritatis Splendor* 27 highlights, the person is made holy, in part, through his *obedience* to the "precepts and love" of Jesus because, again, the primary concern of Church teaching is to lead one to the Father through Jesus.

Since *Veritatis Splendor* 27 speaks of the martyr as one who, guided by the Magisterium, puts the "precepts and love [of Christ] into practice" by the sacrifice of his life, I highlight the implication that the martyr is at least a member of the Church broadly speaking and that he is made holy, in part, through obedience to her teaching. One might ask, however, what makes the martyr different from the other "living voices of the Gospel," whom the Pope enumerates?[16] In the next section, I address this question.

---

[14] John Paul II, *Redemptor Hominis* 10.

[15] John Paul II, *Redemptor Hominis* 10.

[16] The phrase, "the living voice of the Gospel," is taken from the Conciliar document, *Dei Verbum* 8, and it is quoted by John Paul in *Veritatis Splendor* 27.

## "By the Sacrifice of His Life"

An additional point that I emphasize from *Veritatis Splendor* 27 concerns the notion of *sacrifice*. To be sure, both martyrs and non-martyred saints put the "precepts and love [of Christ] into practice."[17] One might ask, then, how a martyr is differentiated from a non-martyr. To anticipate a related question, how is the martyr's death, understood as a contemplation of Christ's face, distinguished from the saintly non-martyr's death? *Veritatis Splendor* 27 differentiates between a saint and a martyr. Clarifying this distinction helps answer further questions that arise when the topic of contemplating the face of Christ enters the discussion.

A careful reading of the text, then, brings to light the following distinction between the saint who is not a martyr and the saint who is a martyr. The saint puts the "precepts and love [of Christ] into practice" by his *life*, while the martyr puts the "precepts and love [of Christ] into practice" by his *death*. Granted, the martyr may live an exemplary life, as well, and such is normally (but not always) the case. For example, some executioners of the martyrs are inspired by the courage, faith and cheerfulness of the martyr. They receive the grace of faith at that moment, and they die as a martyr, themselves, very quickly. They are baptized in their own blood and converted to Jesus in an instant.

Fidelity to Christ and His Commandments certainly characterizes the lives of the Church's saints who are not martyrs. John Paul indicates that the martyr, on the other hand, puts the "precepts and

---

[17] John Paul in *Veritatis Splendor* 27.

love [of Christ] into practice" by his "sacrifice."[18] The martyr sacrifices his life, which is a great good, to be faithful to Jesus, which is an even greater good.

To say that the Church "puts [Christ's] precepts and love into practice in the *lives* of her saints" naturally makes one want to conclude the phrase by saying, "and in the *deaths* of her martyrs," because life and death are opposites when one speaks of the corporal body. It fits, since the sacrifice of which the Pontiff speaks, is the martyr's life. John Paul acknowledges, of course, that the martyr embraces many sacrifices as he moves toward the one, final sacrifice of his life. Since the sacrifice of life means death, the word *death* could be viably interchanged with *sacrifice*.

Why is it important to substitute *death* for *sacrifice*? Does an interchange of words avoid the questions of how *sacrifice* is used and for whom the martyr *sacrifices*? If the martyr puts the "precepts and love [of Christ] into practice" by his *sacrifice*, for whom does the martyr sacrifice? What does he sacrifice? I answer these questions by returning to the notion of *sacrifice* with my explication of *Veritatis Splendor* 27. For the moment, however, I argue why I think an interchange of *death* and *sacrifice* is both a perceptive analysis of the Pontiff's text and a significant contribution toward claiming that the martyr's death, and thus, his contemplation of the face of Jesus Christ, is different from the saintly non-martyr's death.

I believe exchanging the words *death* for *sacrifice* is not only legitimate, but it also contributes to a new understanding of martyr-

---

[18] John Paul in *Veritatis Splendor* 27.

dom. Substituting the word *death* for *sacrifice* emphasizes that the pinnacle of one's life is the moment of death. Similar to the climax of a good story, the final hour of one's physical life culminates in the martyr's putting the "precepts and love [of Christ] into practice" by his *death*. In the case of the martyr, however, the sacrifice of one's life in death also signifies an act of the will. One chooses to die rather than to deny Jesus or His teaching.

Claiming that the moment of one's death marks a precise instance of putting the "precepts and love [of Christ] into practice" also implies an act of the will on the part of the martyr. It further suggests that, because death concludes one's life, it carries a sense of finality. While the Pope characterizes the saint's life as an eminent display of fidelity to Christ and His Commandments, he distinguishes between the saint (who is not a martyr) and the martyr with one word, *sacrifice*, which can be interchanged with *death*. By inferring that the martyr's sacrifice, death, implements the Commandments and the love of Christ, one surmises that the martyr's death, which is the *final* "word," or moment of a human life, is "spoken" by his practice of the "precepts and love" of Christ. The martyr's climatic moment of life, then, summarizes that life as an implementation of the Commandments and the love of Jesus Christ. Because John Paul distinguishes the martyr's death from the saint's death, then, I also distinguish the martyr's death from the saintly non-martyr's death.

## Death Rather Than "An Act Contrary to Faith or Virtue"

By paragraph 76 of *Veritatis Splendor*, John Paul has already explained that "the morality of acts is defined by the relationship of man's freedom with the authentic good;" only the "act in conformity with the good can be a path that leads to life."[19] Thus, the Holy Father brings out the "essential 'teleological' character" of the moral life, which "consists in the deliberate ordering of human acts to God, the supreme Good and ultimate End (*telos*) of man."[20] Further, the Pope has noted various inadequacies, errors, and misunderstandings concerning the object of a moral act, the human will, and human freedom, and he has named various trends that deviate from the person's authentic good up to this point in the encyclical.[21] Still more, John Paul has reminded the reader that human acts must be ordered to God, which is in keeping with the "authentic moral good of man, [and they must be] safeguarded by the Commandments."[22] Finally, John Paul has mentioned, at this point

---

[19] John Paul II, *Veritatis Splendor* 72.

[20] John Paul II, *Veritatis Splendor* 73. John Paul describes human acts as "moral acts because they express and determine the goodness or evil of the individual who performs them" [John Paul II, *Veritatis Splendor* 71]. I further expound upon this definition, drawing out the fact that human acts perfect or destroy the human subject who does them.

[21] John Paul II, *Veritatis Splendor* 74-75.

[22] John Paul II, *Veritatis Splendor* 73. Later in the encyclical, the Holy Father explains that the Commandments, especially the second part of the Decalogue, constitute "the indispensable rules of all social life" [John Paul II *Veritatis Splendor* 97].

in his work, the impossibility of establishing proportions between the moral quality of an act and its consequences.[23]

---

[23] John Paul II, *Veritatis Splendor* 75, 77. What I am referring to is proportionalism. Closely related to it is consequentialism. The Holy Father calls both "false solutions linked...to an inadequate understanding of the object of moral action" and to the free will of the human person [John Paul II, *Veritatis Splendor* 75]. Consequentialism "claims to draw the criteria of the rightness of a given way of acting solely from a calculation of foreseeable consequences deriving from a given choice" [John Paul II, *Veritatis Splendor* 75]. Proportionalism claims that "by weighing the various values and goods being sought," one can learn the correct way of acting based upon "the proportion acknowledged between the good and bad effects of that choice, with a view to the 'greater good' or 'lesser evil' actually possible in a particular situation" [John Paul II, *Veritatis Splendor* 75]. These two theories of moral action are not only erroneous, but also, they are devastating to the human person in the moral realm. For example, they deny intrinsically evil acts. The Holy Father explains as follows. Proportionalism and consequentialism "maintain that it is never possible to formulate an absolute prohibition of particular kinds of behavior which would be in conflict, in every circumstance and in every culture, with those values" [John Paul II, *Veritatis Splendor* 75]. More specifically, "the morality of an act would be judged in two different ways: its moral 'goodness' would be judged on the basis of the subject's intention in reference to moral goods, and its 'rightness' on the basis of a consideration of its foreseeable effects or consequences and of their proportion. Consequently, concrete kinds of behavior could be described as 'right' or 'wrong,' without it being thereby possible to judge as morally 'good' or 'bad' the will of the person choosing them. In this way, an act which, by contradicting a universal negative norm, directly violates goods considered as 'pre-moral' could be qualified as morally acceptable if the intention of the subject is focused, in accordance with a 'responsible' assessment of the goods involved in the concrete action, on the moral value judged to be decisive in the situation" [John Paul II, *Veritatis Splendor*

# Chapter Seven: *Veritatis Splendor* and the Sacrifice of the Martyrs

By the time he begins *Veritatis Splendor* 76, then, John Paul has prepared the reader to understand the magnitude of adherence to the Commandments. By following the Commandments, one safeguards "*the good* of the person, the image of God, by protecting his *goods*."[24] Since the various moral theories he has just enumerated deviate from Church teaching, John Paul warns that "the faithful are obliged to acknowledge and respect the specific moral precepts declared and taught by the Church in the name of God, the Creator and Lord."[25]

As Saint Paul teaches, the love of God and neighbor fulfills the law; that love is lived out by following the Commandments (Romans 13:8-10). John Paul's conclusion to this paragraph, which stresses one's adherence to the Commandments, features martyrdom. Moreover, the Holy Father speaks of martyrdom in light of the obedience one owes to love God and neighbor.

> It is an honor characteristic of Christians to obey God rather than men (cf. Acts 4:19; 5:29) and accept even martyrdom as a consequence, like the holy men and women of the Old and New Testaments, who are considered such because

---

75]. Unfortunately, we see this happening in many different ways in our world today.

[24] John Paul II, *Veritatis Splendor* 13.
[25] John Paul II, *Veritatis Splendor* 76.

they gave their lives rather than perform this or that particular act contrary to faith or virtue.[26]

As John Paul reiterates, the martyr is willing to sacrifice the great good of one's physical life in order to preserve the even greater good of one's spiritual life. Union with God by maintaining faith and virtue is more important than preserving one's earthly life.

**"Obey God Rather Than Men"**

To expound upon *Veritatis Splendor* 76, I divide it into two separate sections. The first part of the quotation I discuss is, "It is an honor characteristic of Christians to obey God rather than men (cf. Acts 4:19; 5:29) and accept even martyrdom as a consequence."[27] The second half of the quotation refers to a number of specific qualifications of the martyr, and it reads as follows: "like the holy men and women of the Old and New Testaments, who are considered such because they gave their lives rather than perform this or that particular act contrary to faith or virtue."[28]

In the first part, "It is an honor characteristic of Christians to obey God rather than men (cf. Acts 4:19; 5:29) and accept even martyrdom as a consequence," the Pope reminds one that obeying God takes prescience over complying with human authority,

---

[26] John Paul II, *Veritatis Splendor* 76. I emphasize the fact that it is precisely the Catholic Church who regards certain people of the "Old and New Testaments," *as holy* [John Paul II, *Veritatis Splendor* 76].

[27] John Paul II, *Veritatis Splendor* 76.

[28] John Paul II, *Veritatis Splendor* 76.

# Chapter Seven: *Veritatis Splendor* and the Sacrifice of the Martyrs

should that authority demand one's action contrary to the law of God.[29] The Pope explains that the obligation to "obey God rather than men (cf. Acts 4:19; 5:29)" might even require "martyrdom as a consequence" of one's obedience to God.[30]

The person stands in obedience to God and to His Commandments even when human authority encourages him to act against one or more of the Commandments. In such a situation, then, the person obeys "God rather than men (cf. Acts 4:19; 5:29);" he accepts martyrdom, should it be required of him.

## *Veritatis Splendor* and Safeguarding the Good of the Human Person

A crucial factor from *Veritatis Splendor* is the notion of the good of the human person. Stressing the good of the person is particularly relevant to *Veritatis Splendor* 76, where the Pontiff exhorts obedience "to God, rather than men" (cf. Acts 4:19; 5:29).[31] Following the Commandments contributes to the "authentic moral good" of the human person.[32] In other words, a person's obedience "to God, rather than men" when another tries to force him to contradict God's commands makes him a morally good human person.

The Holy Father highlights the fact that a person can intuit the "connection between moral good and the fulfillment of his own

---

[29] John Paul II, *Veritatis Splendor* 76.
[30] John Paul II, *Veritatis Splendor* 76.
[31] John Paul II, *Veritatis Splendor* 76.
[32] John Paul II, *Veritatis Splendor* 73.

destiny" as a human being.³³ God is the ultimate Absolute Good, who "attracts us and beckons us," for He is the "origin and goal of man's life."³⁴ Indeed, the person's moral goodness is related to "the Love of God, who is 'the source of man's happiness and…the final end of human activity.'"³⁵ The Pope's insight on God as the Absolute Good of the human person reveals the innate desire for God, which is present in every human being.

In the command to love one's neighbor, for example, one "finds a precise expression of the singular dignity of the human person."³⁶ More specifically, he attains perfection as a human person precisely through his acts, for "he is called to seek his Creator of his own accord and freely to arrive at full and blessed perfection by cleaving to Him."³⁷ The Holy Father explains as follows.

> Human acts are moral acts because they express and determine the goodness or evil of the individual who performs them. …to the extent that they are deliberate choices, they give moral definition to the very person who performs them, determining his profound spiritual traits.³⁸

---

³³ John Paul II, *Veritatis Splendor* 8.

³⁴ John Paul II, *Veritatis Splendor* 7.

³⁵ Servais (Th.) Pinckaers, OP, *An Encyclical for the Future: Veritatis Splendor*, Sr. Mary Thomas Noble, OP, Trans., J. A. DiNoia, OP, Romanus Cessario, OP, eds., in *Veritatis Splendor and the Renewal of Moral Theology*, (Princeton: Scepter Publishers, 1999), 22.

³⁶ John Paul II, *Veritatis Splendor* 13.

³⁷ John Paul II, *Veritatis Splendor* 71.

³⁸ John Paul II, *Veritatis Splendor* 71.

A key factor in the Pontiff's quotation is that every choice the person makes involves a decision about himself. Elsewhere, the Pontiff expresses the same idea in conjunction with human freedom. "Freedom is not only the choice for one or another particular action; it is also, within that choice, a *decision about oneself* and a setting of one's own life for or against the good, for or against the truth, and ultimately for or against God."[39] Because each decision directs one's life "for or against" the good, the truth, and God, one makes oneself into the kind of person one is, with each freely chosen human act. Thus, the human person attains perfection *as* a person precisely through his acts.

> In Jesus Christ and in His Spirit, the Christian is a 'new creation', a child of God; by his actions he shows his likeness or unlikeness to the image of the Son who is the first-born among many brethren (cf. Romans 8:29), he lives out his fidelity or infidelity to the gift of the Spirit, and he opens or closes himself to eternal life, to the communion of vision, love and happiness with God the Father, Son and Holy Spirit.[40]

**The Sacrifice of the Martyr is a Gift of Self to Holy Mother Church**

In the first part of *Veritatis Splendor* 76, extrapolated above, I highlight the importance of obeying "God rather than men" by

---

[39] John Paul II, *Veritatis Splendor* 65.
[40] John Paul II, *Veritatis Splendor* 73.

noting that adherence to the Commandments "safeguards" the authentic good of the human person."[41] The second part of the *Veritatis Splendor* 76 quotation reads as follows. Obeying God over and against another human being or authority sometimes means accepting "even martyrdom as a consequence, like the holy men and women of the Old and New Testaments, who are considered such because they gave their lives rather than perform this or that particular act contrary to faith or virtue."[42]

The section of *Veritatis Splendor* 76 quoted above concerns three aspects. In my interpretation, the Holy Father first presents an example, and second, he identifies two qualities of a martyr. As examples of martyrs, who presumably fit the distinctions he is about to make, the Pope points to "the holy men and women of the Old and New Testaments who are considered such" by the Church.[43] The position that I want to accentuate in this passage is that the Church recognizes certain people who have died as holy. They "are considered holy" based upon the authority of the Catholic Church.

Next, I believe John Paul presents two specific characteristics of the martyr, which, in fact, distinguish him as such: "they gave their lives rather than perform this or that particular act contrary to faith or virtue."[44] First, the martyr *gives* his life and second, he *avoids* performing an "act contrary to faith or virtue." He chooses to offer his life as a gift when such an offering is the consequence of his re-

---

[41] John Paul II, *Veritatis Splendor* 76, 13.
[42] John Paul II, *Veritatis Splendor* 76.
[43] John Paul II, *Veritatis Splendor* 76.
[44] John Paul II, *Veritatis Splendor* 76.

# Chapter Seven: *Veritatis Splendor* and the Sacrifice of the Martyrs

fusal to act in a manner "contrary to faith or virtue."[45] The martyr, who is differentiated from the saintly non-martyr, gives his life precisely when retaining it would mean acting against "faith or virtue."

The manner in which the martyr gives his life hearkens back to *Veritatis Splendor* 27 and to the notion of *sacrifice*, that I explain might be understood as *death*. By his death, the martyr implements the "precepts and love" of Christ.[46] Surrendering one's life to uphold "faith or virtue" highlights the person's self-gift in a vivid manner. In the case of the martyr, his gift of self is a gift given to the entire Church specifically *because* he refrains from acting against either what the Church believes (faith) or how the Church teaches that her beliefs are to be put into action (Commandments). While the death of a saintly non-martyr might also be understood as a gift of self, his death is not the consequence of a refusal to act against "faith or virtue." The martyr's action, which *Veritatis Splendor* 76 highlights, is his acceptance of the consequences for his refusal to act against faith or virtue precisely when it is likely to result in the termination of his physical life.

In *Veritatis Splendor* 76, then, I see John Paul's understanding of martyrdom as a self-gift that results *"as a consequence"* of one's refusal to act against "faith or virtue." One might ask, then, can such a gift, which arises specifically as a *consequence* for one's re-

---

[45] Of course, the saintly non-martyr offers his life as a gift to Holy Mother Church in many other ways.
[46] John Paul II, *Veritatis Splendor* 27.

fusal to act, be properly regarded as a gift?⁴⁷ Is the gift of his life freely given?

Does John Paul regard martyrdom as an example of self-giving, since he indicates that the martyr *gives* his life instead of *doing* an action "contrary to faith or virtue?" If so, does the martyr's gift of self express the person's love for God and neighbor in a manner that is somehow unique from the saintly non-martyr's expression of love? Answering these questions is the task of the next section, which describes the novelty of the martyr's sacrifice in terms of contemplation.

---

[47] One might contend that John Paul uses *self-gift* in many ways, particularly when he speaks of marriage or the consecrated state. Since an analysis of *self-gift* in the writings of John Paul's pontificate would provide ample material for numerous works, I simply speak of one's gift of self as enunciated above in *Salvifici Doloris* 28, and here, with *Veritatis Splendor* 76. My description of self-gift in *Salvifici Doloris* 28 stresses one's fundamental openness to another and it explicates the Conciliar teaching that the human person finds himself "through a sincere gift of himself" [John Paul II, *Salvifici Doloris* 28].

# Chapter Eight

## The Morality of Human Acts and the Existence of Intrinsically Evil Acts

In my discussion above, I highlight particular elements that indicate following the Commandments safeguards the good of the human person. After the Holy Father's reference to martyrdom in *Veritatis Splendor* 76 and before he speaks of it again in paragraph 87, several crucial factors enter into my discussion of his thought on martyrdom. I treat *Veritatis Splendor* 76-83 as a single unit since, with paragraph 84, John Paul begins a new chapter in his encyclical.

With *Veritatis Splendor* 76-83, then, I bring in the Pope's mention of the object of the human act and the existence of intrinsically evil human acts. He stresses the fact that the "primary and decisive element for moral judgment is the object of the human act."[1] One determines the morality of an act based upon its object. Further, he notes the importance of acknowledging the existence of acts that are intrinsically evil.

John Paul's teaching about these two factors, the object of the human act and the existence of intrinsically evil human acts, presupposes the "existence of an 'objective moral order.'"[2] I also expound upon the objective moral order, to which the Pontiff refers. I limit myself to discussing these three factors, which underscore

---

[1] John Paul II, *Veritatis Splendor* 79.
[2] John Paul II, *Veritatis Splendor* 82.

crucial elements regarding martyrdom, rather than engaging in specific details of moral theology.

## "The Object of the Human Act" and the Existence of Intrinsically Evil Acts

John Paul notes the fact that, since the "morality of the human act depends primarily and fundamentally on the 'object' rationally chosen by the deliberate will," one's good intention is not sufficient, in itself, to make an act morally good.[3] In other words, the morality of an act is determined by the freely chosen object. The "human act depends on its object, [and] whether that object is capable of being ordered to God, to the One who 'alone is good,' and thus brings about the perfection of the person."[4]

The Holy Father emphasizes the point that there are certain "objects of the human act which are, by their nature, 'incapable of being ordered' to God because they radically contradict the good of the person made in His image."[5] Here, I want to highlight two facts that the Pope relates. First, an act that can never be ordered to God is intrinsically evil.[6] Second, doing an act that is intrinsically evil harms the human person. Intrinsically evil acts, therefore, can never perfect the human person, made in God's image.[7] Thus, the Ho-

---

[3] John Paul II, *Veritatis Splendor* 78.

[4] John Paul II, *Veritatis Splendor* 78.

[5] John Paul II, *Veritatis Splendor* 80, 115.

[6] The Pope discusses intrinsically evil acts in several places, such as John Paul II, *Veritatis Splendor* 56, 67, 80-83, 90, 95-96, 110, 115.

[7] John Paul II, *Veritatis Splendor* 80, 115.

## Chapter Eight: The Morality of Human Acts

ly Father reiterates his teaching that, by choosing to do an intrinsically evil act, one offends God because he acts contrary to his own good.[8]

An additional element that John Paul accentuates, prior to his next mention of martyrdom, is the "existence of an 'objective moral order.'"[9] John Paul reaffirms that the "moral quality of human acting is dependent on this fidelity to the Commandments, as an expression of obedience and love."[10] He recognizes that the moral order is objective by referring to erroneous teachings, which exaggerate both the intention of the moral agent and the expected consequences of the act.

> ...[T]he opinion must be rejected as erroneous which maintains that it is impossible to qualify as morally evil according to its species the deliberate choice of certain kinds of behavior or specific acts, without taking into account the intention for which the choice was made of the totality of the foreseeable consequences of that act for all persons concerned.[11]

---

[8] As Saint Thomas teaches, "God is not offended by us except in so far as we act against our own good" [Saint Thomas Aquinas, *Summa Contra Gentiles*, Book III, Question 122]. Thus, the Holy Father reiterates the fact that breaking the Commandments goes against one's own good as a human person.

[9] John Paul II, *Veritatis Splendor* 82.
[10] John Paul II, *Veritatis Splendor* 82.
[11] John Paul II, *Veritatis Splendor* 82.

One's intention does not make an act morally good or bad. If one did not maintain the "rational determination of the morality of human acting," as John Paul explicitly teaches, it "would be impossible to affirm the existence of an 'objective moral order' and to establish any particular norm, the content of which would be binding without exception."[12] Thus, by explicitly stating the existence of the objective moral order, the Holy Father reiterates a central issue of morality, which serves to safeguard the human person. Following the Ten Commandments protects and promotes the person.

Ever intent upon the human person, John Paul acknowledges that the questions, which concern the morality of human acts and whether intrinsically evil acts exist, focus upon "the question of man himself, of his truth and of the moral consequences flowing from that truth."[13] Again, the Pope's concern, which is the Church's concern, is to defend the truth of the human person.

Upholding the inherent worth of the human person, created in the image of God, is of prime importance for the Pope. Near the end of *Veritatis Splendor* 83, the Holy Father states this obligation again in light of the present focus on the existence of intrinsically evil acts. He highlights the person by reiterating his intent. He desires to "remain faithful" to the human person, himself: "by acknowledging and teaching the existence of intrinsic evil in given human acts, the Church remains faithful to the integral truth about

---

[12] John Paul II, *Veritatis Splendor* 82. Elsewhere, John Paul notes the "universal and permanent validity of the precepts prohibiting intrinsically evil acts" [John Paul II, *Veritatis Splendor* 95].

[13] John Paul II, *Veritatis Splendor* 83.

## Truth's Splendor: Jesus Christ

My detailed account of *Veritatis Splendor* 76-83 culminates in the final point to which the Pope draws one's attention. By addressing this encyclical to bishops, John Paul exhorts them to "show the inviting splendor of that truth which is Jesus Christ Himself" by their lives of fidelity to Christ and to His Commandments.[15] A familiar passage in Sacred Scripture brings out the same fact: Jesus is "the Way, the Truth, and the Life" (John 14:6). The crucial aspect that John Paul nuances, however, is that the Truth, who is Jesus Christ, radiates an inherent, "inviting splendor."[16] Recall that John Paul's introduction to this encyclical initially opens the reader to the notion of truth's splendor. He writes as follows.

> The splendor of truth shines forth in the works of the Creator and, in a special way, in man, created in the image and likeness of God (cf. Genesis 1:26). Truth enlightens man's intelligence and shapes his freedom, leading him to know and love the Lord. Hence the Psalmist prays: 'Let the light of Your face shine on us, O Lord' (Psalm 4:6).[17]

---

[14] John Paul II, *Veritatis Splendor* 83.
[15] John Paul II, *Veritatis Splendor* 83.
[16] John Paul II, *Veritatis Splendor* 83.
[17] John Paul II, *Veritatis Splendor* Prior to the *Introduction*. Other renditions of Psalms 4:6 include the following: "Lift up the light of Thy

It is precisely this "splendor" of Christ, who *is* Truth, Christ, whose precepts and love the martyr puts into practice by his death, which, I argue, martyrdom radiates.[18] In other words, the martyr shows Jesus Christ to others by radiating *Christ's* splendor and not one's own. He radiates the splendor of Truth, who is Jesus Christ Himself.[19] The martyr's contemplation of truth embraces the totality of his life with a response to God's love. And, his martyrdom expresses not only his contemplation and his total self-offering, but also, his martyrdom, itself, is a response to the love of God.[20]

John Paul's assertion that martyrdom shows "that the splendor of moral truth" cannot be darkened by "the behavior and thinking of individuals and society," which I discuss in *Veritatis Splendor* 93, is a key factor in asserting how the martyr radiates truth.[21] Substantiating my claim, however, requires bringing out the contemplative dimension of martyrdom, which I show in a later section, and it further engages the notion of moral truth's radiant splendor.

---

countenance upon us, O Lord" (RSV)! "Lord, show us the light of Your face" (NAB)! "The light of Thy countenance O Lord, is signed upon us: Thou hast given gladness in my heart" (Psalms 4:6-7, DRA).

[18] John Paul II, *Veritatis Splendor* 27.

[19] John Paul II, *Novo Millennio Ineunte* 16.

[20] As Ide points out, "the Pope tends to speak of the gift of oneself as a 'response to the gift of God'" (le pape parle volontiers du don de soi comme d'une 'réponse' au don de Dieu" [Ide, *Une Théologie du Don (première partie)*, p. 174]. I highlight the notion of *response* in the sentence above.

[21] John Paul II, *Veritatis Splendor* 93.

## Chapter Eight: The Morality of Human Acts

### The "Essential Bond Between Truth, the Good and Freedom"

Paragraph 84 begins the third and final chapter of *Veritatis Splendor*, which is the section containing the longest and most pertinent passages that John Paul offers the Church on the subject of martyrdom. For this reason, I look with greater detail not only at the Pontiff's explicit references to martyrdom, but also at the intermediate paragraphs of *Veritatis Splendor* 84-86, prior to his next mention of the topic, in paragraph 87.

Various moral theories, against which the Pontiff warns in this encyclical, attack the connection between the human person's freedom and the Commandments of God.[22] The central gist of these theories extols personal freedom to the detriment of authentic human freedom. To combat these errors, John Paul aims to highlight "the relationship between freedom and truth" in *Veritatis Splendor* 84. He explains as follows.

> According to Christian faith and the Church's teaching, 'only the freedom which submits to the truth leads the human person to his true good. The good of the person is to be in the truth and to *do* the truth.[23]

---

[22] John Paul II, *Veritatis Splendor* 84. Unmarked quotations in this section refer to *Veritatis Splendor* 84.

[23] John Paul II, *Veritatis Splendor* 84. The Pontiff emphasizes the importance of "doing" the truth by italicizing the word, *do*, in the original text.

The Holy Father stresses the fact that there exists an "essential bond between Truth, the Good and Freedom," and, to the detriment of the human person, this bond is obscure in society today.[24] John Paul places such strong emphasis on the bond between "Truth, the Good and Freedom," that he speaks of its recovery as an urgent mission of the Church. His exhortation to "be in the truth and to *do* the truth" suggests that recovering the "essential bond between Truth, the Good and Freedom" comes about by living in the truth.[25] I reflect upon what it means to "be in the truth and to *do* the truth" in this section.

The Holy Father explains the depth of loss resulting in today's ambiguity of the "essential bond between Truth, the Good and Freedom" with the example of Pontius Pilate who asks, "What is truth" (John 18:38)?[26] John Paul remarks that Pilate's question regarding truth points to the "distressing perplexity of a man who often no longer knows who he is, whence he comes and where he is going."[27] Indeed, the contemporary human person seems to have lost his own identity, as well.

The Pope continues to explain the severity of the condition in the world today regarding the obscurity of knowing that Truth, the Good, and Freedom are inseparable. Various "situations of gradual self-destruction" include the person who sees no need to "acknowledge the enduring absoluteness of any moral value."[28] In

---

[24] John Paul II, *Veritatis Splendor* 84.
[25] John Paul II, *Veritatis Splendor* 84.
[26] John Paul II, *Veritatis Splendor* 84.
[27] John Paul II, *Veritatis Splendor* 84.
[28] John Paul II, *Veritatis Splendor* 84.

fact, the Pope identifies relativism as the gravest situation in which the person finds himself today. The fact that certain things are true and others are false is rejected by the relativist. In addition, the relativist spurns the objective moral good. Some human acts are good, and others are bad. Confusion abounds when one loses such a basic distinction between the true and the false and between what is good and what is evil. Indeed, relativism is a dangerous plague upon contemporary human society.

John Paul elaborates upon relativism as the situation of the human person when he "is no longer convinced that only in the truth can he find salvation. The saving power of the truth is contested, and freedom alone, uprooted from any objectivity, is left to decide by itself what is good and what is evil."[29] In other words, relativism advocates the individual as the sole arbiter of his person.

The Pope further explains that, in theology, relativism becomes "a lack of trust in the Wisdom of God, who guides man with the moral law. Concrete situations are unfavorably contrasted with the precepts of the moral law, nor is it any longer maintained that…the law of God is always the one true good of man."[30] Thus, the Pope identifies relativism as a grave danger because its proponents claim to possess no objective, absolute truth other than the utter conviction that truth is not objective, which contradicts one's own position as a relativist.

Based upon the Holy Father's warning against relativism in *Veritatis Splendor* 84, one might draw out some thoughts upon the

---

[29] John Paul II, *Veritatis Splendor* 84.
[30] John Paul II, *Veritatis Splendor* 84.

martyr in relation to the relativist. If, as the relativist maintains, one truth is as valid as another is, then he believes the martyr dies to uphold his own opinion. On the other hand, if the relativist somehow comes to acknowledge that the martyr is *not* a fool, then he is forced to accede that relativism itself is void precisely *because* the martyr's death, as John Paul maintains, upholds the objectivity of the moral order.

There *is* right and wrong, and the martyr defends that objective moral order by his death. Indeed, martyrdom reveals that the position of the relativist is both erroneous and, in fact, ridiculous. Despite what the relativist contends, the world is run based upon certain things being either true or false and either good or evil. For example, the legal system is based upon certain actions being good or evil.

From the Holy Father's remarks on relativism in *Veritatis Splendor* 84, then, one can surmise the following conclusions. First, the martyr directly opposes relativism because his death witnesses to the objectivity of the moral order. By his death, which puts the "precepts and love [of Christ] into practice," the martyr upholds the moral law, the objectivity of which beckons obedience to the truth inscribed in the person.[31]

One can draw a second conclusion from the flip side of my point regarding the martyr's death affirming the objectivity of the moral order. Noting the Holy Father's depiction of relativism in paragraph 84, one might conclude by saying that, accepting "even

---

[31] John Paul II, *Veritatis Splendor* 27.

martyrdom as a consequence," the martyr is willing to give his life in order to bear witness to t/Truth.[32]

Instead of the "distressing perplexity of a man who often no longer knows who he is, whence he comes and where he is going," the martyr knows t/Truth; he dies with the confident certitude of a person who knows *exactly* "who he is, whence he comes and where he is going."[33] The death of the martyr, then, indicates that the Commandments testify to the truth of the human person. To defy them would be to destroy the human person, himself.

A third conclusion results from the previous two. If the martyr's death proclaims the objectivity of the moral order, and, if the martyr's death bears witness to t/Truth, then he is not only "in the truth," but he also "*does* the truth."[34] The martyr's *doing* of the truth suggests that he recovers the "essential bond between Truth, the Good and Freedom" by his death.[35]

---

[32] John Paul II, *Veritatis Splendor* 76.
[33] John Paul II, *Veritatis Splendor* 84.
[34] John Paul II, *Veritatis Splendor* 84.
[35] John Paul II, *Veritatis Splendor* 84.

# Chapter Nine

## John Paul's Description of Human Freedom: Christ Crucified "Reveals the Authentic Meaning of Freedom"

While the Pope's focus in *Veritatis Splendor* 84 highlights the gravity of relativism and its denial of an objective moral order, in paragraph 85 John Paul addresses the same matter through the lens of one who is doubtful about truth's objectivity. With paternal attention, he first acknowledges the fear and uncertainty gripping many people today. He expresses this unrest with the following question. "How can obedience to universal and unchanging moral norms respect the uniqueness and individuality of the person, and not represent a threat to his freedom and dignity?"[1]

In *Veritatis Splendor* 90, the Pope explains that the moral norm is a universal, immutable principle, which both reveals and protects one's human dignity and inviolability.[2] John Paul opens *Veritatis*

---

[1] John Paul II, *Veritatis Splendor* 85.

[2] John Paul II, *Veritatis Splendor* 90. John Paul speaks of moral norms, which are "universal and permanent," throughout *Veritatis Splendor* [John Paul II, *Veritatis Splendor* 53]. He brings out the fact that moral norms protect "the inviolable personal dignity of every human being" [John Paul II, *Veritatis Splendor* 97]. Upholding the "universal and unchanging" nature of moral norms, he reiterates the fact that the human person is not his own lawgiver; reason does not "create values and moral norms," and neither is the Church the "author or arbiter" of moral norms [John Paul II, *Veritatis Splendor* 96, 40, 95]. The autonomy of reason from its participation "in the wisdom of the divine Creator and

*Splendor* 85, then, by acknowledging the disquiet that many people have regarding whether obedience to objective moral norms endangers one's individual freedom and dignity. The Holy Father seeks to dispel the unease of the person who questions whether adherence to objective moral norms threatens individual freedom and human dignity.

Earlier in *Veritatis Splendor*, John Paul speaks of human freedom, which "abides in the truth and conforms to human dignity" through one's "obedience to the divine law."[3] In *Veritatis Splendor* 85, he explains that living "in accordance with the truth" is a sure way to uphold one's authentic human freedom and dignity. With great love for the person, he affirms that the Church strives to "help all the faithful to form a moral conscience which will make judgments and lead to decisions in accordance with the truth."[4] Indeed, the Holy Father understands human freedom, itself, to be "self-determination."[5] In other words, freedom is the "person's ca-

---

Lawgiver," contradicts Church teaching on "the truth about man" [John Paul II, *Veritatis Splendor* 40].

[3] John Paul II, *Veritatis Splendor* 42.

[4] John Paul II, *Veritatis Splendor* 85.

[5] See Karol Wojtyła, *Love and Responsibility*, 47, 135; *Persona e Atto*, 977-81, 985, 1007, 1026, 1035; "The Personal Structure of Self-Determination," in *Person and Community*, 190; John Paul II, *Man and Woman He Created Them*, 15.2, 186. All references are from Adrian J. Reimers, *Truth about the Good: Moral Norms in the Thought of John Paul II* (Ave Maria, FL: Sapientia Press of Ave Maria University, 2011), 177 footnote #53.

## Chapter Nine: John Paul's Description of Human Freedom

pacity to govern himself and to direct himself toward ends that he recognizes as…good."[6]

Understanding the magnitude of the Church's task of assisting the faithful in the formation of their conscience, John Paul notes in *Veritatis Splendor* 85 that the Church finds the "secret" of her strength by "constantly looking to the Lord Jesus." The Pope further specifies that "looking to Jesus" means looking at the Crucified Christ. The "Church finds the answer" to the troubling question of how "obedience to universal and unchanging moral norms" respects the person and upholds his freedom and dignity in Christ Crucified.[7]

John Paul's concluding sentence in *Veritatis Splendor* 85 explains that Christ Crucified defends the person's freedom and dignity, and, by looking to her Crucified Savior, the Church's high regard for freedom and dignity become evident. The death of Christ reveals "the authentic meaning of freedom" for many reasons, perhaps, but the Holy Father particularly highlights one: the Crucified Christ reveals freedom's true face because it is a "total gift of Himself," laid down for the salvation of the entire human race. His own words are as follows. "The Crucified Christ reveals the authentic meaning of freedom; He lives it fully in the total gift of Himself and calls His disciples to share in His freedom."[8]

Reflecting upon *Veritatis Splendor* 85 leads to the following conclusions. From the text, one might first infer that, because

---

[6] Adrian J. Reimers, *Truth about the Good: Moral Norms in the Thought of John Paul II*, 177.

[7] John Paul II, *Veritatis Splendor* 85.

[8] John Paul II, *Veritatis Splendor* 85.

Christ Crucified "reveals the authentic meaning of freedom," He is the reference point for John Paul's notion of freedom. This conclusion, however, raises a question: What does it mean to claim that Christ Crucified reveals freedom's true face?

Because John Paul explicitly speaks of Christ *Crucified*, I suggest that the death of Christ reveals that human freedom is that which opens the human person as a gift to God and to another person. Further, because Jesus reveals the human person to himself, one might infer that the Crucified Jesus also shows the human person to himself by understanding what it means to be genuinely free. As John Paul maintains, Christ Crucified evokes the notion of opening oneself as a gift, in authentic freedom, because of Christ's own self-emptying on the Cross (Philippians 2:5-8).

A second reflection ensues from *Veritatis Splendor* 85. Working from the Holy Father's notion of the "total gift" of the Christ Crucified, I state the obvious conclusion that the gift of Himself is freely given, in obedience to the Father's will, to each human person.

A third conclusion also results. To say that Christ Crucified "reveals the authentic meaning of freedom" by living it "fully in the total gift of Himself" recalls *Gaudium et Spes* 22 and 24, that I develop above. Because the person "cannot fully find himself except through a sincere gift of himself," one might conclude that the ultimate gift of self is in Christ's death on the Cross.[9]

Further, with *Salvifici Doloris* 28, I develop the notion that the gift of self opens the "I" of oneself to another person who is suffer-

---

[9] Second Vatican Council, *Gaudium et Spes* 24.

## Chapter Nine: John Paul's Description of Human Freedom

ing.[10] John Paul's mention of one's "availability" toward another human person, which I elucidate above as a stopping "beside the suffering of another," suggests that human freedom liberates the person to accompany another who suffers. Combining this thought with the martyr, one finds that in his freedom, the martyr accompanies those who suffer the tragic loss of uncertainty or unbelief in the objective order of morality.

As I explain with *Veritatis Splendor* 84, the martyr's *doing* of the truth implies the recovery of the "essential bond between Truth, the Good and Freedom" with his death. With *Veritatis Splendor* 85, I add the following. Because the martyr holds together in his person the "essential bond between Truth, the Good and Freedom," this "holding together" might be interpreted as the martyr's accompanying of another person who suffers.[11] His death expresses his presence with another who suffers, and the greatest suffering is the loss of God.

One might immediately object that the martyr suffers more than those who inflict his death. From a physical perspective, this is certainly true. The perpetrators of martyrdom, however, suffer as well, perhaps for many reasons. In particular, they suffer because of the loss of God. They lack "living in the truth," which the martyr undeniably possesses. While the martyr "does the truth," his perpetrators succumb to the numerous divisions and "isms" that arise when one's gaze is not directed to Christ Crucified, such as the

---

[10] John Paul II, *Salvifici Doloris* 28.
[11] John Paul II, *Veritatis Splendor* 84; John Paul II, *Salvifici Doloris* 28.

grave danger of relativism, which claims that truth is not objective.[12]

At the inception of the third chapter of *Veritatis Splendor*, John Paul cites a line from the Letter to the Galatians: "For freedom, Christ has set us free" (Galatians 5:1).[13] One might ask, from what is the person set free? One can give many answers to this question, such as the clear example of Christ's death freeing one from sin.

Interpreting these passages, I might surmise that, in *Veritatis Splendor* 85, Christ is the one who stops "beside the suffering" of every human person in order to reveal the authentic meaning of human freedom to each one. Further, His death on the Cross sets human freedom free—free to *also* stop "beside the suffering" of one's neighbor, as does Jesus. Reading Saint Paul's words in light of *Veritatis Splendor* 85, then, one might infer that Christ's death on the Cross not only reveals perfect freedom, but also it sets human freedom free, as John Paul elucidates in *Veritatis Splendor* 86, to which I now turn.

## Human Freedom and the Integrity of the Person

In *Veritatis Splendor* 86, John Paul continues his reflection on the nature of human freedom. Here, he speaks of freedom in a manner that is highly attractive and particularly appropriate to my discussion on martyrdom. *Veritatis Splendor* 86 shows why, in relation to martyrdom, human freedom is the necessary element that

---

[12] John Paul II, *Veritatis Splendor* 84.
[13] John Paul II, *Veritatis Splendor* 4.

safeguards the very integrity of the human person. The subject of human freedom, which is vast in itself, naturally includes the concepts of both human dignity and conscience. In fact, the Pontiff often links together freedom and dignity, as well as conscience, in his solicitous care of the human person.

In the present work, I highlight freedom and dignity specifically regarding martyrdom in light of *Veritatis Splendor*. Although the two concepts cannot be separated, for the sake of order, I first present human freedom, working especially from ideas presented by the Pope in *Veritatis Splendor* 86, combining it with my work above in paragraphs 84 and 85. After reflecting upon freedom, with an emphasis on *Veritatis Splendor* 86, I discuss human dignity and conscience as well, since John Paul holds that conscience, in particular, determines human dignity.

My initial reflection on freedom, which includes dignity and conscience, forms an integral whole together with the subjects of the good of the human person and human acts. Testifying to the unanimity of freedom, conscience, and human acts, John Paul stresses their inseparable congruity in the following manner. The "relationship between man's freedom and God's law, which has its intimate and living center in the moral conscience, is manifested and realized in human acts."[14] In order to explicate the harmony between freedom, conscience, and human acts in light of the Pope's teaching in *Veritatis Splendor*, I carefully analyze paragraph 86.

---

[14] John Paul II, *Veritatis Splendor* 71.

In *Veritatis Splendor* 86, John Paul brings out several elements that, in speaking to the nature of the human person, likewise serve to enunciate the person who is a martyr. While freedom is an essential part of what makes the human person *human*, it bears special relevance in the martyr who, while seemingly robbed of his freedom, actually preserves it and manifests it most fully. He does so in imitation of Christ Crucified, as *Veritatis Splendor* 85 highlights.

How does paragraph 86 bring out the fact that the martyr, like Christ, reveals authentic human freedom? The martyr's death makes known authentic human freedom for many reasons. As I mention above, freedom concerns self-determination. More specifically, human freedom involves "a *decision about oneself* and a setting of one's own life for or against the Good, for or against the Truth, and ultimately for or against God."[15] Comparing the Pope's teaching with the person who is a martyr, I add the fact that the martyr *shows* authentic human freedom by "*doing* the truth."[16]

---

[15] John Paul II, *Veritatis Splendor* 65.

[16] John Paul II, *Veritatis Splendor* 84. Examples of texts that explain John Paul's understanding of human dignity, insofar as it relates to martyrdom, include the following documents from Pope Saint John Paul II: *Dives in Misericordia*, especially 1, 5, 6, 14; *Redemptor Hominis*, especially 10-12; *Veritatis Splendor*, especially 42, 78-97; *Salvifici Doloris* 23; *Christifideles Laici* 37; *Dominum et Vivificantem* 60. Several homilies, some of which particularly refer to a martyr or numerous martyrs, also express John Paul's notion of human dignity. Examples of these homilies include the following: 5 October 1980; 8 May 1981; 10 October 1982; 27 September 1986; 10 June 1987 and 2 June 1997. Several *General Audiences* of John Paul, commonly referred to as *Theology of the Body*, also speak of

# Chapter Nine: John Paul's Description of Human Freedom

The following text contains crucial aspects of the Pope's understanding of human freedom in *Veritatis Splendor*, which bear relevance to the subject of martyrdom. In my opinion, and, elaborating upon the notion of self-determination, John Paul defines human freedom in *Veritatis Splendor* 86 with the passage below.

> Human freedom belongs to us as creatures; it is a freedom, which is given as a gift, one to be received like a seed and to be cultivated responsibly. It is an essential part of that creaturely image which is the basis of the dignity of the person. Within that freedom there is an echo of the primordial vocation whereby the Creator calls man to the true Good, and even more, through Christ's Revelation, to become His friend and to share His own divine life. It is at once inalienable self-possession and openness to all that exists, in passing beyond self to knowledge and love of the other. Freedom then is rooted in the truth about man, and it is ultimately directed towards communion.[17]

Relating *Veritatis Splendor* 86 to martyrdom, I note that John Paul's definition of human freedom is vital to my work for many reasons. First, the Pope brings out the fact that freedom, which is an essential component to the very nature of the human person, is a gift given precisely "to be cultivated responsibly." Second, he stresses that freedom is intrinsic to the person, who is created in

---

human dignity: 3 December 1980 (6) and 22 April 1981 (3) in my section on human dignity. See also John Paul II *Veritatis Splendor* 65.

[17] John Paul II, *Veritatis Splendor* 86.

the image of God. In my ensuing discussion, I accentuate a third pertinent element in the Pontiff's description of freedom, which is the person's openness to all that exists.

A fourth reason why the Pope's definition of freedom in *Veritatis Splendor* 86 is imperative to martyrdom is due to the link he makes between freedom and dignity: freedom is "the basis of the dignity of the person." Elsewhere, John Paul expresses the same idea regarding the inseparable union between freedom and dignity by explaining that freedom is "the condition and basis for the human person's true dignity."[18] The connection between human freedom and human dignity is a key issue in my discussion of martyrdom, and I return to a fuller explication of it in a moment.

Perhaps the most notable factor John Paul captures in *Veritatis Splendor* 86, however, is the beauty of human freedom, which opens the person to his Creator. Within freedom, the Pope explains, the human person is called "to the true Good," who is God Himself. Since freedom is essential to the human person—it characterizes one *as* a human being—and, since freedom indicates the person's openness to his Creator, then one can assert that, from the very nature of the human person, one is fundamentally open to God. If the person is intrinsically open to God, then human freedom not only orients him toward his Creator, but also, as John Paul indicates, it leads to communion with other human beings, and to everything else that exists, as well.

It is a recognized fact, however, that human freedom is weak and it is "inclined to betray this openness to the True and the

---

[18] John Paul II, *Redemptor Hominis* 12.

Good, and that all too often he actually prefers to choose finite, limited and ephemeral goods" rather than genuine goods that lead a person to God.[19]

Admittedly, the person's ability to choose contrary to his own good is a mysterious factor in human freedom. In other words, when human freedom chooses against the authentic good of the human person, it actually works toward the destruction the person, himself. With the following, the Pope explains the "deep rebellion" that can entangle a person in the web of his own self-destruction.

> What is more, within his errors and negative decisions, man glimpses the source of a deep rebellion, which leads him to reject the Truth and the Good in order to set himself up as an absolute principle unto himself: 'You will be like God' (Genesis 3:5). Consequently, freedom itself needs to be set free. It is Christ who sets it free: He 'has set us free for freedom' (cf. Galatians 5:1).[20]

Although human freedom orients the person toward his Creator, freedom can stray from its noble e/End, and John Paul acknowledges this factor in the quotation above. Further, he communicates the fact that human freedom "is real but limited: its absolute and unconditional origin is not in itself, but in the life within which it is situated" and that life represents for freedom "both a limitation and a possibility."[21] Still, the Holy Father concludes by

---

[19] John Paul II, *Veritatis Splendor* 86.
[20] John Paul II, *Veritatis Splendor* 86.
[21] John Paul II, *Veritatis Splendor* 86.

noting that Christ sets human freedom free. By employing the notion of self-gift, my work in the following section explains, based upon *Veritatis Splendor* 86, how Christ Crucified sets human freedom free.

## A Development of One's "Primordial Vocation"

As I have shown in *Veritatis Splendor* 85, John Paul maintains that Christ Crucified "reveals the authentic meaning of freedom…[with] the total gift of Himself."[22] From what I have just explicated, I combine the following two thoughts. First, John Paul teaches in *Veritatis Splendor* 86 that freedom is a gift from God to the human person. It is an intrinsic element of his being. This gift of freedom summons the person to God, who is his true Good.

Second, the Pope's depiction of freedom as "inalienable self-possession and openness to all that exists" specifies, once again, the person's fundamental openness to God and to another human person. In addition, one might surmise that the person is open to all that exists. Freedom, then, is the means by which the human person possesses himself (self-determination), and, by possessing himself, he is open to others.

Combining this double facet of human freedom, which is self-possession and openness to another, together with John Paul's conviction that Christ Crucified "reveals the authentic meaning of freedom," I infer the following points about the martyr. First, considering human freedom as self-possession indicates that the mar-

---

[22] John Paul II, *Veritatis Splendor* 85.

tyr has something to give—himself—since he possesses himself. Because I see Christ Crucified as the reference point for John Paul's concept of freedom, one might conjecture that the martyr imitates the Crucified Christ, who, by His death on the Cross, shows that genuine freedom is expressed in the total gift of self.

If the martyr's freedom as self-possession indicates his own availability as a gift, then a second point follows. This factor builds upon the concept of human freedom's "openness to all that exists." Because the martyr is free, his openness extends to God, to another person, and to all reality, as *Veritatis Splendor* 86 indicates. For the moment, I focus specifically upon the martyr's openness to another person, and I describe that openness as *accompanying* another human person in his suffering.[23] In other words, the martyr's freedom

---

[23] John Paul II, *Veritatis Splendor* 85. The word I use to express this idea of the martyr's openness to another is *accompany*, not *compassion*, and certainly not *pity*. The etymology of the word *compassion* (*compassio, -ōnis*), literally specifies this idea of *suffering <u>with</u>* another person. Unfortunately, the modern connotation of *compassion* often involves *sympathy*, almost in the sense of *pity*, for another person. *Accompany*, however, denotes being *together with* another who suffers. Because *accompany* implies *movement <u>with</u>* another person, and, since I highlight the martyr's openness toward another, *accompany* best expresses the martyr's availability toward another who suffers [John Paul II, *Salvifici Doloris* 28]. A second point deserves to be made. Granted that the martyr suffers, one must note, as well, that the perpetrators of martyrdom *also* suffer. Supposing their freedom is greatly weakened, they simply do not have the availability, or openness to another person, that the martyr possesses. More specifically, while *availability* characterizes the martyr, *unavailability* describes those who inflict martyrdom. One might even call it a *busy-ness* or a *preoccupation* that fails to attend to the other.

(openness) toward another indicates an availability of himself, which accompanies another who suffers. Indeed, human freedom encapsulates the notion that one truly "finds" oneself when a person makes a gift of oneself to another.[24]

The martyr is especially able to accompany another suffering human person precisely because he possesses himself. Thus, "in passing beyond self to knowledge and love of the other, the martyr offers his "availability" toward another who suffers.[25] The Holy Father justifiably claims that freedom is "ultimately directed towards communion," for the martyr draws another human person to himself, and through himself, he opens the person to God.

Martyrdom, then, might be described as a vivid portrait of human freedom, which embodies the truth of the human person. Again, the truth of the human person is that he finds himself when he makes "a sincere gift of himself" to another.[26] Recalling my anthropological component above, as well as my work on *Veritatis Splendor* 84-86, one might argue that the martyr's freedom is, indeed, "rooted in the truth about man." Created in the image of God, freedom encapsulates his self-understanding, self-possession, and self-gift to God and to another human person(s). Human freedom discloses the integrity of the human person, then, because it indicates his essential openness to God and to another person (or persons) as a gift.[27]

---

[24] Second Vatican Council, *Gaudium et Spes* 24.
[25] John Paul II, *Salvifici Doloris* 28.
[26] Second Vatican Council, *Gaudium et Spes* 24.
[27] John Paul II, *Veritatis Splendor* 86.

Ironically, what expresses the martyr's human freedom is his availability to suffer with another, on account of his "self-possession and openness to all that exists," under the most physically dramatic circumstances. If human freedom is "inalienable self-possession and openness to all that exists" as the Holy Father describes, and, if the martyr expresses self-possession and openness *as* self-gift, then what is this gift of self?

The martyr's self-gift is his availability of stopping beside the suffering of another human person, much in the same way as did the Good Samaritan (Luke 10:29-37). Now I add the fact that, the martyr's availability might be characterized as an "attitude toward" human dignity, which John Paul expresses in *Redemptor Hominis* 12, and which I address in a moment. Eventually, I contend that the martyr's attitude toward the dignity of another suffering person suggests a contemplative dimension of martyrdom.[28] Human freedom's intrinsic openness plays a vital role to my argument that the death of the martyr expresses a contemplation of Christ's face because, as I ultimately claim, it is precisely human freedom that lies at the heart of this speechless attitude toward human dignity, an attitude which the martyr's death embodies.

Understanding human freedom, then, insofar as it relates to the intrinsic openness of the human person, helps show that the martyr's acceptance of death "as a consequence" of not performing an "act contrary to faith or virtue," is the most reasonable "statement"

---

[28] John Paul II, *Redemptor Hominis* 12.

a human person can "utter."²⁹ In other words, by his death, the martyr silently expresses human freedom—and, consequently, human dignity—in the most compelling manner possible.³⁰ Such an understanding of the person and of freedom is crucial to my study on the martyr, for the martyr's freedom, which is shaped by truth, is the "place" from which his resplendence shines.³¹

Continuing to develop my interpretation of *Veritatis Splendor* 86, I seek to expound upon the notion of human dignity in light of the martyr's self-gift of accompanying another suffering human person. The martyr's attitude toward human dignity, in conjunction with his own availability to another who suffers, is brought to the fore of human existence at his death.

---

²⁹ John Paul II, *Veritatis Splendor* 76. The quotation marks around the words, "statement" and "utter" indicate the silent articulation of human freedom by the martyr's death.

³⁰ Because the human person generally strives to avoid suffering and to delay death, the martyr's voluntary acceptance of death offers a testimony in "the most compelling manner possible" precisely because he willingly undergoes the suffering and death that martyrdom entails. No intellectual argument can compare with the inaudible witness given by one's own physical death, which provides evidence of the truth for which one dies.

³¹ John Paul II, *Veritatis Splendor* Prior to the *Introduction*. "Truth enlightens man's intelligence and shapes his freedom, leading him to know and love the Lord" [John Paul II, *Veritatis Splendor* Prior to the *Introduction*].

# Chapter Ten

## From Human Freedom to Human Dignity

In a major encyclical, John Paul claims that human freedom is "the condition and basis for the human person's true dignity."[1] In another substantial document, the Holy Father maintains that martyrdom manifests the "supreme glorification of human dignity."[2] Why does the Pope make these assertions? Although the subject of human dignity is vast, the Pontiff's weighty remarks dictate its inclusion in my description of martyrdom. Having first examined human freedom in light of *Veritatis Splendor* 86, my next step is to consider human dignity.

In the thought of the Pope, the truth of the human person rests upon his freedom and dignity. My work above, including the *Veritatis Splendor* texts examined thus far, serve to substantiate this claim. The crucial factor for John Paul is that both human dignity and human freedom are intrinsically connected with truth, whose "splendor…shines forth…in a special way, in man, created in the image and likeness of God."[3] After examining human dignity, particularly as it relates to freedom and to the martyr, I show that freedom is the locus of the person's contemplation of Christ's face in what follows.[4]

---

[1] John Paul II, *Redemptor Hominis* 12.
[2] John Paul II, *Dominum et Vivificantem* 60.
[3] John Paul II, *Veritatis Splendor* Prior to the *Introduction*.
[4] John Paul II, *Redemptor Hominis* 12.

My first task, then, is to offer a definition of human dignity, and I do so by employing the Holy Father's description of it from *Christifideles Laici*. Second, I show the interdependence of human freedom and human dignity upon each other, with *Dominum et Vivificantem* 60. In addition to connecting freedom and dignity, *Dominum et Vivificantem* plays an important role in my discussion of martyrdom because this passage offers a surprising contribution toward understanding the Pope's definition of martyrdom.

**A Definition of Human Dignity**

In *Christifideles Laici* 37, John Paul offers a lucid definition of human dignity.[5] He teaches that, because of the "uniqueness and irrepeatability of every person," one's human dignity "is the indestructible property of every human being;" indeed, it is one's "most precious possession."[6] Because human dignity expresses the inherent worth of the human person, the Holy Father's logical conclusion is to insist upon the fact that "the value of one person trans-

---

[5] John Paul speaks of human dignity throughout his pontificate by defending the human person and by opposing what violates his inherent worth. Having examined several passages where the Holy Father speaks of human dignity, I include his description from *Christifideles Laici* 37 for the following reasons. First, it offers a concise, yet comprehensive, definition of human dignity. Second, *Christifideles Laici* 37 offers a suitable link to expound upon concepts presented above. Third, since my focus is on martyrdom rather than human dignity, *per se*, *Christifideles Laici* 37 offers the most fitting articulation for my purpose.

[6] John Paul II, *Christifideles Laici* 37.

cends all the material world."⁷ Each person is precious in the sight of God. John Paul captures the essence of human dignity, enumerating the many facets it includes, with the following definition.

> The dignity of the person is manifested in all its radiance when the person's origin and destiny are considered: created by God in His image and likeness as well as redeemed by the most Precious Blood of Christ, the person is called to be a 'child in the Son' and a living temple of the Spirit, destined for the eternal life of blessed communion with God.⁸

In the quotation above, the Holy Father not only draws together the unique elements that comprise human dignity, but also, he reiterates and deepens key factors that describe the person's unsurpassable worth. As noted earlier, highlighting one's creation in the image of God indicates the love of God for the human person. His love is principally apparent in Christ's Passion and death.

The Pope's explanation of human dignity in *Christifideles Laici* 37 further serves to articulate God's love for the person, which raises human nature to "a dignity beyond compare" by Christ's Passion, and which restores the person's "likeness to God which had been disfigured ever since the first sin."⁹ In other words, the

---

⁷ John Paul II, *Christifideles Laici* 37.
⁸ John Paul II, *Christifideles Laici* 37.
⁹ John Paul II, *Redemptor Hominis* 8. While *Christifideles Laici* stresses the mystery of the Incarnation as the "most radical and elevating affirmation of the value of every human being," I highlight the Passion and death of Christ to further develop the concept. Especially with *Redemptor*

person's inherent dignity is due to his creation in the image of God and to his restoration as a child of the Father by Christ's Redemption.

In *Christifideles Laici*, John Paul upholds a similar conviction for the incomparable value he places upon the human person when he specifies that considering "the person's origin and destiny" reveal the peak of human dignity. With the *Christifideles Laici* text, John Paul identifies the person's "origin" as his creation by God and his redemption by Christ; the person's "destiny" is eternal life, enveloped in Trinitarian love. The person is created by God for eternal life with Him, if he but follows the Commandments and continually asks for God's mercy.

The Holy Father's thought concerning one's destiny explains that each human person is "called to be a 'child in the Son' and a living temple of the Spirit, destined for the eternal life of blessed communion with God."[10] Given the person's origin and destiny, then, the Pope unmistakably identifies the sublimity, and even the *task*, of human dignity. The person's "task," anchored in human dignity, is to use one's free will in accord with the will of God.

A final point from the *Christifideles Laici* text depicts human dignity in strikingly vivid terms and it describes each human person as *good*. John Paul comments upon the following words of Jesus: "For what does it profit a man to gain the whole world and to forfeit his life" (Mark 8:36)?[11] The Pope interprets this Scripture

---

*Hominis* 8-10, I note God's love for the human person, markedly apparent in Christ's Redemptive act.

[10] John Paul II, *Christifideles Laici* 37.

[11] John Paul II, *Christifideles Laici* 37.

# Chapter Ten: From Human Freedom to Human Dignity

passage by stressing the innate dignity and goodness of the human person in the following manner.

> The words of Jesus...contain an enlightening and stirring statement about the individual: value comes not from what a person 'has—even if the person possessed the whole world!—as much as from what a person 'is': the goods of the world do not count as much as the goods of the person, the good which is the person individually.[12]

The key factor in John Paul's concept of human dignity, then, insofar as *Christifideles Laici* articulates, portrays the person's inherent worth. Created by God, redeemed by the Son, and destined for eternal life, the value of each individual person "transcends all the material world."[13]

**The Interplay Between Freedom and Dignity in Regard to the Martyr**

As *Redemptor Hominis* 12 indicates, freedom is "the condition and basis for the human person's true dignity."[14] And, as *Christifideles Laici* 37 brings out, human dignity specifies the person's unsurpassable worth. Having elucidated freedom and dignity, then, I now analyze the link between them. Because *Dominum et Vivifi-*

---

[12] John Paul II, *Christifideles Laici* 37.
[13] John Paul II, *Christifideles Laici* 37.
[14] John Paul II, *Redemptor Hominis* 12.

*cantem* 60 offers a fitting description of the interplay between freedom and dignity, it serves as the link connecting the two concepts.

Pointing to the Holy Spirit, John Paul explains that the Spirit helps the human person to discover and accomplish "the full measure of [his] true freedom."[15] Here, John Paul does not claim that all of these "witnesses" are martyrs, but he does say that many of them "often mark with their own death by martyrdom the supreme glorification of human dignity." Martyrdom is the highest expression of the dignity of the human person that one can attain during his life on earth.

> This revelation of freedom and hence of man's true dignity acquires a particular eloquence for Christians and for the Church in a state of persecution—both in ancient times and in the present—because the witnesses to divine Truth then become a living proof of the action of the Spirit of truth present in the hearts and minds of the faithful, and they often mark with their own death by martyrdom the supreme glorification of human dignity.[16]

From the *Dominum et Vivificantem* quotation above, one learns that human freedom reveals human dignity. When a person uses his free will to adhere to Christ, His teaching and His Commandments in the face of death, that act of the will, made possible and enlivened by grace, indicates the transcendent dignity of the

---

[15] John Paul II, *Dominum et Vivificantem* 60.
[16] John Paul II, *Dominum et Vivificantem* 60.

person. Combining this idea with *Veritatis Splendor* 85, that Christ Crucified "reveals the authentic meaning of freedom," one might now assert that Christ's death also reveals the innate dignity of each human person.[17]

The *Dominum et Vivificantem* quotation above adds the fact that human dignity identifies the person's prominence because he is "made in the image and likeness of God, a greatness shown by the mystery of the Incarnation." John Paul reiterates elsewhere that the Incarnation is the "most radical and elevating affirmation of the value of every human being," because by the Incarnation, Christ unites "Himself with each man."[18] To recapitulate my work thus far, it is both the Incarnation and the salvific death of Christ on the Cross that testify to the human person's inherent worth and incomparable value.

An additional factor from the *Dominum et Vivificantem* passage above highlights the Church, specifically the Church *under persecution*. John Paul stresses the "particular eloquence" that human freedom and human dignity acquire when the Church is being persecuted, and he enumerates two reasons for this "eloquence." First, the "witnesses to divine Truth" become, under persecution, "a living proof of the action of the Spirit of truth present in the hearts and minds of the faithful." This presence of the Spirit in the "hearts and minds of the faithful" is the reason why

---

[17] John Paul II, *Veritatis Splendor* 85.

[18] John Paul II, *Christifideles Laici* 37; John Paul II, *Redemptor Hominis* 3.

"truth...shines forth...in a special way, in man, created in the image and likeness of God."[19]

A second reason why freedom and dignity acquire "particular eloquence" when the Church is being persecuted is because *some* of the witnesses "mark with their own death by martyrdom the supreme glorification of human dignity." Enveloped by the Holy Spirit, the witness who is a martyr radiates "the full measure" of his human freedom, thus upholding, at the same time, "the supreme glorification" of his own dignity. Because of the action of the Holy Spirit, then, one might claim that the martyr manifests the "supreme glorification of human dignity," precisely because his death implies human freedom to another human person.

One might raise several objections, either to the *Dominum et Vivificantem* text above, or to my interpretation of it. For example, one might observe that, in times of persecution, the human person has been gravely offended in the most de-humanizing circumstances.[20] Because the martyr often suffers severe humiliations and

---

[19] John Paul II, *Dominum et Vivificantem* 60; *Veritatis Splendor* Prior to the *Introduction*.

[20] See, for example, the following sources. William Bush, *To Quell the Terror: The Mystery of the Vocation of the Sixteen Carmelites of Compiègne Guillotined July 17, 1794* (Washington, D.C.: Institute of Carmelite Studies Publications, 1999); Alexander Scholynizitsen, *The Solzhenitsyn Reader: New and Essential Writings 1947-2005*, Edward E. Ericson, Jr. and Daniel J. Mahoney, eds. (Wilmington, DE: Intercollegiate Studies Institute, 2006). When seemingly devoid of human dignity, the martyr actually preserves it by accepting degrading circumstances rather than forsaking the principles and truths upon which he bases his life.

countless attacks against his personal dignity, how can he manifest the "supreme glorification of human dignity?"

Acknowledging the violence against the human person's inherent dignity that martyrdom entails actually advances my argument. Recall the way John Paul defines martyrdom. He maintains that the martyr obeys "God rather than men," accepting "martyrdom as a consequence" for his refusal to "perform this or that particular act contrary to faith or virtue."[21] Further, the martyr puts the "precepts and love [of Christ] into practice" by his death.[22] Therefore, it is exactly *when* he is being put to death, at the moment when his integrity as a human person is most viciously attacked, that human dignity shines forth most radiantly. When the person is persecuted to the point of death, and he *accepts* that death because it serves to uphold the precepts of Christ and the objectivity of the moral law, *then* freedom and dignity become evident. In other words, because the martyr is willing to die, often under severely offensive conditions, one's persistent stance in the truth expresses the most tangible witness to human freedom. The martyr refuses to "act contrary to faith or virtue" under the most horrific, frightening and extreme conditions.[23]

*Dominum et Vivificantem* 60, then, shows the close interconnection between freedom and dignity as follows. By calling the martyr's death "the supreme glorification of human dignity," the Pope upholds dignity in a highly perceptible manner. By staking one's life against false precepts, the martyr not only reveals the per-

---

[21] John Paul II, *Veritatis Splendor* 76.
[22] John Paul II, *Veritatis Splendor* 27.
[23] John Paul II, *Veritatis Splendor* 76.

son's inherent freedom, as *Veritatis Splendor* 86 shows, but he also makes known the summit to which human dignity attains, by his death. The martyr's human freedom, then, is vividly captured in his acceptance of death "as a consequence" of his obedience to "God rather than men."[24]

Human freedom, then, both underlies dignity, and it requires dignity.[25] Martyrdom, understood within the context of the truth of the human person, embodies one's inherent dignity and freedom. It reveals that the martyr's exercise of freedom in his self-gift expresses an attitude toward human dignity that he cannot compromise. His attitude toward human dignity, synthesized by his death, illuminates the "uniqueness and irrepeatability of every person," created by God, redeemed by the Son, and called to be a "temple of the Spirit, destined for the eternal life."[26] I further expound upon the martyr's attitude toward human dignity with *Redemptor Hominis* 12. First, however, I continue to draw upon *Dominum et Vivificantem* 60, now illuminating a new perspective.

## The Concept of Witness

*Dominum et Vivificantem* 60 not only specifies the interplay between human freedom and human dignity, but also, it makes a significant contribution to the Holy Father's concept of the martyr (martyrdom). More specifically, the *Dominum et Vivificantem* text offers a key insight on the Pope's definition of martyrdom, which

---

[24] John Paul II, *Veritatis Splendor* 76.

[25] John Paul II, *Redemptor Hominis* 12.

[26] John Paul II, *Christifideles Laici* 37.

## Chapter Ten: From Human Freedom to Human Dignity

suggests that he retains and furthers the traditional notion of *martyr* as *witness*. Consequently, a careful study of *Dominum et Vivificantem* 60, from the perspective of how John Paul uses the word *witness*, is especially appropriate at this point. In light of human dignity, *Dominum et Vivificantem* 60 contributes toward a more fruitful understanding of *Veritatis Splendor*, which I resume momentarily.

In *Dominum et Vivificantem* 60, John Paul clearly asserts that the daily life of the Christian, with the suffering and persecution it sometimes entails, often witnesses to human dignity. The Holy Father states these "witnesses to man's authentic dignity," are obedient "to the Holy Spirit," and they "contribute to the manifold 'renewal of the face of the earth,'" and yet, not all these witnesses are martyrs.[27]

At the same time, the Holy Father uses the word, *witness*, which means *martyr*, perhaps indicating that those who witness to "man's authentic dignity" undergo some sort of suffering in so doing. Nevertheless, John Paul is about to include martyrs in this paragraph, noting that "the witnesses to divine Truth…often mark with their own death by martyrdom the supreme glorification of human dignity."[28] One might argue, then, that not all witnesses, according to John Paul, are martyrs. The Pope's exact words, which support this understanding, are as follows.

---

[27] John Paul II, *Dominum et Vivificantem* 60.

[28] The Greek word μάρτυς means *witness*. As John Paul indicates in *Dominum et Vivificantem* 60, not all *witnesses* are *martyrs*. Elsewhere, he states, "a *witness*, in biblical language, means *martyr*" [John Paul II, *Homily* 8 June 1979 (5)].

Also in the ordinary conditions of society, Christians, as witnesses to man's authentic dignity, by their obedience to the Holy Spirit contribute to the manifold 'renewal of the face of the earth,' working together with their brothers and sisters in order to achieve and put to good use everything that is good, noble and beautiful in the modern progress of civilization, culture, science, technology and the other areas of thought and human activity. They do this as disciples of Christ who—as the Council writes—'appointed Lord by His Resurrection...is now at work in the hearts of men through the power of His Spirit.[29]

From the unambiguous evidence of John Paul's words, which mark the fact that not all witnesses are martyrs, one gains the following insights. First, by acknowledging the daily witness given to "man's authentic dignity" in *Dominum et Vivificantem*, and, by noting his use of the word *witness*, John Paul retains and deepens the traditional understanding of *martyr* as *witness*.[30]

---

[29] John Paul II, *Dominum et Vivificantem* 60.

[30] If *witness* includes the daily testimony offered to "man's authentic dignity," as *Dominum et Vivificantem* 60 brings out above, then one might contest that John Paul uses *martyr* in a metaphorical sense, by referring to the daily sufferings of the Christian. John Paul notes, however, that a *witness* is *sometimes* a martyr, but not *always* a martyr. His concept of witness *includes* the martyr, which seemingly substantiates the argument that he speaks of *martyrdom* metaphorically. Because not *all* witnesses are *literally* martyrs, however, I maintain that he does not use *martyrdom* in a metaphorical sense.

## Chapter Ten: From Human Freedom to Human Dignity

There is a difference, however, between the Christian's *daily* testimony to human dignity, through obedience to the Spirit, and the martyr's *final* testimony to human dignity, by his death. John Paul makes this distinction in the *Dominum et Vivificantem* passage I am pondering. The differentiating characteristic between the daily witness to human dignity and the martyr's witness to dignity is that the martyr's witness offers a testimony of finality, which is summarized by his death. Thus, the Holy Father justifiably indicates that the person marks with his "own death by martyrdom the supreme glorification of human dignity."[31] The death of the martyr highlights the finality of his offering; once the sacrifice of his life is given, his witness to human dignity reaches its apex. His death, which is his concluding statement on human dignity, cannot be retracted. The martyr's witness to human dignity, then, is encapsulated by his death.

*Dominum et Vivificantem* 60, analyzed from the perspective of *witness*, offers two significant thoughts for my work. First, the Holy Father maintains that not all witnesses are martyrs. Thus, while a martyr *is* a witness, his witness contains something further. Second, the Holy Father insists upon the fact that the difference between the witness of daily suffering and the witness of the martyr is the martyr's *death*. Again, the sense of finality that death evokes is significant. As the Pope clearly expresses, the martyr's death is what marks "the supreme glorification of human dignity."[32] *Dominum et Vivificantem* 60, then, reiterates the difference between the

---

[31] John Paul II, *Dominum et Vivificantem* 60.
[32] John Paul II, *Dominum et Vivificantem* 60.

martyr's death and the saintly non-martyr's death. While both are witnesses, the martyr's death seals his testimony.

## The Martyr's Attitude Toward Human Dignity

My elucidation of *Veritatis Splendor* 86 contains several key insights on freedom and dignity, and their relation to martyrdom. A final consideration, before the next mention of martyrdom in paragraph 87, involves my interpretation of the Pope's concept of human dignity and how it relates to martyrdom. Combining several insights from *Christifideles Laici* 37 and *Dominum et Vivificantem* 60, I offer an analysis of the martyr's *attitude toward* human dignity, which suggests a contemplative element. It is precisely the martyr's speechless attitude toward human dignity that I claim is contemplative; human freedom is the locus from which this attitude develops. The understanding of the martyr's attitude toward human dignity that I am proposing is grounded in *Redemptor Hominis* 12.

In his first encyclical, the Holy Father explains, "the human person's dignity itself becomes part of the content of proclamation, being included not necessarily in words but by an attitude towards it."[33] While this attitude toward human dignity brings out the Church's missionary activity, one recalls that the "Church is missionary by her very nature."[34] Just as John Paul speaks of the missionary proclamation of the Gospel in *Redemptor Hominis* 12, so

---

[33] John Paul II, *Redemptor Hominis* 12.
[34] John Paul II, *Redemptoris Missio* 5.

## Chapter Ten: From Human Freedom to Human Dignity

also does the Church's missionary character underly any discussion on the Church.

With *Christifideles Laici* 37, the Holy Father speaks of human dignity as "the indestructible property of every human being;" each person possesses dignity due to his sublime "origin and destiny" as a "child in the Son." In *Redemptor Hominis* 12, John Paul describes human dignity as "part of the content of...proclamation" of the Gospel.

To say that the martyr reveals human freedom as accompanying (*being present with*) another who is suffering indicates a profound respect for human dignity. I elucidate the martyr's profound esteem for human dignity according to *Redemptor Hominis* 12, where the Pope speaks in terms of an *attitude toward* it. It is this *attitude* that captures the essence of human freedom's openness to another most dramatically.[35]

John Paul reiterates the Conciliar teaching that, "when Christ and...His Apostles proclaimed the truth that comes not from men but from God...they preserved...a deep esteem for man, for his intellect, his will, his conscience and his freedom."[36] This passage seems to suggest that one's regard for human dignity is a key factor in the proclamation of the Gospel, and thus, in the life of the Church.

Building upon Conciliar teaching, the Holy Father explains that one's attitude toward dignity is part of the missionary proclamation. The implication is that one's *attitude toward* human dignity is

---

[35] John Paul II, *Redemptor Hominis* 12; John Paul II, *Veritatis Splendor* 86.

[36] John Paul II, *Redemptor Hominis* 12.

not expressed by words, but by actions. Thus, the silent testimony offered to human dignity lies at the very heart of proclaiming the Gospel. The evangelist desires to bring the saving message of Jesus to "all nations" so that all might "be saved and…come to the knowledge of the truth" (Matthew 28:19; 1 Timothy 2:4).

In *Redemptor Hominis* 12, John Paul refers to "apostolic and missionary unity," which dictates that "all Christians must find what already unites them, even before their full communion is achieved." He describes this "apostolic and missionary unity" as that which "enables us to approach all cultures, all ideological concepts, all people of good will…with the esteem, respect and discernment that, since the time of the Apostles, has marked…the attitude of the missionary." Again, like Christ, the desire of the Catholic is for the salvation of the human race. For this he prays and works.

The Holy Father describes this missionary attitude as that which "begins with a feeling of deep esteem for 'what is in man,' for what man has himself worked out in the depths of his spirit concerning the most profound and important problems."[37] Moreover, the Pope notes that the conversion "begun by the mission is a work of grace, in which man must fully find himself again."[38]

To say "man to fully find himself again" is to imply that something has been lost. The inference is that the missionary's attitude toward human dignity helps another recover who he is as a human person. But further, because Christ reveals to the human person

---

[37] John Paul II, *Redemptor Hominis* 12.
[38] John Paul II, *Redemptor Hominis* 12.

## Chapter Ten: From Human Freedom to Human Dignity

who he is, one might further suppose that each person who possesses this attitude toward human dignity *knows* who he is because he knows Jesus Christ.

John Paul's passage continues by indicating that "the truth revealed to us by God imposes on us an obligation."[39] Possessing an especially "great sense of responsibility for this truth," the Pope looks "towards Christ Himself, the first evangelizer, and also towards His Apostles, martyrs and confessors."[40] The Holy Father expresses these thoughts as follows.

> [W]hen Christ and, after Him, His Apostles proclaimed the truth that comes not from men but from God ('My teaching is not Mine, but His who sent Me' (John 7:16), that is, the Father's), they preserved, while acting with their full force of spirit, a deep esteem for man, for his intellect, his will, his conscience and his freedom. Thus, the human person's dignity itself becomes part of the content of that proclamation, being included not necessarily in words but by an attitude towards it.[41]

Two points follow upon the text above. One concerns the martyr, and the other focuses upon the missionary attitude toward human dignity, which I claim the martyr possesses, but I still have yet to prove. Jesus gave the Apostles and their successors the power to teach in His authority all things necessary for eternal salvation.

---

[39] John Paul II, *Redemptor Hominis* 12.
[40] John Paul II, *Redemptor Hominis* 12.
[41] John Paul II, *Redemptor Hominis* 12.

Thus, one would naturally expect the Pope to mention the Apostles, as well as their successors. But one would not normally anticipate explicit mention of the martyr in this context. By imitating Jesus, the martyr and the Apostles help fulfill the Church's mission of teaching the truth.[42] One might conjecture that the martyr also guards and teaches revealed truth. A martyr, however, is a martyr precisely because he is martyred; he is put to death "as a consequence" for not performing an "act contrary to faith or virtue."[43] Thus, one might surmise that the exact moment of the martyr's death guards and teaches revealed truth.

The Holy Father explains that the attitude toward human dignity is crucial to the world today because "various systems and individuals" propagate *as* freedom, what is, in fact, *not* authentic human freedom.[44] Thus, the Pope reiterates that "the Church, because of her divine mission," is the guardian of human freedom, which is "the condition and basis for the human person's true dignity."[45]

Immediately following the Holy Father's statement in *Redemptor Hominis* 12, he mentions truth, which I explain above in my discussion on human freedom and dignity. According to John Paul, "Jesus Christ meets the man of every age, including our own, with: 'You will know the truth, and the truth will make you free' (John 8:32)."[46] His focus upon these words entails "both a funda-

---

[42] Note that the Pope includes *confessors*, together with *martyrs*.
[43] John Paul II, *Veritatis Splendor* 76.
[44] John Paul II, *Redemptor Hominis* 12.
[45] John Paul II, *Redemptor Hominis* 12.
[46] John Paul II, *Redemptor Hominis* 12.

mental requirement and a warning: the requirement of an honest relationship with regard to truth as a condition for authentic freedom, and the warning to avoid every kind of illusory freedom, every superficial unilateral freedom, every freedom that fails to enter into the whole truth about man and the world."[47]

Jesus "brings man freedom based on truth, frees man from what curtails, diminishes and as it were breaks off this freedom at its root, in man's soul, his heart and his conscience."[48] Jesus Christ renews the human person from within, from inside his soul, heart, and conscience.

Because Christ brings the human person "freedom based on truth," and, since Christ "reveals the human person" to himself, one infers that true freedom, attained by the martyr, shows that the martyr, himself, is genuinely free. John Paul highlights this revelation of authentic freedom by noting the "stupendous confirmation" given by "those who, thanks to Christ and in Christ, have reached true freedom and have manifested it even in situations of external constraint!"[49] By the grace of God, the martyr is truly free.

In *Redemptor Hominis* 12, the Pope refers to Jesus before Pilate, which is a scenario that he also depicts in *Veritatis Splendor* 84. The Holy Father speaks of Christ's mission to bear witness to the truth.[50] He teaches that Jesus Christ Himself "has made an appearance at the side of people judged for the sake of truth" and even more, that He has "gone to death with people condemned for the

---

[47] John Paul II, *Redemptor Hominis* 12.
[48] John Paul II, *Redemptor Hominis* 12.
[49] John Paul II, *Redemptor Hominis* 12.
[50] John Paul II, *Redemptor Hominis* 12.

sake of truth."[51] Christ Jesus who is Truth, cannot desert the human person, created in the image and likeness of God, who lives in the truth and who suffers for it.

Since John Paul focuses upon the requirement and the warning of freedom established in the truth, my aim is to show that knowing the truth demands an "honest relationship" between the person and the truth in order to bring about authentic freedom.[52] Moreover, knowing the truth presupposes heeding the Pontiff's warning to reject trivial and deceptive freedom, which "fails to enter into the whole truth about man and the world."[53] As I show above, one's openness to God, to another human person, and to all of reality particularly characterizes authentic human freedom.

The connection between knowing the truth and human freedom, then, serves as the bedrock of John Paul's concept of martyrdom. Martyrdom is "the supreme glorification of human dignity" since the martyr "witnesses to divine Truth;" he bears witness to t/Truth and makes human freedom known.[54] As I continue my project, two questions remain. According to John Paul, how does martyrdom witness to truth? How does that witness reveal the person's authentic freedom?

---

[51] John Paul II, *Redemptor Hominis* 12.
[52] John Paul II, *Redemptor Hominis* 12.
[53] John Paul II, *Redemptor Hominis* 12.
[54] John Paul II, *Dominum et Vivificantem* 60.

Chapter Ten: From Human Freedom to Human Dignity 189

**Human Dignity and Conscience**

As I mention in my discussion on human dignity, John Paul maintains that dignity is revealed "when the person's origin and destiny are considered" as one who is created by God, redeemed by the Son, called to be a temple of the Holy Spirit, and destined for eternal life.[55] Further, by using John Paul's works, I explain how he regards freedom and dignity as being inseparably connected. The new factor I now consider is his assertion that conscience determines human dignity.[56] The claim, itself, is provocative: if each person is created in God's image and redeemed by Christ, one possesses dignity even before one knows right from wrong. At the same time, each person becomes who he is by his own deliberately chosen human acts. Thus, to affirm that conscience determines dignity needs further explanation.

My reflection on conscience shows that the Pope regards it as playing an integral role in human freedom. Consequently, then,

---

[55] John Paul II, *Christifideles Laici* 37.

[56] John Paul often mentions the fact that conscience determines human dignity. Among numerous references, see the following documents of John Paul II: *Veritatis Splendor* 54-63; *Dominum et Vivificantem* 35, 3. At the same time, the Pope upholds the dignity of the human person from conception until natural death. See, for example, the following documents of John Paul II: *Evangelium Vitae* 19; *Homily* 4 March 1981 (1) and *Homily* 4 June 1997 (2). See also the following: "We receive the gift [of life] freely and, in gratitude, we must never cease to respect and defend it, from its beginning to its natural conclusion. From the moment of conception, human life involves God's creative action and remains forever in a special bond with the Creator, who is life's source and its sole end" [John Paul II, *Ecclesia in Asia* 35].

martyrdom emerges as a chief witness to both human dignity and human freedom. As one would logically anticipate, martyrdom testifies to conscience, as well.

John Paul indicates that the "relationship between man's freedom and God's law, which has its intimate and living center in the moral conscience, is manifested and realized in human acts."[57] Again, one sees the central role of human acts in the thought of the Pope. Further, in *Veritatis Splendor* 54, he cites *Gaudium et Spes* 16, which defines and explains the nature of conscience. The Holy Father cites the familiar Conciliar text.

> In the depth of his conscience man detects a law which he does not impose on himself, but which holds him to obedience. Always summoning him to love good and avoid evil, the voice of conscience can, when necessary, speak to his heart more specifically: 'do this, shun that.' For man has in his heart a law written by God. To obey it is the very dignity of man; according to it he will be judged (cf. Romans 2:14-16).[58]

John Paul explains that conscience derives its dignity from the truth.[59] The Holy Father once more defends the "essential bond between Truth, the Good and Freedom," that I mention above with *Veritatis Splendor* 84. Elsewhere, the Pope teaches that one of the chief results of "an upright conscience is…to call good and evil by

---

[57] John Paul II, *Veritatis Splendor* 71.
[58] John Paul II, *Veritatis Splendor* 54.
[59] John Paul II, *Veritatis Splendor* 63.

### Chapter Ten: From Human Freedom to Human Dignity

their proper name."[60] Connecting the conscience with the martyr, then, shows that the clarity of vision, which results from a properly formed conscience, is embodied by him because he upholds truth and assures the objectivity of the moral order in a world that often obscures truth and calls "evil good, and good evil" (Isaiah 5:20). In *Veritatis Splendor* 60, John Paul expresses these thoughts by affirming that the "judgment of conscience does not establish the law; rather it bears witness to the authority of the natural law and of the practical reason with reference to the supreme Good, whose attractiveness the human person perceives and whose Commandments he accepts."[61]

Authentic freedom, as the Pope teaches, is always freedom in the truth. Freedom is a *living* of the truth and a *doing* of truth, as *Veritatis Splendor* 84 testifies. Since the conscience summons one "to love good and avoid evil," it impels one to live in the truth. Further, by obeying a rightful conscience, one perfects himself as a person, for truthfulness cannot be separated from the conscience. Indeed, freedom, truth and conscience are tightly bound together, for "freedom of conscience is never freedom 'from' the truth but always and only freedom 'in' the truth."[62]

The intellect strives for truth, and truthfulness is inseparable from conscience. Twentieth-century philosopher, Josef Pieper, defines truth as that which "cannot be exhausted by any (human) knowledge; it remains therefore always open to new formula-

---

[60] John Paul II, *Dominum et Vivificantem* 43.
[61] John Paul II, *Veritatis Splendor* 60.
[62] John Paul II, *Veritatis Splendor* 64.

tion."⁶³ While truth is known in history, John Paul teaches that "it also reaches beyond history," for truth transcends historical times and cultures.⁶⁴ Because the conscience beckons one to follow "a law which he does not impose on himself, but which holds him to obedience," it assists the human person to live in the truth.⁶⁵

*Veritatis Splendor* 84-86, together with supplemental texts cited above, provide a needed opportunity to discuss human freedom, dignity and conscience, in light of the martyr. Still close to the beginning of chapter three in *Veritatis Splendor*, John Paul's next mention of martyrdom is found in the subsequent paragraph, which is number 87. As one might anticipate given the Pope's emphasis on human freedom, the subject resumes in the next section.

## The "Acceptance of Truth is the Condition for Authentic Freedom"

In *Redemptor Hominis* 12, John Paul highlights the intimate connection between freedom and truth, and he warns against an illusory freedom, which "fails to enter into the whole truth about man and the world"⁶⁶ Further, in *Veritatis Splendor* 86, he mentions that freedom is embedded in the truth about the human person.⁶⁷ With the next paragraph, the Pope continues his teaching on

---

⁶³ Josef Pieper, *The Silence of Saint Thomas* (South Bend: Saint Augustine's Press, 1999), 103.
⁶⁴ John Paul II, *Fides et Ratio* 95.
⁶⁵ John Paul II, *Veritatis Splendor* 54.
⁶⁶ John Paul II, *Redemptor Hominis* 12.
⁶⁷ John Paul II, *Veritatis Splendor* 86.

## Chapter Ten: From Human Freedom to Human Dignity

human freedom, adding several key ideas. He opens *Veritatis Splendor* 87 by reiterating the intrinsic connection between truth and human freedom, which he highlighted with *Veritatis Splendor* 84.

The Holy Father explains that Christ's words, "You will know the truth, and the truth will set you free" contain the teaching that "the frank and open acceptance of truth is the condition for authentic freedom."[68] Basing one's freedom upon his acceptance of truth draws attention, once again, to the fact that truth and freedom are intimately linked. If authentic human freedom demands the open acceptance of truth, then it also follows that rejecting truth supplies the condition for human enslavement. After expressing these initial thoughts in paragraph 87, John Paul immediately refers to martyrdom. The person who accepts the truth is not only free, but also, he is strengthened to suffer martyrdom, should the circumstances arise.

> Christ reveals, first and foremost, that the frank and open acceptance of truth is the condition for authentic freedom: 'You will know the truth, and the truth will set you free' (John 8:32). This is truth which sets one free in the face of worldly power and which gives the strength to endure martyrdom.[69]

---

[68] John Paul II, *Veritatis Splendor* 87.
[69] John Paul II, *Veritatis Splendor* 87.

The martyr's freedom in the truth implies truth's motivating force. Building upon John Paul's thoughts in *Veritatis Splendor* 86 in conjunction with paragraph 87 seem to suggest that the stirring power of truth impels the person in authentic human freedom toward God, toward another person, and toward all reality.[70] Not only does truth liberate the human person from the domination of "worldly power," then, which inspires the martyr to "obey God rather than men," but also, it provides "the strength to endure martyrdom."[71] Needless to say, the martyr's death is not easy. One's acceptance, however, of truth, which frees and strengthens a person, is the first dimension of John Paul's thought in *Veritatis Splendor* 87.

Accepting the truth, as *Redemptor Hominis* 12 makes clear, is part of the attitude toward human dignity, that I maintain the martyr embodies. The martyr's attitude shows that human freedom involves a striking openness to another human person.[72] Accepting the truth and being set free, despite opposing forces, provide not only "the strength to endure martyrdom," but also they specify the martyr's attitude as an event that occurs in full human freedom.[73] His attitude implies a contemplative being *present with* another suffering human person, which suggests that human freedom, to be authentically free, must be anchored in Jesus Crucified. Christ Je-

---

[70] John Paul II, *Veritatis Splendor* 86.

[71] John Paul II, *Veritatis Splendor* 76, 87.

[72] John Paul II, *Redemptor Hominis* 12; John Paul II, *Veritatis Splendor* 86.

[73] John Paul II, *Veritatis Splendor* 87.

## Chapter Ten: From Human Freedom to Human Dignity

sus "reveals the authentic meaning of freedom."[74] The Pope continues with the following.

> So it was with Jesus before Pilate: 'For this I was born, and for this I have come into the world, to bear witness to the truth' (John 18:37). The true worshippers of God must thus worship Him 'in spirit and truth' (John 4:23): in this worship they become free. Worship of God and a relationship with truth are revealed in Jesus Christ as the deepest foundation of freedom.[75]

John Paul suggests that the one who worships God "in spirit and truth" accepts truth and, by worshiping God, he becomes free. Because Jesus *is* Truth, one's "frank and open acceptance of truth," with either a capital *T* or a lowercase *t*, ultimately implies openness to Jesus Christ. In other words, the human person worships God the Father in and through Jesus Christ, who is God the Son Incarnate. Jesus is the One Mediator with the Father. Consequently, a person cannot have an authentic worship of God without a relationship with Truth, who is Jesus. Truth is objective. For example, only one religion is correct. Jesus is God and He started one Church.

If one brings the martyr into this discussion, as does the Holy Father, one notes the following. The Pope first tells his audience that truth makes one "free" (John 8:32). Despite opposing authori-

---

[74] John Paul II, *Veritatis Splendor* 85.
[75] John Paul II, *Veritatis Splendor* 87.

ties, a compelling factor of truth is that it "gives the strength to endure martyrdom."[76] This statement, followed by John Paul's remarks on worshipping God, imply that the human person's authentic worship of God rouses hostile forces. But worshipping God frees the human person to an even greater extent. With its "strength to endure martyrdom," truth impels the martyr onward to give authentic worship to God. That witness to the truth by death, should the circumstances arise, is the worship of God "in spirit and truth."[77] Further, the very act that makes a martyr a martyr, which is his willing acceptance of death (martyrdom) in order to uphold faith and/or morals, specifies that *by* his death, he offers authentic worship to God.

One might object that the martyr's death cannot illustrate the worship of God. How can one construe *dying* as *worshipping*? Since the martyr is dying, how can he worship, by giving "adoration and honor given to God," while he undergoes death?[78] Further, provided the martyr does give worship to God, one might maintain that his physical suffering and his death do not worship God in "spirit," but rather, in the "flesh."[79]

I suggest that the martyr's death is unquestionably an act of worshiping God "in spirit and truth," because the martyr offers himself in sacrifice, with Jesus, to the Father. Further, as John Paul teaches, "the deepest foundation of freedom" is located in the worship of God and in one's relationship with truth. Thus, "in this

---

[76] John Paul II, *Veritatis Splendor* 87.
[77] John Paul II, *Veritatis Splendor* 87.
[78] *Catechism of the Catholic Church* 2096.
[79] John Paul II, *Veritatis Splendor* 87.

## Chapter Ten: From Human Freedom to Human Dignity

worship [he] becomes free."[80] Because he willingly undergoes death in order to stand in the truth of faith and morals, he worships the Father "in spirit and truth" by giving Him the "adoration and honor" due to God alone.[81] Moreover, claiming that worshiping God "sets man free from turning in on himself, from the slavery of sin and the idolatry of the world," is another way of saying that, in his freedom, the martyr is open "to all that exists."[82]

As John Paul states in *Veritatis Splendor*, freedom and truth are not only intimately connected, but also, as I suggest with paragraph 84, the martyr's *doing* of the truth by accepting death "makes visible" the "essential bond between Truth, the Good and Freedom."[83] Since the worship of God "in spirit and truth" frees the human person, then, the martyr is truly free (John 4:23).[84]

In *Veritatis Splendor* 86, I discuss the Holy Father's definition of freedom as a gift given to the human person, the foundation of one's dignity, and "inalienable self-possession and openness to all that exists."[85] In the next paragraph, he qualifies this definition still further: freedom is not only a gift given by God to the human person, but it is also "the gift of self in service to God and one's breth-

---

[80] John Paul II, *Veritatis Splendor* 87.

[81] *Catechism of the Catholic Church* 2096.

[82] *Catechism of the Catholic Church* 2097; John Paul II, *Veritatis Splendor* 86.

[83] John Paul II, *Veritatis Splendor* 84; John Paul II, *Salvifici Doloris* 28.

[84] One might even hope that the freedom of the martyr and the Truth to whom he bears witness, releases, in at least a small way, the confinement of martyrdom's perpetrators. At times, those who inflict martyrdom turn, and become martyrs themselves.

[85] John Paul II, *Veritatis Splendor* 86.

ren." Having received freedom as a gift, one gives oneself back to the Father. Further, since authentic freedom opens one to another human person, one gives oneself to another, as well, in the Love who is the Holy Spirit.

Although John Paul specifies the innate quality of human freedom in paragraph 86, recall that he also notes that human freedom must be "cultivated responsibly."[86] With the understanding, then, that one possesses freedom both as a gift and as that which one needs to cultivate, the Holy Father explains the sense in which human freedom is nourished. In addition, when he describes how one obtains freedom, John Paul defines *love*, as well. Freedom is "acquired in love, that is, in the gift of self" since one "finds himself" in making himself a gift for another.[87] Love is expressed in the gift of self. John Paul captures these thoughts as follows.

> Jesus reveals by His whole life, and not only by His words, that freedom is acquired in *love,* that is, in the *gift of self.* The One who says: 'Greater love has no man than this, that a man lay down his life for his friends' (John 15:13), freely goes out to meet His Passion (cf. Matthew 26:46), and in obedience to the Father gives His life on the Cross for all men (cf. Philippians 2:6-11).[88]

---

[86] John Paul II, *Veritatis Splendor* 86.
[87] Second Vatican Council, *Gaudium et Spes* 24.
[88] John Paul II, *Veritatis Splendor* 87.

## Chapter Ten: From Human Freedom to Human Dignity

Here, the Holy Father again implies that the Crucified Christ is the reference point for his understanding of freedom.[89] In *Veritatis Splendor* 85, John Paul explains that the death of Christ reveals "the authentic meaning of freedom" in the "total gift of Himself" on the Cross.[90] In *Veritatis Splendor* 87, the Holy Father reiterates this point in slightly different terminology: "Jesus reveals by His whole life...that freedom is acquired in love, that is, in the gift of self." In this significant passage, then, the Pope suggests that freedom is the gift of self, given in love, in order to serve both God and neighbor.

In the same passage, the Holy Father continues to speak of the contemplation of the Crucified Christ. Such contemplation, the Holy Father teaches, is the key to understanding the full meaning of freedom. "Contemplation of Jesus Crucified is thus the highroad which the Church must tread every day if she wishes to understand the full meaning of freedom: the gift of self in service to God and one's brethren."[91] John Paul concludes, "Communion with the Crucified and Risen Lord is the never-ending source from which the Church draws unceasingly in order to live in freedom, to give of herself and to serve."[92]

An additional factor to consider, then, is that the martyr not only imitates Christ in persecution and death, but he also radiates Christ to others in the gift of himself, offered in the freedom of his will. Christ Crucified not only reveals authentic freedom in the gift of Himself, but also, contemplating the Crucified is vital in order to

---

[89] John Paul II, *Veritatis Splendor* 87; 85.
[90] John Paul II, *Veritatis Splendor* 85.
[91] John Paul II, *Veritatis Splendor* 87.
[92] John Paul II, *Veritatis Splendor* 87.

fully understand human freedom. By contemplating Christ Crucified, one learns that the gift of oneself, offered in love and in freedom, makes one genuinely free.

Meditating upon the Crucified, the Holy Father reveals how each person, and not just the martyr, participates in the suffering of Christ. John Paul explains as follows.

> The Church, and each of her members, is thus called to share in the *munus regale* of the Crucified Christ (cf. John 12:32), to share in the grace and in the responsibility of the Son of Man who came 'not to be served but to serve, and to give His life as a ransom for many' (Matthew 20:28).[93]

The centrality of Christ Crucified in John Paul's concept of human freedom is evident in his insistence upon the fact that Jesus is the "living, personal summation of perfect freedom in total obedience to the will of God" the Father.[94] He gives the gift of Himself in freedom, in love, and in obedience to the Father's will. Jesus' life and death encapsulate the Pope's teaching that "freedom is ac-

---

[93] John Paul II, *Veritatis Splendor* 87. It is worth noting that the Latin word, *munus, muneris* may be translated a number of ways. Thus, when John Paul writes that the "Church, and each of her members, is called to share in the *munus regale* of the Crucified Christ," he specifies that the person's participation in the royal offering (or gift), of the Crucified Christ, which the martyr does by his death, is a participation the gift of Christ to His Church. Like every saint, the canonized martyr is a gift for Holy Mother Church.

[94] John Paul II, *Veritatis Splendor* 87.

## Chapter Ten: From Human Freedom to Human Dignity

quired in love, that is, in the gift of self."[95] The gift of oneself, then, is inherently linked to obedience to the Father's will. John Paul explains these thoughts with the following words.

> Jesus, then, is the living, personal summation of perfect freedom in total obedience to the will of God [the Father]. His crucified Flesh fully reveals the unbreakable bond between freedom and truth, just as His Resurrection from the dead is the supreme exaltation of the fruitfulness and saving power of a freedom lived out in truth.[96]

**Final Prelude to John Paul's Central Passages on Martyrdom**

In order to elucidate John Paul's understanding of the martyr, I assert in my *Introduction* that the martyr is a prime example of a believer. To justify this claim, I first offer a short definition of faith from *Veritatis Splendor* 88. This description of faith precedes the Pope's primary teaching on martyrdom.[97]

*Veritatis Splendor* 88 brings out the necessity of *living* faith, to which the martyr's death bears particular relevance, on account of its finality. John Paul's emphasis on the vitality of faith in the life of the believer captures the heart of his definition of faith elsewhere,

---

[95] John Paul II, *Veritatis Splendor* 87.

[96] John Paul II, *Veritatis Splendor* 87.

[97] Paragraph 89 also contains central factors relating to John Paul's understanding of faith. I add further qualifications to the definition of faith presented in *Veritatis Splendor* 88 in my subsequent treatment on martyrdom.

as one's "obedient response to God."[98] In addition, *Veritatis Splendor* 88 helps show how faith lifts, in part, the "human spirit...to the contemplation of truth."[99] Further, the Holy Father's definition of faith in *Veritatis Splendor* 88 contributes toward understanding the martyr's death as a contemplation of Christ's face, which is the task that remains.[100] A careful analysis of faith, then, is crucial to his understanding of the martyr because, as I show, the martyr lives faith in a profound manner.

The Pope's interplay of faith and truth in paragraph 88 continues to uphold the relationship between freedom and truth, which he has been defending thus far in chapter three of the encyclical.[101] With *Veritatis Splendor* 88, John Paul argues that setting "freedom in opposition to truth...is the consequence, manifestation and consummation of another more serious and destructive dichotomy, that which separates faith from morality."

Separating faith and morality is characteristic of secularism, whereby the person lives "as if God did not exist."[102] Instead of the person holding faith as "a new and original criterion for thinking and acting in personal, family and social life," one's faith, influenced by secularism, is "weakened and loses its character."[103] The Pontiff emphasizes the profound effects of a de-Christianized culture: the "criteria employed by believers themselves in making

---

[98] John Paul II, *Fides et Ratio* 13.
[99] John Paul II, *Fides et Ratio* Prior to the *Introduction*.
[100] John Paul II, *Veritatis Splendor* 88.
[101] Note, especially, paragraphs 84, 86 and 87, which I discuss above.
[102] John Paul II, *Veritatis Splendor* 88.
[103] John Paul II, *Veritatis Splendor* 88.

## Chapter Ten: From Human Freedom to Human Dignity

judgments and decisions often appear extraneous or even contrary to those of the Gospel."[104]

In light of the widespread secularization of society, John Paul begins to describe faith, defining it in all of its decisive strength. By exhorting Christians to rediscover faith, he implies its "newness" and its "power to judge a prevalent and all-intrusive culture."[105] The Holy Father reminds one of faith's inner dynamic with his definition in following passage.

> It is urgent to rediscover and to set forth once more the authentic reality of the Christian Faith, which is not simply a set of propositions to be accepted with intellectual assent. Rather, faith is a lived knowledge of Christ, a living remembrance of His Commandments, and a truth to be lived out. A word, in any event, is not truly received until it passes into action, until it is put into practice.[106]

For John Paul, the fundamental ingredient to faith is its lived reality: "faith is a lived knowledge of Christ, a living remembrance of His Commandments and a truth to be lived out."[107] This rich

---

[104] John Paul II, *Veritatis Splendor* 88.

[105] John Paul II, *Veritatis Splendor* 88.

[106] John Paul II, *Veritatis Splendor* 88. To be sure, John Paul upholds the fact that faith certainly does include "a set of propositions to be accepted with intellectual assent" [John Paul II, *Veritatis Splendor* 91]. He explains elsewhere that faith is "knowledge of the truth that comes from the testimony of God Himself" [John Paul II, *Homily*, 25 April 1982]. Such "knowledge" implies acceptance of God's Revelation.

[107] John Paul II, *Veritatis Splendor* 88.

notion of faith teaches several valuable lessons. First, the fact that "faith is a lived knowledge of Christ" specifies that the human person, in whom faith resides, knows Jesus Christ in a living and active manner. In other words, the believer's knowledge of Jesus is evident in the way he lives his life.

The second stipulation that faith requires is "a living remembrance of His Commandments."[108] The connotation of these words also conveys faith's inner vitality: faith entails that an active, living remembrance of the Commandments is evident in the life of the believer. While faith certainly includes "a set of propositions to be accepted with intellectual assent," faith is also more; it is not "simply" this "set of propositions."[109] While faith's "living remembrance" necessarily contains a "set of propositions" to be believed, the person defends and protects those propositions precisely *by* putting them into action. Indeed, by encapsulating them within one's life, the believer has an active and "living remembrance" of both the Decalogue (Exodus 20:1-17) and the Commandments of the New Law, which are the love of God and neighbor (Matthew 22:36-40) and the Beatitudes (Matthew 5:3-12).

Seeming to elaborate upon the notion that faith *includes* propositions, but also that it encompasses *more than* those propositions, John Paul speaks of the nature of a word. He notes that a word "is not truly received until it passes into action, until it is put into practice."[110] Applying this notion to faith suggests that the "set of propositions" must be received *by* the person; he must have a

---

[108] John Paul II, *Veritatis Splendor* 88.
[109] John Paul II, *Veritatis Splendor* 88.
[110] John Paul II, *Veritatis Splendor* 88.

"frank and open acceptance" of the truth that faith's propositions include. In addition, the person's reception of this "set of propositions" suggests an active embracing of God's Commandments.[111]

In John Paul's definition of faith as "a lived knowledge of Christ, a living remembrance of His Commandments, and a truth to be lived out," the final dimension that remains for comment is the Holy Father's description of faith as "a truth to be lived out."[112] In fact, identifying faith as "a truth to be lived out" recapitulates the other two facets. To say that faith is a truth lived throughout one's life is to suggest that truth includes both a dynamic knowledge of Christ and an animated, vibrant presence of the Commandments in one's life. Explaining faith as a truth that demands recognition by one's actions means that faith is identifiable by the way one lives.

John Paul's definition of faith in *Veritatis Splendor* 88 contains an additional stipulation. The following text explains, in my opinion, exactly *how* faith is "a lived knowledge of Christ, a living remembrance of His Commandments, and a truth to be lived out." As the Holy Father shows, faith is not only a living practice of what one believes, but it also involves one's will; the person decides to love Christ in each aspect of one's life. The Pope expresses these thoughts in the following passage, which further enunciates his description of faith.

---

[111] John Paul II, *Veritatis Splendor* 87, 88.
[112] John Paul II, *Veritatis Splendor* 88.

> Faith is a decision involving one's whole existence. It is an encounter, a dialogue, a communion of love and of life between the believer and Jesus Christ, the Way, and the Truth, and the Life (cf. John 14:6). It entails an act of trusting abandonment to Christ, which enables us to live as He lived (cf. Galatians 2:20), in profound love of God and of our brothers and sisters.[113]

In this explanation of faith, John Paul draws upon the connection he makes between faith and truth in *Veritatis Splendor* 86. In paragraph 86, the Pope explains that freedom is "rooted in the truth about man, and it is ultimately directed towards communion."[114] He explains "communion" as part of the very nature of human freedom, which is "openness to all that exists, in passing beyond self to knowledge and love of the other."[115]

Because John Paul speaks of faith as that which unites the believer with Christ, so that he might "live as He lived," in union with God and neighbor, the new element in paragraph 88 is that faith infers human freedom. Freely deciding to encounter Christ in a communion of love, the believer opens himself both to God and to his neighbor.

Relating John Paul's understanding of faith to the martyr, one might surmise the following. By his death, the martyr lives out the truth of faith, in freedom, by putting into action the word ("set of propositions") he has received. That action of initiating the re-

---

[113] John Paul II, *Veritatis Splendor* 88.
[114] John Paul II, *Veritatis Splendor* 86.
[115] John Paul II, *Veritatis Splendor* 86.

## Chapter Ten: From Human Freedom to Human Dignity

ceived word expresses "the newness of the faith and its power to judge a prevalent and all-intrusive culture." He judges a de-Christianized culture by his death. The martyr's death expresses faith because it clearly expresses "a decision involving one's whole existence."[116] One chooses to die rather than deny faith and morals.

The martyr's death, which is sums up his faith as "a truth to be lived out," shows that his life culminates in an intimate "dialogue, a communion of love and of life" between the martyr and Jesus Christ, who is "the Way, and the Truth, and the Life."[117] What reflects this intimacy is the martyr's imitation of the Crucified Christ, who "reveals the authentic meaning of freedom" with the "total gift of Himself" on the Cross.[118] At the moment of death, the martyr's faith reaches its pinnacle in an "act of trusting abandonment to Christ," enabling him "to live as [Jesus] lived."[119] How did Jesus live" His whole visible life on earth expresses the "profound love of God [the Father] and of our brothers and sisters" that is evident in

---

[116] John Paul II, *Veritatis Splendor* 88. Before he became Pope, Cardinal Ratzinger reflects upon *faith* by commenting upon its totality as decision encompassing the person's entire life, but from a different angle. He explains that faith firmly establishes one's life in God and in His revealed word: faith "appears as a holding on to God through which man gains a firm hold for his life. *Faith* is thereby defined as taking up a position, as taking a stand trustfully on the ground of the word of God" [Joseph Cardinal Ratzinger, *Introduction to Christianity*, J. R. Foster, trans. (San Francisco, CA: Ignatius Press, 1990), 39].

[117] John Paul II, *Veritatis Splendor* 88; John 14:6 quoted in John Paul II, *Veritatis Splendor* 88.

[118] John Paul II, *Veritatis Splendor* 85.

[119] Galatians 2:20 quoted in John Paul II, *Veritatis Splendor* 88.

the total gift of Himself on the Cross. Truly He loved us "unto the end" (John 13:1).

As I explain in the next section, the martyr's death reflects the suffering face of the Crucified Christ, who abandons Himself, in obedience, into the loving hands of His Heavenly Father. John Paul's elaboration of faith in relation to martyrdom, from *Veritatis Splendor*, as well as from other texts, is particularly significant in supporting my claim that the martyr's death reveals the face of Christ. For the moment, however, I continue my study on *Veritatis Splendor*, which now halts at John Paul's central teaching on martyrdom.

# Chapter Eleven

## Descriptions of the Term *Martyr*

John Paul brings out the *living* aspect of faith in *Veritatis Splendor* 88: faith is a "truth to be lived out." In paragraph 89, which begins his central teaching on martyrdom, he elucidates the "moral content" of faith, itself.[1] To say that faith possesses "a moral content" brings to the fore the believer's lived reality of faith in the world. That lived reality is particularly evident since faith facilitates, according to John Paul, one's love of God and neighbor.[2] As the Pope mentions in the present paragraph, living one's faith in the world, a "living remembrance" of God's Commandments, often evokes hostility, and can even result in martyrdom for the believer.[3]

The Holy Father elaborates upon his remark from *Veritatis Splendor* 88, that faith is a "decision involving one's whole existence," by quoting the First Letter of John. This Scripture passage also elucidates the preceding paragraph that describes faith as "a truth to be lived out."[4] John Paul explains this additional thought, that faith concerns morality, with the following words.

---

[1] John Paul II, *Veritatis Splendor* 89.
[2] John Paul II, *Veritatis Splendor* 89, 88.
[3] John Paul II, *Veritatis Splendor* 88, 89.
[4] John Paul II, *Veritatis Splendor* 88.

Faith also possesses a moral content. It gives rise to and calls for a consistent life commitment; it entails and brings to perfection the acceptance and observance of God's Commandments. Saint John writes, "God is light and in Him there is no darkness at all. If we say we have fellowship with Him while we walk in darkness, we lie and do not live according to the truth...And by this we may be sure that we know Him, if we keep His Commandments. He who says 'I know Him' but disobeys His Commandments is a liar, and the truth is not in him; but whoever keeps His word, in him truly love for God is perfected. By this we may be sure that we are in Him: he who says he abides in Him ought to walk in the same way in which He walked" (1 John 1:5-6; 2:3-6).[5]

John Paul expounds upon the vibrant reality of faith, with its summon to live the Commandments. Because faith is perceptible by one's fidelity to the Commandments, the believer witnesses, before the face of God, to others. He explains, "Through the moral life, faith becomes 'confession,' not only before God but also before men: it becomes witness."[6] One's faith becomes "confession," or "witness" before God and before another human person when the believer lives his faith by fidelity to the Commandments. That "living remembrance of the Commandments," as John Paul expresses in *Veritatis Splendor* 89, is the gift of self to God and to others,

---

[5] John Paul II, *Veritatis Splendor* 89.
[6] John Paul II, *Veritatis Splendor* 89.

## Chapter Eleven: Descriptions of the Term *Martyr*

which encapsulates the two great Commandments of love: the love of God and the love of neighbor (Matthew 22:36-40).[7]

The Pope elucidates the "gift of self" by noting that the believer's "good works," which glorify the "Father who is in Heaven" (Matthew 5:14-16), are telling signs to a world marked by unbelief.[8] The Holy Father extrapolates these "good works" as expressions of the gift of oneself, in charity and in human freedom, with the passage below.

> These works are above all those of charity (cf. Matthew 25:31-46) and of the authentic freedom which is manifested and lived in the gift of self, even to the total gift of self, like that of Jesus, who on the Cross 'loved the Church and gave Himself up for her' (Ephesians 5:25).

The quotation above draws together several key ideas in the Pontiff's thought on the human person; thus, it can be applied to the person who is called to martyrdom. John Paul again connects human freedom with the gift of oneself by directing one's attention to the Crucified Jesus, who is the epitome of freedom.[9] The Holy Father's account of human freedom in paragraph 89, as the lived gift of oneself, draws upon his preceding reflection. Previously, he spoke of human freedom as the possession of oneself, which opens

---

[7] John Paul II, *Veritatis Splendor* 88.
[8] John Paul II, *Veritatis Splendor* 89.
[9] John Paul II, *Veritatis Splendor* 89, 85.

the person to "all that exists" and to the "knowledge and love of the other."[10]

The Pope's present analysis of freedom explains that one's faith in Christ Crucified is a living out of one's "knowledge of Christ," and the firm remembrance of His Commandments, whereby the person expresses his decision to love God and neighbor.[11] Continuing his reflection in *Veritatis Splendor* 89, the Pope highlights charity. Here, he explains what Christ's sacrificial death on the Cross means for the believer.

> Christ's witness is the source, model and means for the witness of His disciples, who are called to walk on the same road: 'If any man would come after Me, let him deny himself and take up his cross daily and follow Me' (Luke 9:23). Charity, in conformity with the radical demands of the Gospel, can lead the believer to the supreme witness of martyrdom. Once again this means imitating Jesus who died on the Cross: 'Be imitators of God, as beloved children,' Paul writes to the Christians of Ephesus, 'and walk in love, as Christ loved us and gave Himself up for us, a fragrant offering and sacrifice to God' (Ephesians 5:1-2).[12]

John Paul's accentuation of charity underscores one's self-gift, which is given in imitation of Christ, who laid down His life to re-

---

[10] John Paul II, *Veritatis Splendor* 86.
[11] John Paul II, *Veritatis Splendor* 88.
[12] John Paul II, *Veritatis Splendor* 89.

deem the human person.¹³ One might infer, then, that the person's charity depicts one's human freedom, which is articulated in the gift of self, in imitation of Jesus Christ Crucified. The Pope's words support the thought that giving oneself reveals true freedom. Authentic freedom "is manifested and lived in the gift of self, even to the total gift of self, like that of Jesus, who on the Cross 'loved the Church and gave Himself up for her' (Ephesians 5:25)."¹⁴

The key sentence in the quotation above, however, draws the connection between charity and martyrdom. "Charity, in conformity with the radical demands of the Gospel, can lead the believer to the supreme witness of martyrdom."¹⁵ Here, John Paul names martyrdom as the "supreme witness" of the believer, who imitates Christ's "total gift of self" on the Cross.

Freedom is central in this discussion. In my opinion, the Pope refers to the text from Ephesians precisely to emphasize the significance of human freedom. "Christ loved us and *gave Himself up*"

---

¹³ To be sure, the martyr imitates Christ not only in laying down his life for his neighbor (John 15:13), but also, he reflects Christ's victory [John Paul II, *Novo Millennio Ineunte* 19]. Further, in the Holy Father's homily for the canonization of Saint Maximilian Kolbe, he speaks of him who "became a sign of victory." Saint Maximilian's death "was [a] victory won over all the system of contempt and hate for man and for what is divine in man, a victory like that won by our Lord Jesus Christ on Calvary" [John Paul II, *Homily* 10 October 1982 (7)]. For additional references to Saint Maximilian and his witness to charity, see John Paul II, *Homily* 13 June 1987 and John Paul II, *Homily* 26 August 1982.

¹⁴ John Paul II, *Veritatis Splendor* 89.

¹⁵ John Paul II, *Veritatis Splendor* 89.

(Ephesians 5:25), in freedom, out of love for the human person.[16] With the full force of His human will and His divine will, Jesus freely went to the Cross for our salvation. Look to Jesus, who, "having joy set before Him, endured the Cross" (Hebrews 12:2).

## Martyrdom is "the exaltation of the inviolable holiness of God's law"

In *Veritatis Splendor* 90, John Paul highlights the relationship between faith and morality by using the example of martyrdom. Reaffirming the existence of intrinsically evil acts, he teaches that human dignity necessitates their prohibition. *Veritatis Splendor* 90 contains a concise description of the moral norm, as a universal, immutable principle that both makes known and protects the human person's dignity and inviolability.[17] He expresses these thoughts in the following manner.

> The relationship between faith and morality shines forth with all its brilliance in the unconditional respect due to the insistent demands of the personal dignity of every man, demands protected by those moral norms which prohibit without exception actions which are intrinsically evil. The universality and the immutability of the moral norm make

---

[16] John Paul II, *Veritatis Splendor* 89.

[17] John Paul II, *Veritatis Splendor* 90. In my study of *Veritatis Splendor* 85, I offer a definition of *moral norm*, noting paragraph 90. Again, the moral norm is "universal and permanent" [John Paul II, *Veritatis Splendor* 53].

## Chapter Eleven: Descriptions of the Term *Martyr*

manifest and at the same time serve to protect the personal dignity and inviolability of man, on whose face is reflected the splendor of God (cf. Genesis 9:5-6).[18]

The universality and immutability of moral norms, as the Pope stresses, both reveal and safeguard the dignity of the human person. Describing the connection between moral norms and dignity accentuates the value of each human person. Moreover, adherence to moral norms defends the good of the person, as *Veritatis Splendor* 76 highlights. In *Veritatis Splendor* 90, the Pope incorporates the fact that, because moral norms are universal and unchangeable, if the human person's actions are in accord with them, then his acts are consonant with his dignity. If he acts contrary to moral norms, then the person wounds himself.

With the second half of *Veritatis Splendor* 90, the Holy Father warns against various theories that reject the existence of negative moral norms. In this context, he speaks of martyrdom as "a particularly eloquent" way in which negative moral norms are endorsed. *Veritatis Splendor* 90 specifically highlights the martyr who confirms by his death the existence of negative moral norms that are valid without exception.[19] The Pope describes this thought in the following manner.

---

[18] John Paul II, *Veritatis Splendor* 90.

[19] Saint Maximilian is an example of a martyr who volunteered to accept death, thus defending the negative moral norm, "you shall not kill." By bearing the violence of its violation upon himself, he defends innocent human life. In his homily proclaiming Maximilian Kolbe a saint, John Paul speaks of the martyr's death as a gift of oneself and a "sign of victo-

The unacceptability of 'teleological,' 'consequentialist' and 'proportionalist' ethical theories, which deny the existence of negative moral norms regarding specific kinds of behavior, norms which are valid without exception, is confirmed in a particularly eloquent way by Christian martyrdom, which has always accompanied and continues to accompany the life of the Church even today.[20]

Building upon a point from *Veritatis Splendor* 76, that the martyr accepts death "as a consequence" for performing an "act contrary to faith or virtue," paragraph 90 introduces the following.[21] First, the martyr's death upholds his own dignity because he insists *with his life* that certain actions, regardless of the circumstances, are intrinsically evil. Because they are intrinsically evil, one must avoid them.

Second, one might infer that *Veritatis Splendor* 90 continues to sustain John Paul's desire to "remain faithful" to the human per-

---

ry," as noted above. In addition, he highlights the significance of Saint Maximilian's human act, made in freedom, and the many points to which that death bears witness. "Maximilian did not die, but 'gave his life...for his brother.' In that death, terrible from the human point of view, there was the whole definitive greatness of the human act and of the human choice: he spontaneously offered himself up to death out of love. And in this human death of his there was the clear witness borne to Christ: the witness borne in Christ to the dignity of man, to the sanctity of his life and to the saving power of death, in which the power of love is made manifest" [John Paul II, *Homily* 10 October 1982 (7)].

[20] John Paul II, *Veritatis Splendor* 90.
[21] John Paul II, *Veritatis Splendor* 76.

son, on account of the martyr's death, which he sees as an endorsement of human dignity.[22] Because the martyr confirms the existence of negative moral norms by his death, he also, like the Church, "remains faithful to the integral truth about man," thus contributing to the respect due to each human person's dignity.[23]

Reflection upon paragraph 90 results in a third consideration. Drawing together *Redemptor Hominis* 12 with *Veritatis Splendor* 90, one finds confirmation that the martyr's self-gift is a witness to human dignity. The martyr's attitude toward human dignity, as I note above, is verified by his death. Because that death upholds the "existence of negative moral norms," it communicates his gift of self as a witness to the truth of the human person, "upon whose face is reflected the splendor of God."[24]

**Martyrdom and "fidelity to God's holy law"[25]**

In *Veritatis Splendor* 91, John Paul offers examples of martyrs, which serve to further define and explain his concept of martyr-

---

[22] John Paul II, *Veritatis Splendor* 83. As I mention throughout my work, John Paul often expresses his solicitude for the human person and his responsibility, which is the Church's task, to uphold human dignity.

[23] John Paul II, *Veritatis Splendor* 83.

[24] John Paul II, *Redemptor Hominis* 12; John Paul II, *Veritatis Splendor* 90.

[25] John Paul II, *Veritatis Splendor* 93. The same notion of martyrdom as "fidelity to God's…law" is located in paragraph 91, with slightly different wording. To avoid unnecessary confusion regarding the definition of martyrdom, I retain the exact words from *Veritatis Splendor* 93 for the title of this section.

dom. His apparent intent is to show the martyr's witness to both the "existence of an 'objective moral order,'" and the existence of intrinsically evil acts.[26] Taking for granted that John Paul's remarks about one specific martyr generally apply to each martyr, I make ample use of his insights.

The Holy Father's first illustration of a martyr in paragraph 91 is Susanna, one of the "admirable witnesses of fidelity" to God's law, "even to the point of a voluntary acceptance of death."[27] With paragraph 91, he introduces the fact that Susanna's "readiness to die a martyr" suffices to qualify her as such.[28] Although she did not shed her blood in the end, John Paul considers her as a "prime example" of the inviolability of God's Law on account of her willingness to die rather than to sin. The Holy Father explains these thoughts as follows.

---

[26] John Paul II, *Veritatis Splendor* 82. As I mention elsewhere, the Holy Father discusses the existence and nature of intrinsically evil acts in several places.

[27] John Paul II, *Veritatis Splendor* 91. One might argue that because Susanna is not a Christian, implying that the Catholic offers the clearest example of a martyr is unfounded. For example, the Pope speaks of Susanna as a "prime example" of a martyr, yet she is not Catholic [John Paul II, *Veritatis Splendor* 91]. While the Church does not refer to the holy people of the Old Testament as saints *per se*, they are regarded as such. For example, Catholic parents still name their children after holy people of the Old Testament and the Carmelite Order, for example, celebrates the feast of Saint Elijah on July 20.

[28] In a subsequent discussion on *Veritatis Splendor* 91 offered below, I answer the question of whether the "readiness to die a martyr," which qualifies one as a martyr in *Veritatis Splendor* 91, includes the concept of being a *confessor* of the faith.

# Chapter Eleven: Descriptions of the Term *Martyr*

In the Old Testament we already find admirable witnesses of fidelity to the holy law of God even to the point of a voluntary acceptance of death. A prime example is the story of Susanna: in reply to the two unjust judges who threatened to have her condemned to death if she refused to yield to their sinful passion, she says: 'I am hemmed in on every side. For if I do this thing, it is death for me; and if I do not, I shall not escape your hands. I choose not to do it and to fall into your hands, rather than to sin in the sight of the Lord!' (Daniel 13:22-23). Susanna, preferring to 'fall innocent' into the hands of the judges, bears witness not only to her faith and trust in God but also to her obedience to the truth and to the absoluteness of the moral order. By her readiness to die a martyr, she proclaims that it is not right to do what God's law qualifies as evil in order to draw some good from it. Susanna chose for herself the 'better part:' hers was a perfectly clear witness, without any compromise, to the truth about the good and to the God of Israel. By her acts, she revealed the holiness of God.[29]

From the Holy Father's quotation above, one gains a plethora of distinctions concerning the Pope's concept of martyrdom. To begin, John Paul differentiates the Old Testament witness from the New in the following manner. As an initial characteristic of an "admirable witness" from the Old Testament, he speaks of Susan-

---

[29] John Paul II, *Veritatis Splendor* 91.

na's "fidelity to the holy law of God."³⁰ With the New Testament, *Veritatis Splendor* 27 indicates that the "precepts and love" of Christ are put "into practice...in the sacrifice of [the Church's] martyrs."³¹ For John Paul, then, faithfulness to the Commandments of God and to His teaching is the first significant factor of either an Old or New Testament martyr, as noted in *Veritatis Splendor* 91.³²

A second characteristic of a martyr, exemplified in the witness of Susanna, is a commitment to God's law that extends "even to the point of a voluntary acceptance of death."³³ With the example of

---

³⁰ John Paul II, *Veritatis Splendor* 91.

³¹ John Paul II, *Veritatis Splendor* 27. As I note in *Veritatis Splendor* 27, the martyr's *sacrifice* is *death*.

³² By "precepts of Christ" one might surmise that John Paul refers particularly to the Beatitudes, for the following reasons. In *Veritatis Splendor* 12, 15, and 16, John Paul speaks of the Decalogue as a "promise and sign of the New Covenant" [John Paul II, *Veritatis Splendor* 12]. In paragraph 15 of *Veritatis Splendor*, John Paul explains the Beatitudes as the means by which "Jesus brings God's Commandments to fulfillment, particularly the Commandment of love of neighbor," which Jesus does "by interiorizing their demands and by bringing out their fullest meaning." The following document implies that fidelity to the New Covenant is to practice the Beatitudes. Sacred Congregation for the Doctrine of Faith, *Alcuni aspetti della "Teologia della liberazione"* 6-7, 10. Another document teaches that the "love of God and neighbor, which sum up the Decalogue, are lived in the spirit of the Beatitudes and constitute the *magna carta* of the Christian life proclaimed by Jesus in the Sermon on the Mount." The same document teaches that the Beatitudes are "the spirit that must permeate the Decalogue" [Pope John Paul II, *General Catechetical Directory* 115, 117].

³³ John Paul II, *Veritatis Splendor* 91.

Susanna, an additional detail is that the martyr's witness encompasses a "*voluntary* acceptance of death." The martyr's death, "a consequence" for his fidelity to the Commandments, is freely chosen; he prefers death rather than transgressing the Commandments.[34] Combining ideas presented in paragraph 88 with paragraph 91, one can say that the martyr's death is the freely chosen result of his own "living remembrance" of God's Commandments.[35]

A third characteristic of this "admirable witness" from the Old Testament concerns the succession of testimonies to which Susanna bears witness. The Pope mentions again "her faith and trust in God," which is, as *Veritatis Splendor* 88 teaches, a living faith that "is a decision involving one's whole existence."[36] Susanna's "faith and trust in God" embodies her determination to accept death.[37] Further, she also bears witness to her "obedience to the truth and to the absoluteness of the moral order."[38] Her "obedience to the truth" compels her to "live out" this truth by accepting death in order to uphold the "absoluteness of the moral order."[39]

Given his example of Susanna, one realizes the magnitude of John Paul's earlier insistence upon the fact that an objective moral order exists.[40] With *Veritatis Splendor* 91, the Pope adds to his con-

---

[34] John Paul II, *Veritatis Splendor* 91, 76.
[35] John Paul II, *Veritatis Splendor* 88.
[36] John Paul II, *Veritatis Splendor* 88.
[37] John Paul II, *Veritatis Splendor* 91.
[38] John Paul II, *Veritatis Splendor* 91.
[39] John Paul II, *Veritatis Splendor* 91, 88.
[40] John Paul II, *Veritatis Splendor* 82.

cept of martyrdom that one's readiness to undergo death upholds the moral order. Susanna's witness to the "absoluteness of the moral order" is her proclamation, made by her acceptance of death, that "it is not right to do what God's law qualifies as evil in order to draw some good from it."[41] Thus, Susanna defends the inviolable integrity of the human person. Her decision to accept death rather than break the law of God presents that law as "the one true good of man."[42]

As a witness to truth, Susanna resists calling "evil good, and good evil" (Isaiah 5:20). In fact, John Paul commends Susanna, noting that she "was a perfectly clear witness, without any compromise, to the truth about the good and to the God of Israel."[43] Thus, her witness to the objective moral order also testifies to "the truth about the good."[44] By embracing "the truth about the good" with a decision that warrants her subsequent death, she reveals "the holiness of God" who is Good.[45]

The Pope's conclusion to the Old Testament event concerning Susanna is, "By her acts, she reveals the holiness of God."[46] In John Paul's understanding of the term, then, a martyr reveals "the holiness of God" by his actions, which concern the resolution to accept death rather than to depart from the law of God. Combining an earlier passage in the encyclical with the present text, one sees in

---

[41] John Paul II, *Veritatis Splendor* 91.
[42] John Paul II, *Veritatis Splendor* 84.
[43] John Paul II, *Veritatis Splendor* 91.
[44] John Paul II, *Veritatis Splendor* 91.
[45] John Paul II, *Veritatis Splendor* 91.
[46] John Paul II, *Veritatis Splendor* 91.

## Chapter Eleven: Descriptions of the Term *Martyr*

Susanna's resolve the fact that only an "act in conformity with the good can be a path that leads to life."[47] By her willing acceptance of death, Susanna also demonstrates the "duty to refrain from performing even a single concrete act contrary to God's love and the witness of faith."[48] Because human freedom "abides in the truth and conforms to human dignity" through the person's "obedience to the divine law," Susanna's actions testify to the sublimity of freedom and dignity; she is the human person she is because of her freely chosen human acts.[49]

A final point that one gains from Susanna's example concerns the contemplative dimension of her choice. When John Paul says, "Susanna chose for herself the 'better part'" (Luke 10:42) he refers to Mary's decision to sit at the feet of Jesus and to listen to His words.[50] Susanna's decision to obey the law of God, then, might also be construed as listening. Her attentive listening to God's law is evident in her decision to accept death rather than to disobey (i.e., *not* listen) to His law. Susanna's contemplative *listening to* the law of God with "a decision involving one's whole existence" characterizes her as a martyr.[51] She is willing to lay down her life that she might remain in the law of God.

---

[47] John Paul II, *Veritatis Splendor* 72.

[48] John Paul II, *Veritatis Splendor* 91.

[49] John Paul II, *Veritatis Splendor* 42, 85, 65, 91.

[50] The passage, Luke 10:42, refers to Mary and Martha's responses to Jesus' visit. The Greek word is *good* (αγαθην), so the text reads, "μαρια δε την αγαθην μεριδα εξελεξατο." Literally, it translates as, "And Mary chose the good part." Idiomatically, one may translate it as *better* or *best*.

[51] John Paul II, *Veritatis Splendor* 88.

Because Susanna is willing to offer her life in order to uphold "the holy law of God," John Paul offers her as the first example of a martyr. With *Veritatis Splendor* 91, then, John Paul adds the following stipulation to his notion of martyrdom. It is "fidelity to the holy law of God" by voluntarily accepting death that merits (for Susanna) the title, *martyr*.[52] Although in the end, Susanna did not shed her blood, death was the foreseeable consequence of her faithfulness to the law of God. Thus, John Paul regards her as a martyr.

## The Literal or Metaphorical Use of "Martyr"

If John Paul includes the willing acceptance of death in his definition of martyrdom, one might wonder whether martyrdom negates my Aristotelian distinction regarding the literal and metaphorical use of a word. Since the Holy Father regards Susanna as a martyr, how does *death* involve martyrdom? Is it a crucial element that determines whether *martyr* is used in a literal or a metaphorical sense of the word?

My answer is that the Pope's example of Susanna does not alter the fact that he uses "martyr" in the literal sense, to specify one's death. Normally, whenever he speaks of martyrdom, John Paul maintains that a person's death, offered in order to uphold God's holy law, qualifies one as a martyr. The exception is his specific mention of Susanna, as an example of a martyr, in *Veritatis Splendor* 91. Thus, bodily death is not the consistent determining factor that merits the title *martyr* in the literal sense of the word. Instead,

---

[52] John Paul II, *Veritatis Splendor* 91.

as John Paul brings out with *Veritatis Splendor* 91, one's "voluntary acceptance of death," or the "readiness to die a martyr," is the continually recurring qualification that names a person a martyr.[53] One would conclude, however, that this "voluntary acceptance of death" requires the impending circumstances by which the death of the person is seemingly about to occur.[54]

John Paul's definition of "martyr," which I claim is a literal use of the word, concerns a further point. He maintains that a martyr accepts death "as a consequence" of one's decision to uphold the law of God, which, accordingly, endorses the objectivity of the moral order.[55] Because Susanna readily consented to death as a testimony to "her obedience to the truth and to the absoluteness of the moral order," she is, according to John Paul's understanding of the term, a martyr in the literal sense of the word.[56]

**Is Susanna a Confessor of God's Holy Law?**

One might offer the objection that the "readiness to die a martyr" more fittingly qualifies one as a *confessor*, rather than a *martyr*. According to Fr. John Hardon's *Catholic Dictionary*, a *confessor* is a "Christian in the early Church who had suffered much for the sake

---

[53] John Paul II, *Veritatis Splendor* 91.
[54] Note that Susanna was literally being led to the place of her execution before God intervened through Daniel [Daniel 13:45].
[55] John Paul II, *Veritatis Splendor* 76.
[56] John Paul II, *Veritatis Splendor* 91.

of Christ but did not die as a result of torture or ill-treatment."[57] Since Susanna did not die, is she properly called a *confessor*, instead of a *martyr*?

In his pontifical writings, John Paul's use of the word *confessor* includes holding onto the faith under persecution, but without suffering death. He also broadens the definition, however, to implicate one's faithful witness to Christ regardless of whether persecution accompanies it.[58] In fact, most of the Holy Father's references to a

---

[57] John A. Hardon, S.J., *Catholic Dictionary* (New York: Image Books, 2013), 104. As well, *The Oxford English Dictionary* defines a *confessor* as "one who avows his religion in the face of danger and adheres to it under persecution and torture, but does not suffer martyrdom [*The Oxford English Dictionary*, Second Edition, Vol. III, Prepared by J. A. Simpson and E. S. C. Weiner (Oxford, England: Clarendon Press, 1989), 704]. In this definition, the word *martyrdom* implies the actual, physical death of the person.

[58] The following evidence upholds the fact that John Paul broadens the definition of *confessor* to include one's daily witness to Christ. In a parish visitation, John Paul delivers a homily in which he exhorts his listener to live as a faithful Christian, and he uses the word *confessor* in this context. *Confessor* in this sense entails the person's daily fidelity to Christ. "There can be no contradiction between the knowledge ('I know him') and the action of a confessor of Christ. Only one who completes his faith with acts remains in the truth" [John Paul II, *Homily* 25 April 1982 (5)]. For additional examples of John Paul using the word *confessor* in this sense, that is, to refer to a person who witnesses to Christ, but who is not persecuted for it, see the following. *Homily* 23 November 1995 (4); *Homily* 28 September 1979 (5); *Homily* 29 June 2000 (2); 20 June 1982 (1) and *Reflections after the Mass of Canonization*, 20 June 1982 (3); *Homily* 25 April 1982 (5); *Homily* 6 February 1983 (7). In another homily, the Holy Father mentions that Bishop Clems-August Graf von Galen, Bishop of Münster, was a "courageous confessor of the faith" [John Paul II, *Homily*,

## Chapter Eleven: Descriptions of the Term *Martyr*

*confessor* have to do with one's daily fidelity to Jesus and His teachings.

A person who is mistreated for his faith, particularly by civil authorities, might possess the "readiness to die a martyr," of which John Paul speaks in *Veritatis Splendor* 91. Although one cannot judge the interior disposition of each person persecuted for the faith, one element is certain. For Susanna, death is guaranteed. She knew that the consequences of her decision would result in her death, and thus, when pointedly faced with the choice, she freely resolved to die rather than to violate the "holy law of God."[59] Although Susanna's decision did not ultimately result in her death, her decision to accept death remains unaltered.

The only ambiguous mention of the word *confessor* in the Pope's writings concerns Saint Thomas the Apostle. This citation is somewhat unclear in regard to how John Paul uses *confessor* because he enumerates three points regarding Saint Thomas: his profession of faith, his Apostleship, and his martyrdom. The passage in question reads as follows.

> Rather let us return in thought to the picture of Thomas who, even though he was an Apostle, was 'unbelieving;' but

---

2 May 1987 (4)]. While he was not a martyr, he did suffer for the faith. Thus, the following text is an example of John Paul using *confessor* to refer to one who was persecuted for his fidelity to Christ. For additional examples of John Paul using *confessor* in this sense (i.e., to refer to a person who suffered for his fidelity to Christ), see the following. *Homily* 27 September 2001 (4); *Homily* 10 October 1982 (9); and *Homily* 2 May 1987 (4).

[59] John Paul II, *Veritatis Splendor* 91.

after meeting the Risen One, he became His zealous confessor: 'My Lord and my God.' Confessor and Apostle, to the shedding of his blood.[60]

In my reading of the text, I continue to maintain that John Paul uses the word *confessor* in two ways: as one who is persecuted for the faith, but does not die, and as one whose witness involves a daily testimony to Christ and His Commandments.[61]

*Confession* may involve persecution, according to John Paul's use of the word, but not in each instance. Saint Thomas' profession of faith, "My Lord and my God," specifies his commitment to Christ and that allegiance makes him a confessor. In contrast, the Apostleship of Saint Thomas *includes* persecution, and it qualifies him as a *confessor*, in a manner that differs from his daily fidelity to Jesus. Finally, the martyrdom of the Apostle separates his confession, in either of the two senses described by John Paul, from the

---

[60] John Paul II, *Homily* 22 April 1990 (6).

[61] In a subsequent passage of the same homily, the Pope is clear that *confession* sometimes includes persecution, and he names various ways by which the faithful have confessed their faith in Christ. "Here my thoughts turn to the ranks of people who in Slovakia too have confessed their faith during these years, in spite of the dangers which it exposed them to. Bishops ending up in prison, humiliated, impeded, mistreated. Priests threatened, assaulted, limited in exercising their ministry. Men religious expelled from religious houses and imprisoned, women religious separated from their roles of serving the poor. Parents forced to curtail the Christian education of their children. Children trained in falsehoods the first example of which was the denial of God. So many, so many people, who have suffered for their faith" [John Paul II, *Homily* 22 April 1990 (7)]!

literal shedding of his blood. The Holy Father's mention of Saint Thomas as a confessor "to the shedding of his blood" implies that martyrdom goes a step beyond confession.[62]

Applying these findings to the case of Susanna, one might infer that she is a *confessor,* understood in the sense of one whose life is marked by daily fidelity to God and His law. Sacred Scripture attests to this sense of *confessor,* which describes her as a person who fears God and who has been raised "according to the law of Moses" (Daniel 13:2-3). John Paul's second use of the word *confessor,* as one who suffers persecution but is not martyred, does not apply to Susanna because death was the expected result of her adherence to God's law, as I explain above.

**Saint John the Baptist and the Compelling Impetus of Truth**

John Paul's second example of a martyr is John the Baptist. A key factor in the Baptist's martyrdom is the driving force of truth. As the Holy Father expresses in *Veritatis Splendor* 87, truth not only "sets one free," but it also gives one the "strength to endure martyrdom."[63] John the Baptist is an example of such a person, who is so convinced of the truth of God's law that he cannot refrain from speaking this truth, even at the risk of persecution and death. Compelled by truth, the Baptist's martyrdom is characterized by his energetic insistence upon it, for John Paul calls him a "witness

---

[62] John Paul II, *Homily* 22 April 1990 (6).
[63] John Paul II, *Veritatis Splendor* 87.

to truth and justice."⁶⁴ He conveys these thoughts in the following manner.

> At the dawn of the New Testament, John the Baptist, unable to refrain from speaking of the law of the Lord and rejecting any compromise with evil, 'gave his life in witness to truth and justice,' and thus also became the forerunner of the Messiah in the way he died (cf. Mark 6:17-29).⁶⁵

In addition to stressing the Baptist's dynamic persistence in truth, the Holy Father also brings out the fact that he is the forerunner of Jesus. By preparing the way for Jesus, who is Truth, Saint John the Baptist bears witness to Him. Quoting a homily by Saint Bede the Venerable, John Paul explains the precursor's role as follows.

> The one who came to bear witness to the light and who deserved to be called by that same light, which is Christ, a burning and shining lamp, was cast into the darkness of prison…The one to whom it was granted to baptize the Redeemer of the world was thus baptized in his own blood.⁶⁶

Combining the Holy Father's remarks on Saint John the Baptist in *Veritatis Splendor* 91 with my discussion in paragraph 87 of the same encyclical, one draws the following implications. First, with

---

[64] John Paul II, *Veritatis Splendor* 91.
[65] John Paul II, *Veritatis Splendor* 91.
[66] John Paul II, *Veritatis Splendor* 91.

*Veritatis Splendor* 87, I note that one's worship of God rouses hostile forces, and I suggest that one's witness to the truth by martyrdom is one way to worship God "in spirit and truth."[67] In paragraph 91, John Paul emphasizes the fact that truth impels the Baptist; it propels him forward to pursue his God-given task. One might explain Saint John's martyrdom, and, in fact, each martyrdom, as the worship of God "in spirit and truth," fired by truth's propelling force.[68]

**The Martyr Accepts Death to "Profess...Faith and...Love for Christ"**

The Holy Father's final examples of martyrs include saints from the New Testament, such as Saints Stephen and James. The Pope characterizes their witness as a profession of "their faith and their love for Christ, unwilling to deny Him."[69] Here, one perceives a shift from the Old Testament emphasis on the law of God to the New Testament focus upon Christ Jesus.

The New Testament martyrs follow Christ's example by testifying to the truth, as He did Himself, before Pilate: "For this I was born, and for this I have come into the world, to bear witness to the truth. Everyone who is of the truth hears My voice" (John 18:37 RSVCE). Just as Jesus confirms "the truth of His message at the cost of His life," so also does the New Testament martyr bear wit-

---

[67] John Paul II, *Veritatis Splendor* 87.
[68] John Paul II, *Veritatis Splendor* 87.
[69] John Paul II, *Veritatis Splendor* 91.

ness to Him and to His teaching by their own blood. John Paul explains as follows.

> In the New Testament we find many examples of followers of Christ, beginning with the deacon Stephen (cf. Acts 6:8-7:60) and the Apostle James (cf. Acts 12:1-2), who died as martyrs in order to profess their faith and their love for Christ, unwilling to deny Him. In this they followed the Lord Jesus who 'made the good confession' (1 Timothy 6:13) before Caiaphas and Pilate, confirming the truth of His message at the cost of His life.[70]

Elsewhere, the Pope focuses upon Saint Stephen, the Protomartyr, as a fitting example of martyrdom because his death involves an act of "hatred against the faith."[71] Saint Stephen is a martyr because his "murderers demonstrate their hatred for the faith…when their violence is directed against the explicit proclamation of the faith, as in the case of Stephen, who declares that he 'sees an opening in the sky, and the Son of Man standing at God's right hand' (Acts 7:56)."[72]

The Holy Father further indicates that martyrdom entails violence which is "hurled against works of charity towards one's neighbor, works which objectively and truly have their justification

---

[70] John Paul II, *Veritatis Splendor* 91.
[71] John Paul II, *Homily* 15 May 1983 (2).
[72] John Paul II, *Homily* 15 May 1983 (2).

and their motive in the faith. They hate whatever flows from faith, showing that they hate that faith which is its source."[73]

With an additional New Testament example in *Veritatis Splendor* 91, John Paul refers to the numerous martyrs who willingly accept "persecution and death" in order to "refrain from performing even a single concrete act contrary to God's love and the witness of faith."[74] With the example of New Testament martyrs, who remain nameless, John Paul highlights the love of God rather than fidelity to the law, for charity is the "fulfillment of the law" (Romans 13:8).[75] Indirectly, John Paul stresses the existence of intrinsically evil acts with his mention of worshipping the emperor. In such an instance, one may not perform "even a single concrete act contrary to God's love and the witness of faith."[76]

---

[73] John Paul II, *Homily* 15 May 1983 (2).

[74] Although the Pope explicitly mentions persecution in this text, because he combines it with death, I see no variance with my earlier conclusions regarding his use of the word *confessor*. Again, *death* is a key factor in John Paul's notion of martyrdom, but not exclusively. As I mention with the example of Susanna, one's "voluntary acceptance of death" in fidelity to the law of God qualifies a person as a martyr [John Paul II, *Veritatis Splendor* 91].

[75] John Paul's emphasis on charity recalls the Second Vatican Council document, *Lumen Gentium*. The document refers to martyrdom as "an exceptional gift and as the fullest proof of love," by which a "disciple is transformed into an image of his Master by freely accepting death for the salvation of the world—as well as his conformity to Christ in the shedding of his blood" [Second Vatican Council, *Lumen Gentium* 42].

[76] John Paul II, *Veritatis Splendor* 91.

Countless other martyrs accepted persecution and death rather than perform the idolatrous act of burning incense before the statue of the emperor (cf. Revelation 13:7-10). They even refused to feign such worship, thereby giving an example of the duty to refrain from performing even a single concrete act contrary to God's love and the witness of faith. Like Christ Himself, they obediently trusted and handed over their lives to the Father, the One who could free them from death (cf. Hebrews 5:7).[77]

As a concluding thought to *Veritatis Splendor* 91, John Paul mentions innumerable martyr-saints, explaining why the Church regards them as martyrs.[78] He addresses the saint's witness to "moral truth," distinguishing it from the martyr-saint's witness, which consists of witness to truth under pain of death. His final word in paragraph 91 also brings out the Church's role in canonizing the martyr as a faithful witness to Jesus.

The Church proposes the example of numerous saints who bore witness to and defended moral truth even to the point of enduring martyrdom, or who preferred death to a single mortal sin. In raising them to the honor of the altars, the Church has canonized their witness and declared the truth

---

[77] John Paul II, *Veritatis Splendor* 91.
[78] Note the fact that the Pope specifically mentions the Catholic Church, by whose authority one is acknowledged as a saint and a martyr. John Paul's explicit mention of the Church indicates her crucial role in declaring a person both a saint and a martyr.

# Chapter Eleven: Descriptions of the Term *Martyr*

of their judgment, according to which the love of God entails the obligation to respect His Commandments, even in the most dire of circumstances, and the refusal to betray those Commandments, even for the sake of saving one's own life."[79]

From the work on *Veritatis Splendor* completed thus far, one concludes that the "witness" of the martyr is his testimony to truth. Because truth is, ultimately, Christ, who *is* Truth, one might posit that the martyr's witness to truth becomes clear in his decision to accept death, as I elucidate above. The martyr's final word, by which he voluntarily accepts death, shows the inviting splendor of Truth, Himself.

As I describe above, the martyr is a witness to the good, to the objective moral order, and to the existence of intrinsically evil acts. At the culmination of *Veritatis Splendor* 91, the Holy Father summarizes the "witness" of the martyr as a testimony to "the love of God," which obliges the person "to respect His Commandments, even in the most dire of circumstances, and the refusal to betray those Commandments, even for the sake of saving one's own life."[80] Summarizing the martyr's testimony as the love of God shows that the law of charity reigns supreme. Making up in one's "own flesh what is lacking in the sacrifice of Christ" (Colossians

---

[79] John Paul II, *Veritatis Splendor* 90.
[80] John Paul II, *Veritatis Splendor* 90.

1:24), the martyr, "like Christ…obediently trusted and handed over [his] life to the Father."[81]

---

[81] John Paul II, *Veritatis Splendor* 90.

# Chapter Twelve

## Martyrdom Affirms the "Inviolability of the Moral Order"

John Paul stresses the objectivity of the moral order throughout *Veritatis Splendor*. For example, as I mention above, the Pontiff warns against erroneous teachings, which negate the existence of intrinsically evil acts and nullify the fact that moral norms prohibiting these acts are "binding without exception."[1] In paragraph 92, the Holy Father reiterates his insistence upon the objective moral order and its protection of the human person. In this framework, he speaks of martyrdom.

In his depiction of martyrdom with *Veritatis Splendor* 92, the Pope brings together several concepts thus presented. Martyrdom affirms both the objectivity of the moral order and the inviolability of each person's dignity. He teaches, "Martyrdom, accepted as an affirmation of the inviolability of the moral order, bears splendid witness both to the holiness of God's law and to the inviolability of the personal dignity of man, created in God's image and likeness."[2]

Upholding the objective moral order, then, reveals both God's holy law and the lofty dignity of each person. John Paul explains that the martyr's death expresses these truths. In other words, the martyr defends the sacredness of the objective moral order and confirms it. His death reinforces the holiness of God's law. One

---

[1] John Paul II, *Veritatis Splendor* 82; 95.
[2] John Paul II, *Veritatis Splendor* 92.

must obey this law, regardless of the cost. One's obedient listening unto death implies that the human person possesses a dignity beyond his corporeal, physical existence.

One's dignity principally affirms my earlier claim regarding God's love for the human person as a creature made in His image and recreated in Christ through His Blood (cf. Colossians 1:13-17).³ One's human dignity, then, as John Paul specifies in paragraph 92, "may never be disparaged or called into question, even with good intentions, whatever the difficulties involved."

Trying to separate the person from the dignity that envelopes him is impossible precisely because he is created out of the love of God. Moreover, as the Puebla *Address* highlights, one's life is futile without reference to God.⁴ Building upon these factors, one understands that the martyr's death expresses his union with God: his death expresses his relationship with God as the "one thing…necessary" (Luke 10:42).⁵ Since one's dignity "is manifested in all its radiance when the person's origin and destiny are considered," as *Christifideles Laici* 37 teaches, the martyr refuses to be separated from his origin, who is God, and his destiny, who is God.⁶

John Paul continues to discuss how martyrdom protects the inviolability of the human person by highlighting its characteristic

---

³ John Paul II, *Redemptor Hominis* 8-10.
⁴ John Paul II, *Opening Address* at Puebla, 28 January 1979 (I.9).
⁵ John Paul II, *Opening Address* at Puebla, 28 January 1979 (I.9).
⁶ John Paul II, *Christifideles Laici* 37.

ability to call good and evil by their proper names.[7] Moreover, human dignity requires that each person avoid intrinsically evil acts. Because the martyr refuses to comply with an action that is "not capable of being ordered to God," he acts in accord with human dignity.[8] Thus, martyrdom supports and promotes human dignity by testifying to the martyr's defense of it.

## Martyrdom is "the Exaltation of a Person's Perfect 'Humanity' and of True 'Life'"

In *Veritatis Splendor* 92, the Pope highlights the fact that performing morally good acts perfects a person, while morally evil acts not only harm the one who does them, but they also violate one's "humanity."[9] Because the martyr both performs morally good acts and refuses to commit those which are evil, John Paul explains martyrdom as "the exaltation of a person's perfect 'humanity' and of true 'life'" in the following manner.

> Martyrdom rejects as false and illusory whatever 'human meaning' one might claim to attribute, even in 'exceptional' conditions, to an act morally evil in itself. Indeed, it even more clearly unmasks the true face of such an act: it is a

---

[7] In the *Veritatis Splendor*, the Holy Father often refers to the ability of the properly formed conscience to know good from evil. For examples, see John Paul II, *Veritatis Splendor* 32, 35, 44, 65. See also *Dominum et Vivificantem* 43. In my analysis of *Veritatis Splendor* 93 below, I return to this topic.

[8] John Paul II, *Veritatis Splendor* 82.

[9] John Paul II, *Veritatis Splendor* 92.

violation of man's 'humanity,' in the one perpetrating it even before the one enduring it. Hence martyrdom is also the exaltation of a person's perfect 'humanity' and of true 'life,' as is attested by Saint Ignatius of Antioch, addressing the Christians of Rome, the place of his own martyrdom: 'Have mercy on me, brethren: do not hold me back from living; do not wish that I die... Let me arrive at the pure light; once there I will be truly a man. Let me imitate the Passion of my God.'[10]

Conscientious toward the good of each human person, John Paul stresses the effects of acting in a morally upright way. *Veritatis Splendor* 92 portrays the martyr as an embodiment of both human freedom and human dignity, which he summarizes with the above quotation concluding this paragraph. Referring to Saint Ignatius of Antioch's *Letter to the Romans*, the Holy Father draws out several enlightening factors that contribute toward understanding martyrdom as an expression of human freedom and human dignity. The words of Saint Ignatius suggest that the apex of freedom and dignity is being with Jesus in Heaven.

John Paul's reference to the *Letter to the Romans* in paragraph 92 deserves reflection in my discussion on martyrdom. In light of *Veritatis Splendor* 92, one might interpret this *Letter* as the epitome of a person who understands human freedom as being with God on earth, through fidelity to His Commandments, and in Heaven, through beatitude. Human dignity, as a revelation of one's origin

---

[10] John Paul II, *Veritatis Splendor* 92.

and destiny, is now expressed as one's immersion in God: absorbed in love by the Passion of Christ, the saint's only longing is "to be God's."[11] Articulating human dignity as one's immersion in God makes a person truly free, according to the dynamic *Letter* of Saint Ignatius. Offering a longer excerpt portrays these ideas.

> All the ends of the earth, all the kingdoms of the world would be of no profit to me; so far as I am concerned, to die in Jesus Christ is better than to be monarch of earth's widest bounds. He who dies for us is all that I seek; He who rose again for us is my whole desire. The pangs of birth are upon me; have patience with me, my brothers, and do not shut me out from life, do not wish me to be still born. Here is one who only longs to be God's; do not make present of him to the world again or delude him with the things of the earth. Suffer me to attain to light, light pure and undefiled; for only when I am come thither shall I be truly a man. Leave me to imitate the Passion of my God. If any of you has God within himself, let that man understand my longings, and feel for me, because he will know the forces by which I am constrained.[12]

In my analysis, this excerpt from the *Letter to the Romans* offers a key insight into the martyr. The Heavenly Father, through the martyr, draws people together in Christ Jesus. This uniting factor of the martyr's death is not, however, exclusive to the martyr,

---

[11] Saint Ignatius of Antioch, *Letter to the Romans* 105.
[12] Saint Ignatius of Antioch, *Letter to the Romans* 105-106.

but it is a vehicle for uniting mankind together in Jesus. Indeed, holiness is contagious and the holiness is Christ's. My explanation of this thought is brought out by a careful study of the original text of Saint Ignatius.

It is interesting to note that neither the Greek nor the Latin texts read, "shall I be truly a man," although some English translations render it as such.[13] As the Greek brings out, once Saint Ignatius is martyred, then, in the "pure light" (φως λαβειν) of Heaven, he will "befriend mankind" (παραγενόμενος άνθρωπος έσομαι).[14] The specific passage in question reads as follows.

σύγγνωτέ μοι, αδελφοί. μη εμποδίσητέ μοι ζήσαι, μη θελήσητέ με αποθανειν, τον του θεου θέλοντα ειναι κόσμψ

---

[13] Saint Ignatius of Antioch, *Letter to the Romans* 105-106. Various English texts often translate the saint's presence in Heaven as having achieved the full stature of manhood: "once there, I will be truly a man" [John Paul II, *Veritatis Splendor* 92]. A second example that translates "I [will] be truly a man" is the Staniforth text to which this footnote refers. A third example is Quasten's rendition in *Patrology*: "Once arrived there, I shall be a man" [Johannes Quasten, *Patrology*, vol. I *The Beginnings of Patristic Literature* (Utrecht Brussels: Spectrum Publishers, 1950), 71]. Quasten's rendition is the most literal translation of the Latin, which reads as follows. "Ignoscite mihi, fratres! Ne me vivere impediatis, ne velitis me mori, me dei esse cupientem mundo ne tradatis neque per materiam me seducatis, sinite me purum lumen percipere; ubi illuc advenero, homo ero" [Ignatii, *Epistula ad Romanos* VI, 2 in *Patres Apostolici*, vol. 1, Franciscus Xaverius Funk, ed. (Tubingæ: In libraria Henrici Laupp, 1901), 261]. The Latin brings out the notion that once the saint reaches the "pure light (purum lumen)" of Heaven, then, having attained his goal, he becomes the person he was meant to be all along.

[14] Ignatii, *Epistula ad Romanos* VI, 2 in PA 260.

## Chapter Twelve: Martyrdom Affirms "Inviolability of Moral Order" 243

μη χαρίσησθε μηδε ὑλη εξαπατήσητε. ἀφετέ με καθαρον φως λαβειν. εκει παραγενόμενος ἀνθρωπος ἐσομαι.[15]

The words παραγενόμενος ἀνθρωπος ἐσομαι are difficult to translate.[16] ἐσομαι is the first person singular future tense of the future infinitive, ἐσεσθαι. When used in conjunction with ἐσομαι, the term παραγενόμενος best translates as *befriend*.[17] If one posits that any martyr might hold the same thoughts expressed by Saint Ignatius of Antioch, then one infers the following insights.

As the *Letter* from Saint Ignatius of Antioch suggests, "befriending mankind" implies that, having reached one's final end through the grace of God, the martyr is both with God and he unites others together in himself, presenting them to Jesus.[18] In his own martyred flesh, through which he imitates the Passion of Jesus, the martyr is a channel drawing mankind together in Him. The martyr "befriends mankind," or unites others to Jesus Christ because, as *Veritatis Splendor* 84 shows above, his *doing* of the

---

[15] Ignatii, *Epistula ad Romanos* VI, 2 in PA 260.

[16] Ignatii, *Epistula ad Romanos* VI, 2 in PA 260. The Latin rendition of παραγενόμενος ἀνθρωπος ἐσομαι, which differs from the Greek, perhaps indicates the complexity of the phrase. Here, Saint Ignatius signifies that, once he dies and comes to the "pure light" (purum lumen) of Heaven, he "will be a man (homo ero)."

[17] I am indebted to Theodosios Kyriakides for help with the fuller meaning of παραγενόμενος ἀνθρωπος ἐσομαι. A Greek himself, Theodosios checked his intuition of this phrase with a Greek philologist.

[18] Ignatii, *Epistula ad Romanos* VI, 2 in PA 260.

truth recovers the "essential bond between Truth, the Good and Freedom."[19]

Since truth is objective, the moral order is also objective. It is not the result of the majority vote. The martyr, who bears witness to these objective realities by his death, draws others together precisely because truth and the moral order do not change.[20] Since Jesus *is* Truth, and the Church is entrusted with safeguarding His teachings, the martyr draws others to Him through his own witness to Jesus and to His teachings. The teachings of Jesus, which are the teachings of the Church, testify, in turn, to the objectivity of the moral order. The martyr's witness to the universal, immutable nature of truth affects all people of all time because each human person is called to live "in the Truth."[21]

Given the Pope's straightforward description of martyrdom in *Veritatis Splendor* 92 and analyzing it in conjunction with the *Letter to the Romans*, one might infer that the martyr preserves the person's humanity because he supports the primacy of the moral law over an act contrary to that law. The martyr knows that a per-

---

[19] Ignatii, *Epistula ad Romanos* VI, 2 in PA 260; John Paul II, *Veritatis Splendor* 84.

[20] In paragraph 113, John Paul clearly expresses the fact that moral teaching is not "established by following the rules and deliberative procedures typical of a democracy" [John Paul II, *Veritatis Splendor* 113]. By witnessing to truth's objectivity, the martyr's death unites others to Jesus, according to my interpretation of the *Letter* of Saint Ignatius of Antioch. The martyr's death also unites others to Jesus on account of the nature of proclamation, rendered in *Redemptoris Missio*. I discuss this aspect of proclamation with my forthcoming analysis of *Redemptoris Missio*.

[21] John Paul II, *Veritatis Splendor* 84.

son's act against the law of God violates one's own humanity. The martyr not only preserves one's humanity, then, but his very act of preservation infers the social dimension of the human race.

The martyr's embrace of mankind, with his choice to uphold the objective moral order, might be expressed differently. As I explain above, the martyr's death expresses freedom and dignity as openness to another human person who suffers. His willing acceptance of death affects all mankind because each person suffers, at times, by not being authentically free and by offenses against his dignity. The martyr's acceptance of death, however, shows freedom and dignity at their summit.

Because suffering is part of the fabric of human life, the martyr is open to another who suffers precisely because he suffers in order to uphold faith and morals and to defend the objective moral order, the denial of which is "the gravest situation" facing the person today.[22] Given that the universality and immutability of the moral norm both reveals and protects freedom and dignity, the martyr, as a child of God the Father, unites humanity in one's "true life" that he might attain "light pure and undefiled."[23]

---

[22] John Paul II, *Veritatis Splendor* 84. As I discuss above, the Holy Father identifies *relativism* as the refusal to "acknowledge the enduring absoluteness of any moral value" [John Paul II, *Veritatis Splendor* 84].

[23] John Paul II, *Veritatis Splendor* 90; Saint Ignatius of Antioch, *Letter to the Romans* 105. Recall, as well that *Redemptor Hominis* 9 explains, "human beings predestined from eternity in the first-born Son to be children of God and called to grace, called to love" [John Paul II, *Redemptor Hominis* 9. In this passage, John Paul refers to Romans 8:29-30 and Ephesians 1:8].

The excerpt from the *Letter* of Saint Ignatius contains an additional facet of martyrdom's exceptional ability to unite mankind in Jesus Christ. The martyr's capacity to bring others together in Him is due to the singularity of his rapt attention upon Christ. In the *Letter* of Saint Ignatius, the martyr holds Christ Jesus to be his greatest treasure, beyond "all the ends of the earth, [and] all the kingdoms of the world."[24] The martyr regards his relationship to Jesus, which is of greater value than ruling the world, as the only good—the *one* good. As I bring out with *Veritatis Splendor* 91, the contemplative dimension of martyrdom regards Mary's listening to Jesus as the *"one thing"* necessary (Luke 10:42). Combining this thought with the *Letter to the Romans* shows that each martyr holds his life with Jesus, that is, eternal life, as the greatest good.[25]

The *Letter to the Romans* of Saint Ignatius reveals that the martyr clings to Jesus with all his strength, certain that it is better to die in His friendship than to live as a king who transgresses His law: "to die in Jesus Christ is better than to be monarch of earth's widest bounds."[26] The martyr focuses solely upon Jesus, convinced of His great love for him. "He who dies for us is all that I seek; He who rose again for us is my whole desire."[27]

---

[24] Saint Ignatius of Antioch, *Letter to the Romans* 105-106.

[25] By referring to the martyr's life with Jesus as his greatest good, I imply that his relationship with Him is marked by faith. With John Paul, I explain faith as "a lived knowledge of Christ, a living remembrance of His Commandments, and a truth to be lived out" [John Paul II, *Veritatis Splendor* 88].

[26] Saint Ignatius of Antioch, *Letter to the Romans* 105-106.

[27] Saint Ignatius of Antioch, *Letter to the Romans* 105-106.

## Chapter Twelve: Martyrdom Affirms "Inviolability of Moral Order"  247

As I note above, God creates the human person out of His immense love and Jesus restores the person to the Father's friendship through His Passion and death.[28] The martyr is convinced of these truths. Saint Ignatius expresses these truths, regarding his own creation and redemption, in his *Letter to the Romans*. The perceptive notions of the martyr becoming closely united with mankind by his death and of mankind becoming tightly bound to Christ through the martyr are thoughts I continue to ponder below. By the grace of God, the martyr's capacity to serve is a means through which one comes to Christ.

Continuing to comment upon the *Letter to the Romans*, one finds that the martyr regards his death as a life-giving event: he is born into eternal life. Saint Ignatius describes his death using perhaps the most naturally, physically painful human experience possible, which is giving birth. The point to be pondered is that the martyr, here, Saint Ignatius of Antioch, acknowledges his physical suffering as a *real, intense, human* experience. He does *not* nonchalantly cast aside his physical suffering, and this is significant. Too often, the temptation is to downplay the physical suffering of martyrdom to the detriment of the lesson that it teaches. Saint Ignatius does not miss the opportunity to instruct others, and he begins by depicting his immanent physical sufferings in a riveting manner. "The pangs of birth are upon me; have patience with me, my brothers, and do not shut me out from life; do not wish me to be still born."[29]

---

[28] John Paul II, *Redemptor Hominis* 8.
[29] Saint Ignatius of Antioch, *Letter to the Romans* 105-106.

The pain of martyrdom is real and one naturally dreads the suffering at hand. As John Paul reminds his reader, "death through martyrdom is always a torment; but the secret of that death is the fact that God is greater than the torment. Great is the trial of suffering, that 'testing like gold in the furnace'" purifies.[30] Throughout one's suffering, then, the martyr's central focus is God and his union with God. The Holy Father continues, "love is greater than the trial, that is, grace is stronger" than suffering and death.[31] What is humanly impossible, God makes possible with His superabundant grace (cf. Matthew 19:26; Mark 10:27; Luke 18:27).

If the martyr's own death is necessary in order for him to remain united with God, then he willingly suffers it regardless of the suffering accompanying it. In fact, the pain one experiences by his martyrdom is *real, intense, human* suffering. That reality of intense suffering bears witness, in a perceptible, vivid manner, that the martyr's single concern is to be with God. He refrains from anything that might separate him from God in a way that others can see and understand, since human suffering is foreign to no human being. In light of these ponderings, the words of Saint Ignatius of Antioch show the martyr's one point of focus. "Here is one who only longs to be God's; do not make present of him to the world again or delude him with the things of the earth."[32]

Saint Ignatius continues to imply that his union with God is his singular concern. In fact, he writes with full knowledge that his relationship with God can only be sustained by accepting the violent

---

[30] John Paul II, *Homily* 18 June 1983 (4).
[31] John Paul II, *Homily* 18 June 1983 (4).
[32] Saint Ignatius of Antioch, *Letter to the Romans* 105-106.

death appointed for him. He accepts it as God's will. The death of Saint Ignatius of Antioch, then, is the means through which God makes him to be the person He wants him to be, thus bringing the saint to full stature as a human person. Saint Ignatius sees himself as an imitator of Christ, by his own arduous death. "Suffer me to attain to light, light pure and undefiled; for only when I am come thither shall I be truly a man. Leave me to imitate the Passion of my God."[33]

Finally, one recalls from *Veritatis Splendor* 87 that truth not only sets a person free, as the Gospel maintains, but also, truth's invigorating nature imparts the "strength to endure martyrdom."[34] As paragraph 91 especially brings out with the example of Saint John the Baptist, truth has a compelling impetus.[35] With the Pope's example of Saint Ignatius of Antioch in *Veritatis Splendor* 92, one is thus easily able to grasp the martyr's urgency. "If any of you has God within himself, let that man understand my longings, and feel for me, because he will know the forces by which I am constrained."[36] In sum, Saint Ignatius, and every martyr, dies as a "witness to truth and justice."[37] That truth urges him to endure the suffering that the sacrifice of his life entails.

---

[33] Saint Ignatius of Antioch, *Letter to the Romans* 105-106.
[34] John Paul II, *Veritatis Splendor* 87.
[35] John Paul II, *Veritatis Splendor* 91.
[36] Saint Ignatius of Antioch, *Letter to the Romans* 105-106.
[37] John Paul II, *Veritatis Splendor* 91.

## The "Inviolability of the Moral Order"

As John Paul mentions in *Veritatis Splendor* 92, martyrdom "bears splendid witness...to the holiness of God's law." In paragraph 93, he highlights martyrdom as an "outstanding sign of the holiness of the Church."[38] He expresses this holiness in terms of the Church's missionary character, emphasizing again that martyrdom consists of "fidelity to God's holy law, witnessed to by death."[39]

> Finally, martyrdom is an outstanding sign of the holiness of the Church. Fidelity to God's holy law, witnessed to by death, is a solemn proclamation and missionary commitment *usque ad sanguinem*, so that the splendor of moral truth may be undimmed in the behavior and thinking of individuals and society.[40]

A concise definition of martyrdom, offered in the *Veritatis Splendor* 93 passage above, is "fidelity to God's holy law, witnessed to by death." The martyr's commitment to the law of God shows that Christ's teaching, which has been entrusted to the Church, is holy. Because the Church has received from Jesus the mandate to "teach [μαθητευστε] all nations" (Matthew 28:19) her missionary commitment extends *to the point of blood (usque ad sanguinem)*.[41]

---

[38] John Paul II, *Veritatis Splendor* 91.
[39] John Paul II, *Veritatis Splendor* 93.
[40] John Paul II, *Veritatis Splendor* 93.
[41] John Paul II, *Veritatis Splendor* 93. The Latin preposition *ad* takes the accusative case. In other words, it expresses *movement toward* its ob-

# Chapter Twelve: Martyrdom Affirms "Inviolability of Moral Order"

In other words, the missionary carries the teaching of Christ to others, even if it cost him his life. That is how important the Gospel message is.

The martyr's death, then, both radiates "the splendor of moral truth," and it insists upon that splendor being continually "undimmed in the behavior and thinking of individuals and society."[42] I said that the martyr's death *continually* bears witness to moral truth in order to incorporate a point that I bring out with *Veritatis Splendor* 92. In my elucidation of the extract from Saint Ignatius of Antioch, I explain how martyrdom encompasses the notion of the martyr "befriending mankind" by drawing all together in Christ.[43] The death that each martyr endures, then, incessantly bears witness to the "essential bond between Truth, the Good and Freedom."[44] In sum, the martyr's death constantly witnesses to the truths for which he dies precisely because he gives his life in order to uphold them. His testimony remains present to all people of all time, beyond his physical life on earth. The Holy Father suggests, in fact, with paragraph 93, that the martyr's witness endures because his

---

ject, which, in this case, is *sanguinem*. To draw out the meaning of this familiar phrase, one might translate the adverb *ūsque* in a variety of ways, such as *thoroughly, entirely, at every point, continuously, everywhere,* or *constantly*. If one reads each of the possible translations for *ūsque*, then one captures, even more vividly, the depth of the Church's missionary mandate. Christ's command to "teach all nations" extends *continuously, at every moment, entirely toward* the shedding of blood, or death for the sake of the Gospel.

[42] John Paul II, *Veritatis Splendor* 93.
[43] Ignatii, *Epistula ad Romanos* VI, 2 in PA 260-261.
[44] John Paul II, *Veritatis Splendor* 84.

death shows that moral truth is "undimmed in the behavior and thinking of individuals and society."[45]

In *Veritatis Splendor* 93, the notion of martyrdom's testimony to the objective moral order is implicit. Given the martyr's correctly formed conscience, what the Pope accentuates is the capacity of martyrdom to call good and evil by their proper names. The martyr's death characteristically witnesses to the existence of the objective moral order and to the summons of the human person's obedience to the truth that is inscribed in him.[46] The Holy Father expresses these concepts in the following manner.

> This witness makes an extraordinarily valuable contribution to warding off, in civil society and within the ecclesial communities themselves, a headlong plunge into the most dangerous crisis which can afflict man: the confusion between good and evil, which makes it impossible to build up and to preserve the moral order of individuals and communities.[47]

---

[45] A canonized martyr is continually before the Church Militant as both an intercessor with God and as an example for emulation. The constant witness that the martyr's death offers to the faithful naturally includes the Church's celebration and invocation. The unremitting testimony of the martyr's death also witnesses to the "splendor of moral truth [that it might] be undimmed in the behavior and thinking of individuals and society" [John Paul II, *Veritatis Splendor* 93].

[46] John Paul II, *Veritatis Splendor* 27, 82; John Paul II, *Dominum et Vivificantem* 43.

[47] John Paul II, *Veritatis Splendor* 93.

Again, the Holy Father's concern is to uphold human freedom and dignity; living "in accordance with the truth" is thus imperative.[48] The martyr's death contributes toward the Church's task of assisting the faithful in the formation of an upright conscience by showing that "judgments and...decisions in accordance with the truth" cut through "the confusion between good and evil," which is prevalent in society.[49] Martyrdom depicts the truth of the moral order in the most vividly convincing manner because the natural human instinct is to preserve one's own life. Yet, the martyr chooses to forfeit the great good of his physical human life for an even greater good. The sacrifice of his life speaks to the avid distinction between good and evil, thus preserving "the moral order of individuals and communities."[50]

The Holy Father offers an impressive description of the martyr's testimony. Although he speaks of "all the Church's saints" rekindling the moral sensitivity of his day, he differentiates between the martyr and the other canonized saints. His mention of the martyr precedes his reference to the saint who is not a martyr. John Paul presents the martyr as follows.

> By their eloquent and attractive example of a life completely transfigured by the splendor of moral truth, the martyrs and, in general, all the Church's saints, light up every period of history by reawakening its moral sense. By witnessing fully to the good, they are a living reproof to those who

---

[48] John Paul II, *Veritatis Splendor* 85.
[49] John Paul II, *Veritatis Splendor* 93, 85.
[50] John Paul II, *Veritatis Splendor* 27, 93.

transgress the law (cf. Wisdom 2:12), and they make the words of the Prophet echo ever afresh: 'Woe to those who call evil good and good evil, who put darkness for light and light for darkness, who put bitter for sweet and sweet for bitter' (Isaiah 5:20)![51]

One might ask what the difference is between the martyr and any other saint, since both "light up every period of history by reawakening its moral sense."[52] As the Holy Father indicates, both the martyr and the non-martyr saint witness to moral truth, and thus, to the objectivity of the moral order. Further, both the martyr and the non-martyr saint, by their lives of faithful service to Christ and to His Gospel teachings, witness to the truth and to the distinction between good and evil.

Another text suggests that both the martyr and the non-martyr saint "light up every period of history."[53] In a homily that refers to Saint Stephen's vision of the heavens opening at the moment of his death, John Paul writes that the "saints of every age…lived in this vision of the 'heavens opened.' They are witnesses to the Son of Man, who chose to enter history and to journey in it, so as to become for everyone 'the Way, the Truth and the Life' (cf. John 14:6)."[54] Because both the martyr and the non-martyr saint "lived

---

[51] John Paul II, *Veritatis Splendor* 93.
[52] John Paul II, *Veritatis Splendor* 93.
[53] John Paul II, *Veritatis Splendor* 93.
[54] John Paul II, *Homily* 28 May 1995 (5).

## Chapter Twelve: Martyrdom Affirms "Inviolability of Moral Order"

in this vision of the 'heavens opened,'" one might question the difference between these witnesses to Christ.[55]

Fully acknowledging the contribution that both the martyr and the non-martyr saint offer to the Church and to the world, I do not intend to downplay the testimony of the saint who is not a martyr, or to say that the martyr's contribution is somehow better than the testimony of the saint. I note above how all of Christ's followers "contribute to the manifold 'renewal of the face of the earth,'" making it clear that not all of them are martyrs.[56] Martyrdom is a special gift of God's election, given to only a few.

*Dominum et Vivificantem* 60 provides further evidence of the viable witness that the non-martyr saint offers. My specific intent in analyzing paragraph 60 was to explain first, that the Pope maintains that not all witnesses are martyrs, and second, that the distinction between the witness of daily sufferings and the witness of the martyr is, according to *Dominum et Vivificantem* 60, the death endured by the martyr.

Again, the martyr's "voluntary acceptance of death," which he offers in "fidelity to the holy law of God," specifies the distinguishing characteristic between the martyr and the saint who is not a martyr.[57] Both the martyr and the non-martyr saint put the "precepts and love [of Christ] into practice," one by his sacrifice (death) and the other by his life.[58] Thus, I wholly accept John Paul's unmis-

---

[55] John Paul II, *Homily* 28 May 1995 (5).

[56] John Paul II, *Dominum et Vivificantem* 60.

[57] John Paul II, *Dominum et Vivificantem* 60; John Paul II, *Veritatis Splendor* 91.

[58] John Paul II, *Veritatis Splendor* 27.

takable stance that both the martyr and the non-martyr saint serve as beacons of light to the world.

Because each person is called to show Christ to others by his life and death, the point of divergence is located in the dramatic visibility of offering one's life in order to uphold Christ's teachings. Thus, the martyr's death embodies his faith, and his faith embodies his death, in a dramatic, perceivable manner. While the actual degree of faith in any one person is known only to God, the difference between the martyr's embodiment of faith and the non-martyr's living of faith, which is a "truth to be lived," in either case, is in one's acceptance of death in fidelity to Christ and His Commandments.

While not discounting the witness of the saint who is not a martyr, I highlight the martyr's testimony. In addition, I ponder the reason why the Pope explicitly stresses the martyr's capacity to distinguish between good and evil. As John Paul contests in *Veritatis Splendor*, the martyr's death proclaims the objectivity of the moral order in a manner that is quite remarkable. The testimony that he offers, with his willing acceptance of death in order to "*do the Truth*," speaks forcefully.[59] Resuming my analysis of texts on martyrdom, I continue to reflect upon the convincing testimony that the martyr's death signifies.

With the last section of paragraph 93, the Holy Father answers my question regarding the point of distinction between the martyr and the non-martyr saint, conscious of the fact that both "light up

---

[59] John Paul II, *Veritatis Splendor* 84.

every period of history by reawakening its moral sense."⁶⁰ Here, John Paul explains that martyrdom "represents the high point of the witness to moral truth," thus differentiating the martyr from the non-martyr. Combining this fact with the martyr's willing acceptance of death in order to remain faithful to God's law, one might surmise that death, or the voluntary acceptance of death, as Susanna's case qualifies, is the apex of witnessing to truth. Similar to his thought in *Dominum et Vivificantem* 60, the Pope again expresses the daily witness of Christians, noting the "suffering and grave sacrifice" that one's fidelity to Christ can sometimes evoke.

> Although martyrdom represents the high point of the witness to moral truth, and one to which relatively few people are called, there is nonetheless a consistent witness which all Christians must daily be ready to make, even at the cost of suffering and grave sacrifice. Indeed, faced with the many difficulties which fidelity to the moral order can demand, even in the most ordinary circumstances, the Christian is called, with the grace of God invoked in prayer, to a sometimes heroic commitment. In this he or she is sustained by the virtue of fortitude, whereby—as Gregory the Great teaches—one can actually 'love the difficulties of this world for the sake of eternal rewards.'⁶¹

---

⁶⁰ John Paul II, *Veritatis Splendor* 93.
⁶¹ John Paul II, *Veritatis Splendor* 93.

Martyrdom, then, represents the paradigm of one's witness to moral truth. The willing acceptance of death by the martyr leaves no doubt in the minds of others where that person stands regarding Christ Jesus and the Commandments. Although most are not called to martyrdom, each follower of Jesus must be prepared to offer the sacrifice of his life should circumstances require it.

**"Out of Love of Physical Life," Do Not "Lose the Very Reason for Living"**

In *Veritatis Splendor* 94, one might find it surprising that the Holy Father does not directly refer to martyrdom. In fact, John Paul's next mention of martyrdom does not occur until paragraph 102. In my reading of paragraph 94, however, I find a summary of his teaching on martyrdom, and thus, I place *Veritatis Splendor* 94 together with what I regard as the Pontiff's central teaching on martyrdom.

To recapitulate, in the *Introduction* to my project, I offer an initial, but comprehensive definition of martyrdom according to John Paul. Throughout my work, I analyze of this definition, drawing together the Pope's noteworthy statements on martyrdom in an orderly and systematic manner. As I show, martyrdom centers on "fidelity to God's holy law, witnessed to by death."[62] With the *Veritatis Splendor* account, I further explain the martyr's death as an affirmation of "the inviolability of the moral order [that] bears splendid witness" to "the holiness of the Church," to "the holiness

---

[62] John Paul II, *Veritatis Splendor* 93.

## Chapter Twelve: Martyrdom Affirms "Inviolability of Moral Order"

of God's law and to the inviolability of the personal dignity" and freedom of the human person.[63] Moreover, martyrdom is "the exaltation of a person's perfect 'humanity' and of true 'life,'" which paragraph 92 highlights, and which the *Letter to the Romans* of Saint Ignatius of Antioch particularly elucidates.[64] As paragraph 93 explains, the martyr's testimony, differentiated from that of the non-martyr's witness by death, "represents the high point of the witness to moral truth."[65]

In *Veritatis Splendor* 94, John Paul supports his claims regarding both the universality of truth and the objectivity of the moral order. Because truth is objective, it is not confined to the Catholic Church. Neither is truth limited to Christianity, since the "interior and mysterious workings of God's Spirit are not absent" in other religious denominations and sapiential traditions.[66] Thus, the Pope calls upon the fidelity of all people to witness to the "absoluteness of the moral good."[67]

Regardless of one's religious denomination, then, accepting the truth strengthens a person, as John Paul expresses in *Veritatis Splendor* 87. Whether or not one is martyred, truth is objective; consequently, "there are truths and moral values for which one must be prepared to give up one's life."[68] The Holy Father express-

---

[63] John Paul II, *Veritatis Splendor* 92, 93, 90.
[64] John Paul II, *Veritatis Splendor* 92.
[65] John Paul II, *Veritatis Splendor* 93.
[66] John Paul II, *Veritatis Splendor* 94.
[67] John Paul II, *Veritatis Splendor* 94.
[68] John Paul II, *Veritatis Splendor* 94.

es below what the objectivity of the moral order means for all people of all time.

> In this witness to the absoluteness of the moral good Christians are not alone: they are supported by the moral sense present in peoples and by the great religious and sapiential traditions of East and West, from which the interior and mysterious workings of God's Spirit are not absent. The words of the Latin poet Juvenal apply to all: 'Consider it the greatest of crimes to prefer survival to honor and, out of love of physical life, to lose the very reason for living.'[69]

Given the fact that John Paul specifies "the moral sense present" in others, one might question the validity of highlighting the martyr who is Catholic. Since truth is objective, it does not—it *cannot*—depend on one's religious affiliation. Nonetheless, everything that Jesus Christ teaches through His Church, which is the Catholic Church, that is, Sacred Scripture and Sacred Tradition, is objectively true. When any person knows that truth, he is set "free in the face of worldly power."[70]

In order to support the fact that one cannot confine martyrdom to Catholicism, I offer a number of incisive texts from the Conciliar document, *Lumen Gentium*. First, Jesus both established and continues to sustain the Catholic Church, "through which He communicated truth and grace to all," including those outside full

---

[69] John Paul II, *Veritatis Splendor* 94.
[70] John Paul II, *Veritatis Splendor* 87.

membership.⁷¹ Second, as the Conciliar document testifies, some Christians who are not Catholic have been strengthened by Christ "to the extent of the shedding of their blood," because "elements of sanctification and of truth are found outside of [the] visible structure" of Holy Mother Church."⁷² Martyrdom exists within other ecclesial communities, as the Pope explains in *Ut Unum Sint*, and the basis for martyrs of other ecclesial communities is rooted in the

---

⁷¹ Second Vatican Council, *Lumen Gentium* 8. Moreover, the Conciliar document explains that non-Catholic Christians are united in some way to the Catholic Church, although they are without full membership. *Lumen Gentium* explains, "in some real way they [Christians who are not Catholic] are joined with us [the Church] in the Holy Spirit, for to them too He gives His gifts and graces whereby He is operative among them with His sanctifying power" [Second Vatican Council, *Lumen Gentium* 15]. *Lumen Gentium* defines full membership in the Church in paragraph 14. "They are fully incorporated in the society of the Church who, possessing the Spirit of Christ accept her entire system and all the means of salvation given to her, and are united with her as part of her visible bodily structure and through her with Christ, who rules her through the Supreme Pontiff and the bishops. The bonds which bind men to the Church in a visible way are profession of faith, the sacraments, and ecclesiastical government and communion. He is not saved, however, who, though part of the body of the Church, does not persevere in charity. He remains indeed in the bosom of the Church, but, as it were, only in a 'bodily' manner and not 'in his heart.' All the Church's children should remember that their exalted status is to be attributed not to their own merits but to the special grace of Christ. If they fail moreover to respond to that grace in thought, word and deed, not only shall they not be saved but they will be the more severely judged" [Second Vatican Council, *Lumen Gentium* 14].

⁷² Second Vatican Council, *Lumen Gentium* 15, 8.

fact that truth is objective and the law of God is objective.[73] Again, truth and the law of God, which *is* truth, is, for all people of all time, objectively true. Finally, *Lumen Gentium* explains that all are called to salvation through Jesus Christ.

> All men are called to be part of this Catholic unity of the people of God which in promoting universal peace presages it. And there belong to or are related to it in various ways, the Catholic faithful, all who believe in Christ, and indeed the whole of mankind, for all men are called by the grace of God to salvation.[74]

With the clarity of these *Lumen Gentium* passages in mind, I note that, because the Church founded by Jesus Christ "subsists in the Catholic Church," her martyrs are witnesses to the *fullness* of truth, which the Catholic Church safeguards.[75] As *Dominus Iesus*

---

[73] Several key paragraphs from John Paul II, *Ut Unum Sint*, already cited above, include 1, 10, 83, 84, and 86. I further expound upon John Paul's articulation of martyrdom in *Ut Unum Sint* in the next chapter.

[74] Second Vatican Council, *Lumen Gentium* 13.

[75] John Paul quotes, in *Ut Unum Sint* 10 and 86, the Conciliar teaching on this subject, which is located in *Lumen Gentium* 8. *Dominus Iesus* 16 offers precise clarification of the term, *subsist*. The document explains that the Church, "'constituted and organized as a society in the present world, subsists in [*subsistit in*] the Catholic Church, governed by the Successor of Peter and by the Bishops in communion with him.' With the expression *subsistit in*, the Second Vatican Council sought to harmonize two doctrinal statements: on the one hand, that the Church of Christ, despite the divisions which exist among Christians, continues to exist fully only in the Catholic Church, and on the other hand, that 'outside of her structure,

makes clear, "the fullness of Christ's salvific mystery belongs...to the Church, inseparably united to her Lord."[76] Thus, the Catholic is the clearest example of the martyr because, beyond a shadow of doubt, he professes the fullness of truth found in the Catholic Church.[77] He is willing to die to uphold her teaching in faith and morals.

Nonetheless, because the moral law is objective, its own objectivity implies that each person must be ready to die in order to uphold it. The obligation is placed upon every human person, because truth's objectivity means it does not depend upon one's religious denomination, one's interpretation, or upon a government's ideologies. The natural law is imprinted on the heart of every person. Consequently, "every rational creature knows it," to a greater or lesser extent, at least in regard to "the common principles of the natural law."[78] In addition, the Holy Father implies, and *Lumen Gentium* infers, that the existence of an objective moral order places certain demands upon each human being. These demands sug-

---

many elements can be found of sanctification and truth,' that is, in those Churches and ecclesial communities which are not yet in full communion with the Catholic Church. But with respect to these, it needs to be stated that 'they derive their efficacy from the very fullness of grace and truth entrusted to the Catholic Church'" [Congregation for the Doctrine of the Faith, *Dominus Iesus* 16].

[76] Congregation for the Doctrine of the Faith, *Dominus Iesus* 16.

[77] At the same time, numerous martyrs of the Church, such as the early Christian martyrs, offered their lives without full knowledge or full understanding, perhaps, of the teachings of Christ and His Church. Thus, God's grace provides, and His grace does not depend upon human knowledge.

[78] Thomas Aquinas, *Summa Theologiae* I-II, 93, 2.

gest, once again, that martyrdom entails the sacrifice of one's life in order to uphold the teaching of faith and the objective moral order. John Paul explains these thoughts as follows.

> The voice of conscience has always clearly recalled that there are truths and moral values for which one must be prepared to give up one's life. In an individual's words and above all in the sacrifice of his life for a moral value, the Church sees a single testimony to that truth which, already present in creation, shines forth in its fullness on the face of Christ. As Saint Justin put it, 'the Stoics, at least in their teachings on ethics, demonstrated wisdom, thanks to the seed of the Word present in all peoples, and we know that those who followed their doctrines met with hatred and were killed.'[79]

In the passage above, one finds additional support for focusing upon the martyr who is a full member of the Catholic Church. The Holy Father mentions that the Catholic Church perceives and judges that "single testimony" to the truth "which, already present in creation, shines forth in its fullness on the face of Christ."[80]

The *Veritatis Splendor* 94 quotation, then, raises two factors. First, the Church, as Mother and Teacher, sees and judges truth "present in creation." Second, the fullness of truth "shines forth in its fullness on the face of Christ." In other words, the Church

---

[79] John Paul II, *Veritatis Splendor* 94.
[80] John Paul II, *Veritatis Splendor* 94.

founded by Jesus Christ subsists in the Catholic Church, and the Church safeguards the fullness of truth, found in Christ's teachings. Further, Jesus, who is Truth, calls all people to Himself, praying that all might be one with Him, embracing the fullness of truth (cf. John 14:6; 17:21-23).

One might summarize my extrapolation of *Veritatis Splendor* 94 as follows. The "moral sense present" in others, of which the Pope speaks, reiterates the fact that all "are bound to seek the truth…and to embrace the truth they come to know, and to hold fast to it."[81] Since truth is objective, it *cannot* depend upon a person's religious affiliation. Nonetheless, the "many elements of sanctification and of truth" that are found outside of the Church's visible structure, "gifts properly belonging to the Church of Christ, possess an inner dynamism towards Catholic unity."[82] Thus, highlighting the *Catholic* who is a martyr offers clear testimony to the

---

[81] Second Vatican Council, *Dignitatis Humanae* 1.

[82] John Paul II, *Ut Unum Sint* 10. This text recalls the Conciliar teaching that "elements of sanctification and of truth are found outside of [the] visible structure" of the Church with the following passage. "This is the one Church of Christ which in the Creed is professed as one, holy, catholic and apostolic, which our Savior, after His Resurrection, commissioned Peter to shepherd, and him and the other Apostles to extend and direct with authority, which He erected for all ages as 'the pillar and mainstay of the truth.' This Church constituted and organized in the world as a society, subsists in the Catholic Church, which is governed by the successor of Peter and by the Bishops in communion with him, although many elements of sanctification and of truth are found outside of its visible structure. These elements, as gifts belonging to the Church of Christ, are forces impelling toward Catholic unity" [Second Vatican Council, *Lumen Gentium* 8].

objective moral order and to the profusion of truth, which shines in its "fullness on the face of Christ" since he believes and embraces the fullness of truth. Indeed, he is willing to lay down his life for it.

## The Catholic Church Interprets and Safeguards Moral Norms

In *Veritatis Splendor* 95 to 101, until just before his next mention of martyrdom, John Paul reiterates that the Church is the interpreter of the moral norm and not the "author or the arbiter of this norm."[83] Further, given the connection between one's obedience to moral norms and human dignity, the Pope teaches, "In obedience to the Truth [who] is Christ, whose image is reflected in the nature and dignity of the human person, the Church interprets the moral norm and proposes it to all people of good will."[84] For example, paragraph 95 speaks of the dignity of the human person and the Church's responsibility of safeguarding him. Because "there can be no freedom apart from or in opposition to the truth," the demands of human dignity "must be considered the way and the condition for the very existence of freedom."[85]

In addition to supporting human dignity, the Pope also reaffirms the fact that, for one's own good, intrinsically evil acts are forbidden.[86] Because moral norms protect the human person, particularly those norms, which prohibit intrinsically evil acts, they

---

[83] John Paul II, *Veritatis Splendor* 95.
[84] John Paul II, *Veritatis Splendor* 95.
[85] John Paul II, *Veritatis Splendor* 96.
[86] John Paul II, *Veritatis Splendor* 96.

likewise "help to preserve the human social fabric."[87] John Paul summarizes the moral code by teaching that "only a morality which acknowledges certain norms as valid always and for everyone, with no exception, can guarantee the ethical foundation of social coexistence, both on the national and international levels."[88]

The intervening paragraphs before the Pope's next mention of martyrdom offer him the opportunity to emphasize, once again, the importance of objective truth. Earlier, I mention his teaching on relativism, which endangers the good of the human person because the "saving power of the truth is contested, and freedom alone, uprooted from any objectivity, is left to decide by itself what is good and what is evil."[89] In paragraph 99, the Pope identifies totalitarianism as an additional error that results from the denial of objective truth. Although I extrapolate this text above in order to show the transcendent nature of truth, the Holy Father mentions it in *Veritatis Splendor* for a different purpose.

Since God "constitutes the unshakable foundation and essential condition of morality, and thus, of the Commandments," John Paul explains that the "supreme Good and the moral good meet in truth: the truth of God, the Creator and Redeemer, and the truth of man, created and redeemed by Him."[90] Specifically identifying the human person as created and redeemed by God, one finds a synopsis of the Holy Father's central anthropological concern in paragraph 99. The human person is "the visible image of the invisible

---

[87] John Paul II, *Veritatis Splendor* 96, 97.
[88] John Paul II, *Veritatis Splendor* 97.
[89] John Paul II, *Veritatis Splendor* 84.
[90] John Paul II, *Veritatis Splendor* 99.

God."⁹¹ Specifically because the person has the status of being created in the image of God, John Paul reiterates his concern for human dignity. He notes the fact that modern totalitarianism denies the "transcendent dignity of the human person."⁹²

Before his next mention of martyrdom, John Paul emphasizes a final point that concerns "the risk of an alliance between democracy and ethical relativism."⁹³ I underscore the Pope's thought specifically because he warns that such an alliance might "remove any sure moral reference point from political and social life, and, on a deeper level, make the acknowledgement of truth impossible."⁹⁴ His purpose is to endorse the "ultimate truth" and to defend the human person.

If one rejects objective truth, then "ideas and convictions can easily be manipulated for reasons of power," and that leads to totalitarianism.⁹⁵ Thus, the Pope reiterates the fact that "morality—founded upon truth and open in truth to authentic freedom—renders a primordial, indispensable and immensely valuable service not only for the individual person and his growth in the good, but also for society and its genuine development."⁹⁶ Objective truth binds a people, a nation, and the world together.

---

[91] John Paul II, *Veritatis Splendor* 99.
[92] John Paul II, *Veritatis Splendor* 99.
[93] John Paul II, *Veritatis Splendor* 101.
[94] John Paul II, *Veritatis Splendor* 101.
[95] John Paul II, *Veritatis Splendor* 101.
[96] John Paul II, *Veritatis Splendor* 101.

## "Maintaining a Harmony Between Freedom and Truth"

Having recounted various dangers to the human person that can occur when one denies the objectivity of truth and morality, in the paragraphs leading to his next mention of martyrdom, John Paul reminds the reader that obedience to God's law, which comprises "a harmony between freedom and truth," might demand martyrdom.[97] The Holy Father explains this thought in the following passage.

> Even in the most difficult situations man must respect the norm of morality so that he can be obedient to God's holy Commandment and consistent with his own dignity as a person. Certainly, maintaining a harmony between freedom and truth occasionally demands uncommon sacrifices, and must be won at a high price: it can even involve martyrdom.[98]

Although martyrdom "represents the high point of the witness to moral truth," the human person is inclined to sin.[99] The Pope comes back to the point of differentiating between good and evil by noting the "ultimate source of this inner division of man."[100] Due to original sin, the human person is inclined to be his own arbiter of right and wrong.

---

[97] John Paul II, *Veritatis Splendor* 102.
[98] John Paul II, *Veritatis Splendor* 102.
[99] John Paul II, *Veritatis Splendor* 93; 102.
[100] John Paul II, *Veritatis Splendor* 102.

His history of sin begins when he no longer acknowledges the Lord as his Creator and himself wishes to be the one who determines, with complete independence, what is good and what is evil. 'You will be like God, knowing good and evil' (Genesis 3:5): this was the first temptation, and it is echoed in all the other temptations to which man is more easily inclined to yield as a result of the original Fall.[101]

While he acknowledges the person's inclination to sin, John Paul recognizes the ability to overcome temptation and sin, with the help of God's grace, even in challenging circumstances. Quoting Saint Augustine, John Paul explains that "God does not command the impossible, but in commanding He admonishes you to do what you can and to pray for what you cannot, and He gives His aid to enable you."[102]

## Conclusions to John Paul's Thought in *Veritatis Splendor*

Given my work on *Veritatis Splendor*, paragraph 103 strikes me as a concise statement of the Pope's thought on the human person and martyrdom. While the Holy Father does not specifically mention martyrdom in *Veritatis Splendor* after paragraph 102, one might interpret the following paragraph as a text that specifies the source of the martyr's fidelity to God's law. The source of his fideli-

---

[101] John Paul II, *Veritatis Splendor* 102.

[102] The footnote in John Paul II, *Veritatis Splendor* 102 refers to the Council of Trent's quotation of this well-known passage from Saint Augustine's *De Natura et Gratia*.

ty is nothing other than the grace of God. Every martyr endures suffering, persecution and death only with God's grace, which is absolutely necessary.

Although the Pope does not specify the martyr, since God's grace is available to all, John Paul offers a characteristic word of hope to each person. He teaches that one "always has before him the spiritual horizon of hope, thanks to the help of divine grace and with the cooperation of human freedom."[103] One can pray for grace and one receives grace through the sacraments. The Holy Father enumerates the various means through which God confers His grace.

> It is in the saving Cross of Jesus, in the gift of the Holy Spirit, in the Sacraments which flow forth from the pierced side of the Redeemer (cf. John 19:34), that believers find the grace and the strength always to keep God's holy law, even amid the gravest of hardships.[104]

The next section of *Veritatis Splendor*, 103, offers a synopsis of John Paul's concept of the human person. First, he teaches that "Only in the mystery of Christ's Redemption do we discover the 'concrete' possibilities of man."[105] Earlier, I highlighted the Holy Father's interpretation of the *mystery* of human person as one who, loved by God, has been created by Him and redeemed by the Son. In paragraph 103, John Paul emphasizes the depth of influence

---

[103] John Paul II, *Veritatis Splendor* 103.
[104] John Paul II, *Veritatis Splendor* 103.
[105] John Paul II, *Veritatis Splendor* 103.

Christ's redemption has upon the human person. He expresses the saving power of Christ's act on the Cross by articulating its profundity in formidable language.

> But what are the 'concrete possibilities of man?' And of which man are we speaking? Of man dominated by lust or of man redeemed by Christ? This is what is at stake: the reality of Christ's redemption. Christ has redeemed us! This means that He has given us the possibility of realizing the entire truth of our being; He has set our freedom free from the domination of concupiscence. And if redeemed man still sins, this is not due to an imperfection of Christ's redemptive act, but to man's will not to avail himself of the grace which flows from that act. God's command is of course proportioned to man's capabilities; but to the capabilities of the man to whom the Holy Spirit has been given; of the man who, though he has fallen into sin, can always obtain pardon and enjoy the presence of the Holy Spirit.[106]

Realizing the power of Christ's redemption, the martyr relies upon God's grace to remain faithful to His law, even when it costs his physical life. Moreover, when the human person realizes the immense love of God, poured out upon humanity through the Passion and death of Jesus, the person has the "possibility of realizing the entire truth" of one's being.[107] Living as one who understands

---

[106] John Paul II, *Veritatis Splendor* 103.
[107] John Paul II, *Veritatis Splendor* 103.

## Chapter Twelve: Martyrdom Affirms "Inviolability of Moral Order"

the fact that he has been redeemed by Jesus means that he "avails himself of the grace which flows from that act."[108]

My reading of *Veritatis Splendor* in the present section shows that the martyr is a human person whose realization of God's love for him is articulated in his own dependence upon God's grace. The martyr relies upon the grace of God as he puts the "precepts and love [of Jesus] into practice."[109] He depends upon that grace in the "saving Cross of Jesus, in the gift of the Holy Spirit, [and] in the Sacraments which flow forth from the pierced side of the Redeemer" since only with His grace will he have the "strength always to keep God's holy law, even amid the gravest of hardships."[110]

My second conclusion from *Veritatis Splendor* concerns the contemplative dimension of listening and obedience to the holy law of God. Susanna's example shows one's faith as a contemplative listening to God's law, which involves "one's whole existence."[111] Her faith, described as "trusting abandonment," expresses her innocence and her faithfulness to God's law.[112] In her dialogue with God, she makes "an act of trusting abandonment," which expresses her voluntary acceptance of death in order to remain faithful.[113]

An additional concluding reflection to the encyclical, then, is to see John Paul's wisdom in discussing these subjects. His expressed

---

[108] John Paul II, *Veritatis Splendor* 103.
[109] John Paul II, *Veritatis Splendor* 27.
[110] John Paul II, *Veritatis Splendor* 103.
[111] John Paul II, *Veritatis Splendor* 88.
[112] John Paul II, *Veritatis Splendor* 88.
[113] John Paul II, *Veritatis Splendor* 88.

intent is "to discern in obedience to the moral law a grace and a sign of our adoption in the one Son (cf. Ephesians 1:4-6)."[114] In other words, the underlying theme of each related topic is directed toward the human person's coming to "the stature of the fullness of Christ" (Ephesians 4:13). God wants the person to grow in holiness by one's dependence upon His grace; in this manner, the person becomes a child of God.

My concluding thought from *Veritatis Splendor* 103, then, centers upon the human person's redemption by Christ. Combining the person's redemption with the Holy Father's desire that each person come to "the stature of the fullness of Christ" yields the following inference (Ephesians 4:13). My interpretation of paragraph 103 shows that the martyr's redemption by Christ is an expression of his dependence upon God's grace. But, as *Redemptor Hominis* 9 shows, the renewal of creation is a "tremendous mystery of love." Christ's redemptive act renews creation in and through His own heart: by "the fullness of justice in...the heart of the first-born Son."[115] As the Pope further explains, Christ renews creation in order that the person, the apex of visible creation, "predestined from eternity in the first-born Son," may become a child of the Father who is "called to grace, called to love."[116] The martyr's dependence upon God's grace shows, at the moment of his death, that he has become the child that the Father desires him to be from eternity.

One might ask, what does it mean to say that the martyr depends upon God's grace? Naturally, every person is embraced by

---

[114] John Paul II, *Veritatis Splendor* 115.
[115] John Paul II, *Redemptor Hominis* 9.
[116] John Paul II, *Redemptor Hominis* 9.

God's providential love. Even more, each person needs the grace of God in order to "perform supernatural actions that lead to Heaven."[117] One might interpret the Pope's thought, then, as a depiction of the martyr's dependence upon God's grace expressed as an obedient listening to God, who first loved him.

John Paul explains holiness as listening to "the call of the One who 'first loved us' (1 John 4:19)" and one listens to this call by following the Commandments.[118] He explains, "God asks us to be holy as He is holy (cf. Leviticus 19:2) [and] to be in Christ perfect as He is perfect (cf. Matthew 5:48)."[119] To be sure, the teachings of the Church, particularly her defense of "the universal and permanent validity of the precepts prohibiting intrinsically evil acts," are a sign of God's love.[120] John Paul explains that the demands of the Commandment to love are "based upon God's infinitely merciful love (cf. Luke 6:36), and the purpose of that Commandment is to lead us, by the grace of Christ, on the path of that fullness of life proper

---

[117] Grace is necessary for salvation. No one can reach Heaven without God's grace since the Beatific Vision is a supernatural end beyond man's natural powers and capacities to attain on one's own [John A. Hardon, S.J., *Catholic Dictionary*, "Grace" 195-196; Thomas Aquinas, *Summa Theologiae* I-II, 109, 5; I-II, 114, 2]. Further, "Actual Grace" is "Temporary supernatural intervention by God to enlighten the mind or strengthen the will to perform supernatural actions that lead to Heaven" [John A. Hardon, S.J., *Catholic Dictionary*, "Actual Grace" 9; Thomas Aquinas, *Summa Theologiae* I-II, 110, 1]. As the Angelic Doctor makes clear, the person needs God's grace to abide by His holy law [Thomas Aquinas, *Summa Theologiae* I-II, 109, 4].

[118] John Paul II, *Veritatis Splendor* 115.
[119] John Paul II, *Veritatis Splendor* 115.
[120] John Paul II, *Veritatis Splendor* 95.

to the children of God."[121] The human person is called to love God and neighbor. With God's grace, he can do so.

## Veritatis Splendor and Martyrdom

In the *Introduction* to my project, I connect several of John Paul's statements on martyrdom in order to offer the reader a concise definition. To state it again, in *Veritatis Splendor*, John Paul sees martyrdom as "fidelity to God's holy law, witnessed to by death."[122] This death affirms "the inviolability of the moral order [and] bears splendid witness"[123] to "the holiness of the Church,"[124] to "the holiness of God's law and to the inviolability of the personal dignity of man."[125] Martyrdom "is also the exaltation of a person's perfect 'humanity' and of true 'life,'"[126] and it "represents the high point of the witness to moral truth."[127] Having put forth the Pontiff's teaching on various aspects of this definition, as it arises in *Veritatis Splendor*, one might draw several conclusions.

In my paragraph analysis of *Veritatis Splendor*, one first sees that the distinguishing characteristic between the martyr and any follower of Christ who is faithful to "God's law" is the martyr's willing acceptance of death in order to remain faithful to that

---

[121] John Paul II, *Veritatis Splendor* 115.
[122] John Paul II, *Veritatis Splendor* 93.
[123] John Paul II, *Veritatis Splendor* 92.
[124] John Paul II, *Veritatis Splendor* 93.
[125] John Paul II, *Veritatis Splendor* 92, 90.
[126] John Paul II, *Veritatis Splendor* 92.
[127] John Paul II, *Veritatis Splendor* 93.

## Chapter Twelve: Martyrdom Affirms "Inviolability of Moral Order"

law.[128] While persecution is the guarantee of every faithful follower of Christ (Matthew 5:10-11), thus generating the notion of *martyrdom* in a metaphorical sense, the martyr's willingness to die dispels confusion between actual martyrdom and *martyrdom* used in a metaphorical sense.

In the present section of my project, I focus upon significant concepts that ultimately lead to an interpretation of the martyr's death as a contemplation of Christ's face. For example, from *Veritatis Splendor*, I have brought out the Holy Father's thought on human freedom and "the fundamental values connected with the dignity of the person and the truth of his acts."[129] Further, my extrapolation of *Veritatis Splendor* shows John Paul's insistence upon the objective moral order and the moral norm as a universal, immutable principle that upholds human dignity and inviolability.[130] Another point of emphasis from *Veritatis Splendor* is the Pope's reaffirmation of "the universality and immutability of the moral Commandments, particularly those which prohibit always and without exception intrinsically evil acts."[131]

The martyr's willing acceptance of death is not only an act of human *freedom*, and not *coercion*, but also, his death expresses human freedom as the "high point" of witnessing to moral truth."[132] The martyr's death proclaims human freedom because by it, he makes known his decision about himself in a concrete man-

---

[128] John Paul II, *Veritatis Splendor* 93, 91.
[129] John Paul II, *Veritatis Splendor* 115.
[130] John Paul II, *Veritatis Splendor* 90.
[131] John Paul II, *Veritatis Splendor* 115.
[132] John Paul II, *Veritatis Splendor* 93.

ner. Because the martyr's death upholds the moral law, and because it puts the "precepts and love [of Jesus] into practice," it expresses truth.[133]

As I show above, relativism pivots the human person against "the saving power of the truth," dictating that he decide by himself "what is good and what is evil."[134] The martyr's death testifies to the objectivity of truth and of the moral order, announcing the existence of a higher order of being than one's own individual whim; the human person is *not* the sole arbiter of his person. The martyr's death reverses the relativist's "lack of trust in the wisdom of God, who guides man with the moral law" and becomes instead a human expression of confidence and trust in God's all-wise plan for the human person, which is *His* law; that law "is always the one true good of man."[135]

Precisely *because* death is the summation of one's life upon earth, and *because* the martyr's death expresses the utter conviction of one who knows exactly "who he is, whence he comes and where he is going," sacrificing his life to defend the objective moral order pronounces that truth in a manner that indicates its radiant splendor.[136] Christ Crucified is "the Truth which gives of itself."[137]

My interpretation of *Veritatis Splendor* suggests that the person who lives the truth radiates a brilliance, which "shines forth ... in man, created in the image and likeness of God (cf. Genesis

---

[133] John Paul II, *Veritatis Splendor* 27.
[134] John Paul II, *Veritatis Splendor* 84.
[135] John Paul II, *Veritatis Splendor* 84.
[136] John Paul II, *Veritatis Splendor* 84.
[137] John Paul II, *Veritatis Splendor* 117.

1:26)."¹³⁸ This passage, together with the work on this encyclical extrapolated above, clearly emphasizes the importance of the human person's creation in the image of God. It also specifies the profundity of living in the Truth, who is Jesus Christ. Further, in my opinion, *Veritatis Splendor* shows a link between truth on one hand, and faith and reason on the other hand. Truth, which the martyr vividly radiates, not only "enlightens man's intelligence and shapes his freedom," but also it leads him "to know and love the Lord."¹³⁹

When John Paul teaches that Jesus is "the revelation of God's mercy," one thinks of His redemptive death on the Cross.¹⁴⁰ Further, the Holy Father explains that "No human sin can erase the mercy of God, or prevent Him from unleashing all His triumphant power, if we only call upon Him."¹⁴¹ The Holy Father explains the power of Christ's redemptive act.

> Indeed, sin itself makes even more radiant the Love of the Father who, in order to ransom a slave, sacrificed His Son: His mercy towards us is Redemption. This mercy reaches its fullness in the gift of the Spirit who bestows new life and demands that it be lived. No matter how many and great the obstacles put in His way by human frailty and sin, the Spirit, who renews the face of the earth (cf. Psalms 104:30), makes possible the miracle of the perfect accomplishment

---

¹³⁸ John Paul II, *Veritatis Splendor* Prior to the *Introduction*.
¹³⁹ John Paul II, *Veritatis Splendor* Prior to the *Introduction*.
¹⁴⁰ John Paul II, *Veritatis Splendor* 118.
¹⁴¹ John Paul II, *Veritatis Splendor* 118.

of the good. This renewal, which gives the ability to do what is good, noble, beautiful, pleasing to God and in conformity with His will, is in some way the flowering of the gift of mercy, which offers liberation from the slavery of evil and gives the strength to sin no more. Through the gift of new life, Jesus makes us sharers in His love and leads us to the Father in the Spirit.[142]

Connecting these thoughts with martyrdom, one might surmise the following. While being martyred expresses freedom and dignity by living truth, the perpetrators of martyrdom, one would logically conclude, are enslaved by a false sense of freedom and a distorted notion of truth. But, those who inflict martyrdom, make "even more radiant the love of the Father."[143] Moreover, the martyr is a prime example of a follower of Christ because, in "abandoning oneself to Him, in letting oneself be transformed by His grace and renewed by His mercy," the martyr radiates t/Truth and the face of Christ Jesus.[144] A concluding idea from *Veritatis Splendor* 119 appropriately summarizes this section.

> By the light of the Holy Spirit, the living essence of Christian morality can be understood by everyone, even the least learned, but particularly those who are able to preserve an 'undivided heart' (Psalms 86:11). On the other hand, this evangelical simplicity does not exempt one from facing reality in its complexi-

---

[142] John Paul II, *Veritatis Splendor* 118.
[143] John Paul II, *Veritatis Splendor* 118.
[144] John Paul II, *Veritatis Splendor* 119.

ty; rather it can lead to a more genuine understanding of reality, inasmuch as following Christ will gradually bring out the distinctive character of authentic Christian morality, while providing the vital energy needed to carry it out.[145]

Contrary to the Cross of Christ being "emptied of its power," then, the martyr shows, by his witness to Christ who is Truth, that His Cross is *filled* with power. Jesus sustains the martyr in the suffering and death he endures.

---

[145] John Paul II, *Veritatis Splendor* 119.

# Chapter Thirteen

# Additional Encyclicals on Martyrdom

While John Paul's central teaching on martyrdom lies in *Veritatis Splendor*, several additional texts add certain clarifications, elaborations, or distinctions necessary to the topic. My intent in this section is to offer those texts, which further develop the concept of martyrdom from the Holy Father's writings.

### *Redemptoris Missio*: Bearing "Witness to One's Faith in Jesus Christ"

In *Redemptoris Missio* 11, John Paul speaks of the martyr as the person who witnesses to one's "faith in Christ, the one Savior of mankind, a faith we have received as a gift from on high, not as a result of any merit of our own." The Pope highlights the person's need for Jesus, noting that He reconciles each one to God the Father.

> Christian martyrs of all times—including our own—have given and continue to give their lives in order to bear witness to this faith, in the conviction that every human being needs Jesus Christ, who has conquered sin and death and reconciled mankind to God.[1]

---

[1] John Paul II, *Redemptoris Missio* 11.

*Redemptoris Missio* 11 recalls John Paul's anthropological view that Jesus redeems the human person. Moreover, *Redemptoris Missio* 11 reiterates my conclusion from *Veritatis Splendor* 103, regarding the power of Christ's redemptive death. Because the martyr's death unites a person to Christ, as the *Letter to the Romans* of Saint Ignatius of Antioch confirms, the martyr's witness to Jesus also shows one's deep-seated human need for Him. Indeed, the person is created for God. Nothing else offers lasting satisfaction, happiness, or joy. While each person needs Christ's redemption, the martyr shows Jesus to others by his own death, offered on account of his fidelity to Him.

The Holy Father continues to speak of human freedom within the context of martyrdom. In *Redemptoris Missio* 11, he teaches that since "true liberation consists in opening oneself to the love of Christ" one finds that, in Him, the human person is "set free from all alienation and doubt, from slavery to the power of sin and death."

The Pope's insight on freedom as an opening of "oneself to the love of Christ" recalls the notion from *Salvifici Doloris* 28 that specifies one's opening of oneself to another who suffers. While I have explained above that the human person is ontologically dependent on God, and, therefore, open to Him, turning to Jesus with one's intellect and will, and realizing the love God has for him, frees a person. It is liberating. This redemptive love of Christ involves the entire person, as the Pope explains. The salvation that "Jesus came

## Chapter Thirteen: Additional Encyclicals on Martyrdom

to bring...embraces the whole person and all mankind and opens up the wondrous prospect of divine filiation."[2]

The second significant text on martyrdom from *Redemptoris Missio* is paragraph 45. In this passage, John Paul brings out the fact that, whether one has heard of Jesus, "there already exists in individuals and peoples an expectation, even if an unconscious one, of knowing the truth about God, about man, and about how we are to be set free from sin and death."

In the "unconscious expectation" of which the Pope speaks, one appreciates the human person's longing for truth. But, since proclamation is an act that is always "made in union with the entire ecclesial community," the missionary knows that "he is not proclaiming a human truth, but the 'word of God,' which has an intrinsic and mysterious power of its own (cf. Romans 1:16)."[3] In light of these observations about truth, John Paul explains martyrdom as a *giving* of one's life and an accepting of one's *death*.

> The supreme test is the giving of one's life, to the point of accepting death in order to bear witness to one's faith in Jesus Christ. Throughout Christian history, martyrs, that is, 'witnesses,' have always been numerous and indispensable to the spread of the Gospel. In our own age, there are many: bishops, priests, men and women religious, lay people—often unknown heroes who give their lives to bear witness

---

[2] John Paul II, *Redemptoris Missio* 11.
[3] John Paul II, *Redemptoris Missio* 45.

to the Faith. They are *par excellence* the heralds and witnesses of the Faith.[4]

With *Redemptoris Missio* 45, the Holy Father pointedly uses the word *witness* to refer to the martyr, emphasizing that one's testimony is offered on account of one's faith in Jesus. A noteworthy distinction in paragraph 45 identifies the martyr as both a *herald* and a *witness*. Thus, one might interpret John Paul's focus on the martyr's death as a *heralding* or a proclamation of his faith in Jesus. In the present context, one finds that a herald is one who proclaims his faith in Jesus. Here, John Paul uses the word *witness* to specify a martyr as one who gives his life "to bear witness to the Faith." Finally, the quotation shows that, once again, John Paul employs the martyr as the prime example of the point he makes: the martyr is the leading exemplar of both a herald and a witness to the Faith.

Combining *Veritatis Splendor* with the martyr's death as a heralding of his faith in Jesus, one gains the following insight. First, as *Veritatis Splendor* brings out, truth is objective. The martyr's death unites others in Christ on account of the unchanging nature of truth, and of the moral order, as well.[5] In addition to the martyr's

---

[4] John Paul II, *Redemptoris Missio* 45.

[5] The martyr's death bears witness to the objectivity of truth and to the objectivity of the moral order, as I state above. To be sure, this "bearing witness" unites others to Christ Jesus. But the martyr's death unites others to Jesus for another reason, as well. Because the death of the martyr proclaims Jesus, and, because proclamation is "never a merely personal act," but one that is always "made in union with the entire ecclesial community," then the martyr's death unites others together in Jesus through His Church [John Paul II, *Redemptoris Missio* 45]. In other

death bearing witness to objective truth and thus, to the objective moral order, *Redemptoris Missio* 45 teaches that the martyr's death *heralds*, or proclaims, his faith in Jesus.

Because the death of the martyr makes Christ known, and, since John Paul teaches that proclamation is "never a merely personal act," but one that is always "made in union with the entire ecclesial community," then the martyr's death unites others together in Christ through the Church. In other words, the death of the martyr not only heralds his faith in Jesus, but it also proclaims the truth of the Church's teachings, which are Christ's teachings.

## "Ut Unum Sint" and the "Supreme Demand of Faith"

As Universal Pastor, the Holy Father's encyclical, *Ut Unum Sint*, shows his obvious and necessary care for those not in full communion with the Catholic Church. Spurred on by the Church's preparations for the Year of Great Jubilee, John Paul suggests that the "courageous witness of so many martyrs of our century, including members of Churches and Ecclesial Communities not in full communion with the Catholic Church," might assist the Church's work toward Christian unity.[6] He expresses this hope in the opening paragraph of *Ut Unum Sint*.

---

words, the death of the martyr is a proclamation—by the martyr and by the whole Church, founded by Jesus—of the truth of Jesus Christ's teachings.

[6] John Paul II, *Ut Unum Sint* 1. In *Orientale Lumen*, the Holy Father also speaks of martyrdom and Christian unity in similar terms [John Paul II, *Orientale Lumen* 18, 19, 23]. As John Paul explains elsewhere, "At the

The courageous witness of so many martyrs of our century, including members of Churches and Ecclesial Communities not in full communion with the Catholic Church, gives new vigor to the Council's call and reminds us of our duty to listen to and put into practice its exhortation. These brothers and sisters of ours, united in the selfless offering of their lives for the Kingdom of God, are the most powerful proof that every factor of division can be transcended and overcome in the total gift of self for the sake of the Gospel.[7]

---

end of the second millennium, the Church has once again become a Church of martyrs" [John Paul II, *Tertio Millennio Adveniente* 37]. While priests, religious and laity have been martyred in great numbers around the world, John Paul further notes that the "witness to Christ borne even to the shedding of blood has become a common inheritance of Catholics, Orthodox, Anglicans and Protestants, as Pope Saint Paul VI pointed out in his "Homily for the Canonization of the Ugandan Martyrs" [John Paul II, *Tertio Millennio Adveniente* 37]. Speaking of what is, perhaps, "the most convincing form of ecumenism," John Paul describes "the ecumenism of the saints and of the martyrs," noting that the "*communio sanctorum* speaks louder than the things which divide us" [John Paul II, *Tertio Millennio Adveniente* 37].

[7] John Paul II, *Ut Unum Sint* 1. Elsewhere, John Paul refers to the fact that the heroic example of "witnesses to the Faith is truly precious for all Christians," highlighting the ecumenical aspect of martyrdom [John Paul II, *Homily* 7 May 2000 (3)]. He speaks of them as "brothers and sisters of ours in faith…[who] stand as a vast panorama of Christian humanity in the twentieth century, a panorama of the Gospel, of the Beatitudes, lived even to the shedding of blood" [John Paul II, *Homily* 7 May 2000 (3)]. Echoing ideas contained in *Ut Unum Sint*, John Paul exhorts Christians to unity through the "ecumenism of the martyrs and the witnesses to the Faith," as follows. "Dear Brothers and Sisters, the precious heritage which these courageous witnesses have passed down to us is a patrimony shared

Here, John Paul emphasizes the complete self-gift of the martyr, which flows from one's living faith, as *Veritatis Splendor* recalls. Further, because truth is objective, and thus, the moral code is objective, the martyr reaches beyond strict membership in the Catholic Church. In dying to uphold the objectivity of the moral law, he witnesses to Jesus, who is Truth, Himself.

In his opening paragraph, the Holy Father stresses two central factors. First, the Pope highlights the martyr's gift, which is the "selfless offering" of his life given with his acceptance of death. Second, the Holy Father expresses the reason for the martyr's "total gift of self" as an offering made "for the Kingdom of God," and "for the sake of the Gospel" (i.e., faith and morals). John Paul speaks of martyrdom as the most effective means for obtaining Christian unity because it is "the total gift of self for the sake of the Gospel."[8]

In *Ut Unum Sint* 83, John Paul speaks of the fact that all Christian Communities have "martyrs for the Christian faith." The interesting point for my purpose concerns the fact that the martyr

---

by all the Churches and Ecclesial Communities. It is a heritage which speaks more powerfully than all the causes of division. The ecumenism of the martyrs and the witnesses to the Faith is the most convincing of all; to the Christians of the twenty-first century it shows the path to unity. It is the heritage of the Cross lived in the light of Easter: a heritage which enriches and sustains Christians as they go forward into the new millennium" [John Paul II, *Homily* 7 May 2000 (5)].

[8] John Paul II, *Ut Unum Sint* 1. In *Ecclesia in America* 26, the Holy Father comments upon Matthew 7:21, which speaks of doing the Father's will. His reflection mentions martyrdom as an act of total self-gift. "Openness to the Father's will supposes a total self-giving, including even the gift of one's life: "The greatest witness is martyrdom" [John Paul II, *Ecclesia in America* 26].

has "preserved an attachment to Christ and to the Father so radical and absolute as to lead even to the shedding of blood." Again, the Pontiff's ultimate concern is truth. In paragraph 83, he explains the need for "an ever more profound experience of the truth" in order to achieve full communion.

In light of *Ut Unum Sint* 83, then, one might offer the following remark. To identify the martyr as an "eloquent and attractive example of a life completely transfigured by the splendor of moral truth" naturally leads to the conclusion that martyrdom is a viable means for Christian unity.[9] In other words, because the martyr dies in order to uphold the objective moral order, and, because the martyr's death draws others to Christ, as *Veritatis Splendor* attests, then it follows that the closer one comes to truth, the closer one comes to Jesus. Again, Christ Jesus is the fullness of truth. The more Christians embrace the objective moral order and the pursuit of truth, the closer they come to one another. Christian unity is the result.

In *Redemptoris Missio* 45, one recalls the Pope's focus upon the martyr's witness to his "faith in Jesus Christ." With *Ut Unum Sint* 84, the Holy Father comments that martyrdom is "the supreme demand of faith, manifested in the sacrifice of life itself." Because "God preserves communion among the baptized" in the greatest demand that faith can make, namely, the willing acceptance of death, John Paul concludes the following.[10] Since "one can die for

---

[9] John Paul II, *Veritatis Splendor* 93.
[10] John Paul II, *Ut Unum Sint* 84.

## Chapter Thirteen: Additional Encyclicals on Martyrdom

the Faith…other demands of the faith can also be met."[11] Here, the Pope clearly has in mind Christian unity.

There is a second interesting fact in *Ut Unum Sint* 84. The Holy Father specifies that martyrdom is "the highest point of the life of grace" because it is the "truest communion possible with Christ who shed His Blood." The Pope explains this concept of martyrdom in light of communion among Christian Ecclesial Communities. He argues that communion "is already perfect in what we all consider the highest point of the life of grace, *martyria* unto death."[12] He elaborates upon the point by further stressing that martyrdom is "the truest communion possible with Christ who shed His Blood, and by that sacrifice, [He] brings near those who once were far off (cf. Ephesians 2:13)."[13] The Pope identifies martyrdom, then, as both the "highest point of the life of grace" and the "truest communion possible" with Jesus, because the martyr imitates His sacrificial death.[14]

*Ut Unum Sint* 84 brings to light a third fact. While the martyr is "proof of the power of grace," the Pope also implies that he visibly bears witness "to that power." The Pontiff immediately contrasts the martyr's visible attestation to the power of grace with the "invisible way" in which an incomplete communion exists between Ecclesial Communities. This communion is "truly and solidly grounded," the Pope explains, in the "full communion of the

---

[11] John Paul II, *Ut Unum Sint* 84.
[12] John Paul II, *Ut Unum Sint* 84.
[13] John Paul II, *Ut Unum Sint* 84.
[14] John Paul II, *Ut Unum Sint* 84.

Saints—those who, at the end of a life faithful to grace, are in communion with Christ in glory."

## "Fides et Ratio:" The Martyrs "Declare What we Would Like to Have the Strength to Express"

*Fides et Ratio* 32 offers the final comment upon martyrdom from John Paul's encyclicals. Here, the Holy Father explains the difference between *knowing* and *believing*. He defines *believing* as entrusting oneself "to the knowledge acquired by other people," which, however, is "humanly richer than mere evidence," collected over time, by the believer.[15] Whereas *knowledge* concerns empirical facts, *believing* "involves an interpersonal relationship and brings into play not only a person's capacity to know but also the deeper capacity to entrust oneself to others, to enter into a relationship with them which is intimate and enduring."[16]

In *Fides et Ratio* 32, the Pope emphasizes the fact that the "truths sought in this interpersonal relationship are not primarily empirical or philosophical. Rather, what is sought is the truth of the person—what the person is and what the person reveals from deep within." The notions of entrusting oneself to another, and of

---

[15] John Paul II, *Fides et Ratio* 32. Elsewhere, John Paul explains the person's loving entrustment, which he describes in *Fides et Ratio* 32, as characteristic of a believer. He explains that faith is one's "act of entrusting oneself to God," which is "a moment of fundamental decision which engages the whole person" [John Paul II, *Fides et Ratio* 13]. The Pope explains further that faith "allows individuals to give consummate expression to their own freedom" [John Paul II, *Fides et Ratio* 13].

[16] John Paul II, *Fides et Ratio* 32.

entrusting oneself to the truth of the other person, which is brought out by that entrustment, are both vital to John Paul's concept of the martyr.

The Holy Father develops his thought on the interpersonal relationship that arises when a person entrusts himself to another by believing the other person. Still in paragraph 32, he explains, "Human perfection, then, consists not simply in acquiring an abstract knowledge of the truth, but in a dynamic relationship of faithful self-giving with others." Again, one recalls the total gift of self that the martyr offers.

John Paul brings in the notion of truth by asserting that "knowledge through belief, grounded as it is on trust between persons, is linked to truth: in the act of believing, men and women entrust themselves to the truth which the other declares to them."[17] The Pope's lucid description of *believing* testifies to his lively focus on the human person. A person who believes another entrusts himself both to the other person and to the truth of what the other person says. Should that person lie, his interlocutor rightly suffers the shock and pain of his betrayal.

To offer a concrete example of the believer's act of entrustment to another person and to the truth of what the other says, the Holy Father turns to "the martyrs, who are the most authentic witnesses to the truth about existence."[18] John Paul infers the following. The martyr's self-entrustment both to Jesus Christ and to the truth He teaches results in an intimacy. The Holy Father confirms that noth-

---

[17] John Paul II, *Fides et Ratio* 32.
[18] John Paul II, *Fides et Ratio* 32.

ing would cause the martyr to "abandon the truth which [he has] discovered in the encounter with Christ."[19] In other words, the martyr's act of entrusting himself to the Truth, to Christ, brings forth a vibrant relationship with Him, and the martyr will not betray that intimacy. To act against this intimacy with Christ is to betray the truth of the person, which is the martyr's self-giving. Even more, since the martyr's self-giving is likewise enkindled by his believing entrustment to Christ Jesus, he does not want to betray it.

To emphasize the point, the martyr's self-gift is the "truth of the person," the truth of the martyr, himself, which is sought in his "interpersonal relationship" with Jesus. The martyr knows who he is before Jesus and before another human person because Jesus reveals to the martyr who he is. John Paul describes the martyr's "self-giving" as an encounter with Jesus.

> The martyrs know that they have found the truth about life in the encounter with Jesus Christ, and nothing and no one could ever take this certainty from them. Neither suffering nor violent death could ever lead them to abandon the truth which they have discovered in the encounter with Christ.[20]

In *Fides et Ratio* 32, John Paul depicts the martyr's magnetic influence upon others with impressive terminology. The martyr's impact upon others "continues to arouse such interest, to draw

---

[19] John Paul II, *Fides et Ratio* 32.
[20] John Paul II, *Fides et Ratio* 32.

# Chapter Thirteen: Additional Encyclicals on Martyrdom

agreement, to win such a hearing and to invite emulation." One might ask the reason why the martyr elicits such a reaction from others.

Combining the martyr's effect upon others with a thought from *Veritatis Splendor*, I propose the following. In *Veritatis Splendor*, I comment upon the Holy Father's affirmation that freedom is "ultimately directed towards communion."[21] Since the martyr expresses human freedom, he draws the other human person to himself and, through himself, he opens the other person to God.

*Fides et Ratio* 32 suggests the reason why the martyr draws others to Christ. The martyr offers such vivid testimony, which attracts others to Christ, precisely because he entrusts himself to Jesus Christ and to His teachings. The dynamic relationship between the martyr and Jesus Christ is implied by his loving act of entrustment to Him at death. Continuing with the same thought, John Paul expresses these insights in the following manner.

> This is why to this day the witness of the martyrs continues to arouse such interest, to draw agreement, to win such a hearing and to invite emulation. This is why their word inspires such confidence: from the moment they speak to us of what we perceive deep down as the truth we have sought for so long, the martyrs provide evidence of a love that has no need of lengthy arguments in order to convince. The martyrs stir in us a profound trust because they give voice

---

[21] John Paul II, *Veritatis Splendor* 86.

to what we already feel, and they declare what we would like to have the strength to express.[22]

The Holy Father's moving description of the martyr recalls the Conciliar teaching that Christ reveals to the human person who he is. As I note above, the martyr learns who he is, and he expresses who he is, because of his encounter with Jesus. Entrusting himself to Jesus by his death means that he believes Jesus and he believes what Jesus teaches. The martyr makes an act of self-gift, or self-entrustment to Jesus through his death.

Another insight from the *Fides et Ratio* paragraph concerns the following. Because each person needs Jesus Christ and His redemptive death, which "reconciled mankind to God" the Father, the martyr's death expresses his own trusting love, and his loving trust, for Jesus in its climatic moment.[23] The martyr's death reveals dramatically—*dramatically*, because of the suffering involved—that the human person is only fulfilled in Jesus Christ.

*Fides et Ratio* 32 teaches yet another point. Since the human person "cannot be manifested in the full dignity of his nature without reference…to God," the martyr's death, as an expression of his intimate encounter with Jesus, expresses the truth of God's existence and the holiness of His law.[24] Because these truths—that God exists and that His commands are holy—are revealed by the mar-

---

[22] John Paul II, *Fides et Ratio* 32.
[23] John Paul II, *Redemptoris Missio* 11.
[24] I make this point with the Puebla *Address* above. Here, my quotation is from John Paul II, *Dives in Misericordia* 1.

tyr's death, the Pope can rightly attest that the martyr's "word inspires such confidence."

At the core of the human person, as I show above, the martyr expresses one's fundamental openness to God. The martyr's death implies his openness to the transcendent, to God, Himself, on account of his entrusting love. Truly, then, does the martyr's death "speak to us of what we perceive deep down as the truth we have sought for so long."[25]

As I mention above, the person's inherent openness to the transcendent reveals an innate thirst for God. Insights gained from *Fides et Ratio* 32 indicate how the martyr's innate thirst is present: by his death, the martyr reveals his encounter of love with Jesus Christ. Not only does his death show one's need for Christ's redemption, but it also proclaims the freedom and dignity of *this human person*, the *martyr*, who, redeemed by Christ, avails himself of "the grace which flows from that act."[26]

The martyr's thirst for God is most vividly brought to the fore of human existence because nothing, "neither suffering nor violent death," can cause him "to abandon the truth which [he] has discovered in the encounter with Christ."[27] His death expresses the human person's innate openness to God because he accepts death in order to remain faithful to his encounter with Jesus Christ. Thus, the martyr's thirst might be described as the t/Truth that he has discovered in Christ Jesus and in his encounter with Him. This

---

[25] John Paul II, *Fides et Ratio* 32.

[26] John Paul II, *Redemptoris Missio* 11; John Paul II, *Veritatis Splendor* 103.

[27] John Paul II, *Fides et Ratio* 32.

living, pulsating characterization of thirst is so captivating to others precisely because it expresses the human person's capacity for God. The martyr's contemplative thirst, as I shall highlight, is captured by my interpretation of what it means to contemplate the face of Christ.

The martyr provides "evidence of a love that has no need of lengthy arguments in order to convince" because his love is firmly grounded in his living encounter with Jesus.[28] His charity, which is "in conformity with the radical demands of the Gospel," kindles a person to "a profound trust because [he] gives voice to what we already feel and [he] declares what we would like to have the strength to express."[29]

---

[28] John Paul II, *Fides et Ratio* 32.
[29] John Paul II, *Veritatis Splendor* 89; John Paul II, *Fides et Ratio* 32.

# Chapter Fourteen
## Additional Texts on Martyrdom
## Martyrdom as an "Extraordinary Fruitfulness for the Building Up of the Church"

In *Christifideles Laici* 39, John Paul addresses the topic of freedom of conscience and of religion. In this passage, he discusses human dignity in terms of one's "relation to God [which] is a constitutive element of the very 'being' and 'existence' of an individual" human person.[1] The Pope explains that, whether one believes this truth concerning human dignity, each person has "the *right of freedom of conscience and religious freedom*," which is "the right to be respected for [one's] faith and for [one's] life-choice, individual and communal, that flows from that faith." In the context of religious freedom, then, John Paul speaks of martyrdom.

> The Synod did not forget the many brothers and sisters that still do not enjoy such a right and have to face difficulties, marginization, suffering, persecution, and oftentimes death because of professing the Faith. For the most part, they are brothers and sisters of the Christian lay faithful. The proclamation of the Gospel and the Christian testimony given in a life of suffering and martyrdom make up the summit of the apostolic life among Christ's disciples, just as the love for the Lord Jesus even to the giving of one's life constitutes a source of extraordinary fruitfulness for the building up of

---

[1] John Paul II, *Christifideles Laici* 39.

the Church. Thus, the mystic vine bears witness to its earnestness in the Faith, as expressed by Saint Augustine: 'But that vine, as predicted by the prophets and even by the Lord Himself, spread its fruitful branches in the world, and becomes the more fruitful the more it is watered by the blood of martyrs.'[2]

In *Christifideles Laici* 39, John Paul's remarks on human dignity focus upon the very nature of the human person, which signifies an objective expression of dignity. With *Veritatis Splendor*, he stresses the person's own living in accord with the truth; such a life is the means by which the person testifies to human dignity.[3] As noted by the Council Fathers, following one's well-formed conscience is a sign of the inherent dignity of the person, and such a person lives in accord with truth.[4] Consonant with *Redemptoris Missio*, then, the Pope explains martyrdom, in the quotation above, as enduring "death because of professing the Faith." The profession

---

[2] John Paul II, *Christifideles Laici* 39. Indeed, the blood of the martyrs does increase the Church, as Tertullian's well-known dictum explains. John Paul quotes Tertullian in *Tertio Millennio Adveniente* 37, and further elaborates upon it. The "Church of the first millennium was born of the blood of the martyrs: 'Sanguis martyrum—semen christianorum.' The historical events linked to the figure of Constantine the Great could never have ensured the development of the Church as it occurred during the first millennium if it had not been for the seeds sown by the martyrs and the heritage of sanctity which marked the first Christian generations" [John Paul II, *Tertio Millennio Adveniente* 37].

[3] John Paul II, *Veritatis Splendor* 85.

[4] Second Vatican Council, *Gaudium et Spes* 16-17.

of faith comprises both an adherence to the Gospel message of Jesus as taught by Holy Mother Church and the profession of faith practiced by fidelity to the objective moral order, the precepts of which are the Ten Commandments.

An additional point from *Christifideles Laici* 39 shows that the martyr's death is a "proclamation of the Gospel." John Paul speaks of martyrdom as the "summit of the apostolic life among Christ's disciples," which specifies its remarkable ability to advance and increase the Church. Moreover, he sees martyrdom as an expression of one's "love for the Lord Jesus even to the giving of one's life." Given the *Fides et Ratio* text above, one might add that the expression of love, which is evident in martyrdom, brings to the fore the martyr's encounter with Jesus. One might interpret martyrdom in *Christifideles Laici* 39, then, as a confirmation that love is at the heart of the martyr's sacrifice.

The Holy Father's particularly striking remark in *Christifideles Laici* 39 is that the "Church is born of God's grace." He expresses his gratitude toward those who are persecuted and martyred, thanking them for their "witness to an essential property of the Church: God's Church is born of God's grace," and martyrdom is "an excellent way" to profess this property. As *Veritatis Splendor* shows, the grace of God offers the believer the strength to "keep God's holy law, even amid the gravest of hardships."[5] John Paul explains this testimony "given in a life of suffering and martyrdom" by affirming his gratitude for their "example and…gift."

---

[5] John Paul II, *Veritatis Splendor* 103. See also 93.

The whole Church is profoundly grateful for this example and this gift. These sons and daughters give reason for renewing the pursuit of a holy and apostolic life. In this sense the Fathers at the Synod have made it their special duty 'to give thanks to those lay people who, despite their restricted liberty, live as tireless witnesses of faith in faithful union with the Apostolic See, although they may be deprived of sacred ministers. They risk everything, even life. In this way the lay faithful bear witness to an essential property of the Church: God's Church is born of God's grace, which is expressed in an excellent way in martyrdom.'[6]

## A "Sign of That Greater Love Which Sums Up All Other Values"

In his Bull of Indiction for the Year of Great Jubilee, John Paul dedicates one of only fourteen paragraphs to martyrdom. Both the importance of the event that *Incarnationis Mysterium* announces and his devotion of an entire paragraph to martyrdom in a very short document are noteworthy facts. Another mark of interest is the paragraph's location in the text. The Pope focuses upon martyrdom in paragraph 13, the second to last paragraph of the Jubilee Bull. The placement of martyrdom in the Bull suggests that it occupies a central position as the crescendo reaches its height just before the conclusion. Further, given the fact that the Pope stresses the link between martyrdom and charity, and, since charity fulfills

---

[6] John Paul II, *Christifideles Laici* 39.

## Chapter Fourteen: Additional Texts on Martyrdom

the law (Romans 13:10), one might conclude that the Holy Father intends to draw attention to his paragraph on martyrdom.

In *Incarnationis Mysterium* 13, John Paul strongly exhorts the Church not only to remember the martyrs, but also to make the sacrifice of martyrdom, should circumstances require it. He describes the memory of the martyrs as a powerful "sign of the truth of Christian love" because they gave "their lives for love." In fact, with *Incarnationis Mysterium* 13, John Paul defines the martyr as one who is "a sign of that greater love which sums up all other values." One of the marks of "greater love" is forgiving one's enemy. He explains these thoughts in the following manner.

> A sign of the truth of Christian love, ageless but especially powerful today, is the memory of the martyrs. Their witness must not be forgotten. They are the ones who have proclaimed the Gospel by giving their lives for love. The martyr, especially in our own days, is a sign of that greater love which sums up all other values. The martyr's life reflects the extraordinary words uttered by Christ on the Cross: "Father, forgive them, for they know not what they do" (Luke 23:34).[7]

---

[7] John Paul II, *Incarnationis Mysterium* 13. John Paul seemingly never tires of repeating that one must not forget the witness of the martyrs. He continually exhorts the Church, in various countries of the word, to preserve the memory of their martyrs by keeping careful records. See, for example, John Paul II, *Tertio Millennio Adveniente* 37; John Paul II, *Novo Millennio Ineunte* 7; John Paul II, *Incarnationis Mysterium* 13; John Paul

A second point that the Holy Father offers in the Jubilee Bull concerns one's own Christian vocation. As *Veritatis Splendor* shows, Christian witness concerns fidelity to Christ and to His teachings. Thus, John Paul's mention of the possibility of martyrdom is a logical conclusion that follows from one's life of faithfulness to Christ and to His teachings.

> The believer who has seriously pondered his Christian vocation, including what Revelation has to say about the possibility of martyrdom, cannot exclude it from his own life's horizon. The two thousand years since the birth of Christ are marked by the ever-present witness of the martyrs.[8]

John Paul, himself, seems to help the reader consider the possibility of his own martyrdom when he recounts the numerous martyrs of the twentieth century. These martyrs are characteristically identified for their death in "fidelity to Christ and the Church." He explains as follows.

> This century now drawing to a close has known very many martyrs, especially because of Nazism, Communism, and racial or tribal conflicts. People from every sector of society have suffered for their faith, paying with their blood for their fidelity to Christ and the Church, or courageously facing interminable years of imprisonment and privations of

---

II, *Ecclesia in Africa* 34; John Paul II, *Ecclesia in America* 15; John Paul II, *Ecclesia in Oceania* 7.

[8] John Paul II, *Incarnationis Mysterium* 13.

every kind because they refused to yield to an ideology which had become a pitiless dictatorial regime.[9]

In the next part of the paragraph, I read John Paul's text as a summary of the different elements I discuss up to this point regarding martyrdom. He explains the martyr's death as "the most eloquent proof of the truth of the Faith."[10] Keeping in mind the martyr's defense of both human freedom and human dignity, one might summarize that defense as giving "a human face even to the most violent of deaths," and showing the beauty of one's face "even in the midst of the most atrocious persecutions."[11] In other words, the martyr's death, which upholds human freedom and human dignity, radiates humanity in the midst of inhumanity and it restores a sense of the humane by confronting the inhuman. "From the psychological point of view, martyrdom is the most eloquent proof of the truth of the Faith, for faith can give a human face even to the most violent of deaths and show its beauty even in the midst of the most atrocious persecutions."[12]

The Pope's final word on martyrdom in his Jubilee Bull is to offer a "hymn of thanksgiving to the Father" for the testimony of the martyrs. He encourages the Church to "remain anchored in the testimony of the martyrs and jealously guard their memory." Thus, he exhorts the faithful to follow their example by relying confidently upon the grace of God, should martyrdom be required of them.

---

[9] John Paul II, *Incarnationis Mysterium* 13.
[10] John Paul II, *Incarnationis Mysterium* 13.
[11] John Paul II, *Incarnationis Mysterium* 13.
[12] John Paul II, *Incarnationis Mysterium* 13.

Again, martyrdom is a gift given by God to only a few. One cannot endure martyrdom without the grace of God. The Holy Father explains these thoughts as follows.

> Filled with grace during the coming Jubilee year, we shall be able with new strength to raise the hymn of thanksgiving to the Father, singing: *Te martyrum candidatus laudat exercitus.* Yes, this is the host of those who 'have washed their robes and made them white in the Blood of the Lamb" (Revelation 7:14). For this reason, the Church in every corner of the earth must remain anchored in the testimony of the martyrs and jealously guard their memory. May the People of God, confirmed in faith by the example of these true champions of every age, language and nation, cross with full confidence the threshold of the Third Millennium. In the hearts of the faithful, may admiration for their martyrdom be matched by the desire to follow their example, with God's grace, should circumstances require it.[13]

With *Incarnationis Mysterium* 13, then, John Paul ushers in the Year of Great Jubilee by turning the Church's eye upon her martyrs. Not only does the Holy Father laud their witness, but also, he exhorts the faithful to know and to preserve their memory. Even further, the Pontiff exhorts the faithful to emulate the martyrs with their own witness unto death, should it be required of them, by remaining faithful to the Gospel message of Jesus and His Church.

---

[13] John Paul II, *Incarnationis Mysterium* 13.

# Chapter Fourteen: Additional Texts on Martyrdom

The martyr is both a sign of charity and a model of forgiveness. As the Church enters the new millennium, John Paul emphasizes the martyr's bond to charity by encouraging the faithful to consider the martyr as both "a sign of that greater love which sums up all other values" and as a model of forgiving love.[14] Again, the significance John Paul pays to the martyr dictates that one seriously ponder both his words and the subject of martyrdom, as a whole.

## Martyrdom "Reveals to the World the Very Essence of the Christian Message"

A passage from *Ecclesia in Asia* offers a fitting summary to insights from John Paul's encyclicals (other than *Veritatis Splendor*). In paragraph 49 of *Ecclesia in Asia*, the Holy Father focuses upon martyrdom. He states, aside from "programs of formation and strategies for evangelization," it is martyrdom that "reveals to the world the very essence of the Christian message."[15] In one heroic act, the martyr declares, by his death, the supreme kingship of Jesus Christ and the everlasting value of His divine teaching.

John Paul defines a martyr as a witness who has shed his "blood for Christ [and has] borne the ultimate witness to the true value of the Gospel."[16] The martyr puts into diligent practice the teaching and commands of Jesus such that by beholding the martyr's death one "reads" the Gospel of eternal life offered to each person by Jesus Christ.

---

[14] John Paul II, *Incarnationis Mysterium* 13.
[15] John Paul II, *Ecclesia in Asia* 49.
[16] John Paul II, *Ecclesia in Asia* 49.

Given that the Pope describes the martyr in *Incarnationis Mysterium* as "a sign of that greater love which sums up all other values" his remark in *Ecclesia in Asia* makes a similar claim. The logical summation of the documents suggests that the martyr's love, which is a forgiving love in imitation of the Crucified Savior, lies at the very heart of Christian proclamation. Forgiving love embodies the content of Gospel truth, for love is the fulfillment of the law (Romans 13:10). Thus, *Ecclesia in Asia* 49 suggests that the death of the martyr proclaims the Gospel, which is the "Christian message" of love of God and neighbor.

John Paul recalls the great number of Asian martyrs, and he exhorts the Church in Asia to learn the lessons they teach. He specifies that the primary instruction the martyrs offer is the power and the strength of the Cross of Christ Jesus. One infers that the martyr's death proclaims the power of Jesus Christ Crucified, for His "power is made perfect" in the martyr's "weakness" (2 Corinthians 12:9).

An additional concluding thought that the Holy Father brings out in the following passage is the spiritual fecundity of the martyr's death. He reminds the faithful that the blood of the martyr generates new life in the Church. The Holy Father explains these thoughts in the following manner.

> May the great host of Asian martyrs, old and new, never cease to teach the Church in Asia what it means to bear witness to the Lamb in whose Blood they have washed their shining robes (cf. Revelation 7:14)! May they stand as indomitable witnesses to the truth that Christians are called

always and everywhere to proclaim nothing other than the power of the Lord's Cross! And may the blood of Asia's martyrs be now as always, the seed of new life for the Church in every corner of the continent!"[17]

**The Martyr's Resplendent Character**

Earlier, I spoke of the *mystery* of the human person according to John Paul's interpretation of *Gaudium et Spes* 22 and 24. In the present section, I convey John Paul's notion of the martyr (martyrdom) by linking *Veritatis Splendor* and *Fides et Ratio*. Specifically, I interpret John Paul's description of martyrdom as a vibrant embodiment of being "in the Truth" and "doing the Truth."[18]

By his death, the martyr expresses the pinnacle of living in the truth because he shows that truth demands fidelity, including the offering one's life to remain faithful to it—to Christ—who is Truth. Because the martyr's death is a gift offered in "fidelity to God's holy law," it is an "eloquent and attractive example of a life completely transfigured by the splendor of moral truth."[19] The martyr shows Jesus Christ to others, then, because he refuses to act against the moral law, which is objective. His death indicates that freedom and dignity transcend the forces of those who repel against his fidelity to t/Truth.

The "splendor" of Truth—of Christ, to whom the martyr testifies by his death—offers a description of martyrdom that permits

---

[17] John Paul II, *Ecclesia in Asia* 49.
[18] John Paul II, *Veritatis Splendor* 84.
[19] John Paul II, *Veritatis Splendor* 93.

the development of its contemplative dimension. In what follows, I suggest the contemplative angle of martyrdom by explaining the martyr's obedience to Christ as listening with one's whole being.

I interpret the martyr's fidelity to Christ as *listening obedience* on account of John Paul's notion of freedom. Because freedom is "a *decision about oneself* and a setting of one's own life for or against the good, for or against the truth, and ultimately for or against God," martyrdom implies that one's whole being is directed toward God. In the act of offering his life, the martyr's death embodies his listening. His death is a Christ-like obedience unto death. The martyr's death, in obedience to the law of God, proclaims the truth of the human person as a resplendence of Jesus, who radiates the Father's Love.

Another aspect of *Veritatis Splendor* emphasizes that freedom is "ultimately directed towards communion."[20] I explain John Paul's concept of freedom in relation to the martyr by suggesting that his death expresses human freedom as an openness, or transparency, to another who suffers. Combining *Veritatis Splendor* with the *Letter to the Romans*, one learns that, because truth and the moral order are objective, the martyr's death both testifies to these objective realities and his death draws others to Truth—to Christ—because truth and the moral order are immutable. As the *Letter to the Romans* shows, freedom is being faithful to Christ and human dignity is being captivated and absorbed by the love of God. The martyr unites others to Christ, then, through his faithful

---

[20] John Paul II, *Veritatis Splendor* 86.

witness to Christ, who is Truth, and to the Church, who protects and safeguards His teachings.

Using *Fides et Ratio* 32, I add the fact that the martyr draws another person to Christ Jesus through his own witnessed encounter of self-entrustment. Based upon John Paul's text, then, I make the following claims. When the believer who is a martyr entrusts himself to Jesus, he seeks "the truth of the person." The martyr finds that his act of loving entrustment and his "faithful self-giving" make him, the truth of who he is, the "most authentic witness to the truth about existence."[21] Further, as the Holy Father stipulates, the "truth about existence" is the "truth about life," which the martyr has "discovered in the encounter with Christ." The martyr's death, then, proclaims Christ Jesus to the world precisely because it radiates the believing, loving entrustment of the martyr to God.

In the chapters above, I explain that the person is essentially open to the transcendent because he is created in God's image and likeness. I build upon this teaching by offering a concrete illustration of it: the martyr's death depicts his innate openness to the transcendent as a reality that he accepts and embraces in freedom and love. *Fides et Ratio* 32 supports this interpretation by claiming that the martyr grasps in an instant "the truth we have sought for so long," which is "a love that has no need of lengthy arguments in order to convince."[22] Christ reveals to the martyr "the truth" of his fundamental openness to God. At the same time, the martyr reveals to others the loving entrustment he offers to God. The result

---

[21] John Paul II, *Fides et Ratio* 32.
[22] John Paul II, *Fides et Ratio* 32.

of the martyr's loving entrustment, which is evident by his death, is his intimacy with Christ. The martyr does not and will not betray that intimacy. The martyr's act of entrustment to God, which his death radiates, testifies to his loving and being loved by God.

Perhaps the martyr's encounter with Jesus, which entails reciprocal love, incites such fury in one's persecutors for three reasons. First, one's witness implies God's existence and second, one's witness suggests the mutual love between Christ and the martyr. A third reason entails the martyr's witness to the moral order, which, perhaps, the instigators of martyrdom contradict by their words and their manner of life.

Regardless of the reason, the martyr's death testifies to the fact that the "splendor of moral truth" cannot be darkened by "the behavior and thinking of individuals and society."[23] The martyr's contribution to the world, then, is the clear distinction he shows between "good and evil."[24] Having substantiated my claim that the martyr's death radiates truth, I further explicate its unique dimensions in the following chapters.

---

[23] John Paul II, *Veritatis Splendor* 93.
[24] John Paul II, *Veritatis Splendor* 93.

# Chapter Fifteen
## Contemplating Christ's Face and the Death of the Martyr

In his Bull announcing the Year of Great Jubilee, John Paul writes, "the Church is the cradle in which Mary places Jesus and entrusts Him to the adoration and contemplation of all peoples."[1] Receiving this Child into one's heart in the spirit of adoration and contemplation, then, my first task is to explain how John Paul describes, in his own words, *contemplating the face of Christ*.[2] The primary texts that expound upon this theme are *Novo Millennio Ineunte* and *Rosarium Virginis Mariae*, although I also refer to others. Commenting upon these texts, I offer my own reading of *contemplating the face of Christ* simultaneously.

My second task is to show how one might understand the death of the martyr as a contemplation of Christ's face. Having set forth John Paul's notion of martyrdom previously, I seek to justify my claim that the martyr's death is a contemplation of Christ's face and that the martyr's contemplation shows Christ to others.

---

[1] John Paul II, *Incarnationis Mysterium* 11.

[2] John Paul only employs the concept, *contemplating the face of Christ*, after the Year of Great Jubilee has passed. His first mention of *contemplating the face of Christ* begins with his Apostolic Letter that closes the Jubilee, *Novo Millennio Ineunte*.

## John Paul's Explanation of the Term *Contemplating the Face of Christ*

In his Apostolic Letter that closes the Jubilee, John Paul enumerates several aspects, which he regards as central to it. Among the many he mentions, he identifies one primary factor, or "core" of the Jubilee "legacy."[3] In *Novo Millennio Ineunte* 15, he explains that, while the Jubilee "has left us with many memories," one theme, in particular, stands at the forefront of all.

> But if we ask what is the core of the great legacy it leaves us, I would not hesitate to describe it as the contemplation of the face of Christ: Christ considered in His historical features and in His mystery, Christ known through His manifold presence in the Church and in the world, and confessed as the meaning of history and the light of life's journey.[4]

---

[3] John Paul II, *Novo Millennio Ineunte* 15. In the opening paragraph of *Novo Millennio Ineunte*, John Paul immediately points to this "legacy" as he stresses that the "Church's joy was great this year, as she devoted herself to contemplating the face of her Bridegroom and Lord." Elsewhere, John Paul describes *Novo Millennio Ineunte* as a document in which he gathered together the "fruits of the Great Jubilee" [John Paul II, *Mane Nobiscum Domine* 8]. The fact that contemplating Christ's face is one of those fruits is significant.

[4] John Paul II, *Novo Millennio Ineunte* 15. While the Holy Father identifies contemplating the face of Christ as the core of the Jubilee legacy, recall that the very reason for the Jubilee, itself, is to commemorate the Incarnation of Jesus. Moreover, since the Jubilee is a central event in John Paul's pontificate, pondering the term, in light of what martyrdom

## Chapter Fifteen: Contemplating Christ's Face

John Paul regards the Jubilee Year as a time "to refresh our contact with this living source of our hope," who is Christ Jesus, and one does this by contemplating His face.[5] In the above quotation, the Holy Father defines *contemplating the face of Christ* as pondering Jesus Christ Himself, as He is revealed to us in Sacred Scripture.

More specifically, *contemplating Christ's face* is considering the presence of Jesus in human history, in the Church and in the world, as the One who gives history its meaning and who guides each person's life. Contemplating Christ's face is deeply rooted in pondering the real, divine Person, who is Jesus Christ Himself. Sacred Scripture and Christ's presence and action in the Church and in the world assist the person in his own contemplation of Christ's face.

The central theme in the second chapter of *Novo Millennio Ineunte* contains the Holy Father's thought on what it means to contemplate the face of Jesus Christ. In paragraph 16, John Paul reflects upon the words from Sacred Scripture addressed to Saint

---

teaches, offers a significant contribution to developing the content of his thought. An additional point of interest is that paragraph 15, which defines contemplating the face of Christ, is in the last paragraph of chapter one. By its placement in the text, as well as by John Paul's mention of its "legacy" in the document itself, one grasps the importance of reflecting upon its meaning.

[5] John Paul II, *Novo Millennio Ineunte* 58. In *Orientale Lumen*, John Paul speaks of the monk who "becomes accustomed to contemplating Christ in the hidden recesses of creation and in the history of mankind, which is then understood from the standpoint of identification with the whole Christ" [John Paul II, *Orientale Lumen* 12].

Philip, "We wish to see Jesus (John 12:21)." He notes that the person of today also wants to see Jesus. The Pope explains that *showing* Jesus to others implies that one first *sees* Him, oneself. In addition, John Paul indicates that *showing* Jesus to others is a task of the Church in each age. The Holy Father expresses these thoughts in the following manner.

> 'We wish to see Jesus' (John 12:21). This request, addressed to the Apostle Philip by some Greeks who had made a pilgrimage to Jerusalem for the Passover, echoes spiritually in our ears too during this Jubilee year. Like those pilgrims of two thousand years ago, the men and women of our own day—often perhaps unconsciously—ask believers not only to 'speak' of Christ, but in a certain sense to 'show' Him to them. And is it not the Church's task to reflect the light of Christ in every historical period, to make His face shine also before the generations of the new millennium?[6]

In order to show Jesus to others, then, the believer must first contemplate His face. Given the importance of one's own contemplation of Christ's face, the Pope indicates that this contemplation is "inspired by all that we are told about Him in Sacred Scripture" and that the Gospels provide each person with "a vision of faith based on precise historical testimony."[7] The Pontiff stresses the fact that Jesus Christ and the Gospel accounts that narrate the events of

---

[6] John Paul II, *Novo Millennio Ineunte* 16.
[7] John Paul II, *Novo Millennio Ineunte* 17.

### Chapter Fifteen: Contemplating Christ's Face

His life are rooted in human history. He continues, the "face of the Nazarene emerges with a solid historical foundation," including His Resurrection from the dead.[8] In paragraph 19, John Paul describes the face of the resurrected Christ to bring out the historical reality of this event.

> 'The disciples were glad when they saw the Lord' (John 20:20). The face which the Apostles contemplated after the Resurrection was the same face of the Jesus with whom they had lived for almost three years, and who now convinced them of the astonishing truth of His new life by showing them 'His hands and His side' (John 20:20).[9]

The Apostles and disciples were reluctant to believe in Christ's Resurrection, and the Holy Father notes their incredulity. He explains that, "regardless of how much His Body was seen or touched, only faith could fully enter the mystery of that face."[10] Thus, John Paul reiterates the fact that one needs faith in order to grasp who Jesus is, just as Peter did at Caesarea Philippi: "A grace of 'revelation is needed, which comes from the Father (cf. Matthew 16:17)."[11] In addition, the Pope indicates that silence and prayer are indispensable for coming to know Jesus Christ. The Holy Father summarizes these thoughts as follows.

---

[8] John Paul II, *Novo Millennio Ineunte* 17.
[9] John Paul II, *Novo Millennio Ineunte* 19.
[10] John Paul II, *Novo Millennio Ineunte* 19.
[11] John Paul II, *Novo Millennio Ineunte* 19, 20.

> [W]e cannot come to the fullness of contemplation of the Lord's face by our own efforts alone, but by allowing grace to take us by the hand. Only the experience of silence and prayer offers the proper setting for the growth and development of a true, faithful and consistent knowledge of that mystery which finds its culminating expression in the solemn proclamation by the Evangelist Saint John: 'And the Word became Flesh and dwelt among us, full of grace and truth; we have beheld His glory, glory as of the only Son from the Father' (John 1:14).[12]

With these reflections from *Novo Millennio Ineunte*, one gains the following insights. First, to contemplate the face of Jesus is to ponder Jesus Christ Himself, true God and true Man, who, by His Incarnation, has tangibly made Himself present in human history. Since the time of Christ's Incarnation, the person of every age wants to "see" Him. The follower of Jesus shows Him to others only if *he* has first contemplated His face. A means by which the believer contemplates Christ's face is through reflection on Sacred Scripture and salvation history. The Pope clearly stipulates, however, the necessity of faith, as well as silence and prayer, in order to come to know Jesus Christ.

As I show above, *Veritatis Splendor* indicates that faith is "a lived knowledge of Christ, a living remembrance of His Commandments, and a truth to be lived out."[13] In *Novo Millennio Ine-*

---

[12] John Paul II, *Novo Millennio Ineunte* 20.
[13] John Paul II, *Veritatis Splendor* 88.

*unte*, one learns that faith is the necessary ingredient to know Jesus and to be able to "fully enter the mystery" of His face.[14] Combining the two elements, one might claim that living out the truth of the Commandments implies one's knowledge of Jesus and one's entryway into the mystery of His face. The person of faith puts into action the word he receives.[15] Entering into the mystery of Christ's face means that one's life reflects truth and fidelity to Jesus Christ. Thus, if the life of the believer is an embodiment of his living faith, it also expresses a contemplation of Christ's face.

**The Self-Emptying of Jesus Christ**

With paragraph 22 of *Novo Millennio Ineunte*, John Paul brings out the two natures of Jesus, both divine and human, since both are often under attack. For example, the Holy Father explains the dilemma by stating that faith in Christ's divinity "has become problematic" due to rationalism. Others question Christ's humanity by the subtle "tendency to diminish and do away with the historical concreteness" of it. Given the frequent criticisms against both Christ's divinity and humanity, the Pope affirms their reality: "the Word truly 'became Flesh' and took on every aspect of humanity, except sin (cf. Hebrews 4:15)." Highlighting the fact that the first "self-emptying" of Jesus is His Incarnation, and the second is His Passion and death, John Paul explains that it is "truly a kenosis—a self-emptying"—on the part of the Son of God of that glory which

---

[14] John Paul II, *Novo Millennio Ineunte* 19.
[15] John Paul II, *Veritatis Splendor* 88.

is His from all eternity (Philippians 2:6-8; cf. 1 Peter 3:18)."[16] To contemplate the face of Christ, then, means to reflect upon Jesus in the historical reality that the Gospels reveal and to ponder Jesus, who is true God and true Man.

Connecting these thoughts with martyrdom, one might surmise the following. If the martyr is a prime example of one who *does* the t/Truth, then his life reflects the truth of Christ's teachings. The life of the martyr enters into the mystery of Christ's face because it reflects the truth of the Commandments. His lived knowledge of Christ, which his animate faith enlivens, flows from having contemplated His face. Further, the martyr's kenosis is his own emptying out of self—the self-gift of his human life—offered in order to remain faithful to Jesus. The martyr relinquishes his life to retain and deepen the divinization which is his, as a child of God the Father (cf. Romans 8:29-30; Ephesians 1:4-5). John Paul explains the person's divinization in the next paragraph, *Novo Millennio Ineunte* 23.

With paragraph 23, John Paul introduces *Gaudium et Spes* 22 into his reflection on contemplating the face of Christ. Because Jesus is both God and Man, "He reveals to us also the true face of man, 'fully revealing man to man himself.'" Here, the Holy Father reiterates a point I highlight above: Christ's Incarnation "lays the foundations for an anthropology which...moves toward God Himself, indeed toward the goal of 'divinization.'" The Holy Father explains these thoughts as follows.

---

[16] John Paul II, *Novo Millennio Ineunte* 22. As I note above, the self-gift of accompanying another suffering person expresses authentic human freedom on account of Christ's own self-emptying on the Cross.

### Chapter Fifteen: Contemplating Christ's Face

Jesus is 'the new Man' (cf. Ephesians 4:24; Colossians 3:10) who calls redeemed humanity to share in His divine life. The mystery of the Incarnation lays the foundations for an anthropology which, reaching beyond its own limitations and contradictions, moves towards God Himself, indeed towards the goal of 'divinization.' This occurs through the grafting of the redeemed on to Christ and their admission into the intimacy of the Trinitarian life. The Fathers have laid great stress on this soteriological dimension of the mystery of the Incarnation: it is only because the Son of God truly became man that man, in Him and through Him, can truly become a child of God.[17]

John Paul mentions another element that assists in contemplating Christ's face. That factor concerns Christ's own "self-awareness," which helps the person "enter that 'frontier zone' of the mystery" of His divinity and humanity.[18] But, as paragraph 25 mentions, the "most paradoxical aspect of His mystery" that one confronts when contemplating His face concerns the mystery of His death on the Cross. Focusing upon the agony of Christ in the Garden of Olives, John Paul describes Jesus "alone before the Father," on account of human sin.

In order to bring man back to the Father's face, Jesus not only had to take on the face of man, but He had to burden

---

[17] John Paul II, *Novo Millennio Ineunte* 23.
[18] John Paul II, *Novo Millennio Ineunte* 24.

Himself with the 'face' of sin. 'For our sake He made Him to be sin who knew no sin, so that in Him we might become the righteousness of God' (2 Corinthians 5:21).[19]

This quotation contributes toward an understanding of the Pope's thought on contemplating Christ's face because it highlights the "most paradoxical aspect" of His presence in human history.[20] In the above quotation, John Paul reflects upon Jesus taking "on the face of man" and burdening "Himself with the 'face' of sin" as the way that the person is brought "back to the Father's face." This facet of contemplating His face recalls my emphasis on Christ's re-creation of the human person by His Passion and death. With *Redemptor Hominis* 9, John Paul accentuates Christ, who is "our reconciliation with the Father," and the person's re-creation through Jesus Christ, who reveals the Father's eternal love. Elsewhere, John Paul reflects upon the love that God reveals to the world on the Cross. He explains this love in terms of God's desire to "share with mankind His very life, His love, His holiness."[21]

As John Paul is quick to mention, however, Christ's death on the Cross reveals the victorious Christ, who conquers sin and

---

[19] John Paul II, *Novo Millennio Ineunte* 25. Contemplating the sorrowful face of Christ in *Novo Millennio Ineunte* also recalls the importance of the Church looking to the Crucified Jesus for the authentic meaning of freedom. Christ Crucified "reveals the authentic meaning of freedom; He lives it fully in the total gift of Himself and calls His disciples to share in His freedom" [John Paul II, *Veritatis Splendor* 85].

[20] John Paul II, *Novo Millennio Ineunte* 25.

[21] John Paul II, *World Mission Day* 2002 (3).

## Chapter Fifteen: Contemplating Christ's Face

death. The Holy Father explains the wisdom of the Cross and the lessons it teaches: humility, forgiveness, peace, and communion.

> The Cross is the key that gives free access to 'wisdom which is not of this world, nor of the rulers of this age...God's wisdom, mysterious and hidden' (1 Corinthians 2:6-7). The Cross, in which the glorious face of the Risen Christ already shines, introduces us to the fullness of Christian life and perfect love, because it reveals God's longing to share with mankind His very life, His love, His holiness. In the light of this mystery of the Church, remembering the words of the Lord: 'Be perfect, as your Heavenly Father is perfect' (cf. Matthew 5:48), understands ever more clearly that her mission would be senseless if it did not lead to fullness of Christian life, that is to perfect love and holiness. Contemplating the Cross we learn to live with humility and forgiveness, peace and communion."[22]

John Paul moves back to reflecting upon the face of Jesus as He empties Himself out upon the Cross. The Holy Father offers the reader his own contemplation of Christ's face, the wounded and suffering face of Jesus, by interpreting His cry from the Cross as the "prayer of the Son who offers His life to the Father in love, for the salvation of all."[23] John Paul reflects upon Christ's cry to the Father

---

[22] John Paul II, *World Mission Day* 2002 (3).
[23] John Paul II, *Novo Millennio Ineunte* 26.

as that which brings to light an animated relationship of love and trust.

> At the very moment when He [Jesus] identifies with our sin, 'abandoned' by the Father, He 'abandons' Himself into the hands of the Father. His eyes remain fixed on the Father. Precisely because of the knowledge and experience of the Father which He alone has, even at this moment of darkness He sees clearly the gravity of sin and suffers because of it. He alone, who sees the Father and rejoices fully in Him, can understand completely what it means to resist the Father's love by sin.[24]

Given that John Paul's second chapter of *Novo Millennio Ineunte* is a meditation upon what it means to contemplate the face of Christ, the quotation above teaches that contemplating His face means pondering the events of His life, and in particular, His salvific Passion and death. At the climax of His visible life on earth, the Crucified Christ reveals to mankind that the face of the Father is mercy and love. Elsewhere, John Paul teaches that it is "precisely because sin exists in the world, which 'God so loved...that He gave His only Son' (John 3:16), that God, who 'is Love' (1 John 4:8), cannot reveal Himself otherwise than as mercy."[25]

---

[24] John Paul II, *Novo Millennio Ineunte* 26.

[25] John Paul II, *Dives in Misericordia* 13. As the Innocent Lamb of God reconciling mankind to the Father, the Son shows the face of the Father as love and mercy. Elsewhere, the Holy Father writes, "Jesus reveals the face of God the Father 'compassionate and merciful' (James

God's revelation of Himself as mercy "corresponds not only to the most profound truth of that love which God is, but also to the whole interior truth of man and of the world which is man's temporary homeland."[26] In other words, Jesus shows mankind that the person may abandon himself, with full confidence and trust, into the loving hands of the Father. In addition, Jesus reveals the Father's great love for mankind in a manner that highlights His desire to reconcile sinful humanity with Himself. Thus, contemplating the face of Christ means entrusting oneself, with confidence and love, to the Eternal Father.

Immediately following his reflection of Christ on the Cross, John Paul turns to the example of the saints, whose "lived theology" offers many insights.[27] In paragraph 27, he mentions the mystical experience of the "dark night," and the fact that many "saints have undergone something akin to Jesus' experience of the Cross in the paradoxical blending of bliss and pain." The Holy Father explains his thoughts with several examples.

> In the *Dialogue of Divine Providence*, God the Father shows Catherine of Siena how joy and suffering can be present together in holy souls: 'Thus the soul is blissful and afflicted: afflicted on account of the sins of its neighbor, blissful on account of the union and the affection of charity which it

---

5:11), and with the sending of the Holy Spirit He makes known the mystery of love which is the Trinity" [John Paul II, *Incarnationis Mysterium* 3].

[26] John Paul II, *Dives in Misericordia* 13.
[27] John Paul II, *Novo Millennio Ineunte* 27.

has inwardly received. These souls imitate the spotless Lamb, My Only-begotten Son, who on the Cross was both blissful and afflicted.' In the same way, Thérèse of Lisieux lived her agony in communion with the agony of Jesus, 'experiencing' in herself the very paradox of Jesus' own bliss and anguish: 'In the Garden of Olives our Lord was blessed with all the joys of the Trinity, yet His dying was no less harsh. It is a mystery, but I assure you that, on the basis of what I myself am feeling, I can understand something of it.' What an illuminating testimony! Moreover, the accounts given by the Evangelists themselves provide a basis for this intuition on the part of the Church of Christ's consciousness when they record that, even in the depths of His pain, He died imploring forgiveness for His executioners (cf. Luke 23:34) and expressing to the Father His ultimate filial abandonment: 'Father, into Your hands I commend My spirit' (Luke 23:46).[28]

Connecting these thoughts with martyrdom, one conjectures that the martyr also experiences joy and suffering in a profound manner. The pain that martyrdom entails brings to the fore the martyr's own affliction "on account of the sins of [his] neighbor," who is martyring him. The *Letter* of Saint Ignatius of Antioch, upon which I comment above, shows that the martyr does not brush aside the real pain he experiences: "the pangs of birth are upon me." Nothing could be more real than the instruments used in

---

[28] John Paul II, *Novo Millennio Ineunte* 27.

martyrdom. At the same time, one might surmise that the martyr, sustained by the grace of God, also experiences joy in suffering for Christ.[29] Like Christ Crucified, the martyr forgives his persecutors and abandons himself to the Father, entering into union with Him through the open side of Jesus that bares His heart.

**The "Treasure" and "Joy" of Holy Mother Church: Contemplating Christ's Face**

The Pontiff's final paragraph in his chapter dedicated to contemplating the face of Christ is an exhortation to both pause "in contemplation of this bleeding face, which conceals the life of God and offers salvation to the world," and to contemplate the face of the "Risen One!"[30] In *Novo Millennio Ineunte* 28, John Paul explains the Resurrection as "the Father's response to Christ's obedience." Summarizing what it means to contemplate the face of Christ, the Pope stresses the love with which the Church looks toward Christ, "her treasure and her joy." The Holy Father implies that, having contemplated Christ's face, the Church is now revitalized; thus, she is better able to show His face to others. He explains these thoughts with the following words.

---

[29] As I note above, John Paul teaches that the person is given the "strength to endure martyrdom" [John Paul II, *Veritatis Splendor* 87]. In addition, the Pope explains that "believers find the grace and the strength always to keep God's holy law, even amid the gravest of hardships" [John Paul II, *Veritatis Splendor* 103]. Thus, the martyr is sustained by the grace of God in the *real, intense, human* suffering that he experiences with his death.

[30] John Paul II, *Novo Millennio Ineunte* 28.

Gazing on the face of Christ, the Bride contemplates her treasure and her joy. '*Dulcis Iesus memoria, dans vera cordis gaudia:*' how sweet is the memory of Jesus, the source of the heart's true joy! Heartened by this experience, the Church today sets out once more on her journey, in order to proclaim Christ to the world at the dawn of the Third Millennium: He 'is the same yesterday and today and forever' (Hebrews 13:8).[31]

The quotation above hints at the contemplative dimension of the Church's proclamation, which it must embody, in order to be effective. Contemplating the face of Jesus by reflecting upon the events of His life, deeply rooted in history and attested to by the Gospels, and, especially by pondering His face during the Jubilee year, the Church sets forth to "proclaim Christ to the world."

John Paul's description of contemplating Christ's face in *Novo Millennio Ineunte* evokes the following thoughts in relation to martyrdom. In this Apostolic Letter, the Holy Father teaches that Jesus "identifies with our sin: 'abandoned' by the Father, He 'abandons' Himself into the hands of the Father. His eyes remain fixed on the

---

[31] John Paul II, *Novo Millennio Ineunte* 28. Elsewhere, John Paul describes the importance of contemplating Christ's Resurrection. He teaches, "Contemplating the Risen One, Christians rediscover the reasons for their own faith (cf. 1 Corinthians 15:14) and relive the joy not only of those to whom Christ appeared—the Apostles, Mary Magdalene and the disciples on the road to Emmaus—but also *the joy of Mary*, who must have had an equally intense experience of the new life of her glorified Son" [John Paul II, *Rosarium Virginis Mariae* 23].

# Chapter Fifteen: Contemplating Christ's Face

Father."[32] From *Fides et Ratio* 32, one learns that in believing, the person entrusts oneself to the truth of which the other speaks. In the same paragraph, the Holy Father points to the martyr as an example of one who "entrusts" oneself to Jesus. One might infer, then, that the martyr focuses upon Jesus Christ, and that since Christ's "eyes remain fixed on the Father" from the Cross, the martyr also concentrates upon the Father through his attention on Jesus.[33] In the "dynamic relationship of faithful self-giving" to Christ, then, the martyr does not "abandon the truth which [he has] discovered in the encounter with Christ."[34]

With *Novo Millennio Ineunte*, one learns that Christ on the Cross reveals the Father as mercy and love. Indeed, Jesus makes known the Father's desire to reconcile humanity with Himself through the sacrifice of His Son. *Redemptor Hominis* expresses a similar thought: God reveals His love for the human person in a tangible manner through the redemptive love of His Son, Jesus Christ. *Veritatis Splendor* notes that charity, which "can lead the believer to the supreme witness of martyrdom," imitates "Jesus who died on the Cross."[35]

---

[32] John Paul II, *Novo Millennio Ineunte* 26.

[33] John Paul II, *Novo Millennio Ineunte* 26.

[34] John Paul II, *Fides et Ratio* 32.

[35] John Paul II, *Veritatis Splendor* 89. As John Paul notes, Saint Maximilian Kolbe is a particularly fitting example of a martyr for charity. In the Holy Father's homily for his canonization, he says Saint Maximilian is like Christ, who is the "Model of all Martyrs," by His death on Calvary. "Does not this death, faced spontaneously, for love of man, constitute a particular fulfillment of the words of Christ? Does not this death make Maximilian particularly like to Christ, the Model of all Martyrs, who

*Fides et Ratio* 32 might be interpreted as the martyr's revelation of his redemption by Jesus Christ. Because he entrusts himself to Jesus at death, his self-gift in love specifies his redemption by Christ as a new child of the Father. To recall a point earlier made in the *Letter to the Romans*, Saint Ignatius of Antioch implies that, when he dies, he receives new life. The new life that he enters through his martyrdom, vividly depicted with the imagery of giving birth, suggests that his death is a new living of his divine adoption as a child of the Father. Since the human person is fundamentally open to God, and, since Christ redeems the human race with His Passion and death at Calvary, the martyr's death brings these truths to the fore by his unsurpassed desire "to be God's" child. As the Holy Father specifies, contemplating the face of Christ is contemplating His love, for the person who has "truly contemplated the face of Christ" allows the new Commandment of love (John 13:34) to inform his life.[36] The martyr's entrusting love illustrates this contemplation by his acceptance of the "pangs of birth" as he offers his life as a gift of love.

Jesus does not "come down from the Cross" because He fulfills the Father's will in loving obedience; the martyr does not "abandon the truth which [he] has discovered in the encounter with Christ,"

---

gives His own life on the Cross for His brethren?" [John Paul II, *Homily* 10 October 1982 (8)].

[36] John Paul II, *Novo Millennio Ineunte* 42. The Holy Father also elucidates the contemplation of the face of Christ as that which informs the Church's practice of charity to the poor [John Paul II, *Novo Millennio Ineunte* 49].

## Chapter Fifteen: Contemplating Christ's Face

for nothing can separate him from God.[37] From the Cross, Jesus thirsts for love. At his own death, the martyr's thirst for Jesus strengthens him to endure *his* cross. While Jesus willingly lays down His life, the martyr likewise accepts death in order to remain faithful to Jesus and to His teachings.

Christ's death redeems mankind; the martyr's death shows one's need for redemption. Christ's death, in filial obedience, restores humanity to friendship with the Father; the martyr's death reaches out to another suffering person, thus "befriending mankind" by his own freely made gift of self as a child of the Father.

The Resurrection is "the Father's response to Christ's obedience," for He conquers death and merits life for the world.[38] In comparison, one might see the death of the martyr as new life for the Church. Indeed, the Church becomes "more fruitful the more [she] is watered by the blood of martyrs."[39]

**The Contemplation of Christ's Face is a Reciprocity of Abiding Love**

While John Paul does not explicitly state that the death of the martyr is a contemplation of Jesus's face, I see a correlation between his claims regarding *martyrdom* and *contemplation of Christ's face* in the following texts. With *Incarnationis Mysterium* 13, the Holy Father teaches that martyrdom "reflects the extraordi-

---

[37] John Paul II, *Fides et Ratio* 32.
[38] John Paul II, *Christifideles Laici* 39.
[39] John Paul II, *Christifideles Laici* 39.

nary words [of forgiveness] uttered by Christ on the Cross."[40] In *Novo Millennio Ineunte* 25, he asserts that contemplating the face of Christ brings one to the mystery of "His last hour on the Cross." Thus, by suggesting that the death of the martyr is a contemplation of the face of Jesus, I maintain that it is a reality made evident on account of the martyr's forgiving love, which reflects Jesus's act of forgiveness on the Cross. In addition, the martyr's forgiveness suggests his faith and his loving trust in Jesus.

One might ask, then, whether the martyr's death, as a contemplation of the face of Jesus, is *prayer*. On one hand, some might claim that death cannot be a prayer. Further, showing Christ to others by one's death requires no audible prayer from the martyr. His contemplation of Christ's face, as I describe it, is embodied by the death he endures in fidelity to Christ and His teachings. If my claim is correct, how can the martyr's death be a prayer?

On the other hand, one might regard the martyr's death as *prayer* for three reasons. First, one might construe the death of the martyr as prayer because it raises the questions that "refer to prayer."[41] In other words, the martyr's death evokes the "fundamental

---

[40] In the pontifical writings of John Paul II, a concrete example of a martyr offering forgiveness is Saint Stephen, the Protomartyr. "Therefore Stephen, deacon of Jerusalem, the first martyr, who, stoned by his fellow countrymen, died with words of forgiveness on his lips, in his last words raised this penetrating prayer: 'Lord Jesus, receive my spirit' (Acts 7: 59 )" [John Paul II, *Homily* 18 May 1980 (3)].

[41] John Paul II, *Homily* 19 October 1982 (3).

questions which pervade human life" on account of his clear testimony to life beyond corporeal existence.[42]

Martyrdom's witness to objective truth and to the objective moral law leads one to ask, perhaps unconsciously, questions such as, "Who am I? Where have I come from and where am I going?"[43] John Paul describes questions such as "Who must I be?" and "How must I be?" as inquiries that "refer to prayer."[44] In addition, since the martyr's death radiates the profound certitude of God's existence and of God's holy law, his death offers evidence of a life in "reference...to God."[45] And, living one's life in the dramatic reference to God that martyrdom portrays, suggests that his death is, indeed, *prayer*. His clear *doing* of the t/Truth expresses a heart that responds to God in loving attention, which is the very essence of *prayer*.

The martyr's death is *prayer* for a second reason, as well. Susanna's example in chapter three of *Veritatis Splendor* implies the contemplative dimension of the martyr's free decision. Because "Susanna chose for herself the 'better part'" by obeying the law of God, her obedience describes her "whole existence" as a listener.[46]

---

[42] John Paul II, *Fides et Ratio* 1. The Second Vatican Council puts forward some of the "most basic questions" as well. "What is man? What is this sense of sorrow, of evil, of death, which continues to exist despite so much progress? What purpose have these victories purchased at so high a cost? What can man offer to society, what can he expect from it? What follows this earthly life" [Second Vatican Council, *Gaudium et Spes* 10]?

[43] John Paul II, *Fides et Ratio* 1.

[44] John Paul II, *Homily* 19 October 1982 (3).

[45] John Paul II, *Opening Address* at Puebla, 28 January 1979 (I.9).

[46] John Paul II, *Veritatis Splendor* 88, 93.

From his account of Susanna in *Veritatis Splendor*, one might interpolate that the "one thing" necessary, which the martyr's death characterizes, is the listening obedience that requires one's whole life (Luke 10:42). Further, my discussion of the *Letter to the Romans* of Saint Ignatius of Antioch, to which John Paul refers in *Veritatis Splendor* 92, offers additional evidence that martyrdom highlights one's listening obedience. Here, he depicts martyrdom as "the exaltation of a person's perfect 'humanity' and of true 'life.'"[47]

While the Holy Father does not explicitly state that the martyr's death is prayer, combining the martyr's listening obedience as the "one thing" necessary, with the Pope's definition of *contemplating the face of Christ*, suggests how it might be understood as prayer. As I note above with *Novo Millennio* 15, John Paul maintains that *contemplating the face of Christ* is Jesus Christ "confessed as the meaning of history and the light of life's journey." Combining these thoughts, one might infer that the martyr's death, which "confesses" Christ, shows that Jesus is the "light of life's journey" for the martyr because he dies in order to preserve his (listening) obedience to Christ (cf. Luke 10:42).[48] Since the martyr's death "confesses" his life with Jesus by showing it to be the "one thing" necessary, one might describe that death as a contemplation of His face.[49]

The martyr's death might be interpreted as prayer, then, because it highlights one's listening obedience as the "one thing" nec-

---

[47] John Paul II, *Veritatis Splendor* 92.

[48] John Paul II, *Novo Millennio Ineunte* 15.

[49] John Paul II, *Novo Millennio Ineunte* 15.

essary (Luke 10:42). His life with Christ is even more vital than his own physical life. Listening to Christ—one's obedience to Him—is the single most important command. Indeed, it is another way of depicting the love of God and the love of neighbor on account of one's love for God (Matthew 22:37-40). Martyrdom describes prayer as an act of listening before speaking. Because the martyr listens by offering his life, martyrdom describes prayer as an obedience that acknowledges Jesus as the "light of life's journey" (cf. Luke 10:42).[50]

By reflecting upon *Novo Millennio Ineunte* 32, I see a third reason why the martyr's death is *prayer*. Continuing to elaborate upon the term, *contemplation of Christ's face*, John Paul explains it as a silent reciprocity of an abiding love. If my claim that the martyr's death is a contemplation of Christ's face is accurate, then the inaudible exchange of love, implied in contemplating Christ's face, is rightly called *prayer*.[51] Paragraph 32 supports the Holy Father's description of prayer in terms of an abiding reciprocity between Jesus and the one who prays.

---

[50] John Paul II, *Novo Millennio Ineunte* 15.

[51] While the Pope's theology of prayer is a separate topic, it is interesting to note that, in prayer, a person comes to a deeper knowledge of Jesus and, through knowing Jesus, one comes to know oneself. My anthropological component highlights John Paul's interpretation of *Gaudium et Spes* 22. In addition to my extrapolation of *contemplating Christ's face*, both sections endorse and offer new insight to one's growth in the knowledge and love of God and of oneself. Given the scope of my project, further development upon these themes is not possible at present.

Prayer develops that conversation with Christ which makes us His intimate friends: 'Abide in Me and I in you' (John 15:4). This reciprocity is the very substance and soul of the Christian life, and the condition of all true pastoral life. Wrought in us by the Holy Spirit, this reciprocity opens us, through Christ and in Christ, to contemplation of the Father's face.[52]

If the contemplation of Christ's face means pondering His life narrated by the Gospels and His action in human history (which it does), then it concerns prayer. In the quotation above, John Paul describes prayer as developing one's conversation with Christ; the result makes the person an intimate friend of Jesus. Further, the Pope explains prayer as "reciprocity," which opens the human person to the Father, through Jesus.

The notion of a reciprocal relationship between Jesus and the believer evokes John Paul's idea of the believer entrusting himself to the other and to the truth of what the other says. In this case, the other to whom the believer entrusts himself, is Jesus Christ. With John Paul's articulation of *prayer* from paragraph 32, one infers the following. The martyr's self-entrustment to Christ describes his inaudible prayer as a contemplation of the face of the Father in Christ and through Christ. It further suggests that Jesus, in turn, "entrusts" Himself to the martyr with His grace and with His abiding love. Thus, the martyr's "strength to endure martyrdom" not only refers to the grace and strength needed to remain faithful to

---

[52] John Paul II, *Novo Millennio Ineunte* 32.

# Chapter Fifteen: Contemplating Christ's Face

God's law, but it also specifies, in light of *Novo Millennio Ineunte* 32, Christ's love dwelling in the martyr.[53]

To claim that the martyr's death is a contemplation of Christ's face, of His life narrated by the Gospels, does not require the martyr's audible prayer. Nonetheless, the death of the martyr *is* prayer. Again, John Paul highlights the fact that "Prayer develops that conversation with Christ which makes us His intimate friends." I interpret the conversation between Christ and the martyr as *prayer*. His death, which is *prayer*—his profound communion with the Father through Christ—shows Christ to others through the abiding love between Jesus Christ and the martyr. In other words, the martyr's death depicts the intimacy between Christ and the martyr as a reciprocity of abiding love.

## Trinitarian Implications of Contemplating the Face of Christ

In *Novo Millennio Ineunte* 32, John Paul implies that the reciprocity of abiding love, which is prayer, opens one, through Christ, to a contemplation of the Father's face. Elsewhere, the Pope speaks of not only contemplating the face of *Christ*, but also, of *contemplating the face of the Father*, and *of God*, as well.[54] Of course, Jesus is God and the Father is God. The Son and the Father are two of

---

[53] John Paul II, *Veritatis Splendor* 87, 103.

[54] In *Fides et Ratio* 13, the Pope mentions both the *face of the Father* and *of God*. He explains, "Jesus, with His entire life, revealed the countenance of the Father, for He came to teach the secret things of God. But our vision of the face of God is always fragmentary and impaired by the limits of our understanding" [John Paul II, *Fides et Ratio* 13].

the distinct Persons in the Most Blessed Trinity. The Third Person is the Holy Spirit, about whom I have also spoken. Even still, given John Paul's differentiations between Persons, why do I focus solely on the contemplation of *Christ's* face?

Because Jesus is the one Mediator with the Father, John Paul rightly claims that it is "through Christ and in Christ," that one attains to the "contemplation of the Father's face" (cf. Hebrews 12:24).[55] As Sacred Scripture teaches, "to see Jesus is to see the Father" (John 14:9). Further, in the first paragraph of *Dives in Misericordia*, the Holy Father speaks of the human person and of his lofty calling, which are "revealed in Christ through the revelation of the mystery of the Father and His love." Elsewhere, John Paul explains that "Christ is the way that leads us to the Father in the Spirit."[56] Another way of articulating these thoughts is to say that Jesus reveals the face of the Father. Because the "way" of the human person is Jesus Christ, and, since He is one's "Way 'to the Father's house,'" contemplating the face of Christ is contemplating the Father's face through Jesus.[57]

---

[55] John Paul II, *Novo Millennio Ineunte* 32.

[56] John Paul II, *Rosarium Virginis Mariae* 34.

[57] John Paul II, *Redemptor Hominis* 13. Here, I repeat the quotation that Jesus is the "Way" to the Father because it shows what is good for the human person: communion with the Father through Jesus Christ. Naturally, the reader is drawn to ponder John 14:6: "I Am the Way, and the Truth, and the Life; no one comes to the Father, but by Me" (RSVCE). In *Orientale Lumen*, John Paul explains that, to the person who seeks, "the Father's face will let itself be recognized, engraved as it is in the depths of the human heart" [John Paul II, *Orientale Lumen* 12].

## Chapter Fifteen: Contemplating Christ's Face

At times, John Paul mentions that Jesus shows the face of the Father, and of God, occasionally referencing the Hypostatic Union as he does so. He indicates, for example, that "God takes on a human face" on account of the Incarnation.[58] Elsewhere, the Pope explains that, in Christ Jesus, "God [i.e., the *Father*] has truly blessed us in Him [i.e., Christ Jesus] and has made 'His face to shine upon us' (Psalms 67:1)."[59] Another example of Jesus revealing the face of God the Father is a remark concerning the Transfiguration in *Rosarium Virginis Mariae*. The Pope writes, "The glory of the Godhead shines forth from the face of Christ as the Father commands the astonished Apostles to 'listen to Him' (cf. Luke 9:35)."[60] All of these passages indicate that, because Christ is the "Way 'to the Father's house,'" one may also speak of *contemplating the face of the Father* and *of God* who is Father, Son and Holy Spirit.[61]

John Paul likewise speaks of *contemplating the face of God* in *Incarnationis Mysterium* 3. "In the mystery of the Trinity, the journey of faith has its origin and its final goal, when at last our eyes will contemplate the face of God for ever. In celebrating the Incarnation, we fix our gaze upon the mystery of the Trinity."

At the same time, the Holy Father indicates that Jesus reveals the Father. "Jesus of Nazareth, who reveals the Father, has fulfilled

---

[58] John Paul II, *Fides et Ratio* 12.

[59] John Paul II, *Novo Millennio Ineunte* 23. John Paul continues by explaining that, "God and Man that He is, He reveals to us also the true face of man, 'fully revealing man to man himself'" [John Paul II, *Novo Millennio Ineunte* 23].

[60] John Paul II, *Rosarium Virginis Mariae* 21.

[61] John Paul II, *Redemptor Hominis* 13.

the desire hidden in every human heart to know God."[62] The Pope speaks of contemplating the face of *Christ*, then, because "Jesus reveals the face of God the Father [as] 'compassionate and merciful' (James 5:11), and with the sending of the Holy Spirit He makes known the mystery of love which is the Trinity."[63]

As I show above, the Pope clearly teaches that the truth of the human person is "revealed to us in its fullness and depth in Christ."[64] Since Jesus is the "Way" to the Father, one contemplates the face of the Father by contemplating the face of Jesus Christ.[65] Moreover, "openness to Christ, who as the Redeemer of the world fully 'reveals man to himself,' can only be achieved through an ever more mature reference to the Father and His love."[66] Thus, speaking of *contemplating the face of the Father* or *contemplating the face of God* assists one's self-knowledge and opens one to the Father and His love.

Elsewhere, John Paul defines *contemplating the face of Christ* by emphasizing Christ's relationship to the Father. Because John Paul highlights the fact that Jesus reveals the Father, contemplating the face of Christ can lead one to a more intimate relationship with the Trinity. The terms *contemplating the face of Christ, of the Father*, and *of God*, then, show that contemplation focused upon the face of Jesus Christ also concerns the mystery of the Trinity. In other words, the Pope's emphasis on the face of Christ stresses His hu-

---

[62] John Paul II, *Incarnationis Mysterium* 3.
[63] John Paul II, *Incarnationis Mysterium* 3.
[64] John Paul II, *Dives in Misericordia* 1.
[65] John Paul II, *Redemptor Hominis* 13.
[66] John Paul II, *Dives in Misericordia* 1.

## Chapter Fifteen: Contemplating Christ's Face

man nature, "in which the eternal glory of the Father's only Son shines out," for Jesus is the Second Person of the Blessed Trinity Incarnate, true God and true man. Consequently, the *face of Christ* also emphasizes His divine nature since Jesus is one Divine Person with a human nature and a divine nature. With the quotation below, John Paul highlights the fact that contemplating *Christ's* face is to ponder Jesus, true God and true Man, especially as He is revealed to mankind through the Gospels.

> [The] 'face' of Christ is His human likeness in which the eternal glory of the Father's only Son shines out (cf. John 1:14): 'The glory of the Godhead shines forth from the face of Christ.' Contemplating the face of Christ leads to a deeper, interior familiarity with His mystery. Contemplating Jesus with the eyes of faith impels one to penetrate the mystery of the Trinitarian God. Jesus says: 'He who has seen Me has seen the Father' (John 14:9)."[67]

While John Paul sometimes mentions *contemplating the face of the Father* or *of God*, I employ his preferred term, *contemplating the face of Christ*, which also recalls his emphasis in *Redemptor Hominis* 13 of Christ as the "Way" to the Father. Because Jesus is the fullest revelation of God, He shows that the face of God is mercy and love.

In sum, contemplating the face of Christ is pondering the Incarnate face of God Himself, for He is the fullest revelation "of the

---

[67] John Paul II, *World Mission Day* 2003 (3).

mystery of the Father and His love."[68] The Holy Father concludes that, having contemplated Christ during the Jubilee, one has also "adored the Father and the Spirit, the one and undivided Trinity."[69]

---

[68] Second Vatican Council, *Gaudium et Spes* 22.
[69] John Paul II, *Novo Millennio Ineunte* 5.

# Chapter Sixteen

## Contemplating the Face of Christ with Mary

While John Paul's chief explication of *contemplating the face of Christ* is located in *Novo Millennio Ineunte*, less than two years later he provides the Church with another document, *Rosarium Virginis Mariae*, in which he elaborates upon the same theme.[1] In this Apostolic Letter, the Pope offers a "reflection on the rosary, as a kind of Marian complement to that *Letter* [*Novo Millennio Ineunte*] and an exhortation to contemplate the face of Christ in union with, and at the school of, His Most Holy Mother."[2] John Paul urges the believer to contemplate the face of Christ and to learn *how* to contemplate His face with the Blessed Mother.[3]

---

[1] *Novo Millennio Ineunte* was promulgated on 6 January 2001 and *Rosarium Virginis Mariae* was promulgated on 16 October 2002. Pairing the two *Letters* together, John Paul wants the Church to read *Rosarium Virginis Mariae* in continuity with his Apostolic Letter that introduces the new millennium to more fully understand the truths expressed in each one [John Paul II, *Rosarium Virginis Mariae* 3]. The present section answers this request specifically through a study of his term, *contemplating the face of Christ*.

[2] John Paul II, *Rosarium Virginis Mariae* 3.

[3] John Paul II, *Rosarium Virginis Mariae* 3. John Paul explains the rosary as "a path of contemplation," and thus, it is not the only possible way for one to contemplate the face of Christ [John Paul II, *Rosarium Virginis Mariae* 38]. Later in the document, the Holy Father reminds the reader that the rosary is "a method of contemplation," and thus, not an end in itself [John Paul II, *Rosarium Virginis Mariae* 28].

How does John Paul move from *contemplating the face of Christ* to include contemplating His face *with Mary*? In *Novo Millennio Ineunte*, the Holy Father explains *contemplating the face of Christ* as pondering His life in the Gospels. In *Rosarium Virginis Mariae*, John Paul defines the rosary as a Christocentric prayer, which is a compendium of the Gospel.[4] He teaches, "to rediscover the rosary means to immerse oneself in contemplation of the mystery of Christ who 'is our peace.'"[5] Logically, then, he refers to praying the rosary as a means by which the believer may *contemplate the face of Christ with Mary*.[6]

In paragraph 10 *of Rosarium Virginis Mariae*, John Paul speaks of Mary as an "incomparable model" for contemplating Christ. Mary is the unsurpassed exemplar for the Christian who contemplates Christ's face because "the face of the Son belongs to Mary." To be more specific, the Holy Father elucidates Mary's preeminent

---

[4] John Paul II, *Rosarium Virginis Mariae* 1. While *Rosarium Virginis Mariae* describes the rosary as Christocentric and as a compendium of the Gospels, *Mane Nobiscum Domine* personalizes that description by highlighting its focus "on the name and the face of Jesus as contemplated in the mysteries and by the repetition of the 'Hail Mary'" [John Paul II, *Mane Nobiscum Domine* 9]. The repetitions of the "Hail Mary" represent, as the Pope explains in *Mane Nobiscum Domine* 9, "a kind of pedagogy of love, aimed at evoking within our hearts the same love that Mary bore for her Son." Because the Year of the Eucharist is "meant to be a year of synthesis, the high-point of a journey in progress," one might presume that contemplating the face of Christ reaches a pinnacle in contemplating the Eucharistic face of Jesus Christ [John Paul II, *Mane Nobiscum Domine* 10].

[5] John Paul II, *Rosarium Virginis Mariae* 6.

[6] John Paul II, *Rosarium Virginis Mariae* 1.

## Chapter Sixteen: Contemplating the Face of Christ with Mary

standing as Christ's mother in order to highlight her role as model and teacher. Mary teaches the person to contemplate Christ's face because of her "spiritual closeness" as His mother and because she contemplated His face with unsurpassed fidelity.[7] The Holy Father elaborates upon these themes with exquisite detail that continues to illustrate what it means to contemplate the face of Christ.

> It was in her [Mary's] womb that Christ was formed, receiving from her a human resemblance which points to an even greater spiritual closeness. No one has ever devoted himself to the contemplation of the face of Christ as faithfully as Mary. The eyes of her heart already turned to Him at the Annunciation, when she conceived Him by the power of the Holy Spirit. In the months that followed she began to sense His presence and to picture His features. When at last she gave birth to Him in Bethlehem, her eyes were able to gaze tenderly on the face of her Son, as she 'wrapped Him in swaddling cloths, and laid Him in a manger' (Luke 2:7).[8]

---

[7] Further evidence justifies naming Mary as a teacher and a model of *contemplating Christ's face*. For example, she teaches each person about Jesus because "no one knows Christ better than Mary; no one can introduce us to a profound knowledge of His mystery better than His Mother" [John Paul II, *Rosarium Virginis Mariae* 14]. In addition, the Pontiff maintains that contemplating the mysteries of the rosary "in union with Mary is a means of learning from her to 'read' Christ, to discover His secrets and to understand His message" [John Paul II, *Rosarium Virginis Mariae* 14].

[8] John Paul II, *Rosarium Virginis Mariae* 10.

In the quotation above and in the remainder of *Rosarium Virginis Mariae* 10, John Paul offers a contemplation of Christ's face through Mary's eyes. One might articulate this contemplative gaze, "ever filled with adoration and wonder," as Mary's fidelity; her eyes "would never leave Him."[9] The contemplation of Christ's face by Mary, then, brings out the faithfulness and singularity of one who remains focused upon Christ. The Holy Father reflects upon Mary's contemplation of the face of Christ by highlighting various events in Sacred Scripture.

> At times it would be a questioning look, as in the episode of the finding in the Temple: 'Son, why have you treated us so?' (Luke 2:48); it would always be a penetrating gaze, one capable of deeply understanding Jesus, even to the point of perceiving His hidden feelings and anticipating His decisions, as at Cana (cf. John 2:5). At other times it would be a look of sorrow, especially beneath the Cross, where her vision would still be that of a mother giving birth, for Mary not only shared the Passion and death of her Son, she also received the new son given to her in the beloved disciple (cf. John 19:26-27). On the morning of Easter, hers would be a gaze radiant with the joy of the Resurrection, and finally, on the day of Pentecost, a gaze afire with the outpouring of the Spirit (cf. Acts 1:14).[10]

---

[9] John Paul II, *Rosarium Virginis Mariae* 10.
[10] John Paul II, *Rosarium Virginis Mariae* 10.

In the quotation above, John Paul shows how Mary facilitates the believer's contemplation of the face of Jesus. The Pontiff describes her contemplation as "a remembering," which, in the "biblical sense of remembrance," makes present the "works brought about by God in the history of salvation."[11] To "remember" the events of salvation history, "in a spirit of faith and love is to be open to the grace which Christ won for us by the mysteries of His life, death and Resurrection."[12]

**Contemplating the Face of Christ Opens One to "The Mystery of Trinitarian Life"**

In *Rosarium Virginis Mariae* 9, John Paul elucidates the *contemplation of Christ's face* by reflecting upon the Transfiguration of Jesus, which he calls "an icon of Christian contemplation."[13] By gazing upon the face of Christ, one ponders His life, suffering, death, and Resurrection. Further, contemplating His face leads one to receive "the mystery of Trinitarian life," which is, perhaps, the

---

[11] John Paul II, *Rosarium Virginis Mariae* 13.

[12] John Paul II, *Rosarium Virginis Mariae* 13. John Paul further explains, "If the Liturgy, as the activity of Christ and the Church, is a saving action par excellence, the rosary too, as a 'meditation' with Mary on Christ, is a salutary contemplation. By immersing us in the mysteries of the Redeemer's life, it ensures that what He has done and what the liturgy makes present is profoundly assimilated and shapes our existence" [John Paul II, *Rosarium Virginis Mariae* 14].

[13] John Paul II, *Rosarium Virginis Mariae* 9. In the middle of his *Letter*, he adds to the "Gospel compendium" the luminous mysteries of the rosary [John Paul II, *Rosarium Virginis Mariae* 21].

reason why John Paul speaks of *contemplating the face of the Father* and *of God*, at times, as I mention above.[14] The Holy Father expresses this "icon of Christian contemplation" in words that divulge his own contemplation of the sacred face.

> To look upon the face of Christ, to recognize its mystery amid the daily events and the sufferings of His human life, and then to grasp the divine splendor definitively revealed in the Risen Lord, seated in glory at the right hand of the Father: this is the task of every follower of Christ and, therefore, the task of each one of us. In contemplating Christ's face, we become open to receiving the mystery of Trinitarian life, experiencing ever anew the love of the Father and delighting in the joy of the Holy Spirit. Saint Paul's words can then be applied to us: 'Beholding the glory of the Lord, we are being changed into His likeness, from one degree of glory to another; for this comes from the Lord who is the Spirit' (2 Corinthians 3:18).[15]

In the above quotation, then, one finds additional confirmation of the fact that *contemplating Christ's face* means pondering the events of His life, revealed in Sacred Scripture. Every follower of Christ is to contemplate His face because it opens the person "to receiving the mystery of Trinitarian life."[16]

---

[14] John Paul II, *Rosarium Virginis Mariae* 9.
[15] John Paul II, *Rosarium Virginis Mariae* 9.
[16] John Paul II, *Rosarium Virginis Mariae* 9.

# Chapter Sixteen: Contemplating the Face of Christ with Mary

To this description of contemplating face of Christ, to this "icon of Christian contemplation," I add the following. In *Rosarium Virginis Mariae* 34, John Paul defines *contemplation* in reference to *prayer* and to the "essentially Trinitarian structure of all Christian prayer."[17] In this paragraph, he suggests that contemplation—a "proper contemplative tone" of prayer—is "raising the mind as it were to the heights of Heaven and enabling us in some way to relive the experience of Tabor, a foretaste of the contemplation yet to come: 'It is good for us to be here!' (Luke 9:33)."

One might infer, then, from paragraph 34, that John Paul uses *contemplation* of the face of Christ to mean raising "one's mind and heart to God" in prayer.[18] In this paragraph, the Holy Father explains, "Christ is the Way that leads us to the Father in the Spirit." Because the believer prays to the Father through Christ and in the Holy Spirit, contemplating the face of Christ might be interpreted as a key, or hermeneutic, to Christian prayer. In other words, contemplating the face of Christ describes the heart of Christian prayer precisely because it opens one to "the mystery of Trinitarian life." Indeed, Mount Tabor is a prime instance of such prayer.

---

[17] The context in which John Paul speaks of the "Trinitarian structure of all Christian prayer" is his elaboration upon the *Gloria*, which is to "be given due prominence in the rosary" [John Paul II, *Rosarium Virginis Mariae* 34].

[18] John Paul II, *Rosarium Virginis Mariae* 34; *Catechism of the Catholic Church* #2559.

## *Rosarium Virginis Mariae* and "The Truth About Man"

With *Rosarium Virginis Mariae*, I make two points that touch upon the anthropological dimension of contemplating the face of Christ with Mary. First, from paragraph 15, I explain that one who contemplates the face of Christ with Mary—praying the rosary is the Pope's obvious example—enters "naturally into Christ's life" through friendship. Second, from paragraph 25, I discuss the fact that contemplating the face of Christ by praying the rosary leads to a deeper understanding of "the truth about man."[19]

In paragraph 15, the Pope teaches that "Christian spirituality is distinguished by the disciple's commitment to become conformed ever more fully to his Master (cf. Romans 8:29; Philippians 3:10, 12)." One's commitment to become conformed to Jesus, however, necessitates putting on the "mind" of Christ (Philippians 2:5). Because the rosary is a means by which the believer contemplates the face of Christ, John Paul explains that it assists one in thinking and acting like Christ Jesus. More specifically, contemplating the face of Christ with Mary through praying the rosary leads the believer to put on the "mind" of Christ because a friendship between Jesus and the believer results (Philippians 2:5). The Holy Father explains these thoughts as follows.

> In the spiritual journey of the rosary, based on the constant contemplation—in Mary's company—of the face of Christ, this demanding ideal of being conformed to Him is pur-

---

[19] John Paul II, *Rosarium Virginis Mariae* 25.

### Chapter Sixteen: Contemplating the Face of Christ with Mary

sued through an association which could be described in terms of friendship. We are thereby enabled to enter naturally into Christ's life and as it were to share His deepest feelings.[20]

The concepts of friendship and of being able to "enter naturally into Christ's life," recall the Holy Father's reflection, in *Fides et Ratio* 32, of the believer's self-entrustment to another person and to the truth of what he says. Combining *Fides et Ratio* 32 with *Rosarium Virginis Mariae* 15, one might understand this "dynamic relationship of faithful self-giving" between Christ and the martyr as friendship or as entering "naturally into Christ's life."[21]

The "truth of the person," what the "person is and what the person reveals from deep within," finds its full expression by entering into the life of Christ. The "martyrs, who are the most authentic witnesses to the truth about existence," enter into Christ's life through friendship. In other words, the martyr's self-gift of entrustment to Jesus Christ and to the truth He teaches results in an intimacy, which is friendship. The martyr radiates the face of Christ, which his own friendship with Him reveals.

In *Rosarium Virginis Mariae* 25, written near the end of his pontificate, John Paul looks back to a remark he made in an *Angelus Message*: the "simple prayer of the rosary marks the rhythm of human life." Using this comment to enter into a discussion of the anthropological significance of the rosary, the Pope reiterates one

---

[20] John Paul II, *Rosarium Virginis Mariae* 15.

[21] John Paul II, *Fides et Ratio* 32; John Paul II, *Rosarium Virginis Mariae* 15.

of the central themes of his anthropology, extrapolated above. He explains, "Anyone who contemplates Christ through the various stages of his life cannot fail to perceive in Him the truth about man."[22]

The rosary is a contemplation of the life of Jesus, in whom "the mystery of man is seen in its true light;" Christ reveals to the person who He is.[23] Through the rosary, the believer focuses upon Christ and upon following in the "path of Christ, in whom man's path is 'recapitulated,' revealed and redeemed."[24] Through Christ, then, the believer comes "face to face with the image of the true man," who is Jesus Christ.[25] The Holy Father expresses the truth about the human person, which stems from contemplating the mysteries of Christ's life, by praying the rosary.

> [By] [c]ontemplating Christ's birth, they learn of the sanctity of life; seeing the household of Nazareth, they learn the original truth of the family according to God's plan; listening to the Master in the mysteries of His public ministry, they find the light which leads them to enter the Kingdom of God; and following Him on the way to Calvary, they learn the meaning of salvific suffering. Finally, contemplating Christ and His Blessed Mother in glory, they see the goal towards which each of us is called, if we allow ourselves to be healed and transformed by the Holy Spirit. It

---

[22] John Paul II, *Rosarium Virginis Mariae* 25.
[23] Second Vatican Council, *Gaudium et Spes* 22.
[24] John Paul II, *Rosarium Virginis Mariae* 25.
[25] John Paul II, *Rosarium Virginis Mariae* 25.

could be said that each mystery of the rosary, carefully meditated, sheds light on the mystery of man.[26]

By reflecting upon the birth, hidden life, public ministry, suffering, death and Resurrection of Jesus, one learns about Him and about "the mystery of man." Deeply aware of human suffering, the Pontiff reminds the faithful that praying the rosary is handing "over our burdens to the merciful hearts of Christ and His Mother."[27] Thus, the Pontiff closes paragraph 25 by explaining that the rosary "does indeed 'mark the rhythm of human life,' bringing it into harmony with the 'rhythm' of God's own life, in the joyful communion of the Holy Trinity, our life's destiny and deepest longing."

## Contemplating Christ with Mary "in the Living Sacrament of His Body and His Blood"

John Paul writes his last encyclical, *Ecclesia de Eucharistia*, "in continuity with the Jubilee heritage which [he has] left to the Church in the Apostolic Letter *Novo Millennio Ineunte* and its Marian crowning, *Rosarium Virginis Mariae*."[28] The Pope identi-

---

[26] John Paul II, *Rosarium Virginis Mariae* 25.

[27] John Paul II, *Rosarium Virginis Mariae* 25.

[28] John Paul II, *Ecclesia de Eucharistia* 6. Note the fact that John Paul proclaims October 2002 until October 2003 as the Year of the Rosary, writing *Rosarium Virginis Mariae* "as a Marian complement" to *Novo Millennio Ineunte* [John Paul II, *Rosarium Virginis Mariae* 3]. His encyclical *Ecclesia de Eucharistia* is promulgated on Holy Thursday of 2003, as a gift offered to the Church *during* the Year of the Rosary. Recall that

fies these three writings, then, as a trio of his thought regarding the heritage received by the Church in the Year of Great Jubilee.[29] The central focus of these pontifical writings is precisely the contemplation of Christ's face with Mary. Indeed, it is the core of the Jubilee legacy, which sums up her inheritance.

In *Ecclesia de Eucharistia*, John Paul describes contemplating the face of Christ with Mary as "the 'program' which [he has] set before the Church at the dawn of the third millennium, summoning her to 'put out into the deep' on the sea of history with the enthusiasm of the new evangelization." Elsewhere, the Holy Father insists that the "program" is the same for all times, and that "plan

---

John Paul emphasizes, in *Rosarium Virginis Mariae*, that the rosary is Christocentric; it is a means by which the believer may contemplate the face of Christ with Mary [John Paul II, *Rosarium Virginis Mariae* 1]. It is not until the following year, however, that the Pope declares the Year of the Eucharist: from October 2004 through October 2005 [John Paul II, *Mane Nobiscum Domine* 4]. The proximity and the interconnection of these two years of grace with each other makes the contemplation of Christ's face even more noteworthy.

[29] "[D]esirous of contemplating the face of Christ in the spirit which [John Paul] proposed in the Apostolic Letters *Novo Millennio Ineunte* and *Rosarium Virginis Mariae*," he asks the faithful to not fail in developing "this aspect of Eucharistic worship, which prolongs and increases the fruits of our communion in the body and blood of the Lord" [John Paul II, *Ecclesia de Eucharistia* 25]. Further, the Holy Father proclaims the Year of the Rosary to place his twenty-fifth anniversary of the pontificate, "under the aegis of the contemplation of Christ at the school of Mary" [John Paul II, *Ecclesia de Eucharistia* 7]. Thus, he calls the Church to stop before "the 'Eucharistic face' of Christ" and he points out "with new force to the Church the centrality of the Eucharist" [John Paul II, *Ecclesia de Eucharistia* 7].

# Chapter Sixteen: Contemplating the Face of Christ with Mary

[is] found in the Gospel and in the living Tradition" of the Church.[30] In other words, contemplating the face of Christ with Mary is reflecting upon His life, narrated by Sacred Scripture. One might add that the "program" also includes following Christ's teachings, as recorded in Scripture and safeguarded by Tradition. Because the teachings of Christ and His Church are holy, the person who follows them becomes holy; thus, the "program" of the new evangelization is a plan of holiness, which contemplating Christ's face instills in the heart of the person.

A second way in which the Pope describes the contemplation of Christ's face in *Ecclesia de Eucharistia*, concerns, as one would expect, the ability to recognize Him, especially in the Holy Eucharist. The Eucharist is the living Flesh and Blood of Jesus Christ, the Second Person of the Blessed Trinity Incarnate. Thus, John Paul reminds the reader that the "Church draws her life from Christ in the Eucharist."[31] By contemplating the mystery of the Eucharist, the believer comes to recognize Jesus "in the breaking of the

---

[30] John Paul II, *Novo Millennio Ineunte* 29. In *Novo Millennio Ineunte* 29, John Paul elaborates upon this "program" as follows. "It is not therefore a matter of inventing a 'new program.' The program already exists: it is the plan found in the Gospel and in the living Tradition, [and] it is the same as ever. Ultimately, it has its center in Christ Himself, who is to be known, loved and imitated, so that in Him we may live the life of the Trinity, and with Him transform history until its fulfillment in the heavenly Jerusalem. This is a program which does not change with shifts of times and cultures, even though it takes account of time and culture for the sake of true dialogue and effective communication. This program for all times is our program for the Third Millennium."

[31] John Paul II, *Ecclesia de Eucharistia* 6.

bread," just as the disciples recognize Him at Emmaus (Luke 24:35).[32] John Paul explains these thoughts in the following manner.

> To contemplate Christ involves being able to recognize Him wherever He manifests Himself, in His many forms of presence, but above all in the living sacrament of His Body and His Blood. The Church draws her life from Christ in the Eucharist; by Him she is fed and by Him she is enlightened. The Eucharist is both a mystery of faith and a 'mystery of light.' Whenever the Church celebrates the Eucharist, the faithful can in some way relive the experience of the two disciples on the road to Emmaus: 'their eyes were opened and they recognized Him' (Luke 24:31).[33]

With the quotation above, then, John Paul further elucidates his term, *contemplating the face of Christ,* to specify the ability to recognize Him especially in the Holy Eucharist. Contemplating the face of Christ in His Eucharistic Presence is the joy of the Church, who "draws her life from Christ in the Eucharist."[34] Remembering that one learns how to contemplate the face of Christ "at the school of Mary," one learns, from *Ecclesia de Eucharistia,* that her "enraptured gaze" teaches the believer the "unparalleled model of love

---

[32] John Paul II, *Ecclesia de Eucharistia* 6.
[33] John Paul II, *Ecclesia de Eucharistia* 6.
[34] John Paul II, *Ecclesia de Eucharistia* 6.

## Chapter Sixteen: Contemplating the Face of Christ with Mary

which should inspire [each Catholic] every time [one] receive[s] Eucharistic Communion."[35]

The Holy Father's description of *contemplating the face of Christ*, as the ability "to recognize Him wherever He manifests Himself," is akin to His definition from *Novo Millennio Ineunte*. Recognizing Christ "wherever He manifests Himself," then, is to consider Christ "in His historical features and in His mystery" and as He is "known through His manifold presence in the Church and in the world and confessed as the meaning of history and the light of life's journey."[36]

John Paul's addition to contemplating the face of Christ in *Ecclesia de Eucharistia* is, as one would expect, contemplating the Eucharistic face of Jesus in the Blessed Sacrament. As the first and most exemplary model of Eucharistic Adoration, Mary contemplates her Son, truly present in the Holy Eucharist, together with every believer. She also teaches one how to adore Him.

---

[35] John Paul II, *Ecclesia de Eucharistia* 55. Recall my description of Mary, from *Rosarium Virginis Mariae*, that describes her as the best model and teacher for conveying to the believer how to contemplate the face of Christ. For the specific term, contemplating Christ "at the school of Mary," see John Paul II, *Rosarium Virginis Mariae* 1, 3, 14, 43.

[36] John Paul II, *Novo Millennio Ineunte* 15.

# Chapter Seventeen

## The Martyr's Death is a Contemplation of the Face of Christ

According to John Paul's own words, *Novo Millennio Ineunte* contains suggestions for "an ever greater pastoral engagement based on the contemplation of the face of Christ, as part of an ecclesial pedagogy aimed at 'the high standard' of holiness and carried out especially through the art of prayer."[1] In addition, since *Novo Millennio Ineunte* is the Apostolic Letter that closes the Year of Great Jubilee, one might presume that John Paul mentions martyrdom in it, especially since he highlights martyrdom in his Jubilee Bull that announces the Holy Year. Again, martyrdom is one of the central themes of the Year of Great Jubilee.

My next task is to show how holiness connects both contemplating the face of Christ and martyrdom. While I refer to *Tertio Millennio Adveniente* 37 in this section, *Novo Millennio Ineunte* 7 offers a particularly enlightening explanation of holiness, especially as it relates to contemplating Christ's face and to martyrdom. I begin, therefore, with *Novo Millennio Ineunte* 7.

Having discussed John Paul's use of the term, *contemplating the face of Christ*, in significant pontifical works, one might ask whether *Novo Millennio Ineunte* comments upon martyrdom and, if so, exactly what it says. Since I do not include *Novo Millennio Ineunte* in my elucidation of the Pope's thought on martyrdom above,

---

[1] John Paul II, *Mane Nobiscum Domine* 8.

however, one presumes that it contains nothing of further substance regarding his definition of it. Further, John Paul specifies that the contemplation of Jesus' face, which primarily concerns pondering Christ "in His historical features and in His mystery," is directed toward holiness. [2] In addition, one might infer that martyrdom is somehow linked to holiness and to contemplating the face of Christ. My task in this section, then, is to explain why holiness pervades martyrdom and how contemplating Christ's face and martyrdom are inherently connected.

Although *Novo Millennio Ineunte* does not significantly alter or add further substance to John Paul's notion of martyrdom, the document does contain several illuminating corollaries concerning *martyrdom* and the *contemplation of Christ's face*. Again, although the Holy Father does not explicitly connect the martyr's death with the contemplation of Christ's face, several texts in *Novo Millennio Ineunte* suggest, in my opinion, a relation between the two concepts.

The Holy Father's first point concerns the gratitude given to Christ for "granting His Church a great host of saints and martyrs," who have entered "naturally into Christ's life" through friendship.[3] Immediately following his expression of gratitude for the martyrs, John Paul speaks of holiness, which "has emerged more clearly as the dimension which expresses best the mystery of the Church."[4] From their close placement in the text, one might surmise that the

---

[2] John Paul II, *Novo Millennio Ineunte* 15; John Paul II, *Mane Nobiscum Domine* 8.

[3] John Paul II, *Novo Millennio Ineunte* 7, 15.

[4] John Paul II, *Novo Millennio Ineunte* 7.

## Chapter Seventeen: The Martyr's Death

martyr is a prime example of holiness. John Paul continues *Novo Millennio Ineunte* 7 by observing that, "Holiness, a message that convinces without the need for words, is the living reflection of the face of Christ." The Pope clearly expresses, then, that holiness reflects the face of Christ.

With *Fides et Ratio* 32, I reiterate the point that the martyr delivers a silent message, for his death provides "evidence of a love that has no need of lengthy arguments in order to convince." From my extrapolation above, I indicate that the martyr shows the holiness of God, of His law, and of the Church by his willing acceptance of death in order to remain faithful to God's law.[5]

Since holiness reflects the face of Christ, one might surmise that both the law of God and the holiness of the Church also reflect the face of Christ. Further, the martyr witnesses to the holiness of God's law and to the holiness of the Church by his acceptance of death. Thus, he is also holy. By stressing the "fullness of life proper to the children of God," the Pope accentuates holiness. As I indicate above, one's dependence upon God's grace is a means by which one becomes a child of God (cf. Ephesians 4:13).[6] Because holiness reflects the face of Christ, as *Novo Millennio Ineunte* 7 brings out, the martyr likewise reflects His sacred features.

---

[5] John Paul II, *Veritatis Splendor* 91 through 93. Just as one "become[s] good by seeking the Good," so also does one become holy by seeking the Holy One and by doing what is holy, namely, the law of God [J. A. DiNoia, OP, "Veritatis Splendor: Moral Life as Transfigured Life" (pages 1-10) in *Veritatis Splendor and the Renewal of Moral Theology* J. A. DiNoia, OP, and Romanus Cessario, OP, eds. (Princeton: Scepter Publishers, 1999), 2.

[6] John Paul II, *Veritatis Splendor* 115.

In *Novo Millennio Ineunte 7*, John Paul remarks that holiness bears eloquent testimony "without the need for words." This statement recalls the Pope's explanation of holiness as listening to "the call of the One who 'first loved us'" by obeying the Commandments.[7] The martyr's holiness, which his death radiates, is a "living reflection of the face of Christ."[8] That "living reflection" of Him depicts holiness as a crucial factor of the intimate relationship between the martyr and Jesus described in *Fides et Ratio* 32. Again, the martyr's death expresses his act of entrustment to Jesus, which convinces without the "need of lengthy arguments."[9]

One might interpret the martyr's love, described in *Novo Millennio Ineunte 7*, as a convincing love that bears silent witness to the law of God and to the objective moral order. The martyr's love *convinces* precisely because he offers the sacrifice of his life rather than denying Jesus and His holy law. Since death is the final statement of one's life, the martyr's concluding word *convinces* by the faithful love that his death *expresses*.[10] In addition, the martyr's closing word embodies an inaudible testimony to his belief in Jesus and in what He teaches.

As I show above, believing in Christ and in His word is a prayer of abiding reciprocity between Jesus and the martyr.[11] Now, I add

---

[7] John Paul II, *Veritatis Splendor* 115.

[8] John Paul II, *Novo Millennio Ineunte* 7.

[9] John Paul II, *Fides et Ratio* 32.

[10] Notice that I refer to the martyr's *word*. Word is in the singular. That is no mistake, for the martyr's concluding word is *one* Word, Jesus Christ, the Word his death contemplates.

[11] John Paul II, *Novo Millennio Ineunte* 32.

the following. The martyr's prayer of love *needs* no words because his actions fill his entire being with fidelity to Jesus and to His teachings. His abiding, convincing love is also silent because death removes speech.

When John Paul "calls for a Christian life distinguished above all in the art of prayer," the martyr offers an eloquent example, animated by his convincing love, which inaudibly witnesses to the truth of the human person, to the truth of Christ, and to the objective moral law.[12] Further, because prayer "develops that conversation with Christ which makes us His intimate friends," the martyr's love testifies to his refusal to betray that friendship. Moreover, because the martyr abides in Jesus, and Jesus abides in him (cf. John 15:4), as *Novo Millennio Ineunte* 32 brings out, his prayer is a contemplation of Christ's face.[13] One cannot abide in Jesus without keeping His word.[14] Again, the Commandments play a central role in the life of the martyr-contemplator of the face of Jesus Christ. One testifies to his love for Jesus by following the Commandments (John 15:12).

Finally, since this "reciprocity opens us, through Christ and in Christ, to contemplation of the Father's face," and, since the martyr's death reflects the forgiveness "uttered by Christ on the Cross,"

---

[12] John Paul II, *Novo Millennio Ineunte* 32.

[13] John Paul II, *Novo Millennio Ineunte* 32.

[14] Christ's discourse to the Apostles at the Last Supper offers numerous Scripture passages that attest to this truth. For example, Jesus teaches, "If you keep My Commandments, you will abide in My love, just as I have kept My Father's Commandments and abide in His love" [John 15:10]. For more examples of keeping Christ's word in order to abide in Him, see John 15:1-17.

one might understand the martyr's death as a contemplation of the face of Christ, although John Paul does not make this connection explicit.[15] The death of the martyr expresses what it means to contemplate Christ's face on account of his abiding love that *convinces* because he stakes his life on that love. Since the martyr's death embodies forgiving love, it reflects a contemplation of the face of Jesus. Often, the martyr even expresses that forgiveness in words. Saint Maria Goretti (1890-1902) and Blessed Miguel Agustín Pro (1891-1927) serve as examples.

In another document, *Tertio Millennio Adveniente* 37, John Paul highlights the martyr by indicating that the holiness of the Church's members gives "supreme honor to God Himself." He further describes this holiness by pointing to Jesus, who is "at the origin" of the martyr's life and holiness. In other words, the Church honors Christ by venerating the martyr. One might interpret this thought, that the Church's honor is directed to Christ through the martyr, by claiming that the martyr embodies the contemplation of Christ's face by his death. The quotation below, then, suggests the Christocentric heart of martyrdom: Jesus Christ lies at the very center of the martyr's life and death.

> The *martyrologium* of the first centuries was the basis of the veneration of the saints. By proclaiming and venerating the holiness of her sons and daughters, the Church gave supreme honor to God Himself; in the martyrs she venerated

---

[15] John Paul II, *Novo Millennio Ineunte* 32; John Paul II, *Incarnationis Mysterium* 13.

## Chapter Seventeen: The Martyr's Death

Christ, who was at the origin of their martyrdom and of their holiness.[16]

Jesus Christ, Himself, is the center of the martyr's life and death because one accepts death in order to bear witness to Him. By contemplating His face, the martyr entrusts himself to Christ, as I explain above, with his inaudible prayer of convincing love. At the same time, Jesus entrusts Himself to the martyr so much so that He is the "origin of [his] martyrdom and of [his] holiness."[17] Jesus calls the martyr to Himself by means of a death that proclaims one's "fidelity to God's holy law,"[18] affirms "the inviolability of the moral order,"[19] and witnesses to the "holiness of the Church."[20] Highlighting the Christocentric heart of martyrdom, then, John Paul underscores the martyr who "lived fully by the truth of Christ" and thus became holy.[21]

Having described John Paul's meaning of the term, *contemplating the face of Christ*, one might press the point. Why is the death

---

[16] John Paul II, *Tertio Millennio Adveniente* 37.

[17] John Paul II, *Tertio Millennio Adveniente* 37. To claim, as does John Paul, that Jesus is the "origin" of one's martyrdom is to imply that He is the One for whom the martyr offers his life. Again, the martyr does not betray the intimate relationship he has with Jesus, even though it requires his life. The Holy Father's description of Jesus as the "origin" of one's martyrdom, then, offers further evidence that the death of the martyr might be construed as a contemplation of His face.

[18] John Paul II, *Veritatis Splendor* 93.

[19] John Paul II, *Veritatis Splendor* 92.

[20] John Paul II, *Veritatis Splendor* 93.

[21] John Paul II, *Tertio Millennio Adveniente* 37.

of the martyr a contemplation of Christ's face? John Paul does not make that connection explicit.

To be sure, I am not arguing that martyrdom is the only depiction of such contemplation, nor am I suggesting that martyrdom comprises the only legitimate way in which one contemplates Christ's face. Instead, I affirm that the martyr's death describes the human person as a contemplator of the face of Christ Jesus. I explain as follows.

### An Objective Articulation of the Martyr's Death

My first task is to explain how one might understand the martyr's death as a contemplation of Christ's face from an objective perspective. Highlighting the objective dimension justifies my assertion that the death of the martyr is a contemplation of Christ's face. In addition, showing the objective perspective of both *martyrdom* and *contemplation* defends my assertion that the martyr's death is a manifestation, or proclamation of the face of Christ. Because John Paul claims that people "ask believers not only to 'speak' of Christ, but in a certain sense to 'show' Him to them," one might contend that the clearest "speaking," or proclamation, is the "showing" of Christ to others.[22]

Showing Jesus to others hearkens back to my opening comment, at the inception of my work. John Paul states that "our witness...would be hopelessly inadequate if we ourselves had not first

---

[22] John Paul II, *Novo Millennio Ineunte* 16.

## Chapter Seventeen: The Martyr's Death

contemplated His face."[23] While John Paul does not explicitly refer to the martyr's death, from this statement, one can surmise that, if the martyr shows Jesus to others, then he has first contemplated Christ's face, himself. These two points: the *showing* of Christ's face to others by his death (one), from an *objective perspective* (two), are intimately intertwined. They can only be separated with difficulty in order to discuss each one. Thus, I first seek to validate my claim that the martyr's death is, objectively, a contemplation of Christ's face. Once I secure the objective dimension, the *showing* of His face follows.

Describing the objective reality of the martyr's death as a contemplation of the face of Jesus Christ concerns the following. I explain above that the martyr's death radiates the splendor of Truth, of Christ Jesus, who is Truth, by the sacrifice of his life. I explain that his acceptance of death upholds the objectivity of truth, and thus, of the objective moral order, as well. Again, I reiterate the fact that truth is universal and unchangeable. The martyr's death is the anticipated consequence of his fidelity to t/Truth—to Christ and His teachings.

The martyr's death might be described as contemplating the face of Christ, then, because it inherently manifests t/Truth: both objective truth, and Jesus Christ, who is Truth. Again, I am suggesting that the very nature of the martyr's death is an objective reality that shows the face of Jesus to others regardless of the martyr's own personal prayer at that moment.

---

[23] John Paul II, *Novo Millennio Ineunte* 16.

John Paul claims that contemplating the face of Christ confronts "the most paradoxical aspect of His mystery as it emerges in His last hour on the Cross."[24] The martyr's death reflects the mystery of Christ's face because he suffers to bear witness to the t/Truth. Because Jesus reveals the person to himself, as John Paul reiterates from *Gaudium et Spes* 22, the martyr has learned who he is from Jesus. Like Christ, the martyr dies forgiving his persecutors and bearing witness to t/Truth.

In addition, the martyr makes a sincere gift of himself, by accepting death in order to remain faithful to the truth of God's law. This sincere gift is offered with a transparency—an openness—that shows the face of Christ to others *as* forgiving love. The martyr's death, then, describes both the truth of the human person (the martyr) and the Truth of a Divine Person (Jesus Christ). Thus, martyrdom shows the human person's innate openness to God by his testimony to objective truth, and to Jesus Christ, who is Truth. The person's innate openness to God and to truth, expressed by the contemplative obedience that listens unto death, describes the objective reality of the martyr's death as a contemplation of the face of Christ Jesus, Son of the living God.

## An Objective Articulation of Contemplating Christ's Face

As I describe above, the martyr's radiance of t/Truth is contemplative in essence due to his obedience (listening) to the holy law of God. In order to show that the martyr's death (from an ob-

---

[24] John Paul II, *Novo Millennio Ineunte* 25.

jective perspective) is also contemplative (from an objective perspective), I explain as follows.

The martyr's attentive listening, as I show with *Veritatis Splendor*, is characterized by faith that loves unto death. John Paul explains faith as a decision that embodies every dimension of one's life. Thus, the martyr's faith is his loving *living* of t/Truth by attentive listening, or obedience, to Christ. "If you love Me, you will keep My Commandments" (John 14:15 RSVCE).

Because the martyr's death is a willing result of his fidelity to Christ and His teachings, by the very fact of his voluntary acceptance of death, he listens with docile obedience. I explain above that the martyr lives out the truth of faith by putting into action—the "action" that comprises his life and his death—the word, or "set of propositions," he has received. That action, of initiating the received word by martyrdom, may be described as contemplation because it embraces the life of Christ with one's own loving obedient listening unto death.

The martyr's death highlights the contemplative dimension of the human person by his "*doing* the Truth."[25] Martyrdom, then, negates the various "isms" of our day, such as materialism, secularism, and relativism, because the martyr's death both confirms the objectivity of the moral order and it signifies his upright conscience, which calls "good and evil by their proper name."[26] Opposite to a "lack of trust in the wisdom of God, who guides man with the moral law," the martyr's death is *prayer* because it expresses

---

[25] John Paul II, *Veritatis Splendor* 84.
[26] John Paul II, *Dominum et Vivificantem* 43.

confident trust in God's wisdom and mercy, who "guides man with the moral law" to union with his Heavenly Father.[27]

The death of the martyr is an objective contemplation of Christ's face, then, because he reflects in his own life the truth he learns. The truth of the human person is his creation by God and his redemption in Christ. Further, the truth that Christ reveals to the martyr is his inviolable dignity and his status as a child of God the Father. The martyr regards another person as one to whom he extends his love and his self-gift unto death.

In addition, the martyr's (subjective) contemplation of Christ's face—as John Paul maintains is necessary to show Jesus to others—is reflecting upon Christ's life and His Commandment to love with decisions that bring about his own martyrdom. In other words, the martyr's death expresses a contemplative, obedient listening to Christ with a confident resolution that compels him to offer his life to maintain that loving and faithful obedience.

The death of the martyr is an objective contemplation of Christ's face for another reason, as well. His death not only expresses contemplative listening, but it also highlights a contemplative testimony to human dignity. With *Redemptor Hominis* 12, I indicate that the martyr's attitude toward human dignity implies his availability to another who suffers. The martyr's attitude toward the dignity of another suffering person portrays a contemplative dimension of martyrdom because it implies the human person's freedom, in communion with the Church. Thus, to claim that the martyr's death is a proclamation, or a showing of Christ's face

---

[27] John Paul II, *Veritatis Splendor* 84.

to others is to suggest that it is an act "made in union with the entire ecclesial community."[28]

As I show above, the martyr's act of entrustment to Jesus reveals a love that forgives one's persecutors. Human freedom lies at the heart of the martyr's speechless attitude toward human dignity not only because he forgives, but also because he refuses to contradict the truth of the human person by his own actions. Another way of articulating the contemplative dimension of martyrdom, then, is to say that the martyr does not have to argue in order to *be* who he *is*; he *is* who he is on account of his silent testimony, given as he offers his life. In other words, because freedom lies at the heart of the martyr's attitude toward human dignity, his death expresses the contemplative, speechless disposition of his own entrustment to Jesus Christ.

## The Martyr's Death is a Contemplation of Christ's Face

Among the many reasons why the martyr's death might be construed as a contemplation of Christ's face, I offer the following. As I bring out with *Fides et Ratio* 32, the martyr's death radiates his encounter with Jesus. That encounter is his own act of loving entrustment to Christ, and, through Christ, to the Father. The truth of the human person, which the martyr "has discovered in the encounter with Christ," expresses the core of his being as one who is essentially open to God, and "open to receiving the mystery of

---

[28] John Paul II, *Redemptoris Missio* 45.

Trinitarian life," which contemplating His face entails.[29] The innate reality of one's openness to God is implied by the martyr's inaudible loving entrustment to Jesus, which, in turn, indicates a reciprocity of abiding love.

As both *Christifideles Laici* 39 and *Incarnationis Mysterium* 13 help to show, love is at the core of the martyr's sacrifice. Indeed, the martyr "is a sign of that greater love which sums up all other values."[30] One might describe his death as a contemplation of Christ's face, then, because it reflects the martyr's handing over of himself to Jesus, in trusting love. The martyr's entrusting love implies the contemplation of Christ's face because such contemplation entails pondering Jesus Christ, who is the Church's "treasure and...joy."[31]

The martyr's reciprocity of abiding love also vivifies the forgiving love "uttered by Christ on the Cross."[32] As I show with *Ecclesia in Asia*, the forgiving love of the martyr, in imitation of Christ Crucified, comprises the core of Christian proclamation. Because John Paul claims that the "martyr's life reflects the extraordinary words [of forgiveness] uttered by Christ on the Cross," one might conclude that the martyr's death reveals the face of Christ Crucified.[33] One might further conclude that the martyr's death is a contemplation of Christ's face because the martyr's forgiving love re-

---

[29] John Paul II, *Fides et Ratio* 32; John Paul II, *Rosarium Virginis Mariae* 9.

[30] John Paul II, *Incarnationis Mysterium* 13.

[31] John Paul II, *Novo Millennio Ineunte* 28.

[32] John Paul II, *Incarnationis Mysterium* 13.

[33] John Paul II, *Incarnationis Mysterium* 13.

calls "Christ considered...in His mystery," in the "most paradoxical aspect of His mystery, as it emerges in His last hour, on the Cross."[34]

The martyr's death is a contemplation of Christ's face, then, because Christ forgave others both *from* the Cross and *by* His death. As I note above, Christ's death reveals the Father's forgiving love, which is mercy. *Ecclesia in Asia* helps show that the principal teaching the martyr offers is the power of the Cross, which is the strength of Christ Crucified. "For the word of the Cross is folly to those who are perishing, but to us who are being saved it is the power of God" (1 Corinthians 1:18). Because the martyr's death radiates the forgiving love of Jesus Christ Crucified, who, in turn, reveals the face of the Father as love and mercy, one might understand this death as a contemplation of the face of Christ.

## The Martyr's Death is a Visible Proclamation of Christ's Face

As I show above, one might claim that the martyr's death shows the human person's dignity as "part of the content of proclamation" because it expresses his own neediness for Christ's redemptive love.[35] At the same time, the death of the martyr also indicates his own loving embrace of the redemptive love of Jesus. Thus, his attitude toward human dignity is given not in words, but in the testimony of his own blood.

Because the martyr's death is a willing result of his fidelity to Jesus and to His teachings, by the very fact that his death is volun-

---

[34] John Paul II, *Novo Millennio Ineunte* 15, 25.

[35] John Paul II, *Redemptor Hominis* 12.

tarily accepted, he *proclaims* Jesus to others. By his decisions, the consequences of which merit his death, he shows the face of Christ to others because of martyrdom's tangibility and death's finality. In other words, because the martyr offers his life to uphold Christ's teachings, his death expresses a clear and unquestionable testimony to the truth for which he stands.

Another conclusion results from these reflections. To highlight the martyr's death as a proclamation of Christ's face is to express that proclamation, itself, has a contemplative dimension. One cannot show Jesus to others—and showing Jesus lies at the heart of proclamation—unless one first contemplates the face of Jesus for oneself. Again, the contemplation of the face of Christ includes reflecting upon His life, as handed down in Divine Revelation, and recognizing "Him wherever He manifests Himself, in His many forms of presence, but above all in the living sacrament of His Body and His Blood."[36]

In *Fides et Ratio* 32, John Paul implies that the martyr's death is an encounter with Jesus. He explains that the person's encounter shows both a relationship of trusting love with Jesus, and it manifests his essential openness "to receiving the mystery of Trinitarian life."[37] In *Rosarium Virginis Mariae* 9, John Paul says being "open to receiving the mystery of Trinitarian life" describes the contemplation of Christ's face. The martyr's death might also be seen as a contemplation of Christ's face, then, because he willingly dies to

---

[36] John Paul II, *Novo Millennio Ineunte* 15; John Paul II, *Ecclesia de Eucharistia* 6.

[37] John Paul II, *Rosarium Virginis Mariae* 9.

### Chapter Seventeen: The Martyr's Death

retain his relationship with Jesus and to safeguard his own openness with the Trinity.

To reiterate, the death of the martyr might be interpreted as a contemplation of Christ's face, then, on account of his entrustment to Jesus. The martyr testifies to the fact that Jesus gives meaning to his life, especially in the dramatic moment of his death. The martyr's inaudible prayer of abiding love with Christ Jesus, which is the willing sacrifice of his life, testifies to Christ's importance not only in his own life, but also in the lives of others, who make up human history. Again, because his death expresses an attitude toward human dignity, this attitude is directed toward all human beings of all times.

An additional reason why the martyr's death is a contemplation of Christ's face is based upon John Paul's description of contemplation as "Christ considered in His historical features and in His mystery, Christ known through His manifold presence in the Church and in the world, and confessed as the meaning of history."[38] The martyr's death makes Jesus known and it shows His presence in human history because of the martyr's fidelity to His teachings. By his decisions, the consequences of which merit his death, he shows the face of Jesus to others in a tangible manner. In other words, because the martyr offers his life in order to uphold Christ's teachings, his death expresses a clear and unquestionable testimony to Christ's "manifold presence in the Church and in the world," whose presence gives meaning to human history.

---

[38] John Paul II, *Novo Millennio Ineunte* 15.

The martyr's death shows Jesus acting in human history through the courage and grace the martyr receives by obeying His commands, when it requires his own death. The martyr's death is a contemplation of Christ's face, then, because it expresses a reflection of Christ's presence and life, His salvific death, and His action in human history for all people. The death of the martyr not only shows Christ's face to others, but it is also a contemplation of His face, as well.

## The Martyr's Death Expresses a Life "Distinguished...in the Art of Prayer"

One final point deserves to be made. As I explain above, the death of the martyr is a contemplation of the face of Christ, which might be described as an inaudible prayer. Now I add the fact, developed with *Rosarium Virginis Mariae*, that martyrdom expresses "a Christian life distinguished above all in the art of prayer."[39] I support this claim in the following manner.

John Paul speaks of the rosary as "a most effective means of fostering among the faithful that commitment to the contemplation of the Christian mystery."[40] Referring to the genuine "training in holiness" elucidated upon in *Novo Millennio Ineunte*, John Paul identifies the central core of this "holiness" as a life distinguished by "the art of prayer."[41] Since martyrdom reflects the intimate bond

---

[39] John Paul II, *Rosarium Virginis Mariae* 5.
[40] John Paul II, *Rosarium Virginis Mariae* 5.
[41] The Holy Father refers to *Novo Millennio Ineunte* 32 in John Paul II, *Rosarium Virginis Mariae* 5.

## Chapter Seventeen: The Martyr's Death

between Christ and the martyr, and, because this bond is implied by the martyr's fidelity to Him in the face of death, I suggest that martyrdom expresses a life, summarized at the moment of death, by the martyr's love and faith. Further, the martyr's death is "distinguished above all in the art of prayer" because it *is* prayer; the martyr's inaudible cry of abiding love expresses a reciprocal relationship with Jesus Christ Himself.[42] The cry of abiding love lies at the heart of prayer, as the Bride (the martyr, which can also be understood as the Church) rests in the loving gaze of the Bridegroom (Jesus Christ).

As *Incarnationis Mysterium* 13 brings out, the martyr's death reflects the face of Christ Crucified from two perspectives. The first is love and the second is faith. Consequently, the martyr's death, which is a silent cry of abiding love, is made audible by contemplating Christ's face through the offering of self-gift made in love and in faith.

John Paul highlights the fact that the lives of the martyrs reveal the "truth of Christian love."[43] In fact, his depiction of the martyr as "a sign of that greater love which sums up all other values" echoes the words of Saint Paul, which express love as "the fulfillment

---

[42] John Paul II, *Rosarium Virginis Mariae* 5. The Latin word *arte* might be explained, in this context, as follows. The word *arte* may be translated several ways, such as *skill*, *method*, or *technique*, and it can even refer to *conduct* or *character*. Building from these various renditions, then, I develop the following thought. My claim, that the martyr's death is "distinguished above all in the art of prayer," means that his death, as a manner of how he conduct's his life—of living in the truth—forms his life and describes his last moment as an embodiment of prayer.

[43] John Paul II, *Incarnationis Mysterium* 13.

of the law" (Romans 13:10).⁴⁴ Further, John Paul's reference to the martyr as one who gives his life for love recalls Christ's words at the Last Supper. "Greater love than this no man hath, that a man lay down his life for his friends" (John 15:13).

The following passage also confirms that the martyr's death reveals the face of Jesus from the perspective of love. The martyrs "are the ones who have proclaimed the Gospel by giving their lives for love. …The martyr's life reflects the extraordinary words uttered by Christ on the Cross: 'Father, forgive them, for they know not what they do' (Luke 23:34)."⁴⁵ This text recalls Christ's Commandment to "love one another as I have loved you" (John 15:12), thus uniting the martyr, in full freedom, with Jesus and with other persons.⁴⁶ Reading this passage with *Veritatis Splendor* 88, the living faith of the martyr is embodied in "a truth to be lived out." He lives the truth as a "decision involving one's whole existence," and that decision proclaims the "Gospel by giving [his] life for love."⁴⁷ The martyr lays down his life for Jesus and for his neighbor in an act of self-gift. Because of the martyr's forgiving love, then, which recalls the Passion and death of Jesus, one might understand the martyr's death as a contemplation of Christ's face.⁴⁸

A second dimension of the martyr's silent testimony to Christ concerns faith. John Paul explains that the martyr's commitment

---

⁴⁴ John Paul II, *Incarnationis Mysterium* 13.

⁴⁵ John Paul II, *Incarnationis Mysterium* 13.

⁴⁶ John Paul II, *Veritatis Splendor* 86.

⁴⁷ John Paul II, *Veritatis Splendor* 88; John Paul II, *Incarnationis Mysterium* 13.

⁴⁸ John Paul II, *Novo Millennio Ineunte* 15, 25.

## Chapter Seventeen: The Martyr's Death

"to Christ and the Church" gives "eloquent proof of the truth of the faith."[49] More evocatively, the Pontiff refers to faith's ability to give "a human face even to the most violent of deaths and show its beauty even in the midst of the most atrocious persecutions," as *Incarnationis Mysterium* also indicates.

In my reading of *Incarnationis Mysterium*, together with the other documents I cite, I conclude that the martyr's death reflects the face of Christ Crucified on account of his testimony to faith for two reasons. First, the martyr offers his life to uphold Christ's teachings, in which he ardently believes. Second, the martyr gives a "human face" to a violent death by forgiving his persecutors. Thus, the martyr draws others to Christ by radiating his loving entrustment to Him, made audible by his death.

Combining both aspects of the martyr's testimony, his love and his faith, one summarizes the following insight. By making known the beauty of the human face, which reflects "the splendor of God," the martyr radiates Christ Crucified in his love that abides in Him and forgives his persecutors.[50] The martyr's death is the "most eloquent proof of the truth of the faith," then, because he refuses to betray Jesus and His teachings.[51] But, as I also explain above, this refusal to betray Jesus also implies the martyr's unwillingness to deny himself, and the truth of who he is as a human person.

The martyr's refusal to betray Jesus, the truth of the human person, and his own self, manifests both human freedom and hu-

---

[49] John Paul II, *Incarnationis Mysterium* 13.
[50] John Paul II, *Veritatis Splendor* 90.
[51] John Paul II, *Incarnationis Mysterium* 13.

man dignity. In his death that results from this refusal, he reveals the face of Christ Crucified.

# Chapter Eighteen

## Summarizing the Project

In my work, I argue that John Paul's description of martyr's death is a contemplation of the face of Christ. Because the Holy Father does not explicitly make that comparison, understanding his meaning of the two concepts and showing how they correlate are my primary tasks above. Here, I both summarize my project and I deepen it.

First, I draw together the two terms, *martyrdom*, and *contemplation of the face of Christ*. My second task is to deepen this correlation by offering several novel reflections of martyrdom (a contemplation of Christ's face) regarding proclamation, prayer, and the human person. For example, *proclamation* first entails a listening obedience, and John Paul's description of martyrdom indicates such obedience. In addition, the martyr's death, which is an act of entrustment to Jesus, reveals that praying with humility specifies one's entrustment of oneself to the Other and to the Truth that the Other speaks.

### Correlating Martyrdom and Contemplation of Christ's Face with *Gaudium et Spes* 22

To claim that the martyr's death is a contemplation of Christ's face, I begin my work by offering a synopsis of John Paul's concept of the human person. The anthropological component hinges upon two Conciliar texts, central to John Paul's thought, which offer a summary of his reflection upon the person. The Holy Father's interpretation of the Conciliar texts provides the foundation upon which to build my claim concerning the martyr's death as a contemplation of Christ's face.

Resting upon two often-quoted texts from *Gaudium et Spes*, I set forth a number of elements central to John Paul's anthropology. In particular, I focus upon three points that the Holy Father highlights from *Gaudium et Spes* 22 that describe and explain his interpretation of the Conciliar term, the *mystery of man*. With *Redemptor Hominis* 8-10, I bring out the following points from Scripture: the human person is created in the image and likeness of God, he is redeemed by Christ, and his re-creation in Christ flows from God's love for the person.

In *Redemptor Hominis* 8, for example, the Pope affirms the essential goodness of both the person and of human life, itself. The goodness of the human person underscores the command not to take innocent human life. These thoughts, from the Holy Father's interpretation of *Gaudium et Spes* 22, help show that the martyr's willing acceptance of death affirms "the inviolability of the personal dignity of man."[1] On account of the inherent goodness of the person, created in God's image and redeemed by the Passion and death of Christ, each human being possesses an innate dignity that cannot be violated.[2]

---

[1] John Paul II, *Veritatis Splendor* 92.

[2] John Paul II, *Veritatis Splendor* 92. In *Redemptor Hominis* 13, the Pope points to the Church's task of safeguarding the truth of the human

## Chapter Eighteen: Summarizing the Project

Rooted in my analysis of the Pope's interpretation of *Gaudium et Spes* 22, it follows that the martyr's willing acceptance of death in fidelity to God's law is the sacrifice of a great good, of human life, itself, for an even greater good, which is one's fidelity to the Commandments. This greater good, preserving one's union with God by following the Commandments, sometimes results in martyrdom. John Paul describes martyrdom as "the exaltation of a person's perfect 'humanity' and of true 'life.'"[3] I explain these points with *Veritatis Splendor* 92 and Saint Ignatius of Antioch's *Letter to the Romans*.

*Redemptor Hominis* 10 adds that the person's redemption by the Blood of Christ "reveals man to himself" as a person of great worth. The Holy Father calls that "deep amazement at man's worth and dignity...[the] Gospel...the Good News...[and] Christianity." Further, Christ's revelation of the person's *mystery* is that one is a child of God the Father. By His death on the Cross, Jesus makes known one's adoptive sonship by restoring the person to the Father's friendship (cf. Romans 8:14-25; Galatians 4:5-7). One's call to embrace this filial relation with the Father is particularly relevant to my description of the martyr's death. For example, the death of the martyr illuminates a reciprocity of abiding love with the Father through the Son, Jesus Christ. In "abandoning oneself to Him, in letting oneself be transformed by His grace and renewed by His mercy," the martyr radiates Truth who is Jesus Christ.[4]

---

person. As I show in my work, the Church continually upholds the person's innate dignity and freedom.

[3] John Paul II, *Veritatis Splendor* 92.
[4] John Paul II, *Veritatis Splendor* 119.

John Paul's *Opening Address* at the Puebla Conference, in conjunction with *Dominum et Vivificantem* 36, show a second interpretation of his understanding of *Gaudium et Spes* 22. These texts build upon the Pope's explanation, in *Redemptor Hominis* 8-10, of the Father's love for the person. The Puebla *Address* brings out the futility of human existence if one lives without reference to God. The emptiness of life without God highlights, in turn, the fact that because the person is a creature, he is constituted "in a unique, exclusive and unrepeatable relationship with God Himself."

One's ultimate fulfillment by God and the person's unrivaled existence among the rest of creation play into the Pope's concept of martyrdom as the "exaltation of a person's perfect 'humanity' and of true 'life,'" because these points underscore the martyr's death as living in the truth.[5]

Living in the truth means living in a filial relationship with the Father. As the Conciliar document explains, when Jesus reveals "the Father and His love" by His own death on the Cross, then He reveals the truth of the human person. Each person is a beloved child of the Heavenly Father.[6] As my work shows, the truth of the person is filial childhood: "what the person is and what the person reveals" by his very nature is that he is a child of the Heavenly Father.[7] The person is one who "discovers himself as belonging to

---

[5] John Paul II, *Fides et Ratio* 60; John Paul II, *Opening Address* at Puebla, 28 January 1979; John Paul II, *Veritatis Splendor* 92.

[6] Second Vatican Council, *Gaudium et Spes* 22.

[7] John Paul II, *Fides et Ratio* 32.

## Chapter Eighteen: Summarizing the Project

Christ and discovers that in Christ he is raised to the status of a child of God" the Father.[8]

Connecting the truth of the human person with John Paul's teaching on martyrdom highlights the fact that, by one's willing acceptance of death, the martyr shows that one's "perfect 'humanity' and true 'life'" is living as a child of the Eternal Father. In sum, the martyr's "true life" makes known, "from deep within" the person, his filial relation to God the Father.[9] Being the Father's child *that he is* means that he can only be fulfilled by Him. Consequently, each person must be willing to give one's life, if it is required, to remain faithful to Christ, and thus, to the Father (cf. Matthew 10:33). The person's uniqueness among the rest of visible creation dictates his ultimate fulfillment in God alone. Nothing can take that away or erase it from the human person.

As I show with the Puebla *Address* and *Dominum et Vivificantem*, the person's unique creation in the image of God speaks to his dependence upon his Creator. In other words, because the human person exists *as a creature*, he is ontologically dependent upon his Creator for both his existence and his essence. Concerning the person's essence, my work not only highlights his rational nature by discussing human transcendence in *Fides et Ratio* 60, but also, I focus upon the notion of self-gift and one's ability to live in relation to another from *Gaudium et Spes* 24.

As John Paul's teaching makes clear, the object of the human act and the existence of intrinsically evil human acts presuppose

---

[8] John Paul II, *Dominum et Vivificantem* 59.
[9] John Paul II, *Fides et Ratio* 32.

the "existence of an 'objective moral order.'"[10] The person's ontological dependence upon God, then, is significant to the Holy Father's notion of martyrdom because the martyr dies to uphold objective truth, and thus, the objective moral law. Further, as *Veritatis Splendor* 94 shows, the "moral sense present" in the human person obliges that all "are bound to seek the truth…and to embrace the truth they come to know, and to hold fast to it."[11] Thus, the martyr's death, which "represents the high point of the witness to moral truth," describes the martyr as an unquestionable example of one who lives in the truth because the moral order is objective.[12]

Having "defended moral truth even to the point of enduring martyrdom," the martyr clearly "witnesses to divine Truth."[13] Because Jesus Christ is God, He cannot abandon the martyr, who is created in the image and likeness of God and who lives in the truth. Indeed, He has "gone to death with people condemned for the sake of truth."[14]

Another point from John Paul's discussion of the person's transcendence is the notion of one's ability to enjoy God. Recall that in *Augustinum Hipponesem*, John Paul indicates that the Conciliar term, *the mystery of man*, suggests that one's greatness lies in his

---

[10] John Paul II, *Veritatis Splendor* 82.

[11] John Paul II, *Veritatis Splendor* 94; Second Vatican Council, *Dignitatis Humanae* 1.

[12] John Paul II, *Veritatis Splendor* 93.

[13] John Paul II, *Veritatis Splendor* 90; John Paul II, *Dominum et Vivificantem* 60.

[14] John Paul II, *Redemptor Hominis* 12.

## Chapter Eighteen: Summarizing the Project

ability to enjoy God.[15] The human person's ability to delight in God, on account of the transcendent nature of human rationality, is significant for explaining martyrdom as a contemplation of Christ's face because such contemplation necessarily implies delight in God. John Paul teaches that, "In contemplating Christ's face we become open to receiving the mystery of Trinitarian life, experiencing ever anew the love of the Father and delighting in the joy of the Holy Spirit."[16] Contemplating Christ's face brings joy, which corresponds to the fact that human transcendence enables one to enjoy God.

As I show with *Veritatis Splendor* 27, the Church's responsibility of "promoting and preserving the faith and the moral life" infers that obedience to Church teaching assists the person's growth in holiness. One's sanctification, then, also stems from one's obedience to Church teaching. And, the martyr's death reveals fidelity to Church teaching, as John Paul makes clear in *Veritatis Splendor* 76: "It is an honor characteristic of Christians to obey God rather than men…and accept even martyrdom as a consequence" for that obedience. In addition, the "existence of an 'objective moral order'" also stipulates that the "moral quality of human acting is dependent on this fidelity to the Commandments, as an expression of obedience and love."[17] Because the martyr's death reveals the "holiness of God's law" and the "holiness of the Church," it suggests

---

[15] John Paul II, *Augustinum Hipponesem* Chapter II 2. Some have greater or lesser capacities for such enjoyment.

[16] John Paul II, *Rosarium Virginis Mariae* 9.

[17] John Paul II, *Veritatis Splendor* 82.

that love is at the heart of one's obedience and holiness, for God, who is holy, is Love (cf. 1 John 4:8, 16; Matthew 5:48).[18]

Combining the martyr's obedience and holiness with John Paul's term, *contemplating the face of Christ*, means this contemplation is the "light of life's journey."[19] The martyr's contemplative obedience that listens unto death describes his contemplation of Christ's face, the "light of life's journey," as his innate openness to God who is Truth.[20] Such enjoyment, that is, such delight in the Father through the Son, upholds the fact that martyrdom reveals the "holiness of the Church" because love obeys and love is at the core of one's delight in Him.[21] Since the martyr delights in the Father, he reveals both the holiness of God's law and the holiness of the Church He established on earth by his faithful obedience to the Church.

## Correlating Martyrdom and Contemplation of Christ's Face with *Gaudium et Spes* 24

Analyzing the Holy Father's interpretation of *Gaudium et Spes* 24, I focus upon his often-repeated phrase from this Conciliar text, which is that a person finds himself through making a sincere gift of himself to another. While *Redemptor Hominis* 8-10 brings out the centrality of being created in the image of God for Christian anthropology, *Dominum et Vivificantem* 34 highlights the fact that

---

[18] John Paul II, *Veritatis Splendor* 92, 93.
[19] John Paul II, *Novo Millennio Ineunte* 15.
[20] John Paul II, *Novo Millennio Ineunte* 15.
[21] John Paul II, *Veritatis Splendor* 93.

one's creation in God's image is a *gift* that the person receives: each person, "in his own humanity, receives as a gift a special 'image and likeness' to God." In my work above, I make the point that receiving the gift from God suggests that being a gift for another is intrinsic to the very nature of the human person. John Paul explains the point with *Mulieris Dignitatem* 7: being a "person in the image and likeness of God...involves existing in a relationship, in relation to the other 'I.'"

Because living in the truth means *being* who one *is*, the martyr's manner of living in the truth substantiates the fact that he gives his life "as a consequence...rather than perform this or that particular act contrary to faith or virtue."[22] The martyr's death is "the most eloquent proof of the truth of the faith."[23] His death, as a gift of self, also provides further evidence of the concept, brought out with *Veritatis Splendor* 92 and the *Letter to the Romans*, that the martyr's death unites others to Christ. My extrapolation of *Salvifici Doloris* 28 also shows this point: because freedom is "ultimately directed towards communion," and, because the martyr *accepts* death, he draws another person to Christ who is at work in him (cf. Ephesians 1:19-20; 3:17; 20). Through one's martyrdom, Jesus reveals His sacred face, and He opens the other to God the Father.

The martyr's death unites others to Jesus, then, and through Jesus to the Father, because he makes a sincere gift of himself, accepting death rather than betraying the truth of the human person. The person's finding himself "through a sincere gift of self" means,

---

[22] John Paul II, *Veritatis Splendor* 76.
[23] John Paul II, *Incarnationis Mysterium* 13.

for the martyr, that he *becomes* who he *is*: an adoptive child of the Heavenly Father. As John Paul explains in *Dominum et Vivificantem* 59, the "truth about man" indicates that, in Jesus Christ, the human person "is raised to the status of a child of God" the Father. Further, Saint Ignatius of Antioch explains, "to be God's" child through birth into new life means "to attain to light, light pure and undefiled…[to] be truly a man…to imitate the Passion of [one's] God. This manner of *becoming* who one *is* describes the contemplation of Christ's face because the martyr's death confesses Christ "as the meaning of history and the light of [his own] life's journey."[24]

My second point of John Paul's interpretation of *Gaudium et Spes* 24 deepens the notion of one's ontological dependence upon God, which I discuss with the *Opening Address* at Puebla. Interpreting *Dominum et Vivificantem* 59, I describe one's ontological dependence of the person as an intimate relationship between the Father and the human person. Although this "intimacy" lies beyond the subjective realm of the person's active participation in this relationship—because it is an objective reality—the martyr's death implies this relationship.

My third text, which interprets John Paul's notion of *Gaudium et Spes* 24, furthers the person's distinction from the rest of visible creation (*Fides et Ratio*) with the notion of rationality as the basis for human transcendence. In light of the martyr, I elucidate John Paul's concept of self-gift from *Gaudium et Spes* 24 as his availability to another suffering human person. *Salvifici Doloris* 28 helps

---

[24] John Paul II, *Novo Millennio Ineunte* 15.

show that one's openness to another person entails self-giving specifically to another suffering person. One's model for complete self-giving is the Crucified Christ, who shows that freedom is a "total gift of Himself" on the Cross.[25]

John Paul explains, in *Salvifici Doloris* 28, that each person must "stop beside" another human person and this "stopping" means an "availability," and an "interior disposition of the heart," of attending to the suffering of the other person. In my discussion of martyrdom above, I suggest that the martyr's death is a gift of himself that *suffers with* another suffering person, for the following reasons.

First, In *Veritatis Splendor* 87, the Holy Father teaches that "the frank and open acceptance of truth is the condition for authentic freedom." Since that truth "sets one free in the face of worldly power and which gives the strength to endure martyrdom," and, because the martyr lives in the truth of the human person that Christ reveals to him, he is truly free.[26]

Second, as I show with *Veritatis Splendor* 84, the martyr's death implies that his *doing* of the Truth recovers the "essential bond between Truth, the Good and Freedom." Since I explain that the martyr's death affirms the "essential bond between Truth, the Good and Freedom," of which John Paul speaks in *Veritatis Splendor* 84, I suggest that his death *accompanies* another person who suffers. Perhaps the other person he accompanies by his death suffers from the grave loss of uncertainty or suspicion of the objective order of

---

[25] John Paul II, *Veritatis Splendor* 85.
[26] John Paul II, *Veritatis Splendor* 87.

morality. Regardless of the reason, what is certain is that the martyr is free. I explain as follows.

Since "the deepest foundation of freedom" is located in the worship of God and in one's relationship with truth, the martyr is truly free when he worships God by following the Commandments.[27] "If you continue in My word, you are truly My disciples, and you will know the truth, and the truth will make you free" (John 8:31-32 RSVCE).

As the Pope explains, because the martyr accepts a death that "represents the high point of the witness to moral truth," he worships God by giving Him the "adoration and honor" due to Him alone.[28] Thus, the martyr is free; his *doing* of the Truth restores the "essential bond between Truth, the Good and Freedom," which I stress from *Veritatis Splendor* 84. Because freedom is "the gift of self in service to God and one's brethren," the martyr's self-gift by death reveals the totality of his freedom, but also it reveals his love.[29] As the Holy Father declares in *Veritatis Splendor* 87, "freedom is acquired in love, that is, in the gift of self." The martyr's self-gift of love is freely given to another suffering person.

The notion of *sincerity*, that Ide's *Une Théologie du Don* depicts as a pure attitude of "transparency to truth," suggests that the martyr's death reveals this transparency because it "represents the high

---

[27] John Paul II, *Veritatis Splendor* 87.

[28] John Paul II, *Veritatis Splendor* 93; *Catechism of the Catholic Church* 2096.

[29] John Paul II, *Veritatis Splendor* 87.

point of the witness to moral truth."[30] As I show from the Pope's texts, faith is "knowledge of Christ…remembrance of His Commandments, and…truth…lived out."[31]

Because martyrdom "represents the high point of the witness to moral truth," the martyr's death is a living embodiment of faith.[32] Further, in *Ut Unum Sint* 84, the Pope refers to martyrdom as "the supreme demand of faith, manifested in the sacrifice of life itself." The martyr's death, then, reflects a sincerity that allows the truth to be unmistakably perceived. Because the martyr dies in order to remain faithful to "God's holy law," his "sincere gift" of himself reflects the clarity of remaining in the truth of the human person.[33]

**Martyrdom and Contemplating the Face of Jesus Christ**

I highlight the notion of martyrdom, which specifically relates to the contemplation of Christ's face, for the following reason. The Pope speaks of God as the ultimate, Absolute Good who "attracts us and beckons us," because He is the "origin and goal of man's life."[34] Further, as John Paul explains in *Veritatis Splendor* 86, freedom is a gift from God and this gift summons a person to God, who is his true Good. The notion of God as one's true Good helps explain the contemplation of Christ's face, which the Holy Father

---

[30] Ide, *Une Théologie du Don (premiére partie)*, 152; John Paul II, *Veritatis Splendor* 93.

[31] John Paul II, *Veritatis Splendor* 88.

[32] John Paul II, *Veritatis Splendor* 93.

[33] John Paul II, *Veritatis Splendor* 93; Second Vatican Council, *Gaudium et Spes* 24.

[34] John Paul II, *Veritatis Splendor* 7.

describes as "the meaning of history and the light of life's journey."³⁵ Because the martyr remains faithful instead of acting "contrary to faith or virtue," his death reveals that God is the "origin and goal" of his life and "the meaning" of his "journey" of life.³⁶

Next, I extrapolate John Paul's meaning of the term, *contemplating the face of Christ*. The Pope's definition of this term rests upon three documents, which he sees as a trio of his thought on the subject. The core documents include *Novo Millennio Ineunte*, *Rosarium Virginis Mariae*, and *Ecclesia de Eucharistia*.

I then describe the martyr's death as a contemplation of the face of Christ with three points. First, I highlight the objective dimension of my claim, that the death of the martyr is a contemplation of Christ's face. The martyr's death manifests both objective truth, and thus, the objective moral law. And, since Jesus Christ *is* Truth (cf. John 14:6), martyrdom manifests Christ as Truth.

I focus upon the claim, substantiated in this project, which expresses the martyr's death as a contemplative, listening, radiance of t/Truth. Describing the martyr's death as an obedience that listens with his entire being to the holy law of God shows that the martyr, "In contemplating Christ's face…becomes open to receiving the mystery of Trinitarian life."³⁷ Openness to the Trinity, as well as regarding the martyr's death as a contemplation of Christ's face, suggest that martyrdom might be understood as *prayer*. I explain this new insight on martyrdom and prayer above.

---

[35] John Paul II, *Novo Millennio Ineunte* 15.

[36] John Paul II, *Veritatis Splendor* 76, 7; John Paul II, *Novo Millennio Ineunte* 15.

[37] John Paul II, *Rosarium Virginis Mariae* 9.

# Chapter Eighteen: Summarizing the Project

An additional factor explicates the martyr's death as a contemplation of Christ's face based upon *Fides et Ratio* 32. I reflect that the martyr's death is an encounter with Jesus, which shows that the person is essentially "open to receiving the mystery of Trinitarian life."[38] Since John Paul claims, in *Rosarium Virginis Mariae* 9, that being "open to receiving the mystery of Trinitarian life" describes the contemplation of His face, I conclude that the martyr's death is such a contemplation.

A third explanation of the martyr's death, as a contemplation of Christ's face, is based upon the Holy Father's description of the martyr in *Incarnationis Mysterium* 13 as "a sign of that greater love which sums up all other values." The martyr's act of loving entrustment to Jesus implies the contemplation of His face because John Paul depicts such contemplation, in *Novo Millennio Ineunte* 28, as reflecting upon the Church's "treasure and her joy."[39]

A fourth expression of the martyr's death, as a contemplation of Christ's face, considers the forgiving love "uttered by Christ on the Cross."[40] Because the Holy Father teaches, with *Incarnationis Mysterium* 13, that the "martyr's life reflects the extraordinary words [of forgiveness] uttered by Christ on the Cross," one might posit that the martyr's death reflects the face of Jesus Christ Crucified. As I explain above, since the martyr's death imitates the forgiving love of Christ Crucified, and, since Jesus reveals the face of the Father as love and mercy, one might understand the martyr's death as a contemplation of the face of Jesus.

---

[38] John Paul II, *Rosarium Virginis Mariae* 9.
[39] John Paul II, *Novo Millennio Ineunte* 28.
[40] John Paul II, *Incarnationis Mysterium* 13.

I further describe the martyr's death as a contemplation of the face of Jesus by stressing John Paul's point (*Veritatis Splendor* 92) that the martyr's death affirms "the inviolability of the moral order." Because the martyr's death testifies to objective truth, and thus, to the objective moral law, it shows his innate openness to Truth, who is Jesus Christ. Based upon the fact that truth is universal and unchangeable, the martyr's death confirms truth's objectivity. Further, the martyr's contemplative listening, which is an obedience that requires the gift of his life by death, describes his contemplative death as his innate openness to God who is Truth.

Combining martyrdom with contemplating the face of Christ, I note the following. In *Veritatis Splendor* 83, the Holy Father invites one to "show the inviting splendor of that truth, which is Jesus Christ Himself," by one's faithfulness to Him and to His commands. Jesus Christ, who *is* Truth, radiates an intrinsic, "inviting splendor." While the "splendor of truth shines forth...in a special way in man, created in the image and likeness of God," the martyr's death, as a witness to objective truth and to the objective moral law, radiates that truth.[41] The martyr's death radiates truth, and thus, it reflects a contemplation of the face of Jesus Christ, who is Truth, since his death "represents the high point of the witness to moral truth."[42]

Because the martyr accepts death "as a consequence" for his "fidelity to God's holy law," his death shows Jesus to others in a

---

[41] John Paul II, *Veritatis Splendor* Prior to the *Introduction*; 27.
[42] John Paul II, *Veritatis Splendor* 93.

## Chapter Eighteen: Summarizing the Project

physical, tangible manner.[43] Further, the martyr's death shows Jesus to others because death implies his abiding love for Christ, which I further describe as *prayer*. His self-gift through death is offered with a transparency that radiates t/Truth, and thus, it manifests Christ's face to others. Since the martyr's death bears witness to t/Truth, it is a contemplation of the face of Christ.

The "attitude toward" human dignity, which John Paul portrays in *Redemptor Hominis* 12, helps show the connection between the martyr's death and the contemplation of the face of Christ. Recall the Holy Father's definition of human dignity as the "uniqueness and irrepeatability of every person," and the "indestructible property of every human being."[44] In *Redemptor Hominis* 12, he teaches that human freedom is "the condition and basis for the human person's true dignity," and that "the human person's dignity itself becomes part of the content of proclamation, being included not necessarily in words but by an attitude towards it." This "attitude toward" human dignity connects to the attentive suffering with another person that *Salvifici Doloris* 28 elicits. A receptive attitude toward another suffering person suggests a contemplative dimension of martyrdom because human freedom, seen in the martyr's total gift of himself, shows an availability, or openness of himself toward others.

Human freedom is the basis of the martyr's inaudible attitude toward human dignity because his death is the total gift of himself: he "gave [his] life rather than" doing an act contrary to faith or vir-

---

[43] John Paul II, *Veritatis Splendor* 76; 93.
[44] John Paul II, *Christifideles Laici* 37.

tue."⁴⁵ The martyr's acceptance of death upholds human dignity, then, because he refuses to betray the truth of the person and the "inviolability of the personal dignity of man."⁴⁶ His exercise of freedom, with his gift of self, expresses an attitude toward human dignity that portrays the "uniqueness and irrepeatability of every person."⁴⁷ Further, having given himself as a gift, he is "a sign of that greater love which sums up all other values."⁴⁸

Because Mary teaches the believer how to contemplate the face of Christ, and, since Mary contemplated Christ at the foot of the Cross, one might conclude that the martyr's death is a contemplation of Christ's face with Mary: in imitation of Jesus Christ Crucified, the martyr offers his life, in freedom, to uphold human dignity and its "supreme glorification."⁴⁹

*Fides et Ratio* 32 adds another element to the contemplation of Christ's face. This factor builds upon the capacity of the martyr's death for drawing others to Jesus.⁵⁰ *Fides et Ratio* 32 explains that the martyr's act of entrustment to Jesus is his "faithful self-giving," that makes him the "most authentic witness to the truth about existence." His death is seeking "the truth of the person," which Jesus reveals to him. As the Holy Father explains in *Fides et Ratio* 32, the "truth about existence" is the "truth about life." Further, I claim

---

⁴⁵ John Paul II, *Veritatis Splendor* 76.
⁴⁶ John Paul II, *Veritatis Splendor* 92.
⁴⁷ John Paul II, *Christifideles Laici* 37.
⁴⁸ John Paul II, *Incarnationis Mysterium* 13.
⁴⁹ John Paul II, *Dominum et Vivificantem* 60.
⁵⁰ I make this point above with *Veritatis Splendor* 92, the *Letter to the Romans*, and *Salvifici Doloris* 28.

that *Fides et Ratio* 32 shows that the martyr has discovered this truth in his "encounter with Christ." I explain the martyr's death as his encounter of self-entrustment to Jesus. This encounter draws others to Christ Jesus because it indicates the martyr's believing, trusting love for God the Father. Further, since John Paul teaches that the martyr witnesses to moral truth by his death, I claim that the martyr's death reveals a reciprocity of abiding love on account of the martyr's act of entrustment to the Father who created him.[51]

These extrapolations from *Fides et Ratio* 32 suggest that the martyr's death contemplates Christ's face in His "mystery" of revealing the Father's love to the human person, and in "His manifold presence in the Church and in the world."[52] Further, *Novo Millennio Ineunte* 15 explains that contemplating Christ's face means considering His Passion and death, for example, as recorded in Sacred Scripture. Thus, one might conclude that Jesus Crucified teaches the martyr to place himself, with confidence and love, into the loving hands of the Father.

*Fides et Ratio* 32 further shows the contemplation of Christ's face as He is "confessed as the…light of life's journey."[53] In the martyr's entrustment to Jesus, he embraces "true life."[54] As I explain above, *Fides et Ratio* 32 might be understood as the martyr's revelation of his redemption by Christ based upon the "new life" he

---

[51] John Paul II, *Fides et Ratio* 5; John Paul II, *Veritatis Splendor* 88; 93.
[52] John Paul II, *Novo Millennio Ineunte* 15.
[53] John Paul II, *Novo Millennio Ineunte* 15.
[54] John Paul II, *Veritatis Splendor* 92; Saint Ignatius of Antioch, *Letter to the Romans*, 105-106.

receives from Him.⁵⁵ In *Novo Millennio Ineunte* 15, John Paul describes *contemplating Christ's face* as pondering Jesus, who is the One who gives history its meaning and who guides each person's life. The martyr's entrusting love of himself to Jesus shows that Jesus guides the martyr into true life in the world to come.

As the Holy Father maintains, contemplating the face of Christ is allowing the new Commandment of love to inform one's life (cf. John 13:34).⁵⁶ Allowing "grace to take us by the hand," which the Pope says is necessary in order to "come to the fullness of contemplation of the Lord's face," one might surmise that the martyr comes to this "fullness" by letting himself be led by Jesus Christ, into true life.⁵⁷

## The Difference Between the Martyr and the Saintly Non-Martyr

Each believer is to contemplate the face of Christ, and John Paul offers a broad understanding of such contemplation, that identifies it as "being able to recognize Him wherever He manifests Himself, in His many forms of presence, but above all in the living Sacrament of His Body and His Blood."⁵⁸ My work of describing the martyr's death as a contemplation of Christ's face offers a specific, concrete instance of such contemplation.

At the same time, describing the martyr's death as a concrete instance of contemplating the face of Jesus raises the question, ad-

---

[55] Saint Ignatius of Antioch, *Letter to the Romans*, 105-106.
[56] John Paul II, *Novo Millennio Ineunte* 42.
[57] John Paul II, *Novo Millennio Ineunte* 20.
[58] John Paul II, *Ecclesia de Eucharistia* 6.

## Chapter Eighteen: Summarizing the Project

dressed in my presentation, of how the martyr's death is differentiated from the saintly non-martyr's death. One might contest that the distinction between the martyr's death and the non-martyr's death as a contemplation of Christ's face must be inconsequential, because of John Paul's claim in *Veritatis Splendor* 93: "By their eloquent and attractive example…the martyrs and, in general, all the Church's saints, light up every period of history by reawakening its moral sense." How glorious! It is no wonder that they are hated by the world. Even still, since both martyr and saint are able to reawaken the "moral sense" of the world, what is the difference between their contemplation of the face of Christ?

With the concluding remark above from *Veritatis Splendor* 93, John Paul notes that martyrdom "represents the high point of the witness to moral truth," and this "high point of witness," which normally entails death, distinguishes the martyr from the non-martyr. Again, the martyr undergoes death in order to uphold objective truth and the objective moral order. In other words, the martyr lays down his life rather than violate faith or the moral teaching of the Church.

Because each person is to contemplate Christ's face, I distinguish the martyr's death as a contemplation of Christ's face from the saintly non-martyr's death, which might also be regarded as a contemplation of Christ's face. As I note above, Mary is the preeminent example of contemplating the face of Christ. Further, the texts imply that John Paul would consider various actions on the part of the believer throughout his life to be a contemplation of Christ's face.

My reason for focusing upon the martyr's death rather than the saintly non-martyr's virtuous acts in life and in death is due to the fact that martyrdom involves a certain universal willing acceptance of death rather than acting contrary to what one knows is true. In other words, every martyr, the world over, accepts the cessation of his life rather than denying Jesus Christ and His teachings (faith and morals). While the saintly non-martyr accepts death with trusting resignation to the Heavenly Father, he is not in the position of escaping its reality. Sometimes, the martyr is offered wealth, a high position, and many other transitory pleasures if one only denies the truth of faith and acts against the moral law. But again, both the death of the martyr and the death of the saintly non-martyr are contemplations of Christ's face. My work, however, distinguishes between the two kinds of death, rather than various actions in life, which might also be interpreted as a contemplation of Christ's face.

Among other texts that highlight the distinction between the martyr's death and the non-martyr's death, my analysis of *Veritatis Splendor* 27 is particularly helpful since it shows the distinction between the martyr and the saintly non-martyr to be the manner in which they put the "precepts and love [of Christ] into practice." By explaining that the martyr puts the "precepts and love [of Christ] into practice" by his *death*, the martyr stands out from the saintly non-martyr, who practices the "precepts and love" of Christ in his *life*.

Because death entails the explicit finality of a human life, the martyr can make no further statement of his obedience to the "precepts and love" of Jesus than he does by his death. John Paul distinguishes between the martyr and the saintly non-martyr with one word, *sacrifice*, which, as I explain above, can be interchanged with *death*. By highlighting the martyr's *sacrifice* as that which implements the "precepts and love" of Jesus Christ, one concludes that his death is different from the saintly non-martyr's death. Thus, the martyr contemplates Christ's face by putting the "precepts and love [of Christ] into practice" by his death. The manner in which the saintly non-martyr contemplates Christ's face is not specified in *Veritatis Splendor* 27 or in other texts on such contemplation. What *is* clear from *Veritatis Splendor* 27, however, is that the saintly non-martyr puts the "precepts and love [of Christ] into practice in [his] life."

Another distinction between contemplating the face of Christ for both the martyr and for the saintly non-martyr concerns two particular characteristics of the martyr, which John Paul identifies in *Veritatis Splendor* 76: "they gave their lives rather than perform this or that particular act contrary to faith or virtue." As I explicate in my text, the first quality is the martyr's *giving* of his life, while the second is his *avoiding* of acts "contrary to faith or virtue." If the saintly non-martyr's death depicts the contemplation of Christ's face—as one would presume it does—what *Veritatis Splendor* 76 makes clear is that the martyr's death involves offering his life as a gift, in order to avoid acts "contrary to faith or virtue." While the saintly non-martyr's death might be depicted as an offering of his life, his offering is not made in order to avoid acting against "faith or virtue."

I show the difference between the martyr and the saintly non-martyr with *Dominum et Vivificantem* 60, as well. The difference between the martyr's death and the saintly non-martyr's death is that the martyr's death finalizes his testimony, while the saintly non-martyr's death sums up a life dedicated to God in the final analysis. Since persecution plays a role in the life of every believer (cf. Matthew 5:10-12), one presumes that the saintly non-martyr persevered through these various trials and tribulations throughout his life.

To further distinguish between the martyr and the saintly non-martyr, I offer Aristotle's distinction between the *literal* use of a word and the *metaphorical* use of a word. I apply that distinction between the way that *martyrdom* is used literally, and the manner in which it might be used metaphorically. In my project, I find that John Paul uses martyrdom in a *literal* sense—and, when this meaning is unclear, I resolve the point with further study, as my work with the example of Susanna shows. The difference between the martyr and the saintly non-martyr is that the martyr's "voluntary acceptance of death" to remain faithful to the law of God distinguishes the notion of *martyrdom* in a literal sense from *martyrdom* in a metaphorical sense.[59]

---

[59] John Paul II, *Veritatis Splendor* 91.

# Chapter Nineteen

## Concluding Remarks

### Implications of the Martyr's Death as a Contemplation of the Face of Christ

To claim that the martyr's death is a contemplation of Christ's face offers a new way to understand both *martyrdom* and the *contemplation of Christ's face*. Affirming that the martyr's death is a contemplation of Christ's face implies additional new insights, as well. Among the many thoughts that my work provokes, I comment upon the following three. First, the martyr's death, understood as a contemplation of Christ's face, expresses a new way to regard proclamation. Second, the martyr's death, as a contemplation of Christ's face, comments upon a new understanding of the nature of prayer. Third, describing the martyr's death, as a contemplation of Christ's face, contributes toward the transformation of the world and such a transformation suggests a new way of understanding the person and human relationships, in particular.

### The Martyr's Death Expresses a Contemplative Element in Proclamation

First, describing the martyr's death as an objective depiction of contemplating Christ's face indicates that his death *proclaims*, or *shows* Jesus Christ to others. I speak of proclamation as showing Jesus to others for the following reason. As I note in my *Introduc-*

*tion*, John Paul teaches that people today want believers "not only to 'speak' of Christ, but, in a certain sense, to 'show' Him to them."[1] Based upon the fact that one's *actions* that show Christ to others are weightier than one's *words* that speak of Him, I refer to *proclamation* as showing Jesus Christ to others. Because the action of the martyr's death speaks louder than a plethora of words about Jesus, the martyr proclaims (shows) Christ to others by dying for Him.

Proclaiming Jesus by martyrdom is the "seed of Christianity" because it offers an indisputable testimony to Truth, who is Christ.[2] This contemplative aspect suggests that contemplating Christ's face, for example, in "the living sacrament of His Body and His Blood" by Eucharistic Adoration, is crucial to evangelization, but *not only* to evangelization.[3] Contemplating Christ's face is es-

---

[1] John Paul II, *Novo Millennio Ineunte* 16.

[2] By *indisputable*, I mean that one cannot reasonably argue that the martyr rejects what he says, or that he believes it only partially. His willingly acceptance of death insists upon the validity of his claims. While one might object to the truth for which the martyr dies, such a person knows, beyond doubt, that the martyr himself believes what he dies to uphold. If he did not, he would not willingly accept death. In fact, he would do anything he could to get out of being killed.

[3] John Paul II, *Ecclesia de Eucharistia* 6. Although my work is not directed toward evangelization, it supports the Holy Father's appeal that "Evangelization in the third millennium must come to grips with the urgent need for a presentation of the Gospel message which is dynamic, complete and demanding" [John Paul II, *Letter to Priests* 25 March 2001 (15)]. The Pope's strong words match the description I offer of martyrdom: that the martyr's contemplation of Christ's face is *dynamic* because it concerns the summation of a life. The very nature of martyrdom,

# Chapter Nineteen: Concluding Remarks

sential for living a Christian life, and thus, it is vital to Christian spirituality. Although such contemplation is indispensable to evangelization, contemplating Christ's face is primarily both the privilege and the responsibility of each believer.

The death of the martyr, which portrays the face of Christ Jesus, expresses its contemplative element both in obedient listening and in the martyr's attitude toward human dignity. Both obedient listening and a receptive attitude toward a/Another suggest that proclamation, in order to *be* proclamation in the first place, must possess these contemplative elements. I offer a few remarks that build upon the contemplative dimension of martyrdom.

Because the martyr's death radiates the splendor of objective truth and the objective moral order, proclamation, especially the proclamation given each day by the Catholic, essentially describes living in truth. The luminosity that radiates from a human person who *does* the truth is contemplative because it shows that truth informs his life. The voluntary acceptance of death, an obedient listening, in faith, to Jesus and to His teachings, dictates that one first needs to *listen* to Him in order to *speak* of Him to others. As *Veritatis Splendor* 91 shows with the example of Susanna, combined with paragraph 88 from the same document, contemplative listening (obedience) to the law of God involves "one's whole existence."

---

which is the willingness to sacrifice one's life in order to uphold Christ's teachings, requires the totality, or *complete* offering of oneself. The martyr makes a *complete* gift of himself with the consummation of his life. Finally, his death shows the *demanding impetus* of truth, expressed in the "Gospel message" of Jesus Christ, which stipulates a law of love that cannot be betrayed.

The Pope's description of one's "trusting abandonment," then, teaches that proclamation means listening to God's law, regardless of the consequences, before one speaks.[4]

For the believer to proclaim Christ to others, he first listens with filial obedience to Jesus (the Magisterium) and to the truth of the human person. The believer's living faith, an obedient listening to Jesus, *is* contemplative and it *must be* contemplative. His contemplative listening reflects the life and death of Jesus and His command to love (cf. John 13:34).

Listening further implies that faith informs one's life. The person's decisions verify an obedience that obliges even the offering of his life to *listen* to Jesus, should it be required of him. The person's contemplative listening dictates his own obedient acceptance of death, which death the believer willingly endures to retain his inviolable dignity as a human person and as a child of the Heavenly Father, should circumstances require it.

Finally, the believer's self-gift, an availability to another suffering person, can only happen when the person first receives the truth of who he from Christ Jesus. To hear the truth of one's own being, he first entrusts himself to Jesus and to the truth of what He teaches (i.e., the Church's Magisterium). Christ reveals the human person's innate openness to God and He makes known one's status as a child of the Father.

The martyr's attitude toward human dignity, expressed by his death, adds a second stipulation to the notion of proclamation's contemplative element. His self-gift, which I explain as his availa-

---

[4] John Paul II, *Veritatis Splendor* 91; 88.

bility to another suffering human person, dictates that the believer can only proclaim Christ to others if he offers himself in freedom.

The martyr's gift of self upholds human freedom not only because he willingly sacrifices his life, but also because his actions declare the truth of who he is as a person. In order that his proclamation be heard, the self-gift of the believer must be given freely and it must be given in charity for one's neighbor. His self-gift testifies to human dignity, then, because his actions show that the person is a sacred and inviolable being, created in God's image, as a child of the Heavenly Father. As *Ecclesia in Asia* 49 teaches, although martyrdom "reveals to the world the very essence of the Christian message," proclaiming Christ by contemplating His face is central to the life of every believer, whether or not that contemplation is the death of a martyr.

**Martyrdom and Prayer**

Because contemplating the face of Jesus is contemplating His love, for example, in His Passion and death and in His Eucharistic Presence, I describe the martyr's death as *prayer*. As I explain above, the martyr's death is *prayer* because it summons one to ask the deeper questions that arise in life, which "refer to prayer."[5] Second, the martyr's death is *prayer* because it expresses the contemplative aspect of his decision as childlike, obedient listening. Finally, the martyr's death is prayer because it is a silent reciprocity of abiding love between Jesus and the martyr. This inaudible ex-

---

[5] John Paul II, *Homily* 19 October 1982 (3).

change of love is indeed prayer, for prayer, as John Paul describes it in *Novo Millennio Ineunte* 32, "develops that conversation with Christ which makes us His intimate friends." Nothing could be more intimate than the loving words of trustful surrender that a child of the Father utters to Him moments before entering eternity.

Interpreting the death of the martyr as *prayer* also implies several further perspectives on prayer. In fact, claiming that the martyr's death offers a new outlook on prayer suggests that the martyr is "distinguished above all in the art of prayer."[6] Among the many lessons on prayer that the death of the martyr teaches, I comment upon the following three. First, the martyr's death as a contemplation of Christ's face implies that prayer expresses an openness to God that allows one to *become* who he really *is*. One *really is* a child of the Heavenly Father whether or not one knows it. Second, having become the Father's child, the martyr's death as a contemplation of Christ's face suggests that prayer embodies the humility that allows one to entrust oneself to the Heavenly Father. A third aspect of prayer that the death of the martyr conveys is that the heart of prayer lies in fidelity to Jesus Christ. Through Jesus, one reaches the Father, for "no one comes to the Father, but by [Jesus]" (John 14:6).

The martyr teaches that prayer entails humility and humility requires courage. To pray with humility means, in light of John Paul's teaching on martyrdom and contemplation of Christ's face, to entrust oneself to Another, who is God Himself. Prayer is an act of humility because it requires standing before "the truth of the

---

[6] John Paul II, *Rosarium Virginis Mariae* 5.

## Chapter Nineteen: Concluding Remarks

person—what the person is and what the person reveals from deep within."[7]

Like every human person (except the Blessed Mother), the martyr is a sinful, but greatly beloved child of the Heavenly Father.[8] The truth of the person is that he continually needs the grace and mercy of God. To pray with humility, then, in light of the martyr's death as a contemplation of Christ's face, means that one entrusts oneself to the Other—to God—and to the Truth of God, Jesus Christ, so much so that the person does not allow anything to hinder his relationship with the one so loved. But even more, the humility of prayer that martyrdom's contemplation reveals, is to let Christ show the person his inherent worth and dignity as a child of the Father. Humility in prayer requires courage. The martyr's lov-

---

[7] John Paul II, *Fides et Ratio* 32.

[8] Of course, the Blessed Virgin Mary is *the* greatly beloved daughter of God the Father. My point is that, being the Immaculate Conception, she is entirely free of sin. Jesus is entirely sinless, as Sacred Scripture and Church teaching make clear, but He is not a *human* person. He is a *Divine* Person, the Second Person of the Blessed Trinity Incarnate, with a human nature and a divine nature. For more on the impeccability of Christ, see John 8:46 and the term in Fr. John A. Hardon, S.J., *Modern Catholic Dictionary*. As Fr. Hardon notes, the impeccability of Jesus Christ is defined Church teaching. The Council of Florence declares His freedom from original sin (Denzinger 1347), the Council of Chalcedon declares His freedom from personal sin (Denzinger 301), and "the Second Council of Constantinople condemned the theory that Christ became completely impeccable only after the Resurrection" [(Denzinger 434; Fr. John A. Hardon, S.J., *Modern Catholic Dictionary* online version, available at the Catholic Culture website here: (https://catholicculture.org/culture/library/dictionary/index.cfm?id=34113&randomterm=false)].

ing entrustment to the Father not only suggests a new way of seeing the importance of humility in prayer, but also, it echoes the Holy Father's dictum, "Be not afraid" (Luke 5:10; Acts 18:9-10).[9]

Another message that the prayer of the martyr conveys points to the human person's ultimate fulfillment by God. One's creation in His image makes it clear. The prayer that martyrdom teaches is that being open to God makes the human person *become* who he really *is*; pondering the truth of who he is, a child of the Father, the martyr is utterly convinced that he stands in t/Truth. Readily aware that he has been redeemed by Jesus Christ, his prayer realizes one's calling to be holy. His prayer witnesses to his filial adoption by the Father.

In addition to one's subjective awareness of being open to God in prayer—or rather, even before one apprehends the *need* for openness in prayer—the human person already *is* open to God, at an ontological level, on account of his creation in God's image. Thus, the novelty that the prayer of the martyr's death expresses, is an openness to God that allows one to *become* who he really *is*.

One *is* created in God's image, and he *is* intrinsically open to God because of his creation in His image. The person is re-created in Christ and open to the Father on account of human transcendence. Thus, he *becomes* the child of God the Father that he *is* by

---

[9] While John Paul II frequently encourages his youthful listeners at numerous World Youth Day homilies not to be afraid, he also begins his pontificate with this statement. See John Paul II, *Homily* for the Solemn Inauguration of the Pontificate 22 October 1978 (5). See also John Paul II, *Christifideles Laici* 34; John Paul II, *Redemptoris Missio* 88; John Paul II, *Dies Domini* 7.

# Chapter Nineteen: Concluding Remarks

living in "fidelity to God's holy law," whether or not that fidelity requires his death.[10] Martyrdom's "training in holiness" specifies that fidelity to Christ's teachings reflects an innate openness to God, coupled with the martyr's subjective openness in prayer, which illustrates the moment of his death as "distinguished above all in the art of prayer."[11]

Describing the martyr's death as a radiance of abiding love specifies a third aspect of prayer, which is that the heart of prayer involves fidelity to Jesus Christ. The martyr's abiding love, which is his inaudible entrustment to Jesus, and, through Jesus to the Father (John 14:6), testifies to the fact that one conveys love primarily by one's actions. As I show above, the martyr's prayer of love is speechless because his actions fill his being, as a human person, with fidelity to Christ and His teachings.

Living his prayer by his death, the martyr makes Christ audible to the world on account of his faithful love. His inaudible prayer of love testifies to the presence and action of Jesus in his life. Thus, the martyr's death expresses Christ's teachings, encapsulated by the Commandments and the Beatitudes, and it especially highlights Christ's new Commandment of love for one's neighbor. Further, as I show above, Jesus is the "origin of [the martyr's] martyrdom and of [his] holiness."[12]

---

[10] John Paul II, *Veritatis Splendor* 93.

[11] John Paul II, *Novo Millennio Ineunte* 32 quoted in John Paul II, *Rosarium Virginis Mariae* 5.

[12] John Paul II, *Tertio Millennio Adveniente* 37. To claim, as does John Paul, that Jesus Christ is the "origin" of one's martyrdom is to imply that He is the one for whom the martyr offers his life. Again, the martyr

An example of the martyr's death expressing the Commandment to love is found in the *Letter to the Romans*, to which John Paul refers in *Veritatis Splendor* 92. Saint Ignatius of Antioch explains his own death as an entryway into new life. Loving one another as Christ has loved him calls the martyr to offer his life as a gift (John 13:34). The gift of the martyr's life is prayer because it ushers him into this new life, "to be God's" child, which Saint Ignatius describes in his *Letter*.

The martyr's prayer manifests Christ's Commandment of love, and thus, it describes prayer in the following ways. First, the martyr's prayer of abiding love teaches that the prayer of every believer is rooted in love. This love, articulated by *Gaudium et Spes* 24 as a sincere gift of oneself, specifies that love forgives injuries and iniquities against oneself. In addition, the love of the martyr illustrates fraternal charity. More specifically, the martyr's love is prayer "articulated" as the gift of self and as an availability directed toward the suffering of another person. Finally, the martyr's prayer of love teaches that the believer is to regard his relationship with Jesus as the "*one thing*" that is necessary (Luke 10:42).

---

does not betray the intimate relationship he has with Jesus, even though it requires his life. The Holy Father's description of Jesus as the "origin" of one's martyrdom, then, offers further evidence that the death of the martyr might be construed as a contemplation of His face.

# Chapter Nineteen: Concluding Remarks

## The Martyr's Contribution Toward the Transformation of the World

Analyzing the Pope's interpretation of *Gaudium et Spes* 24, I return to the fact that for one's sincere gift of self to be genuine (whether one knows it), that gift must be rooted in the holy Trinity, "who 'exists' in Himself as a transcendent reality of Interpersonal Gift."[13] Further, in *Dominum et Vivificantem* 59, John Paul highlights the fact that the Holy Spirit, given as a gift to the human person, transforms the world through the "hearts and minds" of human people.

Combining these foundational elements with texts about the martyr, I offer some new reflections about how the martyr contributes toward a transformation of the world, with strength from the Holy Spirit, through the "hearts and minds" of others. Further, the transformation of the world that the martyr's death evokes suggests a novel way of regarding not only the human person, but also human relationships, as well.

## The Transforming Impetus of Love

Based upon my study, I conclude by offering several remarks for future deliberation, which suggest a perceptive way of thinking about martyrdom in contemporary society. Rooted in my analysis of martyrdom in the pontifical writings of John Paul and deepened by my evaluation of its contemplative dimension, I suggest that the

---

[13] John Paul II, *Dominum et Vivificantem* 59.

specific quality of the martyr, grounded in his forgiving, abiding love, is his refusal to hate.

Although I do not develop it here, this refusal to hate one's persecutors infuriates those who inflict martyrdom, perhaps due to the simple truth that love conquers. Love offers the final w/Word of forgiveness, proclaimed by the martyr's death. The martyr's forgiving love might enrage the perpetrators of martyrdom because it ruins their desire to control the martyr, the world, the human person, and even God, Himself.

Perhaps the perpetrators of martyrdom desire to control reality—the martyr, the world, (every) human person, and God—by sheer force, by savage violence, or by worldly power. In fact, however, the martyr "controls" reality by his freedom in Jesus Christ, which is his forgiving love, that utterly infuriates and disarms his persecutors. With the martyr's radiance of forgiving love—the abiding love between himself and Jesus evident, although possibly known unconsciously—one easily perceives why John Paul speaks of the martyr as a "sign of that greater love that sums up all other values."[14]

One might express the martyr's refusal to hate in positive terms as a commitment to love. The Pontiff's teaching on the Holy Spirit's transformation of the world through the "hearts and minds" of people offers a concrete example of love, which I apply to the martyr's pledge to love.[15] As I suggest with the martyr's commitment to love, I offer the following illustration of how his abiding, forgiving

---

[14] John Paul II, *Incarnationis Mysterium* 13.
[15] John Paul II, *Dominum et Vivificantem* 59.

## Chapter Nineteen: Concluding Remarks

love serves mankind and contributes toward the transformation of the world.

In *Dominum et Vivificantem* 59, John Paul teaches that the "Holy Spirit as [a] gift to man, transforms the human world from within, from inside hearts and minds." Note that the Holy Father first specifies the heart: *love* is at the center of the transforming power of the Spirit. The Spirit of *Love* is the Spirit of *Truth*. Thus, my second reflection concerns the martyr's contribution toward the transformation of the world, with and in the Holy Spirit, by influencing the hearts and minds of others.

First, the martyr shows his act of entrusting love, which I elucidate as transparency, or openness to God. Thus, one might conclude that the martyr not only draws others to God through his own loving fidelity toward Him, but also, by the power of the Holy Spirit, he contributes toward the transformation of the world through his *heart* by showing forgiving love.

Second, the martyr, by his refusal to betray the law of God, upholds objective moral truth. Again, building upon principles outlined above, one finds that the martyr also contributes toward the transformation of the world, as *Dominum et Vivificantem* 59 helps show, by the transformation of minds. Because of his fidelity to the truth and his refusal to betray Christ's teachings, which would otherwise defy the objective moral law, the martyr's death contributes toward the transformation of minds. He puts on the "mind of Christ" and shares Him with others through his acceptance of death for the sake of the Gospel (1 Corinthians 2:16). Thus, through his actions, he speaks to "people's hearts and minds;" the martyr builds up God's Kingdom, which "is the eternal power of the opening of the Triune God to man and the world, in the Holy Spirit."[16]

To the one who claims truth is *not* objective, martyrdom is regarded as simply a matter of one's personal faith having nothing to do with human reason. To him, the martyr is the most ridiculous of all people (cf. 1 Corinthians 1:20-21). To the one who knows truth's objectivity, martyrdom is the logical course of action when confronted with the choice of whether to act according to conscience. Far from being an isolated, individualistic event, the martyr challenges every human person "about fidelity to [his] own conscience."[17]

The transforming power of love that the martyr's death entails also underlies his faith; it deepens the challenge to the contemporary person regarding "fidelity to [his] own conscience."[18] As *Veritatis Splendor* 88 brings out, since faith unites one with Jesus, so that the person "lives as He lived," faith implies freedom: one freely encounters Jesus in a communion of love, and thus, one opens oneself both to God and to one's neighbor.

By putting into action the truth of faith, the w/Word he has received, his death expresses "the newness of the faith and its power to judge a prevalent and all-intrusive culture."[19] Recall that John Paul defines faith as the "decision involving one's whole existence."[20] Thus, the martyr's ability to judge "a dechristianized cul-

---

[16] John Paul II, *Dominum et Vivificantem* 59.
[17] John Paul II, *Homily*, 22 May 1995 (3).
[18] John Paul II, *Homily*, 22 May 1995 (3).
[19] John Paul II, *Veritatis Splendor* 88.
[20] John Paul II, *Veritatis Splendor* 88.

ture by his death" signifies a death that expresses his faith.²¹ The martyr's faith, a grace given by God, is the impetus resulting in the martyr's death. Faith's "moral content" requires the martyr's life.²²

**Martyrdom Makes t/Truth "Visible" to the World**

Another text explains how the martyr transforms the world—how he serves mankind—by making truth present and "visible." With his opening remark in *Fides et Ratio*, John Paul describes truth as that which "enlightens man's intelligence and shapes his freedom, leading him to know and love the Lord."²³ The contemplation of truth involves a God-given desire to know the truth and to know God. The desire to know God is both answered and deepened by contemplating the face of God Incarnate, who is Jesus Christ. The contemplation of the truth, then, fundamentally concerns Jesus, who is Truth Incarnate. To say that one contemplates the truth is to affirm that one contemplates either Incarnate Truth specifically, or what leads to the Truth, who is Jesus Christ (John 14:6).

Because of the person's God-given desire to know t/Truth, the "human spirit rises to the contemplation of truth" through faith and through human reason.²⁴ "God has placed in the human heart a desire to know the truth—in a word, to know Himself—so that, by knowing and loving God, men and women may also come to

---

[21] John Paul II, *Veritatis Splendor* 88.
[22] John Paul II, *Veritatis Splendor* 89.
[23] John Paul II, *Veritatis Splendor* Introduction.
[24] John Paul II, *Veritatis Splendor* Introduction.

the fullness of truth about themselves."²⁵ Since Jesus is Truth Incarnate, and, since each human person has an innate desire to know Truth Himself, the death of the martyr serves mankind by making t/Truth present and "visible" to the world. As John Paul claims in *Veritatis Splendor* 93, martyrdom shows "that the splendor of moral truth" cannot be dimmed by "the behavior and thinking of individuals and society."

Another way of serving mankind is through living a life of holiness. The person's holiness expresses truth's visibility to the world because the one who is holy lives in the t/Truth. Further, one who is holy does not seek to compromise with the world; instead, he calls good and evil by their proper name regardless of the cost.

As I mention above, the Holy Father stipulates that one of the primary results of "an upright conscience is…to call good and evil by their proper name."²⁶ The martyr's ability to distinguish between good and evil indicates that he lives in the t/Truth. Further, his ability to "call good and evil by their proper name," which his death indicates, "bears witness to the authority of the natural law and of the practical reason with reference to the supreme Good, whose attractiveness the human person perceives and whose Commandments he accepts."²⁷ While the martyr is a clear example of steadfastness in the truth, and thus, of holiness of life, John Paul reminds his listeners that each person must strive to live uncompromising fidelity to God. "The Christian life to be aimed at cannot

---

[25] John Paul II, *Veritatis Splendor Introduction*.

[26] John Paul II, *Dominum et Vivificantem* 43.

[27] John Paul II, *Dominum et Vivificantem* 43; John Paul II, *Veritatis Splendor* 60.

be reduced to a mediocre commitment to 'goodness' as society defines it; it must be a true quest for holiness."[28] In addition to holiness, living "in accordance with the truth" upholds authentic human freedom and dignity.[29]

## Sacrificing One's Corporeal Life Points Toward the Primacy of the Spiritual Life

In this work, I speak of martyrdom as a vibrant radiance of contemplating Christ's face. As a final remark, I want to highlight my comparison of martyrdom which, by its very nature, specifies *death*, with the *life* that contemplating Christ's face entails. My example offers a concluding illustration of how the martyr serves mankind.

Although martyrdom is a self-giving articulation of the human person contemplating the face of Jesus, one might object that it cannot express life since the person dies. As my work shows, however, it is precisely by forfeiting his life that the martyr points to a life beyond the grave, and to eternal Life, Himself (cf. John 3:15-16; 6:40; 14:6). Thus, putting the "precepts and love [of Christ] into practice" by the sacrifice of his life, the martyr indicates that another life that is far more precious.[30]

Laying down one's corporeal life to preserve one's spiritual life makes a statement to both those who propound that all is matter and to those who deny an afterlife. When one willingly sacrifices

---

[28] John Paul II, Letter to Priests Holy Thursday 2001 (15).
[29] John Paul II, *Veritatis Splendor* 85.
[30] John Paul II, *Veritatis Splendor* 27.

the great good of one's own life, one bears witness to the spiritual world and to life after death. Again, martyrdom serves mankind by reawakening the awareness that the human person is more than a physical, corporeal reality. Martyrdom makes known the human person's spiritual life with an undeniable exuberance even while the martyr upholds the sacredness of his corporeal reality.

**The Martyr's Death Expresses Human Relationships in a New Light**

The martyr's death as a contemplation of Christ's face offers a new insight to understanding the human person in light of his relationship with Jesus. In turn, the martyr's union with Jesus suggests a novel way of regarding human relationships. As I comment above, the anthropological component of my work, which highlights the Holy Father's interpretation of *Gaudium et Spes* 22, coupled with my extrapolation of *contemplating Christ's face*, both endorse and offer new insight regarding one's growth in the knowledge and love of God and of oneself. Although the scope of my project does not permit extensive development of these themes, I offer several remarks below.

With the *Letter* of Saint Ignatius, I describe the martyr's distinct capacity of "befriending mankind," as uniting others in Jesus. One might ask, how the martyr draws others to Jesus Christ and why it makes a difference. The martyr's death might be interpreted as drawing others to Jesus because it reveals t/Truth. The martyr's total and complete *doing* of the Truth is marked by his acceptance of death as a consequence for his living of the truth. His death,

## Chapter Nineteen: Concluding Remarks

then, shows "the inviting splendor of that truth which is Jesus Christ Himself" by one's life of fidelity to Him and to His Commandments.[31]

Since, as John Paul claims, "Truth enlightens man's intelligence and shapes his freedom, leading him to know and love the Lord," the martyr's death, which is a showing of the Truth who is Jesus, unites others to Him.[32] The martyr's death serves as a vehicle through which he unites others to Jesus not only because it helps others to know and love Him, but also because it shows the impossibility of acting against "the holiness of God's law."[33]

One might ask why this new insight, of uniting others to Jesus by the martyr's death, makes a difference to contemporary man. The significance of the martyr's death as a vehicle for uniting others to Christ answers the "deeply-felt need for interpersonal contact," that John Paul mentions in his Letter to Priests.[34] Because society today "often leaves people interiorly isolated…[and] involves them in a flurry of purely functional relationships," the martyr's death shows that the heart of any relationship must be rooted in "the inviolability of the moral order" and in the "inviolability of the personal dignity of man."[35] For a human relationship to be fulfilling, both people must be striving for the good. Partnerships in evil lead to ruin and despair, even in this life (Deuteronomy 22:22; Proverbs 24:20; 29:6; Matthew 12:35; Luke 23:12).

---

[31] John Paul II, *Veritatis Splendor* 83.
[32] John Paul II, *Veritatis Splendor* Prior to the *Introduction*.
[33] John Paul II, *Veritatis Splendor* 92.
[34] John Paul II, 2001 Letter to Priests Holy Thursday 13.
[35] John Paul II, *Veritatis Splendor* 92.

If one's relationship with another is rooted in the teachings of Christ, which are consonant with the "personal dignity of man," then even a "purely functional" relationship takes on new meaning. In other words, the "deeply-felt need for interpersonal contact" can only happen at a acutely personal level if the relationship is grounded in the moral order.[36] Rooted in the Truth who is Jesus Christ, the novelty of the martyr's death means that the human relationship is a recovery of the "essential bond between Truth, the Good and Freedom."[37] The martyr's *doing* of the t/Truth sheds new light on human relationships, which unites others in Christ.

---

[36] John Paul II, 2001 Letter to Priests Holy Thursday 13.
[37] John Paul II, *Veritatis Splendor* 84.

# Chapter Twenty

## A Final Exhortation from John Paul II

A fitting closure to the present work offers the opportunity to ponder, once again, the wealth of *Incarnationis Mysterium* 13. Reflecting upon the Holy Father's concluding remarks in paragraph 13, he offers a closing exhortation on martyrdom.

In paragraph 13 of *Incarnationis Mysterium*, already referenced because of its aptness to my project, John Paul recommends to the Church three points. First, he encourages the Church to "remain anchored in the testimony of the martyrs and jealously guard their memory." My hope is that the present work contributes toward a new understanding of the martyr's death, which brings its contemplative dimension to the fore of human thought.

The Holy Father's second wish in *Incarnationis Mysterium* 13 is that "the People of God, confirmed in faith by the example of these true champions of every age, language and nation, cross with full confidence the threshold of the Third Millennium." Although one's entrance into the new millennium has already occurred, "the year of grace is endless;" one has only to "set out anew from Christ."[1] Each day one begins again the search for t/Truth, which is found in Jesus Christ, God Incarnate. My interpretation of the Pope's description of the martyr as one who contemplates the face of Christ by his death shows he is a true victor over death, in union with Christ, who conquered death once for all (cf. Romans 6:9-10).

---

[1] John Paul II, *Message*, World Mission Day 3 June 2001 (7).

The Pope's final exhortation in *Incarnationis Mysterium* 13 is that admiration for the death of the martyr "be matched by the desire to follow [his] example, with God's grace, should circumstances require it."

Although few are called to martyrdom, my work offers a new perspective on the martyr's death and on contemplating the face of Christ. It further shows a novel way of thinking about proclamation, prayer, and the human person. Persevering in such contemplation, may the believer increase in fidelity to Jesus Christ, such that, "should circumstances require it," he is also ready to testify to his abiding love with Him, which martyrdom entails.

In his *Bull of Indiction* for the Jubilee Year, John Paul "expressed the hope that the bimillennial celebration of the mystery of the Incarnation would be lived as 'one unceasing hymn of praise to the Trinity.'"[2] I hope this project contributes to the "unceasing…praise to the Trinity" by showing that, in the witness of the martyrs who contemplate Christ's face, His praises resound.

> "The more you mow us down, the more we grow:
> the blood of the martyrs is the seed of the Christians."[3]

---

[2] John Paul II, *Incarnationis Mysterium* 3 quoted in John Paul II, *Novo Millennio Ineunte* 4.

[3] Tertullian, *Apologeticum*, 50, 13: Jacques Paul Minge, *Patrologia Latina* 1, 534.

# Bibliography

## Primary Literature: Writings of Pope John Paul II

### Encyclicals

John Paul II. *Redemptor Hominis* [The Redeemer of Man]. Vatican Translation. Boston, MA: Saint Paul Books and Media. 1979.

---. *Dives in Misericordia* [On the Mercy of God]. Vatican Translation. Boston, MA: Saint Paul Editions. 1980.

---. *Laborem Exercens* [On Human Work]. Vatican Translation. Boston, MA: Saint Paul Editions. 1981.

---. *Dominum et Vivificantem* [On the Holy Spirit in the Life of the Church and the World]. Vatican Translation. Boston, MA: Saint Paul Editions. 1986.

---. *Redemptoris Mater* [Mother of the Redeemer]. Vatican Translation. Boston, MA: Pauline Books and Media. 1987.

---. *Sollicitudo Rei Socialis* [On Social Concern]. Vatican Translation. Boston, MA: Saint Paul Books and Media. 1987.

---. *Redemptoris Missio* [Mission of the Redeemer]. Vatican Translation. Boston, MA: Saint Paul Books and Media. 1990.

---. *Centesimus Annus* [On the Hundredth Anniversary of Rerum Novarum]. Vatican Translation. Boston, MA: Saint Paul Books and Media. 1991.

---. *Veritatis Splendor* [The Splendor of Truth]. Vatican Translation. Boston, MA: Saint Paul Books and Media. 1993.

---. *Evangelium Vitae* [The Gospel of Life]. Vatican Translation. Boston, MA: Pauline Books and Media. 1995.

---. *Ut Unum Sint* [On Commitment to Ecumenism]. Vatican Translation. Boston, MA: Pauline Books and Media. 1995.

---. *Fides et Ratio* [On the Relationship between Faith and Reason]. Vatican Translation. Boston, MA: Pauline Books and Media. 1998.

---. *Ecclesia de Eucharistia* [On the Eucharist in its Relationship to the Church]. Vatican Translation. Boston, MA: Pauline Books and Media. 2003.

**Apostolic Exhortations**

John Paul II. *Familiaris Consortio* [The Role of the Christian Family in the Modern World]. Vatican Translation. Boston, MA: Saint Paul Editions. 1981.

---. *Reconciliatio et Paenitentia* [Reconciliation and Penance]. Vatican Translation. Boston, MA: Saint Paul Books and Media. 1984.

---. *Christifideles Laici* [The Lay Members of Christ's Faithful People]. Vatican Translation. Boston, MA: Saint Paul Books and Media. 1988.

---. *Redemptoris Custos* [On the Person and Mission of Saint Joseph in the Life of Christ and of the Church]. Vatican Translation. Boston, MA: Saint Paul Books and Media. 1989.

---. *Pastores Dabo Vobis* [I Will Give You Shepherds]. Vatican Translation. Boston, MA: Saint Paul Books and Media. 1992.

---. *Ecclesia in Africa* [The Church in Africa]. (14 September 1995). Available from http://www.vatican.va/holy_father/john_paul_

ii/apost_exhortations/documents/hf_jpii_exh_14091995_eccles ia-in-africa-sp.html. Accessed (Spanish) 9 March 2008.

---. *Ecclesia in America* [The Church in America]. Vatican Translation. Boston, MA: Pauline Books and Media. 1999.

---. *Ecclesia in Asia* [The Church in Asia]. (6 November 1999). Available from http://www.vatican.va/holy_father/john_paul_ ii/apost_exhortations/documents/hf_jpii_exh_06111999 _ecclesia-in-asia-it.html. Accessed (Italian) 7 November 2006.

---. *Ecclesia in Europa* [The Church in Europe]. (28 June 2003). Available from http://www.vatican.va/holy_father/john_paul_ ii/apost_exhortations/documents/hf_jpii_exh_20030628_eccles ia-in-europa-en.html. Accessed (English) 14 January 2007.

**Apostolic Letters**

John Paul II. *Salvifici Doloris* [On the Christian Meaning of Human Suffering]. Vatican Translation. Boston, MA: Saint Paul Books and Media. 1984.

---. *To the Youth of the World – On the Occasion of International Youth Year.* Vatican Translation. Boston, MA: Saint Paul Editions. 1985.

---. *Augustinum Hipponsensem.* (28 August 1986). Available from http://www.vatican.va/holy_father/john_paul_ii/apost_letters/ documents/hf_jp-ii_apl_26081986_augustinum-hipponsensem _en.html. Accessed (English) 23 October 2008.

---. *Mulieris Dignitatem* [On the Dignity and Vocation of Women]. Vatican Translation. Boston, MA: Saint Paul Books and Media. 1988.

---. *Tertio Millennio Adveniente* [On Preparation for the Jubilee of the Year 2000]. Vatican Translation. Boston, MA: Pauline Books and Media. 1994.

---. *Orientale Lumen* [The Light of the East]. Vatican Translation. Boston, MA: Pauline Books and Media. 1995.

---. *Fourth Centenary of the Union of Brest.* (12 November 1995). Available from http://www.vatican.va/holy_father/john_paul_ii/apost_letters/index.htm. Accessed (English) 14 April 2007.

---. *Dies Domini* [On Keeping the Lord's Day Holy]. Vatican Translation. Boston, MA: Pauline Books and Media. 1998.

---. *Novo Millennio Ineunte* [The Beginning of the New Millennium]. Vatican Translation. Boston, MA: Pauline Books and Media. 2001.

---. *Rosarium Virginis Mariae* [On the Most Holy Rosary]. Vatican Translation. Boston, MA: Pauline Books and Media. 2002.

---. *Mane Nobiscum Domine* [Stay with Us, Lord]. Vatican Translation. Boston, MA: Pauline Books and Media. 2004.

## Other Magisterial Documents by John Paul II

John Paul II. Apostolic Constitution *Ex Corde Ecclesiae* [On Catholic Universities]. Available from http://www.vatican.va/holy_father/john_paul_ii/apost_constitutions/documents/hf_jpii_apc_15081990_ex-corde-ecclesiae_en.html. Accessed (English) 9 March 2008.

---. Bull of Indiction of the Great Jubilee of the Year 2000: *Incarnationis Mysterium* [The Mystery of the Incarnation]. Vatican Translation. Boston, MA: Pauline Books and Media. 1998.

---. *Great Pope John Paul II.* [CD-ROM]. Salem, MA: Harmony Media, Inc. 2005.

---. *Man and Woman he Created them: A Theology of the Body.* Translated by Michael Waldstein. Boston, MA: Pauline Books and Media. 2006. 24 October 1979, p. 150. 16 January 1980, p. 185. 6 February 1980, p. 194. 3 December 1980, p. 321. 22 April 1981, 367. 7 April 1982, p. 426. 28 April 1982, p. 436. 5 May 1982, 440. 21 July 1982, p. 459. 28 July 1982, p. 465. 24 November 1982, 517. 5 January 1983, 531.

**Letters**

John Paul II. *Letter to Families.* (2 February 1994). Vatican Translation. Boston, MA: Saint Paul Books and Media. 1994.

---. *Letter to Women.* (29 June 1995). Vatican Translation. Boston, MA: Pauline Books and Media. 1995.

---. *Letter to Priests.* (25 March 2001). Available from http://www.vatican.va/holy_father/john_paul_ii/letters/2001/documents/hf_jpii_let_20010402_priests-holy-thursday_en.html. Accessed (English) 23 October 2008.

**Homilies**

John Paul II. "Feast of the Presentation of the Lord." (2 February 1979). Available from http://www.vatican.va/holy_father/john_paul_ii/homilies/1979/index.htm. Accessed (English) 4 March 2008.

---. "Cathedral of Wavel – Closing of the Archdiocesan Synod." (8 June 1979). Available from http://www.vatican.va/holy_father/john_paul_ii/homilies/1979/index. htm. Accessed (Italian) 10 April 2007.

---. "Mass in Memory of Pope John Paul I." (28 September 1979). Available from http://www.vatican.va/holy_father/john_paul_ii/homilies/1979/index.htm. Accessed (Italian) 10 April 2007.

---. "Visita Pastorale alla Parrocchia del Sacro Cuore di Cristo Re." (18 May 1980). Available from http://www.vatican.va/holy_father/john_paul_ii/homilies/1980/documents/hf_jp-ii_hom_19800518_visita-parrocchia_it.html. Accessed (Italian) 22 June 2009.

---. "Mass in Recife." (7 July 1980). Available from http://www.vatican.va/holy_father/john_paul_ii/homilies/1980/index.htm. Accessed (Italian) 14 April 2007.

---. "Pastoral Visit to Otranto." (5 October 1980). Available from http://www.vatican.va/holy_father/john_paul_ii/homilies/1980/index.htm. Accessed (Italian) 14 April 2007.

---. "Ash Wednesday." (4 March 1981). Available from http://www.vatican.va/holy_father/john_paul_ii/homilies/1981/index.htm. Accessed (Italian) 10 April 2007.

---. "Mass for the Feast of Saint Stanislaw." (8 May 1981). Available from http://www.vatican.va/holy_father/john_paul_ii/homilies/1981/index.htm. Accessed (Italian) 4 March 2008.

Bibliography 433

---. "Pastoral Visit to the Roman Parish of Saints Marcellino and Peter." (25 April 1982). Available from http://www.vatican.va/holy_father/john_paul_ii/homilies/1982/ index.htm. Accessed (Italian) 23 October 2008.

---. "Canonization of Blessed Crispino of Viterbo." (20 June 1982). Available from http://www.vatican.va/holy_father/john_paul_ii/homilies/1982/index.htm. Accessed (Italian) 14 April 2007.

---. "Mass for the Sixth Centenary of Our Lady of Jasna Góra." (26 August 1982). Available from http://www.vatican.va/holy_father/john_paul_ii/homilies/1982/index.htm. Accessed (Italian) 10 April 2007.

---. "Canonization of Maximilian Mary Kolbe." (10 October 1982.) Available from http://www.vatican.va/holy_father/john_paul_ii/homilies/1982/index.htm. Accessed (Italian) 14 April 2007.

---. "Inauguration of the Academic Year of the Ecclesiastical Universities." (19 October 1982). Available from http://www.vatican.va/holy_father/john_paul_ii/homilies/1982/index.htm. Accessed (Italian) 4 March 2008.

---. "Visit to the Roman Parish of Saint Marcella." (6 February 1983). Available from http://www.vatican.va/holy_father/john_paul_ii/homilies/1983/index.htm. Accessed (Italian) 10 April 2007.

---. "Solenne Beatificazione di Monsignor Luigi Versiglis e di Don Callisto Caravario." (15 May 1983). Available from http://www.vatican.va/holy_father/john_paul_ii/homilies/1983

/documents/hf_jp-ii_hom_19830515_due-beatificazioni_it.html. Accessed (Italian) 22 June 2009.

---. "Concelebration in Niepokalanóv, 'City of the Immaculate.'" (18 June 1983). Available from http://www.vatican.va/holy_father/john_paul_ii/homilies/1983/index.htm. Accessed (Italian) 4 March 2008.

---. "Inauguration of the Second Extraordinary Assembly of the Synod of Bishops on the Solemnity of Christ, King of the Universe." (24 November 1985). Available from http://www.vatican.vaholy_father/john_paul_ii/homilies/1985/index.htm. Accessed (Italian) 23 October 2008.

---. "Visit to the Roman Parish of 'Corpus Domini.'" (27 September 1986). Available from http://www.vatican.va/holy_father/john_paul_ii/homilies/1986/index.htm. Accessed (Italian) 14 April 2007.

---. "Mass for Catholics of West Bengala (Calcutta)." (4 February 1986). Available from http://www.vatican.va/holy_father/john_paul_ii/homilies/1986/index.htm. Accessed (English) 7 November 2006.

---. "Eucharistic Concelebration for the Faithful of the Diocese of Essen." (2 May 1987). Available from http://www.vatican.va/holy_father/john_paul_ii/homilies/1987/ index.htm. Accessed (Italian) 10 April 2007.

---. "Eucharistic Celebration in the Cathedral of Krakow." (10 June 1987). Available from http://www.vatican.va/holy_father/john_paul_ii/homilies/1987/index.htm. Accessed (Italian) 6 November 2006.

Bibliography

---. "Liturgy of the Word for the World of Culture and Art in Warsaw." (13 June 1987). Available from http://www.vatican.va/holy_father/john_paul_ii/homilies/1987/ index.htm. Accessed (Italian) 23 October 2008.

---. "Palm Sunday Mass, III World Youth Day." (27 March 1988). Available from http://www.vatican.va/holy_father/john_paul_ii/homilies/1988/index.htm. Accessed (Italian) 9 March 2008.

---. "Inauguration of the Academic Year of the Roman Pontifical Universities." (27 October 1989). Available from the following website located here: http://www.vatican.va/holy_father/john_paul_ii/homilies / 1989/index.htm. Accessed (Italian) 7 November 2006.

---. "Mass for the Faithful of the Archdiocese of Olomouc at the Shrine of Velehrad." (22 April 1990). Available from http://www.vatican.va/holy_father/john_paul_ii/homilies/1990/index.htm. Accessed (Italian) 23 October 2008.

---. "Mass at the Military Airport of Radom." (4 June 1991). Available from http://www.vatican.va/holy_father/john_paul_ii/homilies/1991/index.htm. Accessed (Italian) 10 April 2007.

---. "Beatification of Father Raffaele Chyliński." (9 June 1991). Available from http://www.vatican.va/holy_father/john_paul_ii/homilies/1991/index.htm. Accessed (Italian) 9 March 2008.

---. "Sixth World Youth Day – Czestochowa." (15 August 1991). Available from http://www.vatican.va/holy_father/john_paul_ii/homilies/1991/index.htm. Accessed (Italian) 6 November 2006.

---. "Celebration of the Sacrament of Matrimony at Saint Peter's Basilica." (12 June 1994). Available from http://www.vatican.va/holy_father/john_paul_ii/homilies/1994/index.htm. Accessed (Italian) 23 October 2008.

---. "Beatification of Mother Mary MacKillop at Randwick Racecourse in Sydney." (19 January 1995). Available from http://www.vatican.va/holy_father/john_paul_ii/homilies/1995/index.htm. Accessed (English) 14 January 2007.

---. "Eucharistic Celebration in Honor of Saint Jan Sarkander at the Esplanade of Kaplicówka in Skoczw." (22 May 1995). Available from http://www.vatican.va/holy_father/john_paul_ii/homilies/1995/index.htm. Accessed (Italian) 9 March 2008.

---. "Concelebrazione Eucaristica nella Chiesa di Santa Maria in Vallicella nel 400th Anniversario della Morte di San Filippo Neri." (28 May 1995). Available from http://www.vatican.va/holy_father/john_paul_ii/homilies/1995/documents/hf_jp-ii_hom_19950528_s-filippo-neri_it.html. Accessed (Italian) 22 June 2009.

---. "Eucharistic Concelebration in Palermo." (23 November 1995). Available from http://www.vatican.va/holy_father/john_paul_ii/homilies/1995/index.htm. Accessed (Italian) 14 April 2007.

---. "46th International Eucharistic Congress." (1 June 1997). Available from http://www.vatican.va/holy_father/john_paul_ii/homilies/1997/index.htm. Accessed (English) 7 November 2006.

---. "Gorzow." (2 June 1997). Available from http://vatican.va/holy_father/john_paul_ii/homilies/1997/index.htm. Accessed (English) 9 March 2008.

---. "Shrine of Saint Joseph, Kalisz." (4 June 1997). Available from http://www.vatican.va/holy_father/john_paul_ii/homilies/1997/index.htm. Accessed (English) 23 October 2008.

---. "Easter Vigil." (11 April 1998). Available from http://www.vatican.va/holy_father/john_paul_ii/homilies/1998/index.htm. Accessed (English) 7 November 2006.

---. "Commemoration of the Witnesses to the Faith of the Twentieth Century." (7 May 2000). Available from http://www.vatican.va/holy_father/john_paul_ii/homilies/2000/index.htm. Accessed (English) 14 January 2007.

---. "Saints Peter and Paul." (29 June 2000). Available from http://www.vatican.va/holy_father/john_paul_ii/homilies/2000/index.htm. Accessed (English) 10 April 2007.

---. "Jubilee of Families." (15 October 2000). Available from http://www.vatican.va/holy_father/john_paul_ii/homilies/2000/index.htm. Accessed (English) 14 January 2007.

---. "Closing of the Holy Door on the Solemnity of the Epiphany of the Lord." (6 January 2001). Available from http://vatican.va/holy_father/john_paul_ii/homilies /2001/index.htm. Accessed (English) 23 October 2008.

---. "Apostolic Journey to Armenia, Mass in Latin Rite – External Grand Altar, Etchniadzin." (27 September 2001). Available from http://www.vatican.va/holy_father /john_paul_ii/homilies/2001/index.htm. Accessed (English) 14 January 2007.

**Addresses and Messages**

John Paul II. *Address* "To members of the Third General Conference of the Latin American Episcopate, Puebla - Republic of Mexico." (28 January 1979). Available from http://www.vatican.va/holy_father/john_paul_ii/speeches/1979/january/index.htm. Accessed (English) 4 March 2008.

---. *Message* "Freedom of Conscience and Religion." (1 September 1980). Vatican Translation. Boston, MA: Saint Paul Editions. 1980.

---. *Message* "World Mission Sunday." (3 June 2001). Available from http:// www.vatican.va/holy_father/john_paul_ii/message/missions/documents/hf_jp-ii_mes_ 20010607_world-day-for-missions-2001_en.html. Accessed (English) 10 April 2007.

---. *Message* "World Mission Sunday." (19 May 2002). Available from http://www.vatican.va/holy_father/john_paul_ii/message/missions/documents/hf_jp-ii_mes_20020519_world-day-for-missions-2002_en.html. Accessed (English) 23 October 2008.

---. *Message* "World Mission Sunday." (12 January 2003). Available from http://www.vatican.va/holy_father/john_paul_ii/message/missions/documents/hf_jp-ii_mes_20030221_world-day-for-missions-2003_en.html. Accessed (English) 14 January 2007.

---. *Message* "We Wish to See Jesus: World Youth Day XIX." (22 February 2004). Available from http://www.vatican.va/holy_father/john_paul_ii/messages/youth/documents/hf_jp-ii_mes_20040301_xix-world-youth-day_en.html. Accessed (English) 23 October 2008.

## Other Works by Karol Wojtyła / John Paul II

Wojtyła, Karol. *Acting Person*. In *Analecta Husserliana: The Yearbook of Phenomenological Research*, Vol. X. Translated by Andrzej Potocki. Edited by Anna-Teresa Tymieniecka. Boston, MA: D. Reidel Publishing Company Dordrecht. 1979.

---. *Love and Responsibility*. Translation, Endnotes and Foreword by Grzegorz Ignatik. Boston, MA: Pauline Books and Media. 2013.

---. *Person and Community: Selected Essays*. Translated by Theresa Sandok, OSM. New York, NY: Peter Lang. 1993.

---. *Persona e atto*. Revisione Della Traduzione Italiana e Apparati a Cura di Giuseppe Girgenti e Patrycja Mikulska. Milano e Città del Vaticano: R.C.S. Libri S.p.A.. 2001.

John Paul II. *Crossing the Threshold of Hope*. Translated by Jenny McPhee and Martha McPhee. Edited by Vittorio Messori. New York, NY: Alfred A. Knopf. 1994.

---. *Gift and Mystery: On the Fiftieth Anniversary of My Priestly Ordination*. New York, NY: Doubleday. 1996.

---. *Roman Triptych*. Translated by Jerzy Peterkiewicz. Washington, D.C.: United States Catholic Conference of Bishops. 2003.

---. *Memory and Identity: Conversations at the Dawn of a Millennium*. New York, NY: Rizzoli International Publications, Inc. 2005.

## Bibles

*Bibliorum Sacrorum*. Iuxta Vulgatam Clementinam. Nova Editio. Aloisius Gramatica. Typis Polyglottis Vaticanis. 1959.

*La Sacra Bibbia*. Conferenza Episcopale Italiana. Roma: Unione Editori e Librai Cattolici Italiani. 1974 e 2007.

*Novum Testamentum Graece*. Nestle-Aland. Stuttgart: Deutsche Bibelgesellschaft. 1898 und 1993.

*The Holy Bible*. Douay-Rheims 1899. American Edition. Available from https://www.biblegateway.com. Accessed (English) 27 May 2024.

*The Holy Bible*. Douay Rheims Version. Revised by Bishop Richard Challoner 1749-1752. Rockford, IL: Tan Books and Publishers, Inc. 1989.

*The Holy Bible*. Revised Standard Version Catholic Edition. Available from https://www.biblegateway.com. Accessed (English) 27 May 2024.

*The Holy Bible*. Revised Standard Version Second Catholic Edition. San Francisco, CA: Thomas Nelson Publishing for Ignatius Press. 2006.

*The Jerusalem Bible*. Alexander Jones, L.S.S., S.T.L., I.C.B., General Editor. Garden City, NY: Doubleday & Company, Inc. 1966.

*The New American Bible*. Nashville, TN: Catholic Bible Press Thomas Nelson Publishers. 1987.

# Bibliography

## Church Documents and Other Magisterial Teaching

*Acta Apostolicae Sedis: Commentarium Officiale.* An. et vol. 56 (1964). Città del Vaticano: Typis Vaticanis. *Homily for the Canonization of the Ugandan Martyrs.* Pope Paul VI.

*Acta Apostolicae Sedis: Commentarium Officiale.* An. et vol. 58 (7 December 1966), N. 15. *Sacrosanctum Concilium Oecumenicum Vaticanum II Constitutio Pastoralis de Ecclesia in Muno Huius Temporis,* p. 1025-1120. Città del Vaticano: Typis Vaticanis. 1966.

*Acta Apostolicae Sedis: Commentarium Officiale.* An. et vol. 70 (1978). Homily "Solemn Inauguration of the Pontificate," p. 945-952. (22 October 1978). Città del Vaticano: Typis Vaticanis. 1978.

*Acta Apostolicae Sedis: Commentarium Officiale.* An. et vol. 71 (15 Martii 1979), N. 4. *Redemptor Hominis,* p. 257-324. Città del Vaticano: Typis Vaticanis. 1979.

*Acta Apostolicae Sedis: Commentarium Officiale.* An. et vol. 85 (9 Decembris 1993), N. 12. *Veritatis Splendor,* p. 1133-1228. Città del Vaticano: Typis Vaticanis. 1993.

*Acta Apostolicae Sedis: Commentarium Officiale.* An. et vol. 91 (5 Februarii 1999), N. 2. *Incarnationis Mysterium,* p. 129-143. Città del Vaticano: Typis Vaticanis. 1999.

*Acta Apostolicae Sedis: Commentarium Officiale.* An. et vol. 93 (2001). *Novo Millennio Ineunte,* p. 266-309. Città del Vaticano: Typis Vaticanis. 2001.

*Acta Apostolicae Sedis: Commentarium Officiale.* An. et vol. 95 (7 Januarii 2003), N. 1. *Rosarium Virginis Mariae*, p. 5-36. Città del Vaticano: Typis Vaticanis. 2003.

*Alcuni Aspetti della "Teologia della Liberazione"* in *Enchiridion Vaticanum vol. IX, Documenti Ufficiali della Santa Sede (1983-1985)*, p. 866-927. A cura di Bruno Testacci. Bologna: Centro Editoriale Dehoniano. 1987.

*Catechism of the Catholic Church*, Second Edition. Washington, D.C.: United States Catholic Conference, Inc. Libreria Editrice Vaticana. 1997.

*Catechismus Catholicae Ecclesiae.* Citta del Vaticano: Libreria Editrice Vaticana. 1997.

Congregatio de Cultu Divino et Disciplina Sacramentorum. *Il Martirologio Romano: Teologia, Liturgia, Santità.* Città del Vaticano: Libreria Editrice Vaticana. 2005.

Congregation for the Clergy, *General Directory for Catechesis* (15 August 1997) Vatican City.

*Directorium Generale pro Catechesi* (15 Augusti 1997) in *Enchiridion Vaticanum vol. XVI: Documenti Ufficiali della Santa Sede* (1997), p. 608-1011. A cura di Erminio Lora. Bologna: Centro Editoriale Dehoniano. 1999.

*Dominus Iesus* [On the Unicity and Salvific Universality of Jesus Christ and the Church]. Congregation for the Doctrine of the Faith. Vatican Translation. Boston, MA: Pauline Books and Media. 2000.

Flannery, O.P., Austin. General Editor. *Vatican Council II, Vol. 1: The Conciliar and Post Conciliar Documents*, New Revised Edition. *Ad Gentes* [Decree on the Missionary Activity of the

Church]; *Dei Verbum* [Dogmatic Constitution on Divine Revelation]; *Dignitatis Humanae* [Declaration on Religious Freedom]; *Gaudium et Spes* [Pastoral Constitution on the Church in the Modern World]; *Lumen Gentium* [Dogmatic Constitution on the Church]. *Unitatis Redintegratio* [Decree on Ecumenism]. Northport, NY: Costello Publishing Co. 1996.

Jacques-Paul Migne, *Patrologiae Cursus Completus, Series Latina.* Apud Garnier Fratres, Editores et J.-P. Migne Successores. Parisiis: 1880.

Paul VI, Pope. *Mysterium Fidei* [On the Holy Eucharist]. Vatican Translation. Boston, MA: Saint Paul Books and Media. (3 September 1965). Available from http://www.vatican.va/holy_father/paul_vi/encyclicals/documents/hf_p-vi_enc_03091965_mysterium_en.html. Accessed (English) 14 January 2007.

*Sources of Catholic Dogma.* 30th Edition of Henry Denzinger's *Enchiridion Symbolorum.* Translated by Roy J. Deferrari. Fitzwilliam, NH: Loreto Publications. 1955.

*Sacrosanctum Oecumenicum Concilium Vaticanum II: Constitutiones Decreta Declarationes. Ad Gentes; Dei Verbum; Dignitatis Humanae; Gaudium et Spes; Lumen Gentium; Unitatis Redintegratio.* Citta Del Vaticano: Libreria Editrice Vaticana. 1993.

## Fathers and Doctors of the Church

Aquinas, Saint Thomas. *Summa Contra Gentiles* vol. 3, part 1: *Providence.* Translated by Vernon J. Bourke. Notre Dame, IN: University of Notre Dame Press. 1975.

---. *Summa Theologiae*. Torino: Edizioni San Paolo. 1999.

Ignatius of Antioch. *Early Christian Writings: The Apostolic Fathers*. Translated by Maxwell Staniforth. New York, NY: Dorset Press. 1986.

Migne, J. P., Editorem. *Patrologiae, Cursus Completus: Omnium SS. Patrum, Doctorum, Scriptorumque Ecclesiasticorum, Sive Latinorum, Sive Graecorum [Patrologiae Latinae, Patrologiae Graecae]*.

*Patres Apostolici*, vol. 1. Franciscus Xaverius Funk, Edidit. Tubingæ: In libraria Henrici Laupp. 1901.

Quasten, Johannes. *Patrology, vol. 1: The Beginnings of Patristic Literature*. Utrecht Brussels: Spectrum Publishers, 1950.

Thérèse de l'Enfant-Jésus et de la Sainte-Face. *Histoire d'une Âme: Manuscrits Autobiographiques*. Édition de Référence du Doctorat. Cerf-Pèlerinage de Lisieux. Paris: Editions du Cerf et Desclée De Brouwer. 2007.

---. *Story of a Soul: The Autobiography of Saint Therese of Lisieux*. Translated by John Clarke, O.C.D. Washington, D.C.: Institute of Carmelite Studies Publications. 1976.

## Secondary Sources

### Biographies on Pope John Paul II

Buttiglione, Rocco. *Karol Wojtyła: The Thought of the Man who Became Pope John Paul II*. Grand Rapids, MI: Eerdmans. 1997.

Szulc, Tad. *Pope John Paul II: The Biography*. New York, NY: Scribner. 1995.

Weigel, George. *Witness to Hope: The Biography of Pope John Paul II.* New York, NY: Cliff Street Books, HarperCollins Publishers. 1999.

---. The *End and the Beginning: Pope John Paul II–The Victory of Freedom, the Last Years, the Legacy.* New York, NY: Doubleday. 2010.

Williams, George Huntston. *The Mind of John Paul II.* New York, NY: Seabury. 1981.

## Other Theological Sources on John Paul II

DiNoia, OP, J.A. and Romanus Cessario, OP, Editors. *Veritatis Splendor and the Renewal of Moral Theology.* Princeton, NJ: Scepter Publishers. 1999.

Miller, J. Michael, Editor. *Encyclicals of John Paul II.* Huntington, IN: Our Sunday Visitor. 1996.

Nichols, OP, Aidan. *Pastor and Doctor: The Encyclicals of John Paul II* in *John Paul the Great: Maker of the Post-Conciliar Church.* Edited by William Oddie. Catholic Truth Society and the Catholic Herald. London. 2003.

Ott, Ludwig. *Fundamentals of Catholic Dogma.* Translated by Patrick Lynch. Edited in English by James Canon Bastible, D.D. Fully Revised and Updated by Robert Fastiggi. Virginia Beach, VA: Baronius Press. 2022.

Reimers, Adrian J. *Truth about the Good: Moral Norms in the Thought of John Paul II.* Ave Maria, FL: Sapientia Press of Ave Maria University. 2011.

Saward, John. *Recognizing the Rose: John Paul II and the Causes of the Saints* in *John Paul the Great: Maker of the Post-Conciliar Church*. Edited by William Oddie. Catholic Truth Society and the Catholic Herald. London: 2003.

## Supplemental Historical Articles and Works on Martyrs and Martyrdom

Bergman, Susan. Editor. *Martyrs: Contemporary Writers on Modern Lives of Faith.* San Francisco, CA: Harper. 1996.

Bowersock, G. W. *Martyrdom and Rome.* New York, NY: Cambridge University. 1995.

Bush, William. *To Quell the Terror: The Mystery of the Vocation of the Sixteen Carmelites of Compiègne Guillotined July 17, 1794.* Washington, D.C.: Institute of Carmelite Studies Publications. 1999.

Carroll, Warren H. *A History of Christendom, vol. 1: The Founding of Christendom.* Front Royal, VA: Christendom College Press. 1985.

---. *The Guillotione and the Cross.* Manassas, VA: Trinity Communications. 1986.

---. *The Rise and Fall of the Communist Revolution.* Front Royal, VA: Christendom Press. 1995.

Daniel-Rops, Henri. *The Church of Apostles and Martyrs.* Translated by Audrey Butler. London: J. M. Dent and Sons LTD. New York, NY: E. P. Dutton and Co. Inc. 1960.

de Vaulx, Bernard. *History of the Missions*: Vol. 99 of the *Twentieth Century Encyclopedia of Catholicism,* Section IX: "The Church and the Modern World." Translated by Reginald F. Trevett. Edited by Henri Daniel-Rops. New York, NY: Hawthorn Publishers. 1961.

Malham, Joseph M. *By Fire into Light: Four Catholic Martyrs of the Nazi Camps*. Leuven-Paris-Dudley: Peeters. 2002.

*Passion of SS. Perpetua and Felicity, MM*. Translated by W.H. Shewring. London: Sheed and Ward. 1931. Reprint, Latin / English text. San Francisco, CA: Ignatius Press. 2002.

Rabe, Susan. "Veneration of the Saints in Western Christianity: An Ecumenical Issue in Historical Perspective." *Journal of Ecumenical Studies,* 28, (Winter, 1991); 39-62.

Riccardi, Andrea. *Il Secolo del Martitio: I Cristiani nel Novecento*. Milano: Arnoldo Mondadori Editore. 2000.

Royal, Robert. *The Catholic Martyrs of the Twentieth Century: A Comprehensive World History*. New York, NY: The Crossroad Publishing Co. 2000.

Smith, BD, Gordon Hedderly. *The Missionary and Anthropology: An Introduction to the Study of Primitive Man for Missionaries*. Chicago, IL: Moody Press. 1947.

Solzhenitsyn, Aleksandr Isaevich. *The Solzhenitsyn Reader: New and Essential Writings 1947-2005*. Edited by Edward E. Ericson, Jr. and Daniel J. Mahoney. Wilmington, DE: Intercollegiate Studies Institute. 2006.

Thoonen, J. P. *Uganda Martyrs*. London: 1942.

Volpe, S.J., Michele. *Padre Antonio Capece, S.J., Martire nel Giappone, 1606-1643*. Napoli: Giannini. 1912.

Weibel, Berta. *Edith Stein: Martire per Amore*. Milano: Edizioni Paoline. 1999.

Wood, Diana. Editor. *Martyrs and Martyrologies*. Cambridge: Blackwell. 1993.

Ziliani, Luigi. *Tre Mesi nel Messico Martire: Storia della Persecuzione, Eroismo dei Martiri*. Bergamo: Soc. Ed. S. Alessandro. 1929.

## Supplemental Philosophical Articles and Works

Aristotle. *Topics, Poetics, Rhetoric* in *Basic Works of Aristotle*. Edited by Richard McKeon. New York, NY: Random House, 1941.

Děscartes, Réné. *Discourse on Method for Rightly Conducting One's Reason and for Seeking Truth in the Sciences*. Translated by Donald A. Cress. Indianapolis, IN: Hackett Publishing Company. 1980.

Kupczak, OP, Jarosław. *Destined for Liberty: The Human Person in the Philosophy of Karol Wojtyła / John Paul II*. Washington, D.C.: The Catholic University of America Press. 2000.

Marion, Jean-Luc. *Étant Donné: Essai d'une Phénoménologie*. Paris: Presses Universitaires de France. 1997.

Marion, Jean-Luc, Jean-Noël Dumont, [et al.] *Le don*: Colloque Interdisciplinaire: Lyon, 24-25 Novembre 2001. Lyon: Éditions de l'Emmanuel, Le Collège Supérieur. 2001.

Pieper, Josef. *Problems of Modern Faith*. Translated by Jan van Heurck. Chicago, IL: Franciscan Herald Press. 1985.

---. *The Silence of Saint Thomas*. South Bend, IN: Saint Augustine's Press. 1999.

Pritzl, O.P., Kurt. "Truth in *Fides et Ratio*: Aristotelian Reflections and Recommendations." *Communio: International Catholic Review*, Vol. XXIX, No. 1, (Spring, 2002); 89-106.

Schmitz, Kenneth L. *At the Center of the Human Drama: The Philosophical Anthropology of Karol Wojtyła / Pope John Paul II*. Washington, D.C.: The Catholic University of America Press. 1993.

Sokolowski, Msgr. Robert. *Christian Faith and Human Understanding: Studies on the Eucharist, Trinity, and the Human Person*. Washington, D.C.: Catholic University Press. 2006.

**Supplemental Theological Sources**

Cunningham, Lawrence S. "Saints and Martyrs: Some Contemporary Considerations." *Theological Studies*, 60 (1999); 529-537.

De Silva, Alvaro. "Martyrdom and Christian Morality." *Communio: International Catholic Review*, Vol. XXI, No. 2, (Summer, 1994); 286-297.

Dulles, S.J. Avery. "John Paul II Theologian." *Communio: International Catholic Review*, Vol. XXIV, No. 4, (Winter, 1997); 713-727.

---. "John Paul II and the Advent of the New Millennium." *America*, 173/19, (9 December 1995); 9-15.

Figura, Michael. "Martyrdom and the Following of Jesus." Translated Maria Shrady. *Communio: International Catholic Review*, Vol. XXIII, No. 1, (Spring, 1996); 101-109.

Hardon, S.J., John A. *History and Theology of Grace: The Catholic Teaching on Divine Grace*. Ypsilanti, MI: Veritas Press of Ave Maria College. 2002.

---. *Catechism on the Gospel of Life*. Bardstown, KY: Eternal Life. 1996.

---. *Catechism on the Splendor of Truth*. Bardstown, KY: Eternal Life. 1996.

---. *The Catholic Catechism: A Contemporary Catechism of the Teachings of the Catholic Church*. Garden City, NY: Doubleday & Company, Inc. 1975.

---. *Catholic Dictionary*. New York, NY: Image Books. 2013.

---. *Modern Catholic Dictionary*. Garden City, NY: Doubleday & Company, Inc. 1980.

Ide, Pascal. "Une Théologie Du Don: Les Occurrences de *Gaudium et Spes*, n. 24, §3 Chez Jean-Paul II" (premiére partie). *Anthropotes*, 17/1, (2001); 149-178.

---. "Une Théologie Du Don: Les Occurrences de *Gaudium et Spes*, n. 24, §3 Chez Jean-Paul II" (seconde partie). *Anthropotes*, 17/2, (2001); 313-344.

Ratzinger, Joseph. *Introduction to Christianity*. Translated by J. R. Foster. (San Francisco, CA: Ignatius Press. 1990.

Schonborn, O.P., Christoph. *From Death to Life: The Christian Journey*. Translated by Brian McNeil, C.R.V. San Francisco, CA: Ignatius Press. 1995.

Scola, Angelo. "Following Christ: On John Paul's Encyclical *Veritatis Splendor*." *Communio: International Catholic Review*, Vol. XX, No. 4, (Winter, 1993); 724-727.

Stokes and Strachan. "Old Irish Homily" in *Thesaurus Paelaeohibernicus: A Collection of Old-Irish Glosses, Scholia, Prose and Verse*. 8 Vols. Cambridge: 1903. Vol. II.

Virtue, Rev. William D. Doctoral Dissertation, Pontificia Università S. Tommaso d'Aquino, Teologia. *Mother and Infant: The Moral Theology of Embodied Self-giving in Motherhood in Light of the Exemplar Couplet Mary and Jesus Christ*. Romae: Pontificia Studiorum Universitas. 1995.

Waldstein, Michael. "John Paul II: A Thomist Rooted in Saint John of the Cross." *Faith and Reason*, 30:3 & 4, (2005); 195-218.

Welch, Lawrence J. "*Gaudium et Spes*, The Divine Image and the Synthesis of *Veritatis Splendor*." Communio: International Catholic Review, Vol. XXIV, No. 4, (Winter, 1997); 794-814.

www.ingramcontent.com/pod-product-compliance
Lightning Source LLC
Chambersburg PA
CBHW070746230426
43665CB00017B/2271